Courts, Politics and Constitutional Law

This book examines how the judicialization of politics, and the politicization of courts, affect representative democracy, rule of law, and separation of powers.

This volume critically assesses the phenomena of judicialization of politics and politicization of the judiciary. It explores the rising impact of courts on key constitutional principles, such as democracy and separation of powers, which is paralleled by increasing criticism of this influence from both liberal and illiberal perspectives. The book also addresses the challenges to rule of law as a principle, preconditioned on independent and powerful courts, which are triggered by both democratic backsliding and the mushrooming of populist constitutionalism and illiberal constitutional regimes.

Presenting a wide range of case studies, the book will be a valuable resource for students and academics in constitutional law and political science seeking to understand the increasingly complex relationships between the judiciary, executive and legislature.

Dr Martin Belov is Associate Professor in Constitutional and Comparative Constitutional Law at the University of Sofia 'St Kliment Ohridski', Faculty of Law. He is also Vice Dean of the same law faculty. In addition, he has been a project researcher at Max-Planck Institute for European Legal History (Frankfurt am Main, Germany) and a visiting researcher at the Institute for Federalism (Fribourg, Switzerland). He has specialized at the University of Oxford, UK; Max-Planck Institute for Comparative Public Law and International Law, Heidelberg, Germany; University of Cologne, Germany; and many other European academic institutions.

Comparative Constitutional Change

Series editors:

Xenophon Contiades is Professor of Public Law, Panteion University, Athens, Greece and Managing Director, Centre for European Constitutional Law, Athens, Greece.

Thomas Fleiner is Emeritus Professor of Law at the University of Fribourg, Switzerland. He teaches and researches in the areas of Federalism; Rule of Law; Multicultural State; Comparative Administrative and Constitutional Law; Political Theory and Philosophy; Swiss Constitutional and Administrative Law; and Legislative Drafting. He has been published widely in these and related areas.

Alkmene Fotiadou is Research Associate at the Centre for European Constitutional Law, Athens.

Richard Albert is Professor of Law at the University of Texas at Austin.

Comparative Constitutional Change has developed into a distinct field of constitutional law. It encompasses the study of constitutions through the way they change and covers a wide scope of topics and methodologies. Books in this series include work on developments in the functions of the constitution, the organization of powers, and the protection of rights, as well as research that focuses on formal amendment rules and the relation between constituent and constituted power. The series includes comparative approaches along with books that focus on single jurisdictions, and brings together research monographs and edited collections which allow the expression of different schools of thought. While the focus is primarily on law, where relevant the series may also include political science, historical, philosophical, and empirical approaches that explore constitutional change.

Also in the series:

New Challenges to Constitutional Adjudication in Europe
A Comparative Perspective
Edited by Zoltán Szente and Fruzsina Gárdos-Orosz

The Law and Legitimacy of Imposed Constitutions
Edited by Richard Albert, Xenophon Contiades and Alkmene Fotiadou

Quasi-Constitutionality and Constitutional Statutes
Forms, Functions, Applications
Edited by Richard Albert and Joel I. Colón-Ríos

Courts, Politics and Constitutional Law
Judicialization of Politics and Politicization of the Judiciary
Edited by Martin Belov

For more information about this series, please visit:

www.routledge.com/Comparative-Constitutional-Change/book-series/COMPCONST

Courts, Politics and Constitutional Law

Judicialization of Politics and Politicization of the Judiciary

Edited by Martin Belov

Routledge
Taylor & Francis Group
LONDON AND NEW YORK

First published 2020
by Routledge
2 Park Square, Milton Park, Abingdon, Oxon OX14 4RN

and by Routledge
52 Vanderbilt Avenue, New York, NY 10017

Routledge is an imprint of the Taylor & Francis Group, an informa business

British Library Cataloguing-in-Publication Data
A catalogue record for this book is available from the British Library

Library of Congress Cataloging-in-Publication Data
A catalog record has been requested for this book

ISBN: 978-0-367-27644-7 (hbk)
ISBN: 978-0-429-29706-9 (ebk)

Typeset in Galliard
by Deanta Global Publishing Services, Chennai, India

FSC www.fsc.org MIX Paper from responsible sources FSC™ C013985

Printed in the United Kingdom
by Henry Ling Limited

Contents

Contributors

Enrico Albanesi is Associate Professor of Constitutional Law at the Department of Law, University of Genoa, and Associate Research Fellow at the Institute of Advanced Legal Studies (IALS), University of London, where he co-leads the IALS Law Reform Project. He wrote a monograph on constitutional pluralism and EU infringement proceedings (2018), a handbook on legislative drafting for university students (2013; 2019), and a monograph on committee reports (2010). He had been working for several years as a legal advisor to the President of the *Comitato per la legislazione*, the committee of the Italian Chamber of deputies that scrutinizes the quality of the bills. He was Guest Lecturer at the University of Tartu (Estonia), University of Turku (Finland), and University of Akureyri (Iceland); Visiting Professor in the Erasmus+ Joint Master in Parliamentary Procedures and Legislative Drafting (EUPADRA) at the Universidad Complutense in Madrid and at the IALS; Visiting Scholar at the College of Europe in Bruges (Belgium); and Visiting Research Fellow at the IALS. He has given several presentations overseas (Albania, Bulgaria, Japan, Finland, Israel, Montenegro, Belgium, Algeria, Iceland, UK, Spain) and published articles in peer-reviewed international journals, such as *The Theory and Practice of Legislation* and *European Journal of Law Reform.*

Dr Martin Belov is Associate Professor in Constitutional and Comparative Constitutional Law at the University of Sofia 'St Kliment Ohridski', Faculty of Law. He is also Vice Dean of the same law faculty. In addition, he has been a project researcher at Max-Planck Institute for European Legal History (Frankfurt am Main, Germany) and a visiting researcher at the Institute for Federalism (Fribourg, Switzerland). He has specialized at the University of Oxford, UK; Max-Planck Institute for Comparative Public Law and International Law, Heidelberg, Germany; University of Cologne, Germany; and many other European academic institutions.

He has been a visiting professor and guest lecturer in European and Comparative Constitutional Law in many European universities: University of Girona (Spain), Europa-University 'Viadrina' (Frankfurt/Oder, Germany), European Law and Governance School (Athens, Greece), University of

Södertorn (Stockholm, Sweden), Scuolla Superiore Sant'Anna (Pisa, Italy), University of Lisbon (Portugal), State University of Milan (Italy), University of Cologne (Germany), University of Bari 'Aldo Moro' (Italy), 'Masaryk' University (Brno, Czech Republic), Staatlichen Studienakademie (Dresden/ Bautzen, Germany), University of Warsaw (Poland), etc.

He has held public lectures at the University of Oxford (UK), University 'Pompeu Fabra' (Barcelona, Spain), European Academy of Legal Theory, Goethe University (Frankfurt am Main, Germany), 'Sigmund Freud' University (Vienna, Austria), LUISS 'Guido Carli' (Rome, Italy), University of Lodz (Poland), and others.

He is also a member of several scientific organizations. He is a member of the European Group of Public Law (EGPL), the International Association of Legislation (IAL) as well as of the Advisory Board of the CEE Forum (the Central and Eastern European Forum of Young Legal, Political and Social Theorists). He is a member of the scientific board of several law journals in Italy and Serbia.

He has published 14 books and more than 80 scientific papers. E-mail: martinbelov@yahoo.com

Monica Bonini is Associate Professor at the 'Università degli Studi di Milano Bicocca'. There, she is a member of the PhD committee and of other academic committees, and teaches public law, communication law and policy, and banking law. She is a visiting professor at the University of Konstanz, Germany where she holds courses on Italian constitutional law. Her research interests include public law, comparative constitutional law, and EU law. Prof. Bonini has numerous publications in the above-mentioned academic areas. She is a member of many research groups in the above-mentioned academic fields.

Angela Di Gregorio is Full Professor of Comparative Public Law at the University of Milan, Italy. Her research interests include constitutionalism in new democracies; the dynamics of European integration from the constitutional point of view (i.e. relationships between legal sources and courts); and transitional justice.

Michael Hein works in the field of civic education at the Adult Education Center in Altenburg, Germany. After studying political science, Eastern European Studies, and journalism at the University of Leipzig (2000–2006), he worked as a research associate at the University of Greifswald, where he did his PhD in 2012. Later, he held postdoc positions at the Humboldt University of Berlin (2014–2017) and the University of Göttingen (2017–2019). His main research interests are constitutional politics, constitutional courts, constitutional entrenchment clauses, and politics in South Eastern Europe, especially in Bulgaria and Romania.

Dr Antonios Kouroutakis is Assistant Professor at IE University in Madrid, Spain, and he has taught a variety of law courses and conducted research at the City University of Hong Kong, the Free University of Berlin, FVG Sao Paolo, and Aristotle University of Thessaloniki. Dr Kouroutakis received a DPhil in Law from the University of Oxford and an LLM from UCLA School of Law. Dr Kouroutakis' research interests lie mainly in the field of constitutional engineering, public law, and regulation. In particular, Dr Kouroutakis is interested in the concept of separation of powers, rule of law, emergency legislation, and the regulation of new technologies; he has published widely on these topics in international and peer-reviewed journals, and his work has been cited in numerous reports. His widely reviewed book on the *Constitutional Value of Sunset Clauses* (Routledge 2016) has been quoted at the House of Commons (UK) during the debates about the inclusion of a sunset clause in the Taxation (Cross-border Trade) Bill.

Prof. Dr Konrad Lachmayer is Professor of Public Law, European Law and Foundations of Law, and Vice-Dean of the faculty of law at Sigmund Freud University in Vienna. He is a visiting fellow at Durham Law School (UK). Prof. Lachmayer studied law in Vienna and held visiting or research positions at the University of Cambridge, Faculty of Law (UK), the Max Planck Institute for Comparative Public Law and International Law in Heidelberg (Germany), the Central European University in Budapest (Hungary), the Hungarian Academy of Sciences, Institute of Legal Studies (Hungary), and Durham Law School (UK). His research focuses on Austrian, European, and comparative public law.

Attila Menyhárd is Professor of Civil Law at Eötvös Loránd University, Faculty of Law, Civil Law Department (Budapest). His main research fields are contract law, tort law, property law, company law, human rights and private law, economic analysis of law, and private law in other contexts. He was promoted with a PhD degree in 2003 and habilitated in 2007 in Eötvös Loránd University. He has been a full professor since 2012. Upon the invitation of the Ministry of Justice he contributed to the project for the new Hungarian Civil Code being responsible for the provisions on property law, rent law, and trusts. He is the Hungarian fellow of European Tort and Insurance Law (Wien) and also the fellow of the Institute for Legal Studies at the Centre of Social Sciences of the Hungarian Academy of Sciences (Budapest). E-mail: menyhard@ajk.elte.hu

Prof. Dr Daniel Valtchev is Professor of Jurisprudence and Dean of the Faculty of Law at Sofia University, Bulgaria. Prof. Valtchev studied law in Sofia University and had different specializations. He is Doctor Honoris Causa of Soka University, Tokyo, Japan, and Honorary Professor of Shanghai University, China. His research focuses on Theory and Philosophy of Law, Theory of State, and Human Rights.

Prof. Dr Helen Xanthaki, University College London; Dean, Postgraduate Laws Programmes, University of London; Senior Associate Fellow, Sir William Dale Centre for Legislative Studies, IALS; Visiting Professor, QMUL; President, International Association for Legislation; author of *Drafting Legislation: Art and Technology of Rules for Regulation* (Oxford, Hart Publishing, 2014);

and *Thornton's Legislative Drafting*, 5th edn (London, Bloomsbury, 2013); member of the editorial board of *Theory and Practice of Legislation*. E-mail: h.xanthaki@ucl.ac.uk.

Paul Yowell is Associate Professor, University of Oxford, in the Faculty of Law, and a Fellow of Oriel College. He is the author of *Constitutional Rights and Constitutional Design: Moral and Empirical Reasoning in Judicial Review* (2018) and co-author of *Legislated Rights: Securing Human Rights Through Legislation* (2018). He researches broadly in public law and legal theory, with particular interests in the separation of powers, constitutional theory, comparative constitutional law, and human rights. He did his postgraduate studies at Oxford (DPhil, MPhil, BCL), having previously practiced law and studied in the US (JD, BA, Baylor University).

Mauro Zamboni is Professor of Legal Theory at the Stockholm University (Sweden), Senior Associate Research Fellow at the Institute of Advanced Legal Studies, University of London (UK), and Korea Legislation Research Institute Global Research Fellow (South Korea). His fields of interest are legislative studies and the relationships between law and politics (mostly from a legal theoretical perspective).

Introduction

Martin Belov

There is a well-established belief in both legal theory and socio-political discourse that judges are just experts and courts are institutions which are and should be detached from politics. In fact, they are not. Or at least not to the extent required by the dogma of apolitical judiciary engraved in the normative ideology of Western modernity by key authoritative thinkers such as Montesquieu. Courts are involved in politics in many ways. They adopt legal standards thus participating in the law-making activity of the state. They pave the way for constitutional reform or even may accomplish such reform by virtue of implicit, 'virtual' constitutional amendment or by declaring the unconstitutionality of constitutional amendments. They promote or hamper authoritarian, democratic, lobbyist, or general interests thus engaging with constitutional or sector-specific politics. And vice versa, courts are also exposed to politics and political influence. The political branches have different means of influencing the 'non-political', depoliticized judiciary. This trend is especially visible in the context of democratic backsliding and the so-called 'illiberal democracies' which are currently gaining momentum. However, it is latently also a present danger in liberal democracies.

This book critically assesses the phenomena of judicialization of politics and politicization of judiciary.[1] It explores the rising impact of courts on key constitutional principles, such as democracy and separation of powers, which is paralleled by increasing criticism of this influence from both liberal and illiberal perspectives. The book also addresses the challenges to the rule of law as a principle preconditioned on independent and powerful courts which are triggered by both democratic backsliding and mushrooming of populist constitutionalism and illiberal constitutional regimes.

1 For the general problem of the judicialization of politics and politicization of the judiciary see R. Hirschl, 'The Judicialization of Politics' in: G. Caldeira, R. D. Kelemen & K. Whittington (Eds), *Oxford Handbook of Law and Politics*, Oxford, Oxford University Press, 2008; D. Weiden, 'Judicial Politicization, Ideology, and Activism at the High Courts of the United States, Canada, and Australia', *Political Research Quarterly*, Vol. 64, No. 2, 2011, pp. 335–347; and P. Domingo, 'Judicialization of Politics or Politicization of the Judiciary? Recent Trends in Latin America', *Democratization*, Vol. 11, No. 1, 2004, p. 104 and the following.

The current volume aims to contribute to the discussion on the role of courts in contemporary legal orders. It brings together the analysis of diversified legal systems under the same roof framed by a strong unifying idea around which the various contributors operate. This is the idea of the centrality of the courts in contemporary constitutional orders and their strategic engagement with and exposure to constitutional politics. More precisely, the book engages with some specific discourses which are part of this broader discussion such as: the role of courts in a democratic society; their status, functions, and practical impact on representative democracy and separation of powers; the tension between key constitutional principles such as rule of law on the one hand, and democracy and sovereignty on the other; the impact of the constitutional courts on the constituent power due to their performance as key players in a multilevel constitutional setting; promoters of constitutional change or negative legislators declaring the unconstitutionality of constitutional amendments; the role of courts as legislators or as administrators of justice; and their interaction with the parliament and the government.

The book combines case studies demonstrating specific but rather characteristic problems with the provision of comparative analysis, and the launching of ideas with broader and general theoretical importance. The book is not focused on a single state or even on a specific region. The research provided by the contributors ranges globally from Europe (Italy, UK, Sweden, Germany, France, Hungary, Poland, Bulgaria etc.) to Eurasia (Russia and Turkey), Asia (Nepal), Africa (The Republic of South Africa), and Latin America (Venezuela, Honduras, and Colombia).

The first part of the book comprises the chapters of Daniel Valchev, 'Democracy and courts beyond the ideological banality', and Konrad Lachmayer, 'Disempowering courts: The interrelationship between courts and politics in contemporary legal orders or the manifold ways of attacking judicial independence'. Both chapters are engaged with the discussion of the role of courts in a democratic constitutional order. Valchev highlights the special standing of courts in a constitutional democracy and their contribution to the maintenance of a democratic order whereas Lachmayer outlines the main threats to courts' independence and their impact on democracy and rule of law. The common claim of these two chapters is that the courts are the last bastion of constitutionalism with paramount importance to constitutional ideology, institutional design, and the socio-legal practice of the modern democratic state based on rule of law.

Valchev's chapter reminds us that all regimes are based on a consensus which requires not only logical foundations but also a bit of magic. This is particularly true for modern liberal democracy which has been produced as a result of a consensus on elitist and popular level. Valchev's main claim is that we need to protect the ideological standing and the emotional perception of the courts as safeguards of individual freedom and liberal democracy. The author appeals to us to not disenfranchise the courts from their rather privileged role as islands of expertise in the great sea of majoritarian democracy. He puts forward the provocative question whether the courts can save liberal democracy.

Valchev defines liberal democracy as 'governance founded on elections, which is, for the sake of protecting individual freedom, restrained by procedures, bodies of professional élites, and a normative ideology'. In his account, there is a logical inconsistency enshrined in the foundations of liberal democracy. It consists of the simultaneous belief in democratic legitimacy, people's rule and majority decision-making paralleled by inherent distrust in majoritarian rule. Thus, the author indirectly engages in the current ongoing debate on the intellectual and political divorce between the 'revolutionary', radical democratic and the populist trend of constitutional democracy, and the liberal, counter-majoritarian strain in it.[2] This split is largely debated in the literature on illiberal democracies, democratic backsliding, and especially on populist constitutionalism.

According to Valchev there are three main constraints on majoritarian government and decision-making provided by contemporary liberal constitutionalism. These are procedures, the counter-majoritarian expertise-based institutions, and a particular type of normative ideologies. The author briefly explains the main types of such procedures developed in the course of modern constitutional history and the range of institutional design of counter-majoritarian institutions which is currently available. He emphasizes the role of the courts in this context.

Valchev suggests that the courts' legitimacy is currently grounded on a normative ideology which is centered on human rights and the aim of defense against excessive majoritarianism. The author highlights the role of university professors in preserving the 'magic' of courts. He claims that this magic should not be unspelled for the sake of preserving the courts as the most resilient and reliable fortress against rising authoritarianism and populism. Valchev points to the principle of primacy of EU law over the national constitutions of the member states as an example of well-functioning constitutional magic safeguarding the degree of EU integration which could not have been otherwise produced by political means via the democratically elected institutions. In that regard, the primacy of law is a fundamental principle coined by the Court of Justice of the EU functioning in the context of lacking clear political consensus for such long-lasting political decisions shaped in legal terms.

The chapter by Konrad Lachmayer explores recent developments of increased political influence and pressure on the judiciary. Thus, it is part of the general debates on politicization of judiciary, democratic backsliding, and the rise of illiberal democracies. In that regard, Lachmayer is indirectly engaged in an intellectual dialogue with the chapters of Angela Di Gregorio and Enrico Albanesi, who also raise similar questions. However, it is also a logical continuation of Valchev's chapter exposing the 'magic' of the normative ideology behind judicial independence. In other words, while Valchev pleads not to desacralize the courts Lachmayer shows what happens if we do so.

2 See P. Blokker, *Populist Constitutionalism*, pp. 1–5, available at: Verfassungsblog.de and L. Corrias, 'Populism in a Constitutional Key: Constituent Power, Popular Sovereignty and Constitutional Identity', *European Constitutional Law Review*, Vol. 12, No. 01, 2016, pp. 6–26.

Lachmayer's chapter commences with a brief comparative overview of the infringement of judicial independence in increasingly illiberal democracies such as Poland and Hungary. He outlines the main devices for limitation of judicial autonomy by a populist and illiberal government. Furthermore, the author outlines the main challenges to courts in times of neo-nationalism and rising authoritarian tendencies. He explores the adverse effects of political pressure on courts not only for democracy but also for the rule of law. Thus, Lachmayer implicitly makes the classical suggestion which is typical for liberal constitutionalism that rule of law and authoritarianism should be deemed incompatible. He raises the important claim that 'while international courts are primarily limited by nationalism, national courts have to deal with authoritarianism'. Again, as in the analysis of the Polish and Hungarian cases, Lachmayer outlines the main strategies and tools used by nationalist and authoritarian power centers to put pressure and impose limits on the effects of the decisions of international courts.

Two further observations made by Lachmayer deserve special attention. The author suggests that 'nationalistic approaches create effects on national rule of law systems. While weakening international courts, domestic courts can be attacked much more easily by authoritarian developments on a national level'. Furthermore, 'authoritarian approaches do not only limit domestic courts in their independence, but also affect the acceptance of following judgements of international court'.

An intellectual pillar of Lachmayer's chapter is the thesis that the 'concept of the independence of courts is culturally divergent.' Thus, the author explores the core of the idea of judicial independence, taking into account the fundamental cultural diversity affecting its local manifestations. Claiming that 'cultural diversity cannot serve as justification or legitimation to undermine or destroy judicial independence' the author 'identifies problems and challenges of courts in different legal systems' and provides 'an overview of the different strategies of disempowerment of courts'.

Lachmayer offers an elucidating analysis of the rising prominence of the courts in recent decades. He engages with the general discussion of the legitimacy of the courts' expansion with a view to democracy and separation of powers. Lachmayer provides a critical assessment of the way the national, international, and supranational courts 'gained political control over the constitutional arena'. Thus, he explores the different factors and instruments by virtue of which courts became political factors and produced judicialization of politics that reversely also triggered the politicization of judiciary.

Lachmayer puts special emphasis on the impact of the booming expansion of the executive on the rising importance of courts. Thus, he explores the uneasy interaction between these two institutional players with increasing importance in contemporary constitutional orders. According to the author 'from the perspective of separation of powers, the new rivals of the courts are not the parliaments any more but dominating governments, which are pushing back parliaments and courts alike'. Subsequently, Lachmayer provides us with an interesting analysis of the strategies of the governments and the executive power in general for gaining predominance over the courts.

Consequently, Lachmayer launches an original typology of disempowerment of courts based on the 'authoritarian strategies to limit the role of courts by destructing their judicial independence'. In doing so, he outlines the main features of judicial independence and, vice versa, of tools for undermining it proposed in the scholarship. This enables Lachmayer to systematize the components of the three main dimensions of obstruction of the courts' independence which according to him are the institutional, the personal, and the procedural dimensions. The predominant part of the rest of Lachmayer's chapter is devoted to a profound analysis of these three dimensions. Finally, the author outlines the phenomenon of the erosion of rule of law masqueraded as a sovereigntist and democratic fight against juristocracy and suggests several approaches to strengthen judicial independence.

The second part of the book explores the relationship between courts, parliaments, and the institutions of the executive power. It provides an insightful analysis of courts' engagement with legisprudence, legislation, and legislative power, but also the perception of courts as law-implementing bodies with an administrative outlook. The general idea of the whole second part, which unifies and frames all chapters, is to challenge the traditional understanding of the courts as institutions limited exclusively to the judicial power. Thus, the accomplishment of legislative and administrative functions by the courts equals enhanced engagement in politics. The four contributions in Part II demonstrate that the courts may be extensively engaged in legislation or may be publicly perceived as part of the state administration. The authors demonstrate the advantages and disadvantages of such engagement, its historical roots, and its socio-legal determinants.

Helen Xanthaki's chapter, 'Courts and legislation: Do legislators and judges speak the same language?', is an outline of a communicative theory of legislation focusing on a particular problem – the mismatch between the approaches of legislators and courts to the language of legislation. According to the author

> the hypothesis of this chapter is that recent innovations in drafting techniques have disturbed the continuity of language used by those who produce and those who interpret legislation. Which, in turn, confirms that, currently, legislators and judges speak a different language.

Xanthaki defines 'legislation as a fluid collective task'. She presents her concept of legislation as an inclusive and open-ended process of communication between different stake-holders and key players. In her account, legislation is not limited to the task of the legislator. It also includes the law implementers and law interpreters as well as the addressees of the law. In Xanthaki's words

> if one takes this holistic picture of legislation as a tool for regulation into account [...] drafters can only perform a small, albeit crucial, part in the

> application of governmental policy better expressed as regulation. Legislation becomes a collective task that can only be achieved with the synergy of all actors, including judges.

Xanthaki stipulates that the 'fluidity of legislation' is currently missing. She suggests that 'identifying the users of legislation' in recent empirical surveys 'has led to not one but two earthquakes. First, the law does not speak to lawyers alone. Second, the law does not speak to the "average man".' According to the author these findings have produced a revolutionary change in the approach to legislative drafting. Her main claim, however, is that despite 'this drafting revolution, judges and courts have remained excluded. There seems to be a rather gaping schism between the linguistic perceptions of drafters and interpreters of legislation in the UK today'. The main concern of the author which underpins her whole chapter is that 'judges, as interpreters of legislation, are excluded from the debate on easification, legislative diversity, and effectiveness.'

In the subsequent chapter, 'Text, values, and interpretation: The role of judges and legislative power in private law', Attila Menyhárd suggests a radical realist approach to the role of courts combined with criticism of the traditional syllogistic and mechanic law implementation. In his account,

> interpretation is about establishing the content of the norm. Thus, creation of the law on one hand and application of it on the other hand cannot be distinguished. Interpretation is about establishing the content of the norm which per se means that it is not the legislator but the court that establishes the content of the norm. Thus, in a realistic model of judicial adjudication, the court does not merely state the norm but construes it. This makes the distinction between law-making and application relative; the judgment of the court does not create the norm, but the court, by finding the norm, does.

Menyhárd's theory can be defined as radical legal realism oriented toward the legitimation and establishment of a value-based jurisprudence. The author suggests that 'courts have to implement and enforce the general values prevailing in the society in each of the cases'. He believes that 'theoretically a choice has to be made between textualist (or pure interpretive) model and the supplementer approach'. Moreover, he defines law as a 'mechanism of transmitting and implementing values'.

The radical legal realism of Menyhárd is visible in his thesis that

> the written norm provided by the legislator establishes the basic evaluation only, which can be overruled by the court. This overruling can be performed with different methods. The main tools of such enforcement of values are: interpretation of abstract norms, concretizing general clauses, assessment of "hard cases", or procedural solutions like reversal of burden of proof in cases of information asymmetry. The legislator may also leave the balancing of interests and establishing priorities to the courts.

Furthermore, the author explains, frequently using concrete examples, how these value enforcement devices make possible a flexible and value-oriented concept of law in general and of private law in particular.

According to Menyhárd

> the most precise description of how private law works describes the judgment of the court as a process of evaluation. In this mechanism, the court decides the case on the basis of a closed number of relevant values, counterweighing them in the context of the facts of the case.

Thus, the author adheres to the theory of the flexible system of private law, proposed by Walter Wilburg. Menyhárd suggests that legislation and judicial interpretation are just the two sides of the same coin. He comes to the very provocative conclusion that the difference between judicial and legislative measures cannot be found in hierarchy but in their different legitimacy and efficiency.

Mauro Zamboni's chapter, Supreme courts in Sweden: Are they "real" judges?, presents a very interesting case study. It is a valuable contribution to the comparative constitutional law literature not only because it elaborates an intriguing and peculiar situation in a specific jurisdiction such as Sweden, but also due to the fact that it produces conclusions regarding the compatibility or incompatibility of service-oriented and administration-like attitudes toward the judiciary with democratic orders based on separation of powers. Zamboni poses the fundamental question with broad comparative law importance 'whether a supreme court with a fully judicial nature is a *conditio sine qua non* for every democracy'.

Zamboni's chapter explores the reasons why the Swedish supreme courts 'are considered and consider themselves as part of the larger public administration within legal and constitutional discourse'. Zamboni points out that 'the highest judges tend to operate as an extension of the public administration into the higher legal instance rather than as a third party in disputes among public and private actors'. Thus,

> judges consider themselves as internal reviewers of the public agencies (aiming at shaping a "good administration" according to the criteria set by the legislator) rather than external referees (determining winners and losers in legal disputes, based on the valid law).

This particularly Swedish self-perception of the courts produces peculiar reversed side-effects on the administration. Zamboni is interested in

> how this positioning (on the part of both the judges and the outside actors) of the supreme courts as public agencies, in its turn, fuels another shift: the perception of public agencies not simply as "implementers", but also as authoritative "interpreters" of the law.

He believes that 'there is a perception of the role of judges as a compliance agency as regards public administration decisions, which in turn stimulates the public agencies to operate not only as executive, but also as quasi-judicial actors'.

Zamboni explores the reasons for this specific public and scientific perception of the supreme courts in Sweden as well as self-perception of the Supreme Court judges as being 'a prolongation of the public administration'. He outlines 'three fundamental (interconnected and mutually reinforcing) sets of reasons, related to factors of political, legal, and purely administrative nature'. The first reason according to Zamboni is 'the Swedish or "social-democratic" version of the welfare state – transforming the state into the "house of the people"'. The second reason is 'the Swedish constitutional architecture; one of its major components is a refusal of the principle of division of powers' replaced by the principle of separation of function which conceives the Parliament 'as the only true power (being the only one representing "the people")' while delegating 'the other two functions (judicial and executive) to the courts and the public agencies'. The third reason suggested by the author is the 'specific career system a judge has to follow in order to be likely to be selected for such courts'.

After describing the reasons for the traditional attribution of the courts in general and the supreme courts in particular to the administration, Zamboni identifies also some fragile and initial, but still visible novel trends toward a re-judicialization of the judiciary. According to the author there are five such recent developments. The first one is the increase of judicial activism. The second one is the general reinforcement of the role and status of the courts triggered by Swedish EU membership. The third one is the slow but steady transition toward a post-welfare society. Zamboni explains that one of its central dogmas of this gradually emerging post-welfare is the strong idea of the rule of law. According to the author

> this implies a moving away from the traditional Swedish model of the welfare state and its basic idea that legal actors (and in particular the judicial bodies) should consider and use the law as structurally soft in relation to the values expressed by the political environment (and implemented by the administrative apparatus). In a post-welfare system, it is the other way around: the political, social, and economic discourses are perceived by the judges as generally bending when conflicting with fundamental legal principles, either explicitly in the constitutional documents or through the legal system.

This process leads in Zamboni's view to a situation in which

> the judges operate as a true third party in the disputes, as their focus is mainly inserting and evaluating the disputes under discussion not in relation to the political will or the administrative practices, but rather in relation to the systems of rules and fundamental principles superseding the legal system.

The fourth development is the Swedish constitutional reform of 2011 which has introduced a new system of recruitment to the higher courts. The fifth factor according to Zamboni is that 'the Swedish political, social, and financial atmospheres have changed considerably in the last decade, becoming more conflictual'.

The chapter of Monica Bonini, 'From separation of powers to superiority of rights: The Italian Constitutional Court and end-of-life decisions', is devoted to the relationship between the parliament and the Constitutional Court. This question is of fundamental importance for all constitutional orders. It has central place in constitutional debates on separation of powers, political role of courts, politicization of judiciary, and judicialization of politics. Moreover, it is the focus of the intellectual debates on the proper standing and adequate framework of parliaments in the context of modern liberal democracies. The principal impetus behind this debate is the intrinsic tension between democratic and liberal components of modern constitutionalism. In other words, the intellectual background against which Bonini's chapter should be read is the counter position and cooperation between the parliament as the central representative institution in a democratic constitutional order and the Constitutional Court as the main safeguard of freedom and individual rights.

Bonini engages in the debates on separation of powers and the impact of the concepts of judicial activism, judicial self-restraint, and 'political question' on it. Moreover, the author launches a new concept defined by her as 'parliamentary inertia'. Bonini focuses on the problem of balancing of complex values in the context of two lines of tension: judicial choices versus separation of powers and judicial choices versus parliamentary inertia. She exposes the fragility of our theoretical and normative conceptualization of the relationship between constitutional courts and parliaments in the context of the 'double sided liaison between law and politics', defined by her as '"symbiotic" and conflicting at the same time'. Thus, Bonini engages in the wider conceptual debate on political constitutionalism versus legal constitutionalism[3] existing in the legal theory.

According to Bonini 'under the Italian Constitution, democratic processes and constitutional review should live together in harmony'. However, she demonstrates the huge tensions between these two imperatives of modern constitutionalism in the Italian context on the basis of a case study of the 'end-of-life decisions' of the Italian Constitutional Court. Bonini raises several important questions such as: 'whether the Constitutional Court and other judges are well suited for the purpose of balancing complex values characterizing this specific subject matter' and 'whether the Constitutional Court shall balance complex values when the Parliament refuses to decide upon them'.

One of the aims of Bonini's chapter is 'to reflect upon parliamentary inertia and judicial intervention setting it in the framework of the separation of powers'. In her account, the Constitutional Court should protect human rights against 'parliamentary inertia'. However, 'parliamentary inertia may be a political choice – i.e. a political domain to be strictly left out of the Court's reach.' The

3 See R. Bellamy, *Political Constitutionalism*, Cambridge, Cambridge University Press, 2007, pp. 90–142.

author comes to the conclusion that a delicate balance should be sought between human rights-based judicial activism of the Constitutional Court aiming at protection of rule of law and the due respect of the political discretion of the parliament based on representative democracy and separation of powers.

The third part of the book is devoted to courts, constitution-making, and the separation between constituent and constituted powers. It provides original theoretical views on the role of constitutional courts in constitution-making process, their functioning as negative legislators and as ultimate players in multilevel constituent power games, and their increased engagement with control of constitutionality of the constitutional amendments. Thus, the authors engage in classical discussions, e.g. on the Kelsenian model of constitutional justice, but also in current debates which are gaining momentum such as the scientific discourse on 'unconstitutional constitutional amendments' or the enhanced role of the courts as mediators on the border between the national, international, and supranational constitutional orders. This part of the book combines conceptual contributions to constitutional theory with comparative research and case studies.

The third part starts with Paul Yowell's chapter, 'The negative legislator: On Kelsen's idea of a constitutional court'. Yowell explores Kelsen's view on the role of the constitutional court as negative legislator. He starts with a brief outline of the main features of the Kelsenian model of constitutional courts and constitutional review. He then contrasts it with its theoretical antipode – the American model of constitutional review. Yowell outlines the main differences between both models.

Yowell explains Kelsen's account of human rights as a possible (or actually impossible) object of constitutional review. He provides an insightful analysis of Kelsen's denial of abstract formulas and vague moral formulas as criteria for control for constitutionality of laws. Yowell explains that

> Kelsen opposed giving the constitutional court power to enforce principles formulated in abstract moral language, that is, those which make "an appeal to the ideals of 'justice', 'freedom', 'equality', 'equity', 'decency', and so on". He thought that such terms were legally "vacuous", providing no determinate guidance to judges. They could serve as political norms, directing legislative organs in their creation of law; and law-making is rightly seen as a process that specifies vague principles into positive law. But it would be "highly dangerous" to make the principles a basis for constitutional adjudication, in particular for review of the constitutionality of statutes.

Yowell notes that despite of Kelsen's theoretical influence in Europe most of the European models do not follow all of its postulates very strictly. An important example according to the author is the fact that the European constitutions contain chapters on human rights and allow their constitutional courts to use them as criteria for constitutional review.

Yowell contrasts the Kelsenian and the American approach to the temporal effect of the Constitutional Court decisions. The author contrasts 'Kelsen's practical approach – which is realized in the 1920 Austrian Constitution – with the approach in the American model and other systems'. Yowell provides an informative analysis of the evolution of the practice of the US Supreme Court and other common law courts such as the Australian, Canadian, and Irish Supreme Courts on the concept of initial invalidity of unconstitutional norms and on the retroactive force of the court's decisions. The author highlights key decisions of these courts to show the evolution of their standing on these conceptual problems. He provides an overview of the shift of the jurisprudence of the US Supreme Court from the position of absolute initial invalidity of unconstitutional provisions to a more moderate and compromise stance. Paul Yowell also analyzes the leading decisions of the Irish, Australian, and Canadian supreme courts with regard to the validity of unconstitutional provisions, the effect of the courts' decisions declaring such unconstitutionality, and the subsequent effect on their standing as courts or also as negative legislators. Yowell provides very interesting comparative analysis of the 'void *ab initio*' doctrine with regard to unconstitutional acts in Europe devoting special attention to Germany, Austria, Italy, and Spain.

Yowell thoroughly explores Kelsen's theory of the constitutional court as a negative legislator. He critically assesses Kelsen's functional attribution of legislative power to the constitutional court based on the logic that both the Parliament and the Constitutional Court adopt general norms, in contrast to the courts. In that regard, Yowell's analysis should be read in conjunction with the chapters of Attila Menyhárd and Mauro Zamboni who also provide original views on the status of the courts in the separation of powers especially with a view to the proximity of their functions to institutions belonging to the legislative and the executive power. Both the papers of Menyhárd and Yowell offer refreshing alternative view on the courts as legislators. The difference between them is that Yowell's paper explains the role of the constitutional courts as legislators from the viewpoint of Kelsen's theory.

Furthermore, Yowell provides a thorough analysis of the 'void *ab initio*' debate in the legal theory. The author focuses on 'the relationship between different constitutional practices and doctrines, and the problems they can generate, and legal theory about the precise status (in regard to validity) of an unconstitutional statute'. Before presenting Kelsen's views on that issue Yowell outlines the debate between Supreme Court judges on the matter which constitutes an important contribution of the chapter to the scientific debate. In the author's words 'the debate among judges is also illustrative of tensions in Kelsen's thoughts'. Moreover, Yowell provides an insightful analysis of Hans Kelsen's theory of the status of unconstitutional laws tracing his intellectual evolution throughout the years as objectivized in various publications. Finally, Yowell comes to important conclusions regarding Kelsen's contribution to theory and practice as well as the shortcomings of his theory.

My chapter of the book, 'Constitutional courts as ultimate players in multilevel constituent power games: The Bulgarian case', presents the different roles simultaneously played by the constitutional courts which make them ultimate players in multilevel constituent power games. The constitutional courts are gatekeepers of the bridge between the constitutionalism 'within' and 'beyond statehood'. They are safeguards, promoters, or limitations of constitutional nationalism, constitutional internationalism, constitutional supranationalism, and constitutional globalism. Last but not least, they are mediators of the participation of the member states in the European Union.

The analysis is limited to the Bulgarian case not only due to space constraints, but also because of the principle need to broaden the analysis of the role of constitutional courts to less researched constitutional jurisdictions which do not actively engage in intense judicial dialogue with the Court of Justice of the EU. The Bulgarian case requires attention because the jurisprudence and the general stance of the Bulgarian Constitutional Court with regard to Bulgaria's integration in the EU's multilevel constitutionalism are still rather under-researched.

The chapter commences with research on the impact of the transfer of constitutional competences to the EU as precursor for the increasing role of domestic constitutional courts. Furthermore, I am defining the concept of 'multilevel constituent power game'. This is done in the context of explaining the role of the EU integration in the form of multilevel constitutionalism for the shift in the power schemes provided by the domestic constitutions. The constitutional courts are exposed as gatekeepers of the bridge between national, international, and supranational constitutionalism which allows them to engage in the redefinition of the rules of the multilevel constitutional game thus entering in the domain of the constituent power.

I am demonstrating my general claim that the EU integration makes the constitutional courts insurmountable factors on the edge between constitutionalism 'within' and 'beyond' statehood and on the border between constituent and constituted power on the basis of a case study of the Bulgarian constitutional system. I am outlining the concept of constituent power and external power according to the Bulgarian constitutional model. I am showing that a rigid or semi-rigid constitution in the context of the European integration actually fosters the standing of the constitutional court as ultimate player in multilevel constituent power games. This thesis is also launched by Antonios Kourotakis in the context of the constitutional models he explores in his chapter.

I show that the Bulgarian constitutional court is engaging in 'multilevel constituent power games' related to activist interpretation of the 1991 Constitution, redrawing of the demarcation lines between constituent and constituted powers, paving the way for transfer of sovereignty or, vice versa, for implicit and hidden domestic constitutional protectionism and nationalism. Such engagement of the Bulgarian constitutional court in constitutional politics seems to go against the initial idea of the founding fathers and mothers of the 1991 Constitution for establishment of a moderately rigid constitution and for drawing a clear distinction between constituent and constituted powers. Moreover, the Bulgarian constitutional court is becoming an unexpected player in the external power of the state. Last but not least, the Bulgarian constitutional court has established itself as the gatekeeper of the bridge between the EU and the Bulgarian constitutional orders.

Furthermore, I demonstrate that the procedure for the transfer of constitutional competences to the EU provided by the Bulgarian Constitution is an 'unconstitutional constitutional amendment' that is enhancing the potential of the Bulgarian constitutional court to be the ultimate player in multilevel constituent power games. This is done on the basis of a comparative analysis of the procedure for amendment of the constitution and the procedure for transfer of constitutional amendments to the EU against the background of the case-law of the Bulgarian constitutional court related to the EU integration.

Finally, I come to the conclusion that stringent amendment procedures for domestic constitutional change enhance the role of domestic constitutional courts as players in constituent power games in the context of the EU multilevel constitutionalism. In the light of the Bulgarian case it is highly questionable whether rigid constitutions really protect sovereignty or foster alternative ways for amendment and even surpassing the restraints to EU integration imposed by the domestic constitution. Rigid constitutions may foster 'unconstitutional constitutional amendments' accomplished by alliances of constituted powers – parliaments and constitutional courts – acting as *de facto* constituent powers.

Another important conclusion is that the open texture of the 1991 Constitution, the fuzziness of the EU integration clause, the lack of clear and coherent concept underlying the constitutional foundations of the Bulgarian EU membership, and the already established tradition of judicial activism and jurisprudential virtual amendment of the Constitution make the Bulgarian constitutional court the ultimate player in multilevel constituent power games. The Bulgarian constitutional court is even the ultimate player in the strategic shaping of the framework, principles, and the range of the constituent power. This strategic place of the Bulgarian constitutional court is the result of tactical use of a combination of explicit pro-European activism in seminal decisions paving the way to EU integration and implicit constitutional nationalism in instances that keep the control of the domestic players over the points of interaction between the supranational and the national constitutional orders.

The chapter by Antonios Kourotakis, 'Courts in the constitution-making process: Paradoxes and justifications', explores the role of the judiciary in the constitution-making process in four constitutional orders. These are Colombia, South Africa, Honduras, and Nepal. The author briefly summarizes the classical definition of constituent power launched in modern political and constitutional theory. He reminds us that according to this traditional account the courts are by definition excluded from the constituent power and thus from the accomplishment of constitutional amendment.

However, the author also proves that

> the existence of an interim constitution or a total revision of the existing constitution may grant direct authority to the court to intervene in the constitution-making process, for instance by controlling the constituent assembly, reviewing its acts and even certifying the final constitutional document. In addition, the courts' participation in the constitution-making process might

> be justified on substantive grounds such as natural law principles, common constitutional principles, or the so-called supra-constitutional principles that exist in every democratic society and are pervaded in the general belief of the people.

Kouroutakis explicitly defines the aim of his chapter. This aim is 'to highlight paradoxes but also to offer justifications, both formal and substantive, for the intervention of the Courts in the constitutionalization of a new legal order'.

The author defines the concept of constituent power 'in order to highlight the paradoxes from the judicial intervention in the constitution making process'. Moreover, he presents the limits of the constituent power. Then he outlines the formal and substantial justifications for the courts' intervention. Subsequently Kouroutakis explains the theoretical framework of the total revision of the constitution and argues that 'such process also offers formal justifications for the courts' intervention'. The final part of the chapter provides for insightful case studies of the constitution-making process in Nepal, Colombia, and Honduras with a special emphasis on the role of courts in it.

Kouroutakis suggests that 'the existence of an interim constitution offers the conditions for the participation of the courts in the constitution-making process'. He proves his thesis with a case study of the constitutional amendment process in South Africa using Jon Elster's theory of upstream and downstream constraints on the constituent power. The author believes that excepting the interim constitution there is also one more formal justification for engagement of courts in constituent power. Kouroutakis suggests that this is the explicit recognition of the procedure for total revision of the constitution in the text of the constitution itself.

Kouroutakis contrasts the South African case, where a formal justification for the engagement of the constitutional court was in place, with the cases of Nepal, Colombia, and Honduras. In the last three states a substantial justification was needed. In the part of the chapter devoted to the substantial justifications for the participation of the judiciary in the constitution-making process Kouroutakis also engages in the debate on the unconstitutional constitutional amendments. Kouroutakis explains the role of moral principles, general values, and the suggestion for substantial hierarchy of the constitutional provisions for the engagement of courts in the constitution-making process. Again, his theoretical assumptions are proved on the basis of examples from Nepal, Colombia, and Honduras.

The chapter by Michael Hein, 'The least dangerous branch? Constitutional review of constitutional amendments in Europe', is a valuable contribution to the contemporary debate in constitutional theory and political theory on several interrelated topics. These are the issues of the judicialization of constitutional politics, judicial activism, the engagement of courts in constitutional reform, and unconstitutional constitutional amendments. The key question posed by the author is the following one: 'does constitutional review of constitutional amendments empirically contribute to the protection of modern democracy, or is it endangering the people's democratic right of self-government?' Hein's chapter is engaged in the intellectual debate on the role of constitutional courts in constitutional politics debated by all chapters belonging to Part III of this volume.

One of the most important contribution of Hein's chapter is that it is grounded on impressive empirical research. The author makes us acquainted with 154 decisions that European national courts have made on the constitutionality of constitutional amendments from 1945 until 2016. On the basis of this solid data analysis Hein's main claim and conclusion is 'that when invalidating constitutional amendments, European courts predominantly do so in a democracy-adverse, judicial activist manner'.

Hein starts with the convincing example of the Constitutional Court of Moldova which changed the form of government by striking down a constitutional reform of the procedure for election of the President many years after it had been adopted by the constituent power. After demonstrating the clear need for reflection on the engagement of constitutional courts in constitutional reform and in controlling its substantial and procedural compliance with the constitutional model of the constituent power, Hein carefully explains his methodology and the conceptual framework that lies at the basis of his research. More precisely, the author defines judicial activism, outlines its different manifestations, and contrasts it with judicial self-restraint. He provides an insight into how to identify judicial activism in the constitutional review of constitutional amendments. This is done on the basis of substantive assessment of court decisions which enables the author

> to determine whether they constitute a case of judicial activism encroaching on the people's democratic right of self-government instead of protecting democracy, or a case of judicial restraint, that is, a decision that accepts the people's democratic right of self-government and intervenes only insofar as the court is (at least implicitly) entitled and called upon by the constitution to do so.

Furthermore, Hein develops 'a framework for the substantive analysis of court decisions' and explores the 'phenomenon of constitutional review of constitutional amendments in the literature on judicial activism'. The author provides the reader with a brief overview of the history of the constitutional review of constitutional amendments in Europe since 1945. An important contribution is the provision of typical examples of judicial self-restraint and judicial activism as well as their visualization via comparative tables.

Finally, Hein summarizes his key findings and provides some conclusions regarding 'their implications for the normative debate on and the constitutional practice of reviewing constitutional amendments'. In his account 'constitutional review of constitutional amendments has become an important and regular feature in many European countries' that 'fluctuates between judicial activism and judicial restraint'. Hein's analysis shows that most decisions are either completely or partially restrained non-interventions (interventions which do not produce any real change) or activist decisions. The author concludes that 'constitutional review of constitutional amendments – although theoretically a reasonable feature of the protection of modern constitutional democracy – is empirically the opposite: a threat to democracy'.

The fourth and final part of the book addresses the challenges to courts stemming out of the rise of illiberal democracies, democratic backsliding, and self-assertive executives. While many of the previous chapters explore the judicialization of politics, consisting of the engagement of courts in constituent, legislative, and executive power, the two chapters of Part IV provide an analysis of the reversed problem, namely the political pressure of the political powers on the courts. Thus, Part I and Part IV of the volume frame the book by focusing on the problem of politicization of the judiciary.

Part IV of the book consists of two chapters which are logically interconnected. The chapter by Angela Di Gregorio, 'Constitutional courts in the context of constitutional regression: Some comparative remarks', sets the conceptual framework of the challenges to courts in the context of democratic backsliding whereas the subsequent and final chapter by Enrico Albanesi explores concrete mechanisms, instruments, and procedures that may provide a remedy for violations of the rule of law inflicting infringement of judicial independence by political powers and especially by illiberal executives.

Di Gregorio's chapter is devoted to the 'limitations on the independence of constitutional courts' as 'the main pointers of constitutional regression'. Thus, her chapter should be read in conjunction with the chapter by Konrad Lachmayer addressing the challenges to judicial independence in the context of rising illiberalism, neo-nationalism, and democratic backsliding. Both chapters are a solid theoretical basis paving the way for the research on the effectiveness of possible sanctions of illiberal regimes for infringement of the rule of law in the EU – a topic explored by the last chapter in this volume written by Enrico Albanesi.

Di Gregorio's chapter analyzes 'how the "normalization" or "neutralization" of the courts has triggered and then maintained illiberal degeneration'. This task is settled in the context of a comparative constitutional research combined with a case study of the challenges to constitutional courts' independence in Hungary, Poland, Russia, Turkey, and Venezuela.

The author explores the problem of constitutional regressions challenging the perspective of constitutional transitology and more precisely its 'transition paradigm'. She explains the relationship between the 'degeneration' and 'transition' paradigms used to explain the role of constitutional courts and their independence in fragile, semi-established, or non-established democracies.

Di Gregorio explores the problematic interplay between semi-consolidated democratic and non-consolidated authoritarian features in the emerging illiberal democracies in the context of democratic backsliding with a special emphasis on their effect on constitutional courts. Di Gregorio suggests that there are several factors for 'the involvement of constitutional courts in constitutional regression'.

Some of them coincide with those outlined in Konrad Lachmayer's chapter. In Di Gregorio's account

> the main aspects on which attention should be focused are the ways in which degeneration occurred (through the modification of or derogation from the constitution), the role of the constitutional courts in this regression (as victims or co-protagonists) and after it, the responsibility and failure of supranational actors.

Di Gregorio sets the constitutional, socio-political, and historical context of the development of democratic and authoritarian trends in the countries which are object of her research. She outlines the commonalities and the differences in their constitutional progress as well as in their constitutional regressions. On the basis of this general socio-legal panorama she explains the role of constitutional courts in constitutional regressions. The author traces in detail the historical misuse of courts for the purpose of fostering of political illiberalism and authoritarianism or the ways the executive power has limited or even suppressed judicial independence, blocking the courts as safeguards for rule of law and democracy.

Di Gregorio also engages with the discussion on constitutional identity. In her account, the recourse to constitutional identity may be a way for defense of a policy of resilience against international and supranational courts promoted by some domestic constitutional courts. According to Di Gregorio, in order 'to legitimate constitutional regression a constitutional court must elaborate its own theory of "constitutional identity"'. She explores the divergent ways in which the different national constitutional courts of illiberal democracies develop their own concepts of constitutional identity and use them as shield against international and supranational organizations. Finally, the author offers her conclusions for the future spread of constitutionally masqueraded authoritarian regimes and the role of courts in their overcoming, democratization or, vice versa, maintenance, and further development.

The chapter by Enrico Albanesi, 'The use of the EU infringement procedures to protect *de facto* the rule of law via the development of the parameter: From obligations under the Treaties to the Charter of Fundamental Rights', is a logical continuation of the concerns which were raised in the previous chapters of Konrad Lachmayer and Angela Di Gregorio. Albanesi explores a specific problem related to the emerging illiberal democracies in the EU. His analysis is devoted to the use of the EU infringement procedures to protect the rule of law.

The main task of Albanesi's chapter is to explore which should be the most appropriate procedure to be used as a remedy against rule of law infringements of the Member States. The author stipulates that

> the path under Article 7 TEU is seen as a sort of "nuclear option" because of its politically devastating effects: due to political obstacles, it has not been used so far and it is very unlikely that it will be used.

He highlights the fact that 'the principle of the rule of law and the other EU fundamental values are protected according to Article 7 TEU through mechanisms that are essentially political. These political mechanisms have actually failed in protecting constitutional democracy'. Albanesi explores the use of infringement procedures by the European Commission and the Court of Justice of the EU to protect the EU fundamental values under Article 2 TEU. The author provides several cases serving as examples of such procedures against Hungary and Poland.

Albanesi concludes that although the 'European Commission has always started such types of infringement procedures on the grounds of breach of specific provisions of EU law only' and 'it would be highly unlikely that the European Commission would seek a judgment solely finding an infringement of the values of Article 2', nevertheless it has served a protective function for the rule of law and the other EU fundamental values under Article 2 TEU. According to Albanesi 'the use of infringement procedures to tackle *indirectly* issues concerning the violation of the EU fundamental values under Article 2 TEU and in particular the rule of law, was effective and gained results.'

Part I

Courts and democracy

1 Democracy and courts beyond the ideological banality

Daniel Valchev

1.1 Introduction

In this chapter, I shall not induce arguments in order to prove that *today's liberal democracy* is the only right form of governance in the 21st century. It seems to me that after the *Habermas–Rawls debate* of the 1990s it would be a fruitless effort to point out new arguments in this direction, whether they be of a procedural or a substantial nature.[1] I shall not strive to prove the opposite either – that this is an exhausted political and value paradigm that ought to be forsaken, or at least significantly altered. An attempt at this would offer a certain intellectual temptation but would be futile without outlining a desirable alternate political model, such as contemporary societies have not, as of yet, discovered.

Within this chapter, I shall try to do three things:

(a) present my views on the main internal contradiction of the contemporary democratic paradigms, as well as on how the changing social environment influences this contradiction;

(b) outline the role of the Court in maintaining the contemporary democratic systems of the Western type in a relative balance and what are (in my opinion) the expectations in that respect;

(c) appeal for extreme caution when it comes to disempowerment and especially 'disenchantment'[2] of the Court.

1 I am inclined to agree that the two theories are close on the axis of procedurality/substantiality, as far as John Rawls' *Theory of Justice* justly claims to have the characteristics of a procedural theory, while Jürgen Habermas' *Discourse Ethics* is not at all deprived of presumptive substantial footing.

2 I shall use the word *disenchantment* in the way Max Weber uses the German word *Entzauberung* – meaning 'the breaking of a magic spell', i.e. a process of lifting the delusive enchantment and the illusions as to the origins, the pattern of development, or the meaning of a certain social phenomenon.

1.2 Court and separation of powers – Some banal remarks

The ideological banality requires that we present the Court not only as an important democratic institution, but as one of the most important democratic institutions. The grounds for this are just as banal as the thesis itself – without the Court, there is no way to create a system of mutually controlling authorities (or groups thereof) which guarantees that the democratic order will not be replaced by a dictatorship and, what is more important, without which individual freedom would be in danger. The Court is seldom regarded simply as one of the bodies that participate in the separation of powers. It is believed, by definition, that the court's rulings possess a very high degree of *legitimacy* as ones grounded entirely on law and justice and are thus denuded of any influence by individual or collective interests related to the political conjuncture, which is typical for the decisions of the other two branches of power.

In fact neither John Locke, nor Charles Louis de Montesquieu whom we often point out as the fathers of the theory of separation of powers, grant the Court such a place in the general balance of powers as we do today, often referring to them. As we know, Locke only bestows upon the judiciary peripheral attention, and doesn't consider it necessary to explicitly place it in the balance of powers,[3] whereas Montesquieu, while pointing it out as one of the three powers, adds that it is not a power in the strict sense of the word.[4] Regardless of the differences, they both accentuate the authorities that are involved in the creation of general rules of conduct (the Parliament or the *King in Parliament*).

The French Revolution continues this tradition by sanctioning Rousseau's view that the law is an expression of the general will. However, two of the other central theses in Rousseau's theory are forsaken – first, that the general will is not necessarily the will of the majority (according to him, the criterion is not quantitative at all – even the unanimous will of all may not be the general will), and second, that it can only be formed directly by the sovereign people, which means that it certainly cannot be reached through political representation.[5] The practice

3 In point of fact, we ought to note that Locke appreciates the significance of the function of justice. In the chapter named 'The purposes of political society and government', he points out that the three things which are lacking in the state of nature are 'an established, settled, known law, received and accepted by common consent', 'a known and impartial judge', and 'a power to back up and support a correct sentence, and to enforce it properly'. J. Locke, *Two Treatises of Government, Create Space Independent Publishing Platform*, 2013, II Treatise, Ch. IX.

4 'Of the three powers above mentioned, the judiciary is in some measure next to nothing'. (Original French version: 'Des trois puissances dont nous avons parlé, celle de juger est en quelque façon nulle'.) C. Montesquieu, *De l'Esprit des Lois*, Paris, Librairie de Lecointe, 1832L. XI, Ch. VI.

5 Rousseau considers the general will to be the will of a politically organized community, which he refers to with the interchangeable terms *nation*, *state*, *sovereign*, or *the body politic*. The criterion whether there is *a general will* is not quantitative at all, but whether the will is directed towards the *common interest (intérêt commun)*. Who decides whether something is in the *common interest*, and how, is a matter of complicated sophistic reasoning in Rousseau's theory.

of the French Revolution (especially during the Jacobin period) results in both forsaken theses losing their popularity but does not affect the legitimizing force of the thesis of the law as an expression of the general will.

In the 19th century in the Western world a common understanding of democracy was gradually built. Despite the numerous interpretations democracy is considered a '*system of political representation*' whereby the common will is in the Parliament's possession and the Court is called upon to apply the laws correctly.

In continental Europe the question of the Court's significance in the system of democratic separation of powers is being rediscovered within the *debate for the constitutional courts*.[6] The authority of a professional body, which is, by default, stripped of any claim to political representation, to repeal laws, poses a challenge to the traditional democratic thinking.[7] The result is an obvious paradox – a complicatedly formed collegium of experts rule on behalf of the constitutional legislator, thus controlling the ordinary legislator that creates laws on behalf of the people by whom the latter was elected.

The crisis of the parliamentary models between the two world wars gave new topics for consideration. It turned out that the rapid expansion of voting rights in combination with economic insecurity and social disappointments might give birth to *anxious majorities* with very low loyalty to the established democratic traditions. Consequently, different types of *techniques for limiting the omnipotence of the majority* were developed and refined in the post-war years. In my opinion the existing mechanisms for restraint of the majority that deserve to be considered can be reduced to the following three groups – *procedures, bodies of various professional élites, and normative ideology.*

Why am I even addressing this topic today? In my opinion there are at least three reasons.

First, the rapid development of information and communication technologies in the last decades is beginning to reflect on fundamental constellations in Western societies and cause a crisis of certain fine mechanisms for ensuring the reproduction, or at least a smooth evolution, of the social structures – education, media, cultural environment, a slower accumulation of material wealth etc. Indeed, principles in public law do not traditionally rise via network but are rather hierarchically imposed.[8] But the networks can have a strong destructive charge. It

6 This debate really is rather continental, since in the English-speaking world, the matter was put to discussion much earlier – for example, by A. Hamilton, J. Madison & J. Jay, *The Federalist Papers*, New York, Bantam Classics, 1982, p. 78.

7 This is one of the dimensions of the debate between Hans Kelsen and Carl Schmitt regarding who the guardian of the Constitution is. In the last several years, interest in the two scholars, and especially for this debate, is renewed. See for example, L. Vinx, *The Guardian of the Constitution: Hans Kelsen and Carl Schmitt on the Limits of Constitutional Law*, Cambridge, Cambridge University Press, 2015.

8 I have developed arguments in favour of this thesis in my article 'Legal Principles in Public Law', published in M. Belov (Ed.), *Rule of Law at the Beginning of the Twenty-First Century*, Den Haag, Eleven International Publishing, 2018, pp. 5–8.

is known that in chimpanzees, the young males, coordinated in a network, take the authority of the aged Alpha male away. It is a fact that hierarchy is then re-established – a new hierarchy replaces the temporary network that brought down the old hierarchy. If we follow that logic we may assume that the information and communication networks are unlikely to create new principles in public law but may seriously question the existing ones.

Second, the concept that the world is moving toward a unipolar value and political model of a Western type that flourished 30 years ago has withered, and today exists only in the form of a carefully preserved herbarium. This inevitably leads to the expectation of a new opposition of values and political models, such as a whole new generation do not remember. Furthermore, it is a generation that doesn't have the same sense of order and hierarchy as for instance mine, and that of my parents, do. Thus appear visible difficulties for people who are entering a politically active age to discern between true and false, disputable and indisputable, relatable and non-relatable.

And third, the network communication practices, combined with the lack of obvious rightness of the Western value model, breathe new life into the expectations of a new (similar to that of last century) *crisis of the parliamentary systems* and to the sympathies for those who offer radical solutions and a firm hand. The signals for this are numerous. The decay of the traditional left-right parties and the success of leaders of the populist type are only the tip of the iceberg. This tendency is significantly facilitated by mass consumer culture, which creates superficial and easily alterable tastes, and by the Internet culture of denial and encapsulation in relatively small groups of similarly thinking people.

1.3 The majority principle vs individual freedom

Whatever definition of *democracy* we may give, there is no way to avoid the statement that it is *governance based on majority support.* Every denial of this statement not only leads to a lexical paradox, but problematizes many of the basic parameters of contemporary Western political models (e.g. universal suffrage with a secret ballot and the constituting of the main governing bodies through elections). Along with this, it is impossible to deny that today's understanding of democracy is in a sustainable connection with *the concept of individual freedom.* And not individual freedom as a right of participation in the settling of public matters (as it was, according to Benjamin Constant,[9] considered in Antiquity, as well as by later authors like Rousseau) but as a protected personal perimeter of conscience and conduct – including being protected from the State and the moods of the majority that define public policy.

In my opinion, today's concept of democracy can be expressed like this: *governance founded on elections, which is, for the sake of protecting individual freedom,*

9 See Benjamin Constant, *De la Liberté des Anciens Comparée à Celle des Modernes*, Paris, Mille et Une Nuits, 2010.

restrained by procedures, bodies of professional élites, and a normative ideology. In other words, my thesis is that contemporary liberal democracy contains a fundamental *contradiction* – it is based on the idea of the people's rule (i.e. the collectivist concept of the leading role of the arithmetical majorities), and together with this it suggests a strong individualistic distrust in the decisions of these majorities and therefore restrains them through procedures, bodies, and normative ideology. The verbalization of this contradiction is not a novelty. Quite the contrary; in the last decades different explanations that deny or extenuate this contradiction have been proposed, as well as a great number of ideas and even techniques for overcoming it. But in essence this contradiction exists.

As previously noted, in my opinion, there are three groups of restraints to the majority's decisions that historically were formed and developed. *The procedures* underwent a long evolution – from direct restrictions on suffrage and the vast legislative powers of bodies constituted without elections, to the limitations on the subject and the special procedure for holding of referenda. In order to illustrate the significance of this group of restraints, I will give an example of the prohibition on holding a referendum on matters of the state budget and taxation rates that exist in many countries, Bulgaria included.[10] The obvious reason for the existence of such stipulations is the fear that the majority will probably vote in favor of both – increasing the state budget and decreasing taxes.

The second group of restraints are the *bodies with high requirements for professional competence and professional prestige* that have considerable powers and weight in public life, disproportionate to their representativeness. Typical examples of such bodies are the governing councils of national banks (and, with equal reason, that of the European Central Bank (ECB), audit offices, stock market supervision commissions, and of course, the constitutional courts.

Beyond any doubt the Court plays a key role in every one of the three restraints on majority. Whatever the differences between the procedures that limit the omnipotence of the majority, the final ruling on their compliance with the Constitution or any other high standard, as well as the ruling on their own legal correctness are, in the majority of cases, submitted to the Court. The Court is a bright example of a body with great authority, which is mainly formed on a professional principle (the elections of judges are relatively rare and by default apply only to judgeships in the lower courts).

But the most important thing is that the Court is the main keeper and protector of the *normative ideology*. In my opinion *normative ideology* is a system of

10 Article 9, para 2 of the Direct Citizen Participation in State and Local Government Act: 'The following shall not be subject to a national referendum: 1. issues which fall within the competence of the Grand National Assembly; 2. issues referred to in Article 84 (4), (6), (7), (8), (10), (12), (16), and (17); Articles 91 and 91a; Article 103 (2); Article 130 (3); Article 132a, and Article 147 (1) of the Constitution; 3. issues pertaining to the amount of taxes, charges, and labour as well as public insurance payments and contributions; 4. Issues related to the state budget; 5. issues pertaining to the rules of internal procedure and operation of the National Assembly'.

interrelated moral assertions which are regarded as general legal principles, can serve as a point of reference of the Court's interpretation of a legal case, and, in certain (politically sensitive) cases, are used for justification of legal validity (e.g. the ***Radbruch formula*** and its influence on the rulings of the German Federal Constitutional Court).[11] Another attestation to the importance of the Court's normative ideology is the fact that certain authors place it in the center of their theories on law. According to Alf Ross, for example, legal science is an empirical science and one of the two types of social facts that it examines is namely the normative ideology of the judges.

It is precisely on the field of normative ideology that the Court carries the greatest weight in protecting the individual freedom. After World War II (and to some extent as a result thereof), ***human rights*** were asserted as a leading normative ideology. Its adoption happened gradually and naturally, and today, it continues to be considered generally correct and important for the mass conscience. But should we consider human rights an ideology impossible to abandon? I am not convinced.[12] There are at least four things that evoke concern.

First, the concept of individual freedom, which lies in the foundation of human rights, was put to the test by ***the rise of terrorism*** in the context of the tension between ***liberty*** and ***security***. After the 9/11 attacks the question of restricting freedom (and therefore certain rights) for the sake of security was persistently posed. For the time being, the ideology of human rights withstands the test, but this can easily change in the event of new challenges.

Second, there are no serious prospects of ***the technological revolution*** slowing down or becoming predictable to a greater degree. The permanent changes in the way of living and in the labor market, the rapid changes in the physical environment, in day-to-day communication, and in leisure time, create a favorable environment for ***new anxious majorities***. The situation is very similar to the anxiety of man upon the decline of the Middle Ages described by Erich Fromm – one gains economic and spiritual freedom but loses ***security*** which was previously given by one's belonging to a certain economic and spiritual community.[13] Today man is more liberated in terms of lifestyle and information, but many authors point out that he is increasingly isolated and depersonalized in a world of shaken values and hierarchies, of informational chaos, and of growing economic uncertainty.

11 This matter is considered in the wonderful book by Robert Alexy, *The Argument from Injustice (A Reply to Legal Positivism)*, Oxford, Oxford University Press, 2002.

12 See Manuel Castells, ***Rupture: The Crisis of Liberal Democracy***, Cambridge, Polity Press, 2019.

13 According to Erich Fromm, by the end of the Middle Ages, man gradually becomes doubly free: on the one hand, he is liberated from the medieval feudal and corporative system and gains opportunities for freer economic activity; on the other hand, thanks to the Reformation, he is also released from the burdensome spiritual authority. As a result of the latter two though, he is also free from the bonds that ensure him belonging in the community and guarantee economic and spiritual security. Erich Fromm, *Escape from Freedom*, Oxford, Farrar & Rinehart, 1941, Ch. 3.

Third, although the *migration crisis in Europe* may not be a separate factor, it exposed and radicalized a part of the fears of Europeans. The global communication networks made drawing comparisons possible and led many people to an important conclusion – within the limits of one generation, achieving a better life is much more realistic by changing the country rather than by replacing the government. But from the point of view of the citizens of the host countries, at least two problems emerged. The first one is the fear that migrants would undermine the established way of living (through consummation or importing foreign culture, i.e. values). The second one is how to use liberal democracy not as a means of inclusion in public life but as grounds for exclusion thereof.

And last but not least – the *question of the EU élite*. Bizarre as may be, it is exactly the Brussels élite who are probably based on the most meritocratic patterns of selection and advancement that have surprisingly disproportionally low degree of legitimacy. Ivan Krastev gives a remarkable two-reasons explanation of that phenomenon.[14] On the one hand, he refers to Michael Young, according to whom an entirely meritocracy-based society would be a terrible combination of egoistic and arrogant winners and anxious and desperate losers.[15] On the other hand, most Europeans feel that this international élite are not connected to a specific place, that in the event of a crisis, they will grab their families and leave and will fulfill themselves equally well anywhere in Europe or in the world. The legal élite are traditionally *national*, due to the fact that historically national legal systems were closed systems. But the legal systems of the EU member states are quickly changing and becoming increasingly open. Wouldn't this raise the question of the confidence in the Court in the future?

1.4 Can the courts save liberal democracy?

Will the Court prove equal to these challenges? Not only are the expectations that the Court is capable of settling political matters while keeping its role of an unbiased arbiter undiminished, but expectations have been visibly growing in the last decades. One of the best examples in this regard is the development of the debate about the primacy of the European Union law over the law of the member states.

As is known, within *closed legal systems* the question of legal validity could be easily resolved from a formal point of view. In continental closed legal systems the paradigm of legal validity even possesses a geometrical clarity. Following Hans Kelsen we may assert that every norm in a legal system is legally valid inasmuch as it was created by a person (or a body) who has been empowered to do so by a legal norm that stands higher in the normative hierarchy, and was created following a procedure and based on grounds also specified in the latter norm. Thus

14 Ivan Krastev, *After Europe*, Philadelphia, PA, University of Pennsylvania Press, 2017, pp. 86–93.

15 Michael Young, *The Rise of Meritocracy 1870–2033: An Essay on Education and Society*, Oxford, Thames and Hudson, 1958.

the norms that the decrees of the executive bodies contain draw their legal validity from the norms stipulated in laws which, in turn, do so from the norms of the Constitution. The question of what gives legal validity to the constitutional norms has different possible answers. Regardless of whether we refer to Kelsen's Basic norm hypothesis, to Hart's rule of recognition, to the more complicated circular models of Raz, or to something else, the legal validity of the Constitution is after all, a matter of fact, not of norm. In simpler terms, the Constitution is valid because it is respected as a result of a tacit or explicit consensus.

The matter of legal validity becomes complicated within the *open legal systems.* In the hierarchy within the legal systems of the EU member states, two more type of norms are included – those of public international law, and those of EU law. In many member states, the correlation between the norms of the national law and of public international law is stipulated on a constitutional level. For instance, as per the Bulgarian Constitution, international treaties which have been ratified in accordance with the constitutional procedure, have been promulgated, and have come into force with respect to the Republic of Bulgaria, shall be part of the national legislation and shall have primacy over any conflicting provision thereof (Article 5, para 4). It is beyond doubt that these norms have a primacy over the norms of the national laws but hierarchically stand beneath the constitutional norms.

The question of EU law is more complicated still. As is known, the principle of EU law primacy is not explicitly stipulated in the primary EU law. It is deduced from the practice of the Court of Justice of the European Union (CJEU), established with the widely known ruling in the Case 6/64 *Costa v. Enel* (1964) and developed with a number of later rulings. An attempt was made to explicitly stipulate this principle in the founding treaties (Article I-6 of the Draft Treaty Establishing a Constitution for Europe)[16] but it didn't succeed. In the following Treaty of Lisbon the primacy of the EU law principle was abandoned and was only timidly mentioned in one of the annexed declarations.[17] Even though from a dogmatic point of view it is obvious that a body which does not have the power to amend the Constitution, has still less power to delegate to another body the creation of norms which would hierarchically stand above the Constitution, the principle of EU law primacy formulated by the CJEU is not often openly contested. Logic requires us to ask ourselves why that is.

In my opinion the reason is rooted in the fact that the national political élites who do not share the principle of EU law primacy (if they did, this principle would have simply been stipulated in the Lisbon Treaty) have to overcome not

16 Article I-6 of the Draft Treaty Establishing a Constitution for Europe: 'The Constitution and law adopted by the institutions of the Union in exercising competences conferred on it shall have primacy over the law of the Member States'.

17 Declaration concerning primacy: 'The Conference recalls that, in accordance with well settled case law of the Court of Justice of the European Union, the Treaties and the law adopted by the Union on the basis of the Treaties have primacy over the law of Member States, under the conditions laid down by the said case law'.

the standpoints of other political élites, but *rulings of the Court.* This raises at least two types of problems. On the one hand, the meddling of politicians in 'the purely legal work of the Court' contradicts the established concept of the separation of powers. On the other hand, the rulings of the Court are *a priori* assumed immune political conjuncture and are based solely on law, equity, and justice. There is hardly a doubt that the rulings of the CJEU, which establish and champion the primacy principle, are by far more politically justified than they are legally grounded. They express an obvious *political necessity* – to compensate for the deficiency of political will for a stronger integration. Nevertheless, albeit founded on a political logic, these are *Court rulings* and therefore enjoy a high level of legitimacy. Thus the national political élites found themselves in a difficult situation – opposing the fading legitimacy of representative democracy to the constant legitimacy of law, equity, and justice.

As witnessed, the national political élites found a way to counterbalance this. The formulation of the *principle of national constitutional identity* (first in the Draft Treaty Establishing a Constitution for Europe, and then in the Lisbon Treaty)[18] transformed the debate from one between politicians and a Court into one between courts. Thus, within this debate, the argument for greater legitimacy became invalid, since it would be too unconvincing to claim that the rulings of the *Court in Luxembourg* have a higher level of legitimacy compared to the *Court in Karlsruhe.*[19]

What does this example demonstrate? At first glance the Court also draws its legitimacy from reason and justice, just as the bodies constituted through political representation do. But if we follow Jouvenel's logic there are certain fine distinctions in the source of legitimacy.[20] The legitimacy of the politically constituted bodies is based mainly on arguments of the '*because*' type, i.e. arguments related to the manner of constituting these bodies (case in point, '*because* they were elected by the people'), whereas the legitimacy of the courts is much more based on arguments of the '*in order to*' type, i.e. related to the purposes these bodies were created for (case in point, '*in order to* apply the law accurately and bring equity and justice').

In view of the emerging new crisis of the parliamentary models, the significance of the Court as a keeper and protector of the normative ideology of human

18 Article 4, para 2 of the consolidated version of the Treaty on European Union (after the Lisbon Treaty): 'The Union shall respect the equality of Member States before the Treaties as well as their national identities, inherent in their fundamental structures, political and constitutional, inclusive of regional and local self-government'.

19 The majority of contemporary authors refer to this debate as a *Judicial Dialogue.* See Martin Belov, *Bulgarian Constitutional Identity*, Sofia, Sibi, 2017, p. 24 etc. (in Bulgarian). Like all notions, this one is conceptual. In this case, it is loaded with expectation for a rational conversation, a common search for acceptable decisions, and willingness for mutual compromises without which the development of the EU would be impossible.

20 Bertrand de Jouvenel, *Du Pouvoir (Histoire Naturelle de sa Croissance)*, Paris, Hachette, 1972, pp. 53–54.

rights is growing and will probably continue to grow. But we ought to ask ourselves whether the Court that was unable to oppose the political rise of any of the totalitarian ideologies of the 20th century would be able to do so at the beginning of the 21st century. That, we do not know, but it is certain that, in order for the Court to do so, it would take more than effort. It would take ***magic***.

The 18th century definitely disenchanted the State and put it on rational footing. The end of the 19th and the beginning of the 20th century disenchanted the man and reduced him to an evolved primate with a class conscience and an Oedipus complex. We should not allow the 21st century to ***disenchant the Court***. And it is precisely upon those of us who teach in Faculties of Law that a part of this great responsibility falls. Without necessarily turning law school into Harry Potter's Hogwarts, we must be conscious of the fact that we are among those who are responsible for keeping the magic of the Court alive.

References

R. Alexy, *The Argument from Injustice (A Reply to Legal Positivism)*, Oxford, Oxford University Press, 2002.

M. Belov, *Bulgarian Constitutional Identity*, Sofia, Sibi, 2017 (in Bulgarian).

M. Castells, *Rupture: The Crisis of Liberal Democracy*, Cambridge, Polity Press, 2019.

B. Constant, *De la Liberté des Anciens Comparée à Celle des Modernes*, Paris, Mille et Une Nuits, 2010.

E. Fromm, *Escape from Freedom*, Oxford, Farrar & Rinehart, 1941.

A. Hamilton, J. Madison & J. Jay, *The Federalist Papers*, New York, Bantam Classics, 1982.

B. de Jouvenel, *Du Pouvoir (Histoire Naturelle de sa Croissance)*, Paris, Hachette, 1972.

I. Krastev, *After Europe*, Philadelphia, PA, University of Pennsylvania Press, 2017.

J. Locke, *Two Treatises of Government*, Create Space Independent Publishing Platform, 2013.

C. Montesquieu, *De l'Esprit des Lois*, Paris, Librairie de Lecointe, 1832.

J.-J. Rousseau, *Du Contrat Social*, Bréal, 2015.

D. Valtchev, 'Legal Principles in Public Law', in M. Belov (Ed.), *Rule of Law at the Beginning of the Twenty-First Century*, Den Haag, Eleven International Publishing, 2018.

L. Vinx, *The Guardian of the Constitution: Hans Kelsen and Carl Schmitt on the Limits of Constitutional Law*, Cambridge, Cambridge University Press, 2015.

M. Young, *The Rise of Meritocracy 1870–2033: An Essay on Education and Society*, Thames and Hudson, 1958.

2 Disempowering courts

The interrelationship between courts and politics in contemporary legal orders or the manifold ways of attacking judicial independence

Konrad Lachmayer

2.1 Courts under attack

2.1.1 The Polish situation

The Polish judiciary is under attack in manifold ways nowadays. Based on unconstitutional legislation and pseudo-formal procedures the structures of the Polish judiciary were changed,[1] which now creates a significant impact on the judicial branch in Poland.[2] While the Court of Justice of the European Union (CJEU) already declared the early retirement of Polish judges as contradicting European Union law,[3] manifold issues were created by packing the courts and changing court procedures by the governmentally controlled parliament.[4] The destruction of the independence of the judges is not over yet. A recent development concerns various proceedings against Polish judges for disciplinary reasons.[5]

1 W. Sadurski, 'Polish Constitutional Tribunal Under PiS: From an Activist Court, to a Paralysed Tribunal, to a Governmental Enabler', *Hague Journal on the Rule of Law*, Vol. 11, No. 1, 2019, pp. 63–84.

2 This most significantly also includes the Constitutional Tribunal of Poland. See W. Sadurski, 'Constitutional Crisis in Poland', in M. A. Graber, S. Levinson & M. V. Tushnet (Eds), *Constitutional Democracy in Crisis?*, New York, Oxford University Press, 2018, pp. 257, 260–264.

3 See CJEU Judgement of 17 December 2018 in Case C-619/18, Commission v Poland. The CJEU declared that 'Poland Must Immediately Suspend the Application of the Provisions of National Legislation Relating to the Lowering of the Retirement Age for Supreme Court Judges'. <https://curia.europa.eu/jcms/upload/docs/application/pdf/2018-12/cp180204en.pdf> [Accessed 20 May 2019].

4 'The drafts and laws have produced a mosaic of interlocking provisions, some of which were invalidated by CT, with some of these invalidating judgments remaining unpublished – ending up with a picture totally obscure and incomprehensible to the general public, which probably was just the purpose'. Sadurski, 2019, p. 71.

5 See L. Pech & P. Wachowiec, '1095 Days Later: From Bad to Worse Regarding the Rule of Law in Poland (Part II)', 17 January 2019 <https://verfassungsblog.de/1095-days-later-from-bad-to-worse-regarding-the-rule-of-law-in-poland-part-ii/> [Accessed 20 May 2019].

The president of the Polish Judges Association 'IUSTITIA', Prof. Krystian Markiewicz, describes the situation in the following way:

> For several months now the disciplinary officer Piotr Schab and his two deputies Przemysław Radzik and Michał Lasota have initiated and conducted various proceedings against judges. The way of proceeding infringes the basic standards such as the right of defense. The proceedings are usually initiated against judges who are active in the field of defending the rule of law, among others by educational actions, meetings with citizens, international activity. Such proceedings are also initiated against judges who asked preliminary questions concerning the changes within the judicial system.[6]

The disciplinary commissioner, who is appointed by the Ministry of Justice for a four-year time period, prosecutes the judges. A common court judge with ten years of professional experience can be appointed as a judge of the disciplinary court

> by the Minister of Justice, after consulting the National Council of the Judiciary, for a six-year term of office. All the cases of disciplinary courts at appellate courts are heard by a bench of three judges. The number of judges in disciplinary courts should be specified by the Minister of Justice, by means of an ordinance.[7]

'A judge is liable to disciplinary actions for misconduct, including an obvious and gross violation of legal provisions and impairment of the authority of the office (disciplinary misconduct)'.[8] Furthermore, judges may face disciplinary charges if they 'violate the dignity of judges' profession'.[9] The catalogue of possible disciplinary penalties includes: an admonition, a reprimand, lowering the basic salary by 5–50% for a period up to two years, dismissal from the function held, transfer to another place of service, and dismissal from the office of a judge.

Disciplinary proceedings were started against eight judges and five public prosecutors, especially because of presenting their critical opinion in public media. In conclusion, Poland is repressing critical judges to silence them in public debate but also in their judicial behavior. 'Preliminary disciplinary investigations concern also judges who referred requests for preliminary ruling to the Court of Justice'.[10]

6 See K. Markiewicz, 'A Letter from the Polish Judges Association to Frans Timmermans', <www.rechtersvoorrechters.nl/letter-from-the-polish-judges-association-to-frans-timmermans/> [Accessed 20 May 2019].

7 M. Szuleka & M. Kalisz, 'Disciplinary Proceedings against Judges and Prosecutors', 2019, p. 2<www.hfhr.pl/wp-content/uploads/2019/02/HFHR_Disciplinary-proceedings-against-judges-and-prosecutors.pdf> [Accessed 20 May 2019].

8 Szuleka & Kalisz, 2019, p. 3.

9 Szuleka & Kalisz, 2019, p. 5.

10 See Pech & Wachowiec, 2019.

Poland is following the path of the Hungarian government, which invested much structural energy in influencing the judicial branch over years.[11] One of the starting points was again the early retirement of judges, followed by re-structuring the Curia, changing majorities in the constitutional court by court packing, which then developed new forms of interpretation of a (pre-)historical (un-)constitutional understanding of the constitution. The introduction of newly established administrative courts, which can be even more be influenced by the government, is the latest development.[12] 'The jurisdiction of this new wing of the judiciary, staffed by formed civil servants handpicked by the Minister of Justice will have jurisdiction over a wide range of cases, including – most likely – election disputes'.[13]

2.1.2 Courts in times of nationalism and authoritarianism

Political pressure on courts is not a new phenomenon, but has existed as long as courts have been established. Nevertheless, the recent developments toward authoritarianism as well as nationalism do not only illustrate democracies in decline but deeply affect the rule of law[14] or vice versa, these new attacks on courts do not only have negative effects on the judiciary but are also significant as they affect democracies as well. If courts cannot safeguard the democratic framework (free elections, opposition parties, freedom of speech etc.), neo-authoritarian approaches will have an easier chance to destroy democracy.

This phenomenon is not only limited to pressure on domestic courts but also on international courts. While international courts are primarily limited by nationalism, national courts have to deal with authoritarianism. As illustrated in another paper, the links between these two developments should not be overlooked or underestimated.[15] Thus, attacks on courts shall not only be seen in a limited perspective regarding national courts, but also in the broader context of a network of national and international courts. European Courts, like the CJEU or the European Court of Human Rights (ECtHR), are important transnational actors not only to defend against attacks on the independence of national courts, but might also be challenged by domestic governments with regard to their own judicial authority.[16]

11 G. Halmai, 'A Coup against Constitutional Democracy: The Case of Hungary', in M. A. Graber, S. Levinson & M. V. Tushnet (Eds), *Constitutional Democracy in Crisis?*, New York, Oxford University Press, 2018, pp. 243, 246.

12 R. Uitz, 'An Advanced Course in Court Packing: Hungary's New Law on Administrative Courts', *VerfBlog*, 2 January 2019, <https://verfassungsblog.de/an-advanced-course-in-court-packing-hungarys-new-law-on-administrative-courts/> [Accessed 20 May 2019].

13 Uitz, 2019.

14 A. Jakab, 'Was kann Verfassungsrecht gegen die Erosion der Demokratie und Rechtsstaatlichkeit tun?', *Zeitschrift für Öffentliches Recht*, Vol. 74, 2019 (forthcoming).

15 K. Lachmayer, 'Counter-developments to Global Constitutionalism', in M. Belov (Ed.), *Global Constitutionalism and Its Challenges to Westphalian Constitutional Law*, Oxford, Hart Publishing, 2018, pp. 81, 99–100.

16 See, e.g. S. Michalopoulos, 'Orban Attacks the European Court of Human Rights', 2017 <www.euractiv.com/section/global-europe/news/orban-attacks-the-european-court-of-human-rights-at-epp-congress/> [Accessed 20 May 2019].

The International Criminal Court (ICC), for example, is under current pressure by different domestic governments, like the UK, the Philippines, or the United States. The pressure relates to legal threats to be prosecuted by the international court.[17] The Philippines notified their withdrawal from the Rome Statute.[18] The United States attacked the ICC by announcing that the ICC judges and prosecutors cannot enter the US anymore and their funds in the US will be frozen.[19] In March 2019, the US realized their threats by revoking or denying visas of ICC judges. Moreover, the US also refused to accept an International Court of Justice (ICJ) ruling on Iran[20] by stressing the overall limitations on international courts by domestic governments. Ignoring and not accepting judgments is, thus, not only a strategy against courts on a domestic, but also on an international level.

The ECtHR was facing a referendum in Switzerland, which was opposing the European Convention on Human Rights (ECHR) at 25 November 2018. Although the initiative 'Swiss Law instead of foreign judges' failed significantly (33.8% positive votes; turnout 47.7%),[21] the initiative illustrates nationalistic approaches to limit the international protection of human rights. The UK's discussion of abolishing the Human Rights Act, exiting the ECHR, and enacting a British Bill of Rights can also be mentioned in this context.[22] Finally, the renewed

17 See, e.g. HRW, 'Pressure Point: The ICC's Impact on National Justice Lessons from Colombia, Georgia, Guinea, and the United Kingdom', 2018, <www.hrw.org/sites/default/files/report_pdf/ij0418_web_0.pdf≥ [Accessed 20 May 2019]; T. O. Hansen, 'Complementarity (in)action in the UK?', 2018, <www.ejiltalk.org/complementarityinaction-in-the-uk/≥ [Accessed 20 May 2019].

18 See ICC Press Release, 'ICC Statement on The Philippines' Notice of Withdrawal: State Participation in Rome Statute System Essential to International Rule of Law', 20 March 2018, <www.icccpi.int/Pages/item.aspx?name=pr1371> [Accessed 20 May 2019]. The Philippine context refers to the preliminary examination of the ICC's Prosecutor office to investigate in the 'war on drugs' campaign by the Philippine Government.

19 See BBC News, 'John Bolton Threatens ICC with US Sanctions', 11 September 2018, <www.bbc.com/news/world-us-canada-45474864≥ [Accessed 20 May 2019]; The Guardian, 'US to Deny Visas for ICC Members Investigating Alleged War Crimes', 15 March 2019, <www.theguardian.com/us-news/2019/mar/15/mike-pompeo-us-war-crimes-investigation-international-criminal-court≥ [Accessed 20 May 2019].

20 See N. Turak, 'US Rejects International Court of Justice Ruling on Iran, Continuing Its Isolationist Charge', 5 October 2018, <www.cnbc.com/2018/10/05/us-rejects-international-court-of-justice-ruling-on-iran-continuing-its-isolationist-charge.html≥ [Accessed 20 May 2019].

21 See the official results of the referendum <www.bk.admin.ch/ch/d/pore/va/20181125/det624.html> [Accessed 20 May 2019].

22 See Secretary of State for Justice and Lord Chancellor, The Governance of Britain (2007) p. 60 <https://assets.publishing.service.gov.uk/government/uploads/system/uploads/attachment_data/file/228834/7170.pdf> [Accessed 20 May 2019]; The Ministry of Justice, 'Rights and Responsibilities: Developing Our Constitutional Framework' (2009) pp. 11–62, <https://assets.publishing.service.gov.uk/government/uploads/system/uploads/attachment_data/file/228938/7577.pdf> [Accessed 20 May 2019]; see also Theresa May's promise to abolish the Human Rights Act in 2013: The Guardian, 'Conservatives Promise to scrap Human Rights Act After Next Election', 30 September 2013, <www.theguardian.com/law/2013/sep/30/conservitives-scrap-human-rights-act> [Accessed 20 May 2019].

refusal of the CJEU to join the ECHR illustrates the limited willingness to promote the ECHR even on a European level.[23]

Nationalistic approaches create also effects on the national rule of law. While weakening international courts, domestic courts can be attacked easier by authoritarian governments on a national level. On the other hand, authoritarian approaches do not only limit domestic courts in their independence, but also affect the acceptance of following the judgments of international courts.

2.1.3 Cultural diversity based on the general idea of the independence of courts

A crucial element of this comparative study of the recent authoritarian and nationalistic developments is the cultural divergence of the concept of the independence of courts. Each court system is unique; thus, different elements of judicial independence are relevant when it comes to a specific constitutional order.[24] The following comparison cannot analyze the cultural details of each mentioned legal order, but it can be based on a fundamental understanding of the idea of the independence of courts as a separate branch of government.[25] The general idea of the independence of courts is not expressed by one unified, coherent, or universal court system.[26] Cultural diversity, however, cannot serve as justification or legitimation to undermine or destroy judicial independence. This chapter identifies problems and challenges of courts in different legal systems with the idea to create an overview of the different strategies of disempowerment of courts. By doing so, the chapter seeks to enable democratic systems to understand even small or seemingly minor changes of court systems, which can be the starting point of much bigger attacks on court systems in liberal democracies.[27]

As a starting point for a discussion about political pressure on courts, the rise of courts in contemporary legal orders shall be analyzed (Section 2.2). The legal power as well as the political influence of courts increased significantly in the last 30 years. Based on these developments, the scholarly debate focused on questions of the interrelation between the legislator and the judiciary. In the meantime, we,

23 See CJEU Opinion of 18 December 2014, Opinion 2/13 (para. 258: 'The agreement on the accession of the European Union to the European Convention for the Protection of Human Rights and Fundamental Freedoms is not compatible with Article 6(2) TEU or with Protocol (No 8) relating to Article 6(2) of the Treaty on European Union on the accession of the Union to the European Convention on the Protection of Human Rights and Fundamental Freedoms'.

24 A. Seibert-Fohr, 'Introduction: The Challenge of Transition', in A. Seibert-Fohr (Ed.), *Judicial Independence in Transition*, Heidelberg, Springer, 2012, p. 14.

25 D. Smilov, 'The Judiciary: The Least Dangerous Branch?', in M. Rosenfeld & A. Sajó (Eds), *The Oxford Handbook of Comparative Constitutional Law*, Oxford, Oxford University Press, 2012, pp. 859, 864–866.

26 See with regard to different concepts and expressions, e.g. A. Seibert-Fohr (ed.), *Judicial Independence in Transition*, Heidelberg, Springer, 2012.

27 See with regard to the manifold developments, M. A. Graber, S. Levinson & M. V. Tushnet (Eds), *Constitutional Democracy in Crisis?*, New York, Oxford University Press, 2018.

however, can observe the rise of the executive, which regains power and affects the role of the courts (as well as other actors) (Section 2.3). The consequences, especially in the context of neo-authoritarianism and nationalism, is an attack on courts in manifold ways. The chapter identifies and structures these strategies of disempowerment of courts. This includes an increasing institutional influence on courts and personal pressure on judges, as well as procedural changes, which create possibilities of control and limitation of courts (Section 2.4). In conclusion, an erosion of the rule of law can be identified (Section 2.5). Finally, strategies shall be developed on how courts in transnational networks can support each other and how civil society can strengthen the importance and the resilience of independent courts.

2.2 The rise of the courts

Fifteen years ago Ran Hirschl wrote in his ground-breaking book *Towards Juristocracy* about the 'expansion of judicial power through constitutionalization and the corresponding acceleration of the judicialization of politics' (2004). The political power of courts was on the rise and this gave them strong influence to shape the legal framework of societies. In this chapter it is not possible to give even an overview of these complex tremendous developments. The rise of the political power of courts did not stop on a domestic level but created international networks of courts,[28] including judges meeting each other,[29] citing foreign precedents,[30] and starting judicial dialogues.[31]

These developments led to – primarily academic – discussions of empowering courts in democratic societies on the one hand and the (anti-majoritarian) effects on role of parliaments on the other hand. Courts did not only have a limiting function to guarantee constitutionalism (especially rights) but went further as an innovative power with creative possibilities as a positive legislator.[32] Mark Tushnet pleaded in the context of social rights for 'Weak Courts, Strong Rights'.[33] The debate focused in general on the question of whether democratic legitimized parliaments or the independent judges of supreme/constitutional courts shall have the final say.

28 See A.-M. Slaughter, *A New World Order*, Princeton, NJ, Princeton University Press, 2005, p. 65.

29 See, e.g. the International Association of Judges, <www.iaj-uim.org/home/> [Accessed 20 May 2019].

30 T. Groppi & M.-C. Ponthoreau (Eds), *The Use of Foreign Precedents by Constitutional Judges*, Oxford, Hart Publishing, 2013.

31 See A. Arnull, 'Judicial Dialogue in the European Union', in J. Dickson & P. Eleftheriadis (Eds), *Philosophical Foundations of European Union Law*, Oxford, Oxford University Press, 2012, p. 109.

32 See A. R. Brewer Carías, *Constitutional Courts as Positive Legislators: A Comparative Law Study*, Cambridge, UK, Cambridge University Press, 2011.

33 M. V. Tushnet, *Weak Courts, Strong Rights: Judicial Review and Social Welfare Rights in Comparative Constitutional Law*, Princeton, NJ, Princeton University Press, 2008.

While courts gained more political power, the de-politicization of courts was demanded in the context of the rule of law.[34] Strengthening the independence of courts should create a strong legal system without political influences. A recent discussion even declared judges to be social heroes, referring to 'towering judges'.

> Political towering judges are those that promote a particular ideological, moral or political agenda or change. This change can be liberal, rights-protecting, or globalist (Barak, Mason, Bhagwati, Warren); tied to particular circumstances, such as helping to oust an autocratic regime (Valenzuela); or to integrate the country into the EU (Sólyom).[35]

While an anti-individualist legal culture was identified in Germany, this individualistic approach to judges[36] somehow illustrates the peak of political, legal, and social power of courts. While the uprising challenges will need even more hero judges, it will be much more important not only to look at iconic judges but at the large number of judges who have to uphold the independence of courts in their daily life, with their daily decisions and an overall judicial attitude.

The glory days of courts and judges, however, do not seem to be prolonged in the same way as in the last 30 years. It is important to look closer to the situation in different countries to identify the particular challenges, which are on the rise.

2.3 Separation of powers

The function of courts in a democracy as a separate branch of the state is to grant effective legal protection in civil and criminal law as well as to control the administration's actions. Constitutional and supreme courts with elements of constitutional adjudication go far beyond these basic judicial functions. Guaranteeing human rights, invalidation of statutory law, applying (self-developed) constitutional principles, controlling the rule of law, and stabilizing a federal system are just some of these constitutional competences.[37] In such an extended concept constitutional/supreme courts create a tight conceptual framework for the legislator, which has to be considered in various fields of policies and governmental politics. Principles of

34 See G. Gee, 'The Persistent Politics of Judicial Selection', in A. Seibert-Fohr (Ed.), *Judicial Independence in Transition*, Heidelberg, Springer, 2012, pp. 121, 145.

35 I. Porat & R. Abeyratne, 'Symposium: Towering Judges in Comparative Perspective: Introduction', *IACL-AIDC Blog*, 4 March 2019, <https://blog-iacl-aidc.org/2019-posts/2019/3/4/towering-judges-in-comparative-perspective-introduction-thhnc> [Accessed 20 May 2019].

36 See even cinema films, which declare judges to be heroes; see, e.g. the film about Ruth-Bader Ginsburg: RBG (2018).

37 See, e.g. C. Moellers, *The Three Branches: A Comparative Model of Separation of Powers*, Oxford, Oxford University Press, 2013, pp. 126–142.

reasonableness,[38] the concept of an invisible constitution,[39] or (eternal) principles of constitutional law,[40] like the rule of law or democracy, as well as newly created fundamental rights[41] are applied by constitutional/supreme courts.

These developments introduced and intensified the role of courts in the political sphere. Courts gained political control over the constitutional arena.[42] Their judgments defined the legal framework within which politics could develop further political considerations or initiatives.[43] In many countries, in which constitutional courts have not existed before or a supreme court did not have constitutional functions, the situation changed and an active constitutional/supreme court became a core factor in politics. The German Constitutional Court or the US Supreme Court usually served as an example. Even countries with their own constitutional tradition on supreme/constitutional courts like the UK[44] or France[45] adopted a model which referred to international standards and partly left their particular approach to the rule of law.

This kind of politicization by the courts became even more complex with the rising importance of international courts and the transnational communication of courts. The functions of these networks of courts in the transnational era,[46] especially within the European Union, affected not only domestic but also transnational politics. The primacy of Union law linked with the broad application of the Charter of Fundamental Rights transformed the CJEU into a powerful court, which furthermore was supported by domestic courts to guarantee the application of Union law in Europe. The ECHR did not only develop its human rights case law, but created also institutional guarantees like the independence of courts as a human right (Art 6. ECHR).[47] The network of courts created a transnational

38 See with regard to Austria, M. Stelzer, *The Constitution of the Republic of Austria: A Contextual Analysis*, Oxford, Hart Publishing, 2011, p. 242.

39 See with regard to Hungary, G. A. Tóth, 'Lost in Transition. Invisible Constitutionalism in Hungary', in R. Dixon & A. Stone (Eds), *The Invisible Constitution in Comparative Perspective*, Cambridge, UK, Cambridge University Press, 2018, pp. 541–562.

40 See with regard to Germany, U. K. Preuss, 'The Implications of "Eternity Clauses": The German Experience', *Israel Law Review*, Vol. 44, No. 3, 2011, pp. 429–448.

41 See M. Hailbronner & S. Martini, 'The German Federal Constitutional Court', in A. Jakab, A. Dyevre & G. Itzcovich (Eds), *Comparative Constitutional Reasoning*, Cambridge, UK, Cambridge University Press, 2017, pp. 356, 388–389.

42 R. Hirschl, *Towards Juristocracy: The Origins and Consequences of the New Constitutionalism*, Harvard, Harvard University Press, 2007.

43 Hirschl, 2007.

44 E. F. Delaney, 'Judiciary Rising: Constitutional Change in the United Kingdom', *Northwestern University Law Review*, Vol. 108, No. 2, 2014, pp. 543, 569–572.

45 O. Pfersmann, 'Concrete Review as Indirect Constitutional Complaint in French Constitutional Law, A Comparative Perspective', *European Constitutional Law Review*, Vol. 6, No. 2, 2010, p. 223.

46 See V. C. Jackson, *Constitutional Engagement in a Transnational Era*, New York, Oxford University Press, 2010.

47 See A. Seibert-Fohr, 'Judicial Independence – The Normativity of an Evolving Transnational Principle', in A. Seibert-Fohr (Ed.), *Judicial Independence in Transition, Heidelberg, Springer*, 2012, pp. 1279, 1353–1356.

system of rule of law, within which the courts are dynamically interacting with each other.[48] Within the system of separation of powers these developments shifted political powers toward the judiciary.

In the last years the executive is, however, turning away from these developments of the last 30 years. Nowadays the long-lasting discourse about constitutionalism is confronted with developments of governmental authoritarianism.[49] We can observe a shift of paradigm: instead of limiting government (by constitutionalism) dominating constitutional law (by the government) is the upcoming approach. This shift towards the executive significantly affects the role of courts. From the perspective of separation of powers, the new rivals of the courts are not the parliaments anymore but dominating governments, which are pushing back parliaments and courts alike.

The executive is re-gaining power by different strategies. Although this chapter is not in particular focusing on such strategies, some aspects shall be shortly mentioned, e.g. a constitution-amending majority, the declaration of a state of emergency or governmental empowerment by the legislator.

A constitutional amending majority in Hungary opened the possibility for the Hungarian government to take over control step by step; while controlling the parliament, the president, and the ministries was the starting point, influence on the media and the amendment of the voting system were further steps. The influence on the courts required different strategies, which will be discussed in the next section.

The declaration of a state of emergency becomes an effective possibility for governments to circumvent the parliament to gain further powers and to limit the judicial control at the same time. The French state of emergency has to be mentioned in this regard[50] as well as the state of emergency which was declared by the Trump government in the US.[51]

In the context of the British Brexit debate the empowerment of the government by the EU Withdrawal Act 2018 is not the focus of perspectives. Regarding sec. 8 para. 1 of the European Union (Withdrawal) Act 2018

> [a] Minister of the Crown may by regulations make such provision as the Minister considers appropriate to prevent, remedy or mitigate (a) any failure of retained EU law to operate effectively, or (b) any other deficiency in retained EU law, arising from the withdrawal of the United Kingdom from the EU.

48 K. Lachmayer, 'Between International Standards and Transnational Greed, Providing Transnational Rule of Law in Times of Economic Crisis', *Hague Journal on the Rule of Law*, Vol. 8, No. 2, 2016, pp. 291, 292–294, 306–307.

49 Lachmayer, 2018, pp. 86–89.

50 T. Mariniello, 'Prolonged Emergency and Derogation of Human Rights, Why the European Court Should Raise Its Immunity System', *German Law Journal*, Vol. 20, No. 1, 2019, pp. 46, 52–54.

51 K. L. Scheppele, 'Trump's Non-Emergency Emergency', *VerfBlog*, 2019 <https://verfassungsblog.de/trumps-non-emergency-emergency/> [Accessed 20 May 2019].

In the nationalistic context of Brexit, a huge empowerment of the government creates significant possibilities for the government to change statutory acts, which are usually reserved to be amended by the legislature. Recent developments illustrate the dramatic attacks on the sovereignty of parliament in the UK.

These different developments to strengthen the political power of the governments especially affect courts, who are or have been an important bearer of political powers, which typically increased in the last 20–30 years (through interpretation or new competences). Different strategies and new intensities can nowadays be observed, how courts in general and supreme/constitutional courts are disempowered.

Before focusing on the typologies of disempowerment of courts, it is important to stress the difference between the discourses on the role of courts in democratic societies and the authoritarian destruction of independence. The power of courts in liberal democracies can be limited in different ways without endangering the independence of courts.[52] The following analysis, however, focuses on the authoritarian strategies to limit the role of courts by destroying their judicial independence.

2.4 Typologies of disempowerment

2.4.1 Overview

There is a necessity to create awareness of how pressure was and is put on courts. The importance of this knowledge does not only refer to countries in constitutional decline but also to all other liberal democracies. First attacks on the independence of courts can develop very inconspicuously, but might be relevant for further developments toward authoritarianism. The following typologies of disempowerment of courts shall enable academia and civil society to identify developments toward a weakening of courts. Even seemingly harmless institutional changes to the judiciary can turn out to be subversive strategies to weaken the judiciary from a long-term perspective. As possibilities to influence courts are manifold it is necessary to identify the main concepts to weaken the independence of courts.

Many of these strategies are clearly violating the rule of law and reveal the obvious intention by the government to get the judiciary under control. Controlling the judiciary disables the judiciary to control the government and unleashes the political powers of government. At the same time the rights of individuals are weakened significantly and legal protection loses its function as a tool to guarantee the principle of legality. By these developments the necessity of the government to comply with legal standards is undermined. Moreover, as observed, e.g. in Poland, courts can be misused to support authoritarian strategies of the government.[53]

52 See, e.g. M. V. Tushnet, *Taking the Constitution Away from the Courts*, Princeton, NJ, Princeton University Press, 2000.

53 Sadurski, 2019, pp. 77–81.

Different analyses already identified certain vulnerabilities of court systems. Vicki Jackson identified the following relevant criteria of judicial independence:[54]

- the power to select;
- tenure;
- financial dependence (salaries and pensions);
- recusal, disqualifications, and bans on extrajudicial activities;
- decisional authority and jurisdiction;
- legislative control of procedural rules;
- particular procedures;
- unanimity or separate opinions;
- authority to remove;
- immunity in civil damages;
- working conditions (physical security);
- administrative and budgetary autonomy;
- mandatory judicial education.

In his concept of constitutional resilience Christoph Grabenwarter identifies three Achilles' heels of constitutional courts:

- composition of a court and election of judges;
- modification of procedural law;
- acceptance of the constitutional court and its case-law by government.[55]

Courts are disempowered by different governmental strategies, which have to be analyzed in more detail. Usually, different strategies are combined to increase the influence on courts. Different dimensions can be distinguished in these governmental strategies of disempowerment:

The first dimension refers to courts as an institution and to the institutional design of a court. By legal change or political pressure, the institutional framework can be attacked directly. This creates anti-judicial damage within the court and affects the independence of judges in their daily work, changes majorities in decision-making or limits the effectiveness of proceedings. The government limits the courts' competences and/or the court will be influenced from outside.

The second dimension relates to the judges themselves. Different strategies exist to influence the judges directly. The judge as a person or his personal environment will be influenced in general or in deciding a particular case. Other approaches aims to create conformity with governmental politics or to weaken at least the resistance of the judges.

54 V.C. Jackson, 'Judicial Independence: Structure, Context, Attitude', in A. Seibert-Fohr (Ed.), ***Judicial Independence in Transition***, Heidelberg, Springer, 2012, p. 19.

55 C. Grabenwarter, 'Constitutional Resilience', *VerfBlog*, 6 December 2018, <https://verfassungsblog.de/constitutional-resilience/> [Accessed 20 May 2019].

The third dimension addresses court procedures. Court proceedings depend on a legal framework, which can be limited by the government. Moreover, authoritarian governments create strategies to ignore court judgments or to revise them on unreasonable grounds. This approach can be reached within the hierarchical court system itself or by using the power of legislation.

All three dimensions of disempowerment are usually combined in different ways and mutually dependent. It can be also one measure alone which does the damage. Within these dimensions various governmental strategies exist. Thus, it is not possible to identify all strategies, but to analyze at least some core strategies of different governments. In a comparative approach the following strategies can be observed to obstruct the independence of courts:[56]

- Institutional dimension (influencing/limiting the court):
  - limiting competences of courts;
  - re-organizing courts;
  - creating new supervising authorities/new courts;
  - packing the court;
  - criticizing courts publicly or
  - controlling/reducing the budget of the judiciary.
- Personal dimension (influencing/attacking judges):
  - nomination of judges;
  - introducing early retirement schemes;
  - (personal) threatening of judges/personal restrictions;
  - dividing the judges;
  - silencing the judges, disciplinary measures;
  - recall of judges/removal from office/impeachment or
  - imprisonment of judges.
- Procedural dimension (influencing/changing the judgments):
  - procedural amendments (obstructing and blocking procedures);
  - influencing decision-making directly;
  - changing the procedural setting (e.g. by shortening the decision deadlines, creating immunities for politicians);
  - playing courts off against each other;
  - refusing to publish judgments;
  - revising judgments; or
  - ignoring judgments.

All these anti-judicial approaches of authoritarian or nationalistic governments can be observed on a national level. The very same strategies are also applied to argue that international or European courts should be limited. The attempts to influence and to control international courts can, however, not as easily be achieved by one

56 At least some of these strategies can be used legitimately in liberal democracies to re-shape the role of courts within the domestic separation of powers.

member state. Certain strategies are preferred by states, e.g. to ignore judgments or to implement them only half-heartedly. Exiting international judicial orders also reduces the possibilities for international courts, which can be the result of neo-nationalism on a domestic level. It will typically affect the rule of law in the particular country and strengthen authoritarian tendencies domestically.

The political reasoning of governments for introducing anti-judicial measures are manifold: actual developments, like terrorist attacks or other threats to national security, are used as an argumentation; as well as efficiency arguments to restructure courts or court proceedings; budgetary constraints are instrumentalized as well as organizational matters (e.g. the introduction of new courts to strengthen the court structure).[57] As already mentioned, certain changes of the judiciary can also be implemented for good reasons in liberal democracies which are not shifting toward authoritarianism. The criterion to assess the particular changes is, however, the effect on judicial independence.

Authoritarian tendencies in governments are sometimes concealed in complex ways. Some governments are for example arguing with comparative constitutional law to justify changes in the institutional balance of the state. The reasoning goes the following: the measure which shall be introduced does not contradict the rule of law, because it also exists in other democratic states. Thus, the introduction will not endanger (but maybe even shall improve) the rule of law. The opposite, however, is the case, because when using legal transplants, it is necessary to consider the overall concept of checks and balances as well as the rule of law in a particular country. It is necessary to understand how a certain court or court procedure functions in a particular legal culture. These cultural elements, like the history, politics and society, have to be taken into consideration.

Misusing constitutional ideas with bad intentions can easily turn 'the migration of constitutional ideas'[58] into manipulative creation of authoritarian concepts, which seems to have a legitimate foundation in comparative constitutional law. This kind of constitutional cherry-picking to legitimize the disempowerment of courts is based on a superficial understanding of constitutional law, which often uses constitutional law as a textual façade to hide illiberal and authoritarian politics.

If the authoritarian dissatisfaction with courts gets bigger, the attacks, however, will become more direct. Judges are criticized personally and judgments are attacked harshly. In such cases the attempts to influence courts are not covered with (pseudo-)rational arguments anymore but addressed directly. Influencing courts becomes an official strategy and the independence of court is no longer part of the domestic rule of law. Usually even in this situation the constitutional text still refers to judicial independence. This illustrates that even undermined elements of judicial independence might remain.

57 Uitz, 2019.

58 S. Choudhry, 'Migration as a New Metaphor in Comparative Constitutional Law', in S. Choudhry (Ed.), *The Migration of Constitutional Ideas*, Cambridge, UK, Cambridge University Press, 2006, pp. 1–35.

2.4.2 Institutional dimension (influencing/limiting the court)

Beside the possibility of using existing democratic competences, e.g. the nomination or appointment of loyal lawyers to become judges, the most effective way for authoritarian governments to influence courts is the reorganization of courts by amending statutory law. In times of reorganization of the judiciary, it is easy to exchange judges and to bring in new judges who are estimated to share the ideology of the government or are loyal to the regime. Within the reorganization of courts authoritarian politics do not only restrict the competences of courts, but also marginalize influential judges. The core of judicial independence including the restricted procedures of recusal rules does not apply in times of reorganization. Measures which are linked to these institutional strategies are limiting of competences of courts, reduction of the budget of the judiciary, and establishment of new supervising authorities as well as court packing.

The strategy of the Hungarian government in the year 2010 illustrated how courts can be pressured by limiting their competences.[59] The government reduced possibilities for the constitutional court to review statutory (especially budgetary) law under certain constitutional aspects.[60] Moreover, the government reduced the accessibility of the court by abolishing the *actio popularis* system of the Hungarian constitution.[61]

The reorganization of the court system enables a government to bring new judges into the system and to shift certain areas of judiciary into newly established courts. The recent Hungarian development of the establishment of administrative courts provides such an example. While Austria also established new administrative courts of first instance in 2014 (to comply with European standards for judiciary in administrative law) and thus, strengthened the rule of law significantly, the very same concept will weaken the judiciary in Hungary dramatically. It gives the Hungarian government the power to shift cases from the ordinary courts to the newly established courts, which will be filled up by (loyal) civil servants, who are becoming judges.[62] In contrast to this, in the Austrian system cases were transferred from the legally bound administrative authorities towards the new administrative courts.[63]

Creating new supervising authorities or changing the supervisory powers on the courts builds another authoritarian strategy to influence courts. Poland,

59 See O. W. Lembcke & C. Boulanger, 'Between Revolution and Constitution: The Roles of the Hungarian Constitutional Court', in G.A. Tóth (ed.), *Constitution for a Disunited Nation: On Hungary's 2011 Fundamental Law*, Budapest, CEU Press, 2012, pp. 269–299.

60 See, e.g. N. Chronowski & M. Varju, 'The Hungarian Rule of Law Crisis and Its European Context', in A. Kellerhals & T. Baumgartner (Eds), *Rule of Law in Europe – Current Challenges*, Zürich, Schulthess, 2017, pp. 149, 155–157.

61 See A. Jakab & J. Fröhlich, 'The Constitutional Court of Hungary', in A. Jakab, A. Dyevre & G. Itzcovich (Eds), *Comparative Constitutional Reasoning*, Cambridge, UK, Cambridge University Press, 2017, pp. 394, 430–434.

62 Uitz, 2019.

63 A still existing deficit in the Austrian system relates to missing training for new judges of administrative courts of first instance – in contrast to judges at ordinary courts.

Hungary, Romania, or Turkey are just some examples of countries, which intervened on a supervisory level in the court structure. The effects are new ways of putting formal and informal pressure on judges as well as opportunities to influence the assignment of cases to individual judges or to start disciplinary procedures against judges.

The exchange of majorities of constitutional/supreme courts usually takes a long period of time, which is much longer than the usual office period of a government. Thus, authoritarian governments are using strategies to change majorities faster. One possibility, which was used by the Hungarian government with regard to the constitutional court, was packing the court. The number of judges was increased from 12 to 15 to influence majorities more easily. Packing the court was also a strategy of the Polish government to change majorities in the Polish constitutional court. The Polish strategy included the nomination of pseudo-judges to the constitutional court by ignoring already legitimate appointments to the court.[64] A much broader exchange of judges happened in Turkey, which largely released judges to bring in new loyal judges.[65]

To increase the pressure on courts, it is also possible to keep courts busy. In Poland, procedural measures were implemented to prevent the court from working efficiently.[66] The judges got under higher pressure and could not uphold their standards of judging. Based on arguments toward higher efficiency or budgetary constraints, the reduction of the budget of the judiciary is one possibility to increase pressure on courts. As an example, the Austrian government 2017/2019 shall be mentioned. In 2018 the presidents of the higher court of appeals publicly protested against the dramatic budgetary situation.[67] The government reduced the resources of ordinary courts, which prevented the courts upholding the existing standards of the rule of law in judiciary.

A more general strategy to weaken the courts institutionally is to criticize them in a general approach, which is not focusing on a reasonable discussion with regard to certain case law. The Trump government dealt with the judgments of the US Supreme Court and other courts from the perspective of utility. If a court served the interests of government, the Court's judgments were applauded publicly.[68]

64 Sadurski, 2019, pp. 65–71.

65 O. O. Varol, 'Stealth Authoritarianism in Turkey', in M. A. Graber, S. Levinson & M. V. Tushnet (Eds), *Constitutional Democracy in Crisis*?, New York, Oxford University Press, 2018, p. 339, p. 352.

66 See below.

67 See Der Standard, 'Richter und Staatsanwälte setzen Proteste gegen Einsparungen fort' [judges and public prosecutors are continuing their protest against budgetary savings], 17 April 2018, <derstandard.at/2000078118990/Richter-und-Staatsanwaelte-setzen-Proteste-gegen-Einsparungen-fort> [Accessed 20 May 2019].

68 R. Thebault, 'You Can Hear the Klan's Lawyers': Federal Judge Likens Trump's Attacks on Judiciary to KKK', 13 April 2019, <www.washingtonpost.com/politics/2019/04/13/you-can-hear-klans-lawyers-federal-judge-likens-trumps-attacks-judiciary-kkk/?utm_term=.025a4edefff3> [Accessed 20 May 2019].

If the court judgments did not support the politics of the government, courts were criticized generally in an unreasonable manner.

2.4.3 Personal dimension (influencing/attacking the judges)

The extent to which governments are legally able to influence the appointment of judges is very divergent. On the one hand governmental influence on the appointment of judges is usually considered to establish democratic legitimacy; on the other hand it opens authoritarian governments possibilities of influencing the court by bringing in 'loyal' judges. This strategy can lead to a division of judges as the Polish example illustrates. Dividing judges does not only affect judgments (especially in senates) but also increases the pressure on judges in general.

The nomination of judges is the easiest way to influence a court. Increasing the influence of the government in the nomination procedures while reducing the relevance of internal judicial procedures gives governments the power to shape the composition of the courts. In Romania or Turkey this strategy of influencing the nomination of judges was applied.[69]

Influencing the court by just waiting for new appointments is usually a long-lasting procedure, which lasts far too long if a government wants to gain control over the judiciary. Thus, further measures are taken. The Hungarian government introduced early retirement schemes, to send judges into pension.[70] Such a strategy accelerates the possibilities for appointing new judges (as far as the government can influence this process). Poland copied the Hungarian strategies; both were confronted with the clear position of the CJEU that this strategy does not only violate judicial independence but also the rule of law.[71] The damage was already partly done as the reactivation of retired judges depends on the duration of the proceedings at the CJEU.

Controlling courts often does not restrict itself to influence the appointment and retirement, but also consists of an increase of the pressure on judges. Starting in informal ways, threatening judges can lead to personal restrictions, which can be observed in the US example of sanctioning ICC judges personally.[72] Pressure is also exercised indirectly regarding family members. Public pressure via personal attacks in the media also plays an important role in the attack and intimidation of judges; media attacks usually affect the family of a judge as well.

69 See International Commission of Jurists, 'Turkey: The Judicial System in Peril: A Briefing Paper' (Geneva 2016) 10–15; B. Selejan Gutan, 'New Challenges against the Judiciary in Romania', *VerfBlog*, 22 February 2019, <https://verfassungsblog.de/new-challenges-against-the-judiciary-in-romania/> [Accessed 20 May 2019].

70 See, e.g. Chronowski & Varju, 2017, p. 159.

71 See CJEU Judgment of 17 December 2018 in Case C-619/18, Commission v Poland.

72 The Guardian, 'US to deny visas for ICC members investigating alleged war crimes', 15 March 2019, <www.theguardian.com/us-news/2019/mar/15/mike-pompeo-us-war-crimes-investigation-international-criminal-court≥ [Accessed 20 May 2019].

Finally, different strategies are used to silence judges. The example at the beginning of the paper shows how disciplinary measures are used in Poland to threaten all judges and take the most confident judges out of the court system. Disciplinary measures can increase the burden of judges in many ways, not least by financial pressure, but also by stigmatizing them. This again will have an effect on their career possibilities in the court system. It also creates an atmosphere within the courts which leads to conformity without any further necessity for intervention.

The final destruction of judicial independence is reached when judges are recalled because they decide unfavorable judgments or they are understood as critical opposition to the government. If the government's power includes the possibilities to recall judges, the independence of the courts is already destroyed. The Turkish case illustrated how the whole judicial system was destroyed by an authoritarian cleansing of the courts. The imprisonment of judges for arbitrary reasons (especially because they are inconvenient for the government) constitutes the end of the long road of personal repression of judges.

2.4.4 Procedural dimension (influencing/changing judgments)

Governments do not only influence courts and judges but also intervene in ongoing procedures as well as react in inadequate ways to court judgments. The ways of influencing court procedures start with the statutory framework of the court proceedings. By an amendment of statutory procedural law governments can first of all restrict the existing procedures, e.g. blocking certain ways of judicial access or legal protection. The abolishment of *actio popularis* in Hungary was one of the first steps of the Orban government in 2010.[73] Limiting court proceedings is a way to drying-out the court's power. The opposite development can also be observed, which is overloading the court with cases. By changing court proceedings, the regular work of the courts can also be made quite complicated. In Poland the government blocked the possibilities of prioritizing judgments with regard to their importance. Thus, the constitutional court was overloaded and could not prioritize the important cases. The structuring of the court cases by date of entry completely paralyzed the constitutional court.[74] Overloading of courts also result in long-lasting court procedures, which cannot offer effectiveness of legal procedures nor create a fair trial. Another strategy of overloading is reached by changing the procedural settings, e.g. by shortening the decision deadlines. The quality of the judgment depends on a minimum possible length of proceedings. Shortening procedures create high pressure on courts.

73 See A. Jakab & J. Fröhlich, 2017, pp. 430–434.

74 M. Granat, 'Constitutional Judiciary in Crisis. The Case of Poland', in Z. Szente & F. Gárdos-Orosz (Eds), *New Challenges to Constitutional Adjudication in Europe: A Comparative Perspective*, Abingdon, Routledge, 2017, pp. 132, 140.

Besides the blocking of the court, competences of courts can be shifted to other courts. Part of the authoritarian strategy is also to play courts off against each other. In the Polish case, the governmental takeover of the majority of the constitutional court allowed the government to attack other courts. In the Turkish situation, the courts of first instance took over the functions of constitutional review; thus, the constitutional court was not even necessary to destroy the constitutional system.[75]

When the rule of law framework is not working anymore, influencing decision-making directly becomes easier. This can happen by economic incentives in the context of corruption, but also by influencing the question which judges becomes responsible for a sensitive case.

Finally, the court's relevance is attacked by the treatment of judgments. In a functioning democracy based on the rule of law, court's judgments have to be obeyed. The more the court system loses its independence, the more governments do not feel the importance of complying with court judgments. Usually the starting point is a rhetorical attack of judgments in the public. While criticism of judgments is a part of a vivid democracy, a public unsubstantiated attack on a judgment by the government already undermines the legitimacy of the judgment. In the Austrian coalition government 2000–2006, the influential Carinthian state governor Jörg Haider first attacked the constitutional court, because of opposing a judgment protecting the Slovenian majority. As a next step, he created strategies of ignoring the judgment. He was not prosecuted because of his political influence on the federal government, especially on the Ministry of Justice.[76]

From rhetoric against a judgment to the revision of a judgment it is a big step down the authoritarian road. Again, a statutory act revising judgments might be a possible part of judicial dialogue in a liberal democracy; however, the very same measure can be analyzed as an authoritarian move by a government in a very specific context. A particular problem can be identified when a constitutional court decides in human rights cases and the constitutional legislator amends the constitution to block the specific form of human rights protection. This happened for decades in Austria until the constitutional court declared a constitutional amendment which – constitutionally legitimized – exempted the constitutional court's competence to review a specific area of law to be unconstitutional.[77] The Hungarian government used the very same technique

75 See B. Çal, 'Will Legalism be the End of Constitutionalism in Turkey?', 22 January 2018, <https://verfassungsblog.de/will-legalism-be-the-end-of-constitutionalism-in-turkey/> [Accessed 20 May 2019].

76 See K. Lachmayer, 'Questioning the Basic Values – Austria and Jörg Haider', in A. Jakab & D. Kochenov (Eds), *The Enforcement of EU Law and Values: Ensuring Member States Compliance*, Oxford, Oxford University Press, 2016, pp. 436–455.

77 H. Eberhard & K. Lachmayer, 'Constitutional Reform in Austria', *Vienna Journal on International Constitutional Law*, Vol. 2, No. 2, 2008, p. 112.

to influence the constitutional court, while not having a majority of judges on its side in 2013.[78]

Although the Hong Kong basic law guarantees Hong Kong's judicial independence the final power of interpretation is granted to the National People's Congress of China:[79]

> The 2016 NPCSC Interpretation has created the new situation of the NPCSC seeking to interfere decisively into the decision-making of the HKSAR courts. The time may have come to ask the CFA [Court of Final Appeal] to review its 1999 statements, and its hitherto unqualified acceptance of the binding force of NPCSC interpretations. However, if the CFA is to accept this invitation, it will surely be regarded by the Central Authorities as "turning rogue".[80]

When it is not possible to amend the Act behind the judgment, another strategy, e.g. especially in the context of international treaties, consists in ignoring the judgments. Again, usually the rhetorical attack of the legitimacy of the judgment goes first and in a second step judgments are ignored or not implemented in the system. Russia can serve as such an example in the context of the ECHR.[81] In Poland, the government decided not to publish judgments for a certain period of time.[82]

2.5 Erosion of the rule of law

The role of courts in post-modern societies has to be considered separately from the question of an authoritarian backlash. Courts are not perfect, judges are misusing their powers, courts are blocking legitimate interests, costs of courts can be too high, procedures too long etc. Nevertheless, there are democratic ways of control, debate, and possibilities to change the courts' concept democratically.

78 Z. Szente & F. Gárdos-Orosz, 'Judicial Deference or Political Loyalty? The Hungarian Constitutional Court's Role in Tackling Crisis Situations', in Z. Szente & F. Gárdos-Orosz (Eds), *New Challenges to Constitutional Adjudication in Europe: A Comparative Perspective*, Abingdon, Routledge, 2017, pp. 89, 105.

79 See G. Torode & J. Pomfret, 'Hong Kong's Judges Voice Fears Over China Influence in Judiciary', Reuters, 15 May 2018, <www.reuters.com/article/us-hongkong-law/hong-kongs-judges-voice-fears-over-china-influence-in-judiciary -idUSKCN1GR0LD> [Accessed 20 May 2019].

80 See P. Y. Lo, 'Two Kinds of Unconstitutional Constitutional Interpretations in China's Hong Kong', *International Journal of Constitutional Law*, 23 December 2016, <www.iconnectblog.com/2016/12/two-kinds-of-unconstitutional-constitutional-interpretations/> [Accessed 20 May 2019]; C. Chan, 'The Legal Limits on Beijing's Powers to Interpret Hong Kong's Basic Law', *HKU Legal Scholarship Blog*, 3 November 2016, <http://researchblog.law.hku.hk/2016/11/cora-chan-on-legal-limits-of-beijings.html> [Accessed 20 May 2019]; A. Mason, 'The Rule of Law in the Shadow of the Giant: The Hong Kong Experience', *Sydney Law Review*, Vol. 33, No. 4, 2011, pp. 623–644.

81 L. Mälksoo and W. Benedek, *Russia and the European Court of Human Rights*, Cambridge, UK, Cambridge University Press, 2017.

82 Sadurski, 2019, pp. 74–77.

The governmental pressure on courts can be misunderstood as a way of regaining power, but it is – in the context of constitutional decline – also inextricably linked to a shift from (the rule of) law to (an authoritarian rule of) politics. The erosion of the rule of law opens up an unlimited and legally uncontrolled form of power politics of governments. The rise of populism and the crises of traditional parties create increasingly faster opportunities for movements and (charismatic or unorthodox) leaders to take over governments.

Erosion is a gradual change of a substance over time, which removes this substance step by step. The rule of law as a basic legal concept is implemented in society. It thus has to be upheld by society in an ongoing process. The developments, which we can observe nowadays, are not a sudden *coup d'état* to transform a democratic government into dictatorship.[83] It is much more a creeping development over time, which dismantles, reduces, and removes the constitutional structures of democracy, the rule of law, and human rights. The descriptions of these phenomena are illiberal democracy, semi-authoritarianism, or rule by law. These labels seem to consist of contradictory approaches but just express the process from one concept ('constitutionalism') to another ('authoritarianism'). The in-between concepts, the different levels of grey, make it so difficult to address and to assess the concrete measures exactly. Regarding the analysis of concrete governmental activities, it is important not only to consider the specific measures alone, but also the political background in which it is taken. The analysis of developments in the semi-authoritarian grey area has to consider the direction a governmental action is pointing toward.

The disempowerment of courts is combined with strategies of streamlining courts. The core idea of judicial independence comes under attack. It is important to consider that there are different approaches to conceptualizing the rule of law in different countries. The cultural differences are significant. Although the role of independent courts for the rule of law is, however, undisputed, it is important to consider that certain measures might improve the rule of law in one country while they obstruct the rule of law in another.

Governmental authoritarianism demands conformity of courts to legitimize governmental decisions (neither opposing nor limiting the government). It attempts to control the judiciary institutionally (by introducing supervision of the courts), personally (by selecting judges loyal to the government), and substantially (by influencing the judgments). Usually authoritarian regimes will combine different strategies to create limits on courts. The paradigm shifts from limiting governments to limited courts. Courts under control create preventive political compliance; direct pressure is not necessary anymore. Finally, courts are promoting the authoritarian concept themselves.[84] This, however, means that the rule of law is destroyed in the particular country and the rule of politics carves out the role of law in society.

83 Jakab (forthcoming).
84 Sadurski, 2019, p. 77–81.

2.6 Approaches to strengthen judicial independence

When judicial independence is under attack by governmental authoritarianism, manifold approaches can be applied to support the courts, the judges, and the judgments of the courts. Within these many opportunities two approaches shall be stressed as a conclusion of this chapter: on the one hand a top-down approach is suggested and on the other hand a bottom-up approach could supplement the first.

The top-down approach refers to the support by transnational courts, like the ECtHR or the CJEU, to strengthen domestic courts in their independence. The ECtHR has protected domestic courts already for many years by promoting judicial independence in the member states.[85] In recent years the CJEU is also becoming more active as it can be observed in the context of the Hungarian court system as well as the Polish situation.[86] It is, however, necessary to mention that the same intensity of transnational judicial review does not exist in all areas of world and that transnational courts usually can only interfere very selectively. The role of transnational courts in defending the independence of domestic courts can also create a nationalistic atmosphere opposing transnational courts in the relevant member states. Nevertheless, it is not as easy for a domestic government to influence transnational courts; the implications of a termination of an international agreement are usually quite complex. The example of the Philippines, however, illustrates that an authoritarian government might also be motivated to terminate the membership in an international court system.

To limit this vicious circle of the 'migration of anti-constitutional ideas'[87] it is necessary that courts in contemporary legal orders are not left to defend their role in liberal democracies on their own. Society has to understand the importance of independent courts for overall peace, freedom, and legal certainty in a country and be ready to engage politically in favor of this cornerstone of the rule of law. The bottom up approach, thus, refers to civil societies protecting domestic courts. Courts are first of all a possibility for the people to access justice and to gain legal protection. As observed in Poland, Romania, or Hong Kong, the people rediscover the role of independent courts as part of their political sphere. In times of populism and semi-authoritarian regimes the role of the people is the last stronghold to fight for constitutionalism and to regain democratic power on the long run. Opposing the disempowerment of courts becomes a crucial task of constitutionalism itself.

85 Critical in the Turkish context see B. E. Oder, 'Independent Journalism v. Political Courts: The Cumhuriyet Trial in Turkey and Strasbourg', *VerfBlog*, 4 May 2019 <https://verfassungsblog.de/independent-journalism-v-political-courts-the-cumhuriyet-trial-in-turkey-and-strasbourg/> [Accessed 20 May 2019].

86 See CJEU Case C-619/18, Commission v Poland (17 December 2018); Chronowski & Varju, 2017, pp. 163–167.

87 K. L. Scheppele, 'The Migration of Anti-Constitutional Ideas: The Post-9/11 Globalization of Public Law and the International State of Emergency', in S. Choudhry (Ed.), *The Migration of Constitutional Ideas*, Cambridge, UK, Cambridge University Press, 2006, pp. 347–373.

References

A. Arnull, 'Judicial Dialogue in the European Union', in J. Dickson & P. Eleftheriadis (Eds), *Philosophical Foundations of European Union Law*, Oxford, Oxford University Press, 2012, p. 109.

A. R. Brewer Carías, *Constitutional Courts as Positive Legislators: A Comparative Law Study*, Cambridge, UK, Cambridge University Press, 2011.

S. Choudhry, 'Migration as a New Metaphor in Comparative Constitutional Law', in S. Choudhry (Ed.), *The Migration of Constitutional Ideas*, Cambridge, UK, Cambridge University Press, 2006, p. 1.

N. Chronowski & M. Varju, 'The Hungarian Rule of Law Crisis and Its European Context', in A. Kellerhals & T. Baumgartner (Eds), *Rule of Law in Europe – Current Challenges*, Zürich, Schulthess, 2017, p. 149.

E. F. Delaney, 'Judiciary Rising: Constitutional Change in the United Kingdom', *Northwestern University Law Review*, Vol. 108, No. 2, 2014, p. 543.

H. Eberhard & K. Lachmayer, 'Constitutional Reform in Austria', *Vienna Journal on International Constitutional Law*, Vol. 2, No. 2, 2008, p. 112.

G. Gee, 'The Persistent Politics of Judicial Selection', in A. Seibert-Fohr (Ed.), *Judicial Independence in Transition*, Heidelberg, Springer, 2012, p. 121.

M. A. Graber, S. Levinson & M. V. Tushnet (Eds), *Constitutional Democracy in Crisis?*, New York, Oxford University Press, 2018.

M. Granat, 'Constitutional Judiciary in Crisis. The Case of Poland', in Z. Szente & F. Gárdos-Orosz (Eds), *New Challenges to Constitutional Adjudication in Europe: A Comparative Perspective*, Abingdon, Routledge, 2017, p. 132.

T. Groppi & M.-C. Ponthoreau (Eds), *The Use of Foreign Precedents by Constitutional Judges*, Oxford, Hart Publishing, 2013.

M. Hailbronner & S. Martini, 'The German Federal Constitutional Court', in A. Jakab, A. Dyevre & G. Itzcovich, (Eds), *Comparative Constitutional Reasoning*, Cambridge, UK, Cambridge University Press, 2017, p. 356.

G. Halmai, 'A Coup Against Constitutional Democracy: The Case of Hungary', in M. A. Graber, S. Levinson & M. V. Tushnet (Eds), *Constitutional Democracy in Crisis?*, New York, Oxford University Press, 2018, p. 243.

R. Hirschl, *Towards Juristocracy: The Origins and Consequences of the New Constitutionalism*, Cambridge, MA, Harvard University Press, 2007.

V. C. Jackson, *Constitutional Engagement in a Transnational Era*, New York, Oxford University Press, 2010.

V. C. Jackson, 'Judicial Independence: Structure, Context, Attitude', in A. Seibert-Fohr (Ed.), *Judicial Independence in Transition*, Heidelberg, Springer, 2012, p. 19.

A. Jakab, 'Was kann Verfassungsrecht gegen die Erosion der Demokratie und Rechtsstaatlichkeit tun?', *Zeitschrift für Öffentliches Recht*, Vol. 74 (forthcoming).

A. Jakab & J. Fröhlich, 'The Constitutional Court of Hungary', in A. Jakab, A. Dyevre & G. Itzcovich (Eds.), *Comparative Constitutional Reasoning*, Cambridge, Cambridge University Press, 2017, p. 394.

K. Lachmayer, 'Between International Standards and Transnational Greed, Providing Transnational Rule of Law in Times of Economic Crisis', *Hague Journal on the Rule of Law*, Vol. 8, No. 2, 2016a, p. 291.

K. Lachmayer, *'Questioning the Basic Values – Austria and Jörg Haider'*, in A. Jakab & D. Kochenov (Eds), *The Enforcement of EU Law and Values: Ensuring Member States Compliance*, Oxford, Oxford University Press, 2016b, p. 436.

K. Lachmayer, 'Counter-Developments to Global Constitutionalism', in M. Belov (Ed.), *Global Constitutionalism and Its Challenges to Westphalian Constitutional Law*, Oxford, Hart Publishing, 2018, p. 81.

O. W. Lembcke & C. Boulanger, 'Between Revolution and Constitution: The Roles of the Hungarian Constitutional Court', in G.A. Tóth (Ed.), *Constitution for a Disunited Nation: On Hungary's 2011 Fundamental Law*, Budapest, CEU Press, 2012, p. 269.

L. Mälksoo & W. Benedek, *Russia and the European Court of Human Rights*, Cambridge, Cambridge University Press, 2017.

T. Mariniello, 'Prolonged Emergency and Derogation of Human Rights, Why the European Court Should Raise Its Immunity System', *German Law Journal*, Vol. 20, No. 1, 2019, p. 46.

A. Mason, 'The Rule of Law in the Shadow of the Giant: The Hong Kong Experience', *Sydney Law Review*, Vol. 33, No. 4, 2011, p. 623.

A. Moellers, *The Three Branches: A Comparative Model of Separation of Powers*, Oxford, Oxford University Press, 2013.

O. Pfersmann, 'Concrete Review as Indirect Constitutional Complaint in French Constitutional Law, A Comparative Perspective', *European Constitutional Law Review*, Vol. 6, No. 2, 2010, p. 223.

U. K. Preuss, 'The Implications of 'Eternity Clauses': The German Experience', *Israel Law Review*, Vol. 44, No. 3, 2011, p. 429.

W. Sadurski, 'Constitutional Crisis in Poland', in M. A. Graber, S. Levinson & M. V. Tushnet (Eds), *Constitutional Democracy in Crisis?*, New York, Oxford University Press, 2018, p. 257.

W. Sadurski, 'Polish Constitutional Tribunal Under PiS: From an Activist Court, to a Paralysed Tribunal, to a Governmental Enabler', *Hague Journal on the Rule of Law*, Vol. 11, No. 1, 2019, p. 63.

K. L. Scheppele, 'The Migration of Anti-constitutional Ideas: The Post-9/11 Globalization of Public Law and the International State of Emergency', in S. Choudhry (Ed.), *The Migration of Constitutional Ideas*, Cambridge, UK, Cambridge University Press, 2006, p. 347.

A. Seibert-Fohr (Ed.), *Judicial Independence in Transition*, Heidelberg, Springer, 2012a.

A. Seibert-Fohr, 'Introduction: The Challenge of Transition', in A. Seibert-Fohr (Ed.), *Judicial Independence in Transition*, Heidelberg, Springer, 2012b, p. 14.

A. Seibert-Fohr, 'Judicial Independence – The Normativity of an Evolving Transnational Principle', in A. Seibert-Fohr (Ed.), *Judicial Independence in Transition*, Heidelberg, Springer, 2012c, p. 1279.

A.-M. Slaughter, *A New World Order*, Princeton, NJ, Princeton University Press, 2005.

A. Smilov, 'The Judiciary: The Least Dangerous Branch?', in M. Rosenfeld & A. Sajó (Eds), *The Oxford Handbook of Comparative Constitutional Law*, Oxford, Oxford University Press, 2012, p. 859.

M. Stelzer, *The Constitution of the Republic of Austria: A Contextual Analysis*, Oxford, Hart Publishing, 2011.

Z. Szente & F. Gárdos-Orosz, 'Judicial Deference or Political Loyalty? The Hungarian Constitutional Court's Role in Tackling Crisis Situations', in Z. Szente & F. Gárdos-Orosz (Eds), *New Challenges to Constitutional Adjudication in Europe: A Comparative Perspective*, Abingdon, Routledge, 2017, p. 89.

G. A. Tóth, 'Lost in Transition. Invisible Constitutionalism in Hungary', in R. Dixon & A. Stone (Eds), *The Invisible Constitution in Comparative Perspective*, Cambridge, UK, Cambridge University Press, 2018, p. 541.

M. V. Tushnet, *Taking the Constitution Away from the Courts*, Princeton, NJ, Princeton University Press, 2000.

M. V. Tushnet, *Weak Courts, Strong Rights: Judicial Review and Social Welfare Rights in Comparative Constitutional Law*, Princeton, NJ, Princeton University Press, 2008.

O. O. Varol, 'Stealth Authoritarianism in Turkey', in M. A. Graber, S. Levinson & M. V. Tushnet (Eds), *Constitutional Democracy in Crisis?*, New York, Oxford University Press, 2018, p. 339.

Part II

Courts and their relationship with legislative and executive power

3 Courts and legislation

Do legislators and judges speak the same language?

Helen Xanthaki

3.1 Introduction[1]

Although each legislative act is a unique product, its life is fragmented: the policy process belongs to policy officers, the legislative process belongs to legislators, the drafting process to drafters, its implementation to citizens, its enforcement to enforcers, and its interpretation to judges.[2] This fragmentation invites the contribution of all actors in the policy process, thus leading to the production of a legislative text that, hopefully, encompasses the agreement of all. However, it also invites frictions and diversities that may endanger the efficacy and effectiveness of the whole regulatory package.

In the field of legislation, much praise is placed on modern drafters whose accessibility techniques seem to have borne fruit in bringing legislation to the people. Radical innovations in legislative techniques have been introduced mainly in Europe but also in Australia, New Zealand, South Africa, and elsewhere. The question is whether these innovations, so firmly rooted within legislative cycles, have left the other actors of the policy process isolated.

The hypothesis of this chapter is that recent innovations in drafting techniques have disturbed the continuity of language used by those who produce and those who interpret legislation. This, in turn, confirms that, currently, legislators and judges speak a different language.

1 This chapter is based on the following works: Helen Xanthaki, 'Judges v Drafters: The Saga Continues', in Jeffrey Barnes, Statutory Interpretation, forthcoming; and Helen Xanthaki, 'An "Ordinary Meaning" of Words: Is There Such a Thing?', in Ik-Hyeon Rhee and Wim Voermans (Eds), *Innovation of Legislative Process*, Seoul, KLRI/IAL, 2018, pp. 123–136.

2 Constantin Stefanou, 'Legislative Drafting as a Form of Communication', in Luzius Mader and Marta Tavares de Almeida (Eds), *Quality of Legislation Principles and Instruments*, Nomos, 2011, 308; and also see C. Stefanou, 'Drafters, Drafting and the Policy Process', in Constantin Stefanou and Helen Xanthaki (Eds), *Drafting Legislation: A Modern Approach*, Ashgate, 2008, p. 321.

3.2 Legislation as a fluid collective task: From policy concept to application/interpretation

The UK's Good Law initiative has proven empirically that legislation is read mainly by lay users. If one sees legislation as a mere tool for regulation, then the drafters of legislation must use the language of lay users as a means of explaining clearly how their behavior is expected to change and law reform is to come about. Communicating these messages clearly is the only way in which the legislation can, with the synergy of the other actors of the policy process,[3] achieve the regulatory results required by policymakers.[4] A good law is one that is capable of leading to efficacy of regulation. A good law is an effective law. In addition, ultimately, quality in legislation is effectiveness. Effectiveness is the criterion that drafters use when selecting the most appropriate drafting rule for the problem before them. This qualitative definition of quality in legislation respects and embraces the subjectivity and flexibility of both drafting rules and conventions and, ultimately, of phronetic legislative drafting.[5]

The drafter of legislation cannot be isolated from the many other actors in the process to which the drafter belongs. Leaving aside the necessity for a multiplicity of disciplines to be represented in the drafting process in its narrow sense, one must view the drafter as one of the actors of the drafting process, which is a mere stage of the legislative process, which in turn constitutes a stage of the policy process.[6] If one takes this holistic picture of legislation as a tool for regulation into account, and applies Stefanou's scheme on the three processes, drafters can only perform a small, albeit crucial, part in the application of governmental policy better expressed as regulation. Legislation becomes a collective task that can only be achieved with the synergy of all actors, including judges.

The collectiveness of the task requires fluid and uninhibited homogeneity in the drafting of legislation. This touches upon the conceptualization of legislation, the logic of its structure, and, of course, the linguistic choices involved in legislative expression. The main argument of this chapter is that this fluidity is lacking, at least at the moment. This endangers the quality of the legislation and, ultimately, the success of the regulation that the legislation serves.

3 J. P. Chamberlain, 'Legislative Drafting and Law Enforcement', *American Laboratory Legislation Review*, Vol. 21, 1931, pp. 235–243, p. 243.

4 L. Mader, 'Evaluating the Effect: A Contribution to the Quality of Legislation', *Statute Law Review*, Vol. 22, 2001, pp. 119–131 at p. 126.

5 H. Xanthaki, 'Drafting Manuals and Quality in Legislation: Positive Contribution Towards Certainty in the Law or Impediment to the Necessity for Dynamism of Rules?', *Legisprudence*, Vol. 4, 2010, pp. 111–128.

6 C. Stefanou, 'Drafters, Drafting, and the Policy Process', in Constantin Stefanou and Helen Xanthaki (Eds), *Drafting Legislation: A Modern Approach – In Memoriam of Sir William Dale*, Ashgate, Dartmouth, 2008, pp. 321–332, at p. 323.

Let us explore this argument further by discussing the theory of phronetic drafting that underpins choices related to legislative expression. The values of regulation and legislation present as follows:[7]

The diagram[8] below visualizes these goals and their hierarchy.

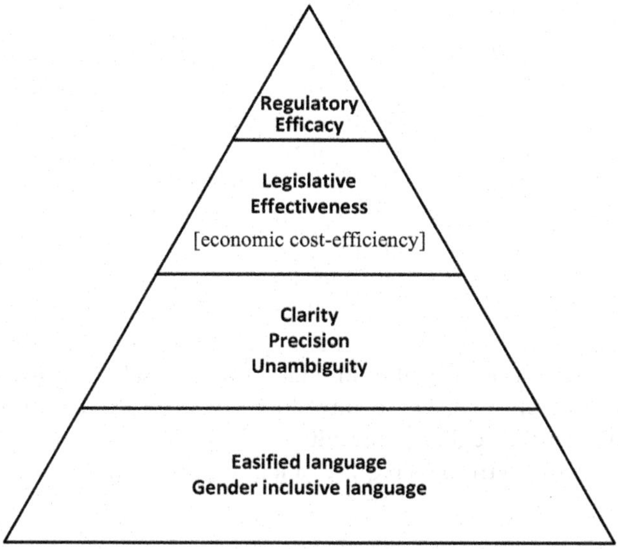

Starting with regulatory efficacy, this is the extent to which regulators achieve their goal.[9] However, achieving the desired regulatory results is not a goal that can be achieved by the drafter alone:[10] legislation requires a solid policy, appropriate and realistic policy measures for its achievement, cost-efficient mechanisms of implementation, and ultimately user willingness to implement and judicial inclination to interpret according to legislative intent.[11]

7 For a first draft of the pyramid, see H. Xanthaki, 'On Transferability of Legislative Solutions: The Functionality Test', in Constantin Stefanou and Helen Xanthaki (Eds), *Drafting Legislation: A Modern Approach – In Memoriam of Sir William Dale*, Ashgate, Dartmouth, 2008, pp. 1–18.

8 See ibid. p. 1. The basis of the diagram remains the same but the entries have been updated for clarity.

9 See ibid., 126; also see M. Mousmouti, 'Operationalising Quality of Legislation through the Effectiveness Test', *Legisprudence*, Vol. 6, 2012, p. 191.

10 See J. P. Chamberlain, 'Legislative Drafting and Law Enforcement', *American Laboratory Legislation Review*, Vol. 21, 1931, p. 235, p. 243.

11 See D. Hull, 'Drafters Devils', *The Loophole*, 2000, www.opc.gov.au/calc/docs/calc-june/audience.htm; also see U. Karpen, 'The Norm Enforcement Process', in U. Karpen and P. Delnoy, (Eds), *Contributions to the Methodology of the Creation of Written Law*, Baden-Baden, Nomos, 1996, p. 51, p. 51; also L. Mader, 'Legislative Procedure and the Quality of Legislation', in U. Karpen and P. Delnoy (Eds), *Contributions to the Methodology of the Creation of Written Law*, ibid, p. 62, p. 68.

The drafter's limited possible contribution to efficacy is effectiveness,[12] defined as the extent to which the observable attitudes and behaviors of the target population correspond to the attitudes and behaviors prescribed by the legislator;[13] or 'the fact that law matters: it has effects on political, economic and social life outside the law – that is, apart from simply the elaboration of legal doctrine';[14] or a term encompassing implementation, enforcement, impact, and compliance;[15] or the degree to which the legislative measure has achieved a concrete goal without suffering from side effects;[16] or the extent to which the legislation influences in the desired manner the social phenomenon which it aims to address;[17] or a consequence of the rule of law, which imposes a duty on the legislator to consider and respect the implementation and enforcement of legislation to be enacted;[18] or a measure of the causal relations between the law and its effects: and so an effective law is one that is respected or implemented, provided that the observable degree of respect can be attributed to the norm.[19] If one attempts to use all of the elements of these enlightened definitions of effectiveness, one could suggest that effectiveness of legislation is the ultimate measure of quality in legislation,[20] which reflects the extent to which the legislation manages to introduce adequate mechanisms capable of producing the desired regulatory results.[21] In its concrete, rather than abstract conceptual sense, effectiveness requires a legislative text that can (i) foresee the

12 See C. Timmermans, 'How Can One Improve the Quality of Community Legislation?', *Common Market Law Review*, Vol. 34, 1997, p. 1229, pp. 1236–1237; 'European Governance: Better Lawmaking', Communication from the Commission, COM (2002) 275 final, Brussels, 5.6.2002; also see High Level Group on the Operation of Internal Market, 'The Internal Market after 1992: Meeting the Challenge – Report to the EEC Commission by the High Level Group on the Operation of Internal Market', *SEC* (92) 2044, 1992; also Office of Parliamentary Counsel, 'Working with OPC', 6 December 2011; and OPC, 'Drafting Guidance', 16 December 2011.

13 See L. Mader, 'Evaluating the Effect: A Contribution to the Quality of Legislation', *Statute Law Review*, Vol. 22, 2001, p. 119, p. 126.

14 See F. Snyder, 'The Effectiveness of European Community Law: Institutions, Processes, Tools and Techniques', *Modern Law Review*, Vol. 56, 1993, p. 19; also F. Snyder, *New Directions in European Community Law*, London, Weidenfeld and Nicolson, 1990, p. 3.

15 See G. Teubner, 'Regulatory Law: Chronicle of a Death Foretold', in Lenoble (Ed.), *Einfuhrung in der Rectssoziologie*, Darmstadt, Wissenschaftliche Buchgesellschaft, 1987, p. 54.

16 See G. Muller and F. Uhlmann, *Elemente einer Rechtssetzungslehre*, Zurich, Schulthess, 2013, pp. 51–52.

17 See I. Jenkins, *Social Order and the Limits of the Law: A Theoretical Essay*, Princeton, NJ, Princeton University Press, 1981, 180; also see R. Cranston, 'Reform through Legislation: The Dimension Of Legislative Technique', *NwULRev*, Vol. 73, 1978–1979, p. 873, p. 875.

18 See W. Voermans, 'Concern about the Quality of EU Legislation: What Kind of Problem, by What Kind of Standards?', *Erasmus Law Review*, Vol. 2, 2009, p. 59, p. 230.

19 See M. Mousmouti, n. 9, p. 200.

20 See H. Xanthaki, 'On Transferability of Legal Solutions', in C. Stefanou and H. Xanthaki (Eds), *Drafting Legislation, A Modern Approach*, n. 7, p. 6.

21 See Office of the Leader of the House of Commons, Post-Legislative Scrutiny – The Governments Approach, March 2008, para. 2.4.

main projected outcomes and use them in the drafting and formulation process; (ii) state clearly its objectives and purpose; (iii) provide for necessary and appropriate means and enforcement measures; and (iv) assess and evaluate real-life effectiveness in a consistent and timely manner.[22]

As a mere expression of the regulatory agenda, legislation inevitably relies on the soundness of the policy goals and regulatory aims set by regulators. Legislation requires a constitutionally, legally, ethically, and democratic (in the sense of acceptable by the majority) policy aim pursued by equally constitutional, legal, ethical, democratic, and cost-efficient means to achieve it. Moreover, it relies on the intent of users and interpreters to comply with it.[23] Of course, this interdependence of policy, regulation, legislation, and implementation works both ways: good legislative expression can accentuate the logic of the policy, can clarify the choice of regulatory tools, and can ultimately incite implementation. However, in the same way that efficacy requires legislative facilitation of regulatory success, it also requires the synergistic contribution of all parts and actors of the drafting process as part of the legislative process, which in turn is part of the policy process.[24]

3.3 The new language of legislation

Legislation aims to communicate the regulatory message to its users as a means of imposing and inciting implementation. It attempts to detail clearly, precisely, and unambiguously what the new obligations or the new rights can be, in order to inform citizens with an inclination to comply how their behavior or actions must change from the legislation's entry into force. The receipt of the legislative message in the way that it was sent by the legislative text is crucial for legislative effectiveness and, ultimately, for regulatory efficacy.

Easified language, as a development of plain language, aims to introduce principles that convey the legislative/regulatory message in a manner that it clear and effective for its audience. Easified language encompasses the analysis of the policy and the initial translation into legislation, the selection and prioritization of the information that readers need to receive, the selection and design of the legislative solution, and choices of legislative expression. Easified language extends from policy to law to drafting.

The blessing of this ambitious mandate comes with a curse of relativity. Easification requires simplification of the text for its specific audience, and thus

22 This is Mousmouti's effectiveness test.

23 Helen Xanthaki, 'The Limits of Legislation as a Product', *Hukim – The Israeli Journal on Legislation*, Vol. 11, 2018, pp. 153–172.

24 See C. Stefanou, 'Legislative Drafting as a Form of Communication', in L. Mader and M. Travares-Almeida (Eds), *Quality of Legislation Principles and Instruments*, Baden-Baden, Nomos, 2011, p. 308; and also see C. Stefanou, 'Drafters, Drafting and the Policy Process', in C. Stefanou and H. Xanthaki (Eds), *Drafting Legislation: A Modern Approach*, Aldershot, Ashgate, 2008, p. 321.

requires an awareness of who the users of the texts will be, and what kind of sophistication they possess. And it must do so in a single document: possible clashes between various instruments at various levels would incite uncertainty in the law, thus making it ineffective anyway.

Answers to these questions were simply not present for legislation until very recently. It was widely accepted that legislative communication involved the drafter (who, at least in the UK, is a trained lawyer with drafting training and experience) and the generic user (who can be anything from a senior judge to an illiterate citizen of below-average capacity). The inequality in the understanding of both common terms (whatever they may be) and legal terms renders communication via a single text a hopeless task. And this is precisely the second limit of legislation: communication from a trained and highly experienced lawyer to a wide circle of possible audiences with vast diversion of general and legal sophistication is simply an impossible task. Much more so if this is attempted by means of a single written text. This deprives the communication sender from the opportunity to gauge reception and make amends by means of further clarification where needed, or by means of intonation or even gestures that are simply not available in written communication.

Until now, identifying the users was a hypothetical and rather academic exercise. Recent empirical data offered by a revolutionary survey of UK's The National Archives in cooperation with the OPC have provided much needed answers.[25] Speaking to the users is a noble pursuit but presupposes an understanding of who uses legislation and what level of legal awareness these users have. At the end of the day identifying the people whose choice to act or not makes government policy a success or a failure[26] is crucial in establishing effective communication with them. But is there one audience for legislation? Can a drafter rely on the common notion of the 'lay person', the 'average man on the street',[27] the 'user'? The theoretical debate over this point has now been answered by the Good Law Initiative survey: at least three categories of people constitute the audience of legislation, and these are lay persons reading the legislation to make it work for them,[28] sophisticated non-lawyers using the law in the process

25 See www.gov.uk/good-law.

26 See D. Berry, 'Audience Analysis in the Legislative Drafting Process', *The Loophole*, 2000, www.opc.gov.au/calc/docs/calc-june/audience.htm.

27 See D. Murphy, 'Plain English-Principles and Practice', Conference on Legislative Drafting, Canberra, Australia, 15 July 1992.

28 See J. J. E. Gracia, *A Theory of Textuality: The Logic and Epistemology*, Albany, State University of New York Press, 1995, pp. 159–163, and pp. 164–165; also see G. L. Pi and V. Schmolka, 'A Report on Results of Usability Testing Research on Plain Language Draft Sections of the Employment Insurance Act: A Report to Department of Justice Canada and Human Resources Development Canada', unpublished, August 2000; and V. Schmolka, 'Consumer Fireworks Regulations: Usability Testing, TR1995-2e', Department of Justice Canada, unpublished, 1995.

of their professional activities, and lawyers and judges. In more detail, there are three categories of users of legislation:

a. non-lawyers who need to use legislation for work, such as law enforcers, human resources professionals, or local council officials; the 'Mark Green' of the survey represents about 60% of users of legislation;
b. lay persons who seek answers to questions related to their personal or familial situation; 'Heather Cole' represents about 20% of users of legislation; and
c. lawyers, judges, and senior law librarians; the 'Jane Booker' persona represents about 20% of users of legislation.[29]

The significance of the survey for plain language and good legislation cannot be understated. The survey provides, for the first time in UK legislative practice, empirical evidence from a huge sample of the two million visitors of www.legislation.gov.uk per month. The survey, whose data relate to users of electronic versions of the free government database of legislation only, destroys the myth that legislation is for legal professionals alone. In fact, legal professionals are very much in the minority of users, although their precise percentage may well be affected by their tendency to use subscription databases rather than the government database, which is not annotated and often not updated. Whatever the exact percentages of each category are, there is significant empirical evidence that in the UK, and most probably in the rest of Europe of which the UK is a representative case study, legislation speaks to three distinct groups of users, whose legal awareness varies from none, to some, to much. But is the legal awareness of the users the only parameter for plain language as a means of effective legislative communication?

Pitching the legislative text to the 'right' level requires an additional consideration. Having realized which are the rough profiles of the audience, the next parameter for plain communication is the topic of the legislative text. Legislative texts are not all aimed at the same readers. Their primary audience varies. For example, the main users of rules of evidence are probably judges and lawyers.[30] The language and terminology used can be sophisticated: paraphrasing the terms 'intent' or '*mens rea*' with a plain language equivalent such as 'meaning to' would lead the primarily legal audience to the legitimate assumption that the legislation means something other than 'intent' and would not easily carry with it the interpretative case-law of 'intent' on to 'meaning to'. Rules of evidence can be drafted in specialist language, albeit with a caveat: a primarily legally sophisticated

29 See A. Bertlin, 'What Works Best for the Reader? A Study on Drafting and Presenting Legislation', *The Loophole*, www.gov.uk/government/uploads/system/uploads/attachment_data/file/326937/Loophole_-_2014-2__2014-05-09_-What_works_best_for_the_reader.pdf, 2014, pp. 27–28.

30 See B. A. Garner 'Guidelines for Drafting and Editing Court Rules', *Federal Rules Decisions,* 1997, pp. 169, 187.

audience cannot serve as a 'carte blanche' for legalese, since non-lawyers may need to, and in any case must, have access to the legislation too. As audiences become more specialized and more educated in technical areas, they expect texts that are targeted to their particular needs.[31]

Moreover, since accessibility of legislation is directly linked to Bingham's rule of law,[32] passing inaccessible legislation under the feeble excuse that its primary audience possesses legal sophistication is not easily acceptable. There is an argument for either the continued use of legal terminology or for the provision of a definition of the new plain language equivalent referring to the legal term used until now.

How easified is legislation currently? Even within the 'Heather Cole' persona, there is plenty of diversity. There is a given commonality in the lack of legal training, but the sophistication, general and legal, of Heather Coles can range from a fiercely intelligent and generally sophisticated user to a rather naïve, perhaps illiterate, and even intellectually challenged individual. Which of those Heather Coles is the legislation speaking to? Certainly not the commonly described 'average man on the street'. To start with, there are also women on our streets, and they are users of legislation too. And then, why are the above or below average people amongst us excluded from legislative communication?[33] Since effectiveness is the goal of legislative texts, legislation speaks to each and every user who falls within the subjects of the policy solution expressed by this specific legislative text. This includes the above average, the average, and the below average people.

This is a rather revolutionary innovation. Identifying the users of legislation has led to not one but two earthquakes. First, the law does not speak to lawyers alone. Second, the law does not speak to the 'average man'.

3.4 The gap between drafters and judges[34]

All through this drafting revolution, judges and courts have remained excluded. There seems to be a rather gaping schism between the linguistic perceptions of drafters and interpreters of legislation in the UK today. Drafters seem to be much more aware of the specific parameters of legislative diversity. And drafting has moved a long way toward achieving real easification.

Awareness of diversity of the legislative users has prompted drafters to start their task by identifying the profile of the main users of the specific legislative

31 See K. A. Schriver, 'Plain Language through Protocol-Aided Revision', in E. R. Steinberg (Ed.), *Plain Language: Principles and Practice*, Detroit, Wayne State University Press, 1991, pp. 148, 152.

32 See Lord Simon of Glaisdale, 'The Renton Report-Ten Years On', *Statute Law Review*, 1985, Vol. 6, No. 1, p. 133.

33 J. Kimble, 'Answering the critics of plain language', *The Scribes Journal of Legal Writing*, Vol. 5, 1994–1995, pp. 51, 59.

34 Helen Xanthaki, 'An "Ordinary Meaning" of Words: Is There Such a Thing?', in Ik-Hyeon Rhee and Wim Voermans (Eds), *Innovation of Legislative Process*, Seoul, KLRI/IAL, 2018), pp. 123–136.

text before them. Aware of the analytics of legislative users in abstract, they can achieve a better understanding of whom the text is addressed to, and, perhaps more importantly, which parts of the legislative story are relevant to each user group. They can therefore pitch the text and its provisions to the right level. In fact, they could (and should) test the provision by means of representative user groups to verify the level of easification achieved by their draft.

Judges, as interpreters of legislation, are excluded from the debate on easification, legislative diversity, and effectiveness. Discussions on methods of statutory interpretation and the 'ordinary meaning' of words remain outside the scope of audience analytics and user diversity. In view of the novelty of the legislative debate, perhaps this mismatch is explained. However, it cannot remain as is. Drafters choose to use words based on the linguistic and legislative characteristics of the user groups of legislation, whilst judges continue to be guided by usage of what is still perceived as the 'average man' and the 'ordinary meaning' of words.

The new empirical data on the analytics of legislative diversity in the UK feeds further breath to what one could view as an archaic debate. The parameters of 'ordinary' can now be identified with some accuracy, thus allowing the judge or statutory interpreter to guess what the meaning of the word could be to a legislative user. However, in order to achieve this enlightened understanding of the true meaning of words, the statutory interpreter must become aware of the debate on legislative diversity, must be privy to the factors of choice used by the drafter and to any user testing results. Purposive interpretation, which puts context to the language of the text, serves well as a guide here.

One wonders where the interpreter could trace these elements of drafting choices. I would suggest that explanatory notes (what civil lawyers would recognize as *traveaux préparatoires*) could be a handy place. Despite erroneous perceptions of the past, explanatory notes are used exclusively by lawyers and judges. They can therefore serve as a source of sophisticated guidance on which user groups were identified, what linguistic and legislative awareness they have, and how this is reflected in the provisions of the text.

3.5 Conclusions

This chapter aimed to prove that recent innovations in drafting techniques have disturbed the continuity of language used by those who produce and those who interpret legislation. Legislative drafting, and legislative studies, have been radically revolutionized by the recent empirical data on legislative usage. There is now compelling empirical evidence that legislation, at least in the UK, is mainly read by lay users, namely users without legal sophistication who read legislation in order to acquire answers to problems related to their everyday life or to the exercise of their professional duties.

To ensure legislative effectiveness as a tool for regulatory efficacy, drafters draft legislation in an easified language. This is language that is understood by the specific users of the particular legislative text. The language choices of drafters seem to clash with the expectation of judges, who continue to interpret legislation by use of the 'ordinary meaning of words' as used by 'the average man'.

This division in the perceived usage of language by legislative users creates a schism between the linguistic choices of drafters and their interpretation by the courts. In turn, this creates a considerable hurdle in the normally fluid seamless passage from conceptualization to drafting to application and interpretation of legislation. To put it simply, at the moment, users are more likely to understand the intended meaning of legislation than the courts.

Aligning language expectations, usage, and interpretation between drafters and judges is not necessarily a hefty task. Purposive interpretation (what civil lawyers recognize as teleological interpretation) has given rise to guidance tools, such as explanatory notes. Although these used to be addressed to lay users, they can serve as a valuable channel of communication with learned users such as judges. They can identify the main legislative audiences and can provide context to judges for the purposes of delimiting and specifying the 'ordinary meaning' of words. For now, one can simply confirm that, currently, legislators and judges speak a different language.

References

D. Berry, 'Audience Analysis in the Legislative Drafting Process', *The Loophole*, 2000, www.opc.gov.au/calc/docs/calc-june/audience.htm.

A. Bertlin, 'What Works Best for the Reader? A Study on Drafting and Presenting Legislation', *The Loophole*, 2014, www.gov.uk/government/uploads/system/uploads/attachment_data/file/326937/Loophole_-_2014-2__2014-05-09_-What_works_best_for_the_reader.pdf.

J.P. Chamberlain, 'Legislative Drafting and Law Enforcement', *American Labor Legislation Review*, Vol. 21, 1931, pp. 235–243 at p. 243.

R. Cranston, 'Reform Through Legislation: The Dimension of Legislative Technique', *North Western University Law Review*, Vol. 73, 1978–1979, p. 873.

European Commission, 'European Governance: Better Lawmaking', Communication from the Commission, COM, 2002, 275 final, Brussels 5.6.2002.

B. A. Garner, 'Guidelines for Drafting and Editing Court Rules', *Federal Rules Decisions*, Vol. 175, 1997, p. 169.

J. J. E. Gracia, *A Theory of Textuality: The Logic and Epistemology*, Albany, NY, State University of New York Press, 1995.

High Level Group on the Operation of Internal Market, 'The Internal Market After 1992: Meeting the Challenge – Report to the EEC Commission by the High Level Group on the Operation of Internal Market', *SEC* (92) 2044, 1992.

D. Hull, 'Drafters Devils', *The Loophole*, 2000, www.opc.gov.au/calc/docs/calc-june/audience.htm.

I. Jenkins, *Social Order and the Limits of the Law: A Theoretical Essay*, Princeton, NJ, Princeton University Press, 1981.

U. Karpen, 'The Norm Enforcement Process', in U. Karpen & P. Delnoy (Eds), *Contributions to the Methodology of the Creation of Written Law*, Baden-Baden, Nomos, 1996, p. 51.

J. Kimble, 'Answering the Critics of Plain Language', *The Scribes Journal of Legal Writing*, Vol. 5, 1994–1995, p. 51.

J. Mader, 'Evaluating the Effect: A Contribution to the Quality of Legislation', *Statute Law Review*, Vol. 22, 2001, pp. 119–131 at 126.

J. Mousmouti, 'Operationalising Quality of Legislation Through the Effectiveness Test', *Legisprudence*, Vol. 6, 2012, p. 191.

G. Muller & F. Uhlmann, *Elemente einer Rechtssetzungslehre*, Zurich, Schulthess, 3. Auflage, 2013, pp. 51–52.

D. Murphy, 'Plain English-Principles and Practice', Conference on Legislative Drafting, Canberra, Australia, 15 July 1992.

Office of the Leader of the House of Commons, 'Post-legislative Scrutiny – The Government's Approach', March 2008, para. 2.4.

Office of the Parliamentary Counsel, 'Working with OPC', 6 December 2011.

Office of the Parliamentary Counsel, 'Drafting Guidance', 16 December 2011.

G. L. Pi & V. Schmolka, 'A Report on Results of Usability Testing Research on Plain Language Draft Sections of the Employment Insurance Act: A Report to Department of Justice Canada and Human Resources Development Canada' (Unpublished, August 2000).

V. Schmolka, 'Consumer Fireworks Regulations: Usability Testing, TR1995-2e' (Unpublished, Department of Justice Canada, 1995).

K. A. Schriver, 'Plain Language Through Protocol-Aided Revision', in E. R. Steinberg (Ed.), *Plain Language: Principles and Practice*, Detroit, MI, Wayne State University Press, 1991, p. 148.

Lord Simon of Glaisdale, 'The Renton Report-Ten Years On', *Statute Law Review*, 1985, Vol. 6, No. 1, p. 133.

F. Snyder, *New Directions in European Community Law*, London, Weidenfeld & Nicolson, 1990, p. 3.

F. Snyder, 'The Effectiveness of European Community Law: Institutions, Processes, Tools and Techniques', *Modern Law Review*, Vol. 56, 1993, p. 19.

C. Stefanou, 'Drafters, Drafting and the Policy Process', in C. Stefanou & H. Xanthaki (Eds), *Drafting Legislation: A Modern Approach*, Ashgate, Dartmouth, 2008, p. 321.

C. Stefanou, 'Legislative Drafting as a Form of Communication', in L. Mader & M.T. de Almeida (Eds), *Quality of Legislation Principles and Instruments*, Nomos, Baden-Baden, 2011, p. 308.

G. Teubner, 'Regulatory Law: Chronicle of a Death Foretold', in Lenoble (Ed.), *Einfuhrung in der Rectssoziologi*, Darmstadt, Wissenschaftliche Buchgesellschaft, 1987, p. 54.

C. Timmermans, 'How Can One Improve the Quality of Community Legislation?' *Common Market Law Review*, Vol. 34, 1997, p. 1229.

W. Voermans, 'Concern about the Quality of EU Legislation: What Kind of Problem, by What Kind of Standards?', *Erasmus Law Review*, Vol. 2, 2009, pp. 59, 230.

H. Xanthaki, 'On Transferability of Legislative Solutions: The Functionality Test', in C. Stefanou & H. Xanthaki (Eds), *Drafting Legislation: A Modern Approach – In Memoriam of Sir William Dale*, Ashgate, Dartmouth, 2008, pp. 1–18.

H. Xanthaki, 'Drafting Manuals and Quality in Legislation: Positive Contribution Towards Certainty in the Law or Impediment to the Necessity for Dynamism of Rules?', *Legisprudence*, Vol. 4, 2010, pp. 111–128.

H. Xanthaki, 'Judges v Drafters: The Saga Continues', in J. Barnes (Ed.), Statutory Interpretation, forthcoming; and H. Xanthaki, 'An 'Ordinary Meaning of Words': Is There Such a Thing?', in Ik-Hyeon Rhee & W. Voermans (Eds), *Innovation of Legislative Process*, Seoul, KLRI/IAL, 2018a, pp. 123–136.

H. Xanthaki, 'The Limits of Legislation as a Product', *Hukim – The Israeli Journal on Legislation*, Vol. 11, 2018b, pp. 153–172.

4 Text, values, and interpretation

The role of judges and legislative power in private law

Attila Menyhárd

4.1 Introduction

This chapter attempts to provide a model for private law which follows a model similar to constitutional law as far as method of interpretation and finding the legal norm are concerned. Furthermore, it makes conclusions about some consequences of this model as to the structure of law and the role of courts and of the legislator. It is a failure to draw a Chinese wall between the legislative and the judicial power. In the context of private law, as well as in the context of constitutional law, making the law cannot be consequently distinguished from its application. If, however, this distinction is to be construed – as is normally done – its validity is necessarily relative.

My starting point is that a legal dispute is a social conflict. Conflicts are wrong. That is why there is a need for lawyers in society. The task of lawyers is to avoid, to resolve, and to close down conflicts. It is especially the task of the courts to resolve or to close social conflicts. As courts decide cases, they eliminate conflicts in order to maintain cooperation amongst the members of society or, at least, to maintain social coexistence and social peace. In the mechanism of judicial decision-making, i.e. resolving social conflict, the court is seeking the answer to whether the plaintiff has a right against the respondent as was stated in the plaintiff's claim. If the court establishes that the plaintiff has the right against the respondent as it was stated in the claim, it decides for the plaintiff. The content of the judgment is determined by the plaintiff's right vis-à-vis the defendant, which, on the other hand, imposes an obligation on the defendant vis-à-vis the plaintiff. In order to resolve the case and to hand the judgment down the court has to establish the content of the law, because it is the legal norm that is the source of the right vis-à-vis the other party. The legal norm is ordered by the law and is to be sought by the judge.

Thus, in the model of judicial decision-making in private law, it is the task of the court to establish rights and obligations. The source of rights and obligations is the law. While establishing the content of private law, it is the source of the law that has to be identified. In this contribution it is argued that private law cannot be identical with written rules. It is much more to be understood as a normative materialization of the values that prevail in society. It is the task of the court to enforce social values via establishing the content of the law. Thus, the task of the court is the very same as the task of the legislator. That is, enforcing social values as between the parties and providing social evaluation of the case. The consequence of this is that the relationship of the courts and of the legislator cannot be described as a hierarchy based on subordination of the courts to the supremacy of the legislator. Hence, as far as establishing the content of legal norms is concerned, there is no difference between legislative and judicial power. The relationship of legislation and the judiciary is much more a division of the tasks of social engineering according to aspects of efficiency and legitimacy than hierarchy.

4.2 Judgments and written norms

It is a failure to think that law is identical with written norms. Written norms themselves cannot be the source of the legal norms as they are to be interpreted. Application of written law is finding the meaning of text (statutes or principles laid down in leading judgments) in order to establish the rule (norm) to be followed in a certain case and confronting the norm with the facts of the case. Interpretation is the way of finding the meaning of text and establishing its content. When it comes to interpretation, theoretically a choice has to be made between textualist (or pure interpretive) model and the supplementer approach. According to the pure interpretive approach, it is the meaning of the text as such that is to be established, while the supplementer approach requires amending the text according to the moral values and customs generally accepted in society.[1]

This choice, however, is not a real option in the case of written legal texts formulated in such an abstract way that it opens the text for judicial interpretation. In the context of such norms, only a supplementer approach can prevail. Typically, the text of constitutions and civil codes are provided on a high level of abstraction, being open for juridical interpretation.

Interpretation is about establishing the content of the legal text in the given case by the court. There are provisions that are so open for such an interpretation that establishing their content is left entirely to the court. These norms are defined as general clauses, because their function is transmitting a social evaluation of the case. General clauses are to be concretized by the court to the specific case. The ultimate role of law and of the court procedure is searching for justice, i.e. searching for the right. That is why our approach can only be correct if we have in our focus the case and judicial decision-making, that is, the process of searching and establishing rights and obligations. In this sense, answers to questions concerning the content of the law are statements about hypothetical judgments of courts trying to predict what conclusion a court would reach about relevant rights and obligations according to the facts of the case. The text of the

1 Thomas C. Grey, 'The Constitution as Scripture', *Stanford Law Review*, Vol. 37, 1984–1985, pp. 1–26.

legal norm plays a role in this assessment only because we assume that the courts would follow the very same pattern of thinking that we predicted. In this sense, one of the main goals of legal theory is making this algorithm transparent and predictable. In the absence of this, legal knowledge cannot be shifted to the level of community of lawyers and made common.

According to the standard model, the legislator makes the law and the court applies it. This approach assumes hierarchy, where the court simply executes the legislator's order. This model, however, is not correct, or at least it is not entirely correct. Judgments assume ranking evaluations and establishing priorities. Values accepted in society play a role, with different weight according to the facts of each of the cases. The priority of values is determined by the balance of the interests that underlie the case.[2] The main principle is that different cases shall be assessed differently while the same cases shall be assessed the same way. The written norm provided by the legislator establishes the basic evaluation only, which can be overruled by the court. This overruling can be performed with different methods. The main tools of such enforcement of values are: interpretation of abstract norms, concretizing general clauses, assessment of 'hard cases', or procedural solutions like reversal of burden of proof in cases of information asymmetry. The legislator may also leave the balancing of interests and establishing priorities to the courts.

4.2.1 Law and interpretation

Interpretation is about establishing the content of the norm. Thus, creation of the law on one hand and application of it on the other hand cannot be distinguished. Interpretation is about establishing the content of the norm which *per se* means that it is not the legislator but the court that establishes the content of the norm. Thus, in a realistic model of judicial adjudication, the court does not merely state the norm but construes it. This makes the distinction between law-making and application relative; the judgment of the court does not the create norm, but the court, by finding the norm, does.

It is relatively easy to understand that it cannot be possible to rely on four-corner interpretation. The Hungarian Constitutional Court, in its first important opinion, established that

> the starting point shall be the Constitution as a whole. The Constitutional Court has to continue its work on elaborating and establishing the conceptual basis of the Constitution and the constitutional rights. The judgments of the constitutional court shall create a coherent system which stands above the Constitution – which is exposed to amendments driven by temporary political interests – as an "Invisible Constitution" and is the permanent standard of assessing the compliance of legal norms with the Constitution

2 Helmut Koziol, 'Das bewegliche System – Die goldene Mitte für Gesetzgebung und Dogmatik', *Austrian Law Journal*, 2017 March, p. 161 ff.

> predictably not colliding with constitutions that are passed in the future as well. The Constitutional Court, in this respect, has a free playground as far as it stands within the frames provided by the concept of constitutionality.[3]

This approach is, however, neither exclusively Hungarian, nor a specifically European one. As John Ely stressed,

> a neutral and durable principle may be a thing of beauty and a joy forever. But if it lacks connection with any value the Constitution marks as special, it is not a constitutional principle and the Court has no business imposing it.[4]

The problem is that if there are conflicting values and there are no preferences to be derived from the written norm, could (or should) the preferences given by the Court be justified. Thus, it is not possible to follow a 'neutral application' model. Consequently, the idea of unwritten or invisible constitution is an inherent element of a legal system referring to the relevant values and interests, much more than a national peculiarity.

4.2.2 General clauses

In legal systems based on written norms provided by the legislator, there is a need for general rules which open the law for moral evaluation of the case if necessary, make the law able to adjust to changing social and economic environment, and give tools into the hands of the judge to decide cases which are not covered with specific provisions (gap-filling). General clauses are broadly defined norms of civil codes and they cannot be interpreted in the traditional sense. They cannot be applied via normal subsuming like other legal norms. Due to their openness their content shall be determined according to the general values of society. These general clauses are inherent part of codified legal systems. Their function is to open the case for judicial evaluation in all types of legal relationship, whether there is a written norm to cover the case or not. These rules can not only fill the gaps left in written law but must also overrule written norms, if their application would not comply with the prevailing social values under the facts and the circumstances of the given case. Requirements of good faith and fair dealing and prohibition of abuse of rights are typical general clauses but they may appear under other concepts in civil codes as well.[5] With the application of such general clauses, courts establish moral evaluation and with their judgments create

3 Resolution no. 23/1990. (X.31.) AB. of the Constitutional Court of the Hungarian Republic on Incompatibility of Death Penalty with the Constitution.

4 John Hart Ely, 'The Wages of Crying Wolf: A Comment on Roe v. Wade', *Yale Law Journal*, Vol. 82, 1973, pp. 920, 949.

5 Treu und Glauben (BGB § 242), correttezza (Codice civile Art 1175), "redelijkheid en billijkheid" (BW § 6:2). In English-American law doctrines (estoppel, *in pari delicto*, etc.) have similar function.

categories under which they are subsuming new cases. This process is similar to the judge-made law where categories or groups of cases are established by courts and eventually play the role of precedents.

The role and interpretation of general clauses may change together with changes in society. The general starting point is that general clauses introduce actual non-legal social norms into the body of law, although they do not necessarily transmit direct policy. In that regard the courts do not simply find the moral values but they shape society and the law just like social engineers. Often, they are ready to implement direct policy too. This has already been well presented in case law of extreme socio-political systems. Comparison of interpretation and concretization of general clauses in extreme socio-economic system may provide a good example of how courts can apply open norms for realizing socio-political aims such as excluding or promoting market mechanisms, providing social justice, or simply using open norms for realizing or strengthening oppression of disqualified groups of society.[6]

4.2.3 Hard cases

Hard cases[7] emerge when there is no clear and direct legislative rule that would address the consequences of the given facts of the case or if the case seems to come under the scope of a rule which was not designed specifically for the given scenario. That is, there is a relevant rule to be found for the case but the result of application of the rule is questionable in context of social evaluation or policy and the legislator does not seem to have had the specific scenario in mind when designing the rule.

In such cases a choice has to be made. The court either will point to the written rule and conclude accordingly or will overrule the written provision according to moral convictions or policy considerations. If the court applies the written rule in spite of the hardly acceptable result, it shifts the responsibility to the legislator. The court gives in this way the message that if the public would not find the conclusion correct, the rule should be amended by legislative measures. If the court, however, overrules the written norm, e.g. making recourse to a general clause, it takes the responsibility of avoiding *summum ius summa iniuria* and provides justice. The court gives in this way the message that although there is a written rule, the case at hand and the cases that are similar do not belong to the scope of the rule. That is, such cases are decided not according to the written norm but according to the underlying principles established by the court instead. It is,

6 Jens Wanner, *Die Sittenwidrigkeit der Rechtsgeschäfte im totalitären State*, Ebelsbach, Aktiv Druck & Verlag GmbH, 1996, p. 267, Bernd Rüthers, *Die unbegrenzte Auslegung. Zum Wandel der Privatrechtsordnung im Nationalsozializmus*, 5. erw. Aufl., Heidelberg, C.F. Müller Verlag, 1997, p. 219.

7 Like the well-known Elmer's case [Riggs v Palmer, 115 N.Y. 506 (1889)]. *Ronald Dworkin, Law's Empire*, Oxford, Hart Publishing, 1998, p. 15 ff.

however, up to the court to decide which way to follow. Opting for the application of a rule with an unjust outcome can be supported by argumentations resting on a pure interpretive model, while overruling the rule for reaching a just result requires further justification, e.g. relying on public moral, policy considerations, reference to protected interests.[8] This is a question of argumentation.

4.2.4 Procedural measures

Procedural rules, especially the ones allocating burden of proof, are provided by legislative measures. These rules allocate burden of proof according to the statements and claims of the parties. Such rules normally shift the burden of proof to the party whose interest is in having the relevant statements accepted as facts by the judge. Courts, however, tend to reverse the burden of proof if maintaining the just risk allocation requires it. This is especially the case if there is an information asymmetry concerning the relevant facts of the case to the detriment of the person to be protected by the law. In the context of tort law, e.g. in medical malpractice cases, the court may require the doctor (in practice the hospital) to prove that even if the doctor complied with the required standard of conduct, the damage would have occurred; that is, there was no causal link between the personal injury and the doctor's negligence. Reversal of the burden of proof shifts the risk of absence of information (i.e. what could have happened in the case of the defendant's conduct being correct) to the defendant.[9]

4.2.5 Playgrounds left open by virtue of decision of the legislator

It is typical that to enforce the inherent rights of persons (e.g. right to privacy, human dignity, bodily integrity, good reputation, freedom of speech) the courts have to decide cases on the basis of counterweighing contending interests of the parties, having regard to the interests of the public as well. In this context the legislator may establish the relevant values but if such values are in conflict in a concrete case, it is up to the judge to decide to which one the priority shall be given over the other. The law of national jurisdictions in this field is built up as pure case law, where the courts shape the underlying doctrines as well. This area of law is a unique interaction of the practice of national ordinary courts, the constitutional courts and the judgments of the European Court of Human Rights. Typical issues like limits to the right to privacy of public persons are also left to

8 In the famous judgment in the case Roe v Wade the American Supreme Court clearly and openly did *not* rely on constitutional text for the content of the substantive principle it referred to in order to invalidate unconstitutional legislation: 'this right of privacy, whether it be founded in the Fourteenth Amendment's concept of personal liberty and restrictions upon state action, as we feel it is, or, as the District Court determined, in the Ninth Amendment's reservation of rights to the people, is broad enough to encompass a woman's decision whether or not to terminate her pregnancy'. Roe v Wade, 410 U.S. 113, 153 (1973).

9 Supreme Court, Legf Bír Pfv III 22.188/2010 – BH 2012 no 10.

the national court practice. In so far as the necessity of changes may be indicated, it is also a message to the courts rather than to the legislator.[10]

4.3 Implementing values via interpretation

Courts have to implement and enforce the general values prevailing in society in each of the cases. In the course of this process, they confront the relevant values according to the relevant facts of the case. This cannot happen otherwise, because it is the task of the state and of the law to implement and to enforce values that prevail in society. If the state and the law fail to do that, they would not comply with the interests of society and would not perform their function in that society properly.

A peculiarity of this transposition of values is that courts do not follow a kind of social majority opinion but attempt to enforce the values of an ideal society, e.g. justice, that function properly. From this point of view, the central issue is not what 'is' (*Sein*), but what 'should be' (*Sollen*). This should be the focus of the scientific interest because this is also the task of judges functioning as social engineers. In the social level of division of labor, the task of the lawyers is not simply to know, understand, and transmit legal scripture but – far more – to identify, keep, and implement the values of the proper society. This is the task and the social responsibility of legal profession. That is why lawyers fight for freedom in oppressive regimes, even against the majority opinion prevailing in the society. This is the legitimacy for fighting against the death penalty, protecting the rights of perpetrators, procedural guarantees, or rights of individuals vis-à-vis the state.

Values become principles or standards of required conduct which are the content of abstract norms including the general clauses. They appear also as content of more concrete rules.[11] From this point of view, law can be described as a mechanism for transmitting and implementing values. Thus, in the course of dispute resolution, the task of the courts and judges is not the duty of the legislator's servant, but to implement the values of a good society. This does not mean that the court can disregard the clear order of the legislator anytime, according to its discretion. It means, however, that the abstract written rules in private law always open the possibility of implementing values. Moreover, general clauses, especially the requirement of good faith and fair dealing and the prohibition of abuse of rights (or the functionally equivalent rules and doctrines) authorize judges to overrule any written norm provided by the legislator in order to enforce the values of the good society. Because of their nature the general clauses become part of the algorithm of application of written norms. Consequently, any written norm provides a right to one party vis-à-vis the other only upon the condition that the exercise of the right does not qualify as an abuse of rights or would not

10 Von Hannover v Germany (2004) (Application no. 59320/00).

11 Jürgen Habermas, *Between Facts and Norms*, Cambridge, Polity Press, Blackwell, 1997, p. 255.

be incompatible with the requirement of good faith and fair dealing. The task and the function of the legislator and of the judge is the very same: implementing and enforcing social values in the course of resolving social conflicts. Values appear as rules of conduct, that is, norms. From the point of view of enforcement, it does not make a difference if the norms were provided as written rules created by the legislator or rules of conduct established by courts and enforced with judgments. Courts and the legislator produce the law with no hierarchy as between them. From this point of view, even if it may sound provocative, as courts also create the law, there is no sense in assuming '*contra legem*' court practice.

4.4 The flexible system of private law

The most precise description of how private law works describes the judgment of the court as a process of evaluation. In this mechanism, the court decides the case on the basis of a closed number of relevant values, counter-weighing them in the context of the facts of the case. The result of such evaluation is establishing if the party does have a right against the other party. According to this model, provided by the Austrian scholar Walter Wilburg, private law should be seen as a flexible system.[12]

In this flexible system, for example, the binding force of a contract depends on counter-weighing four fundamental values: private autonomy, protection of reliance on the other party's conduct and statement, objective evaluation of the intended exchange, and self-reliance.[13] The strength of the value of private autonomy depends on how informed the parties were in the course of contracting and if their decision upon contracting was a voluntary one. Private autonomy is a fundamental value of a market economy and the civil society. Mistake, misrepresentation, and duress, however, are market failures. If the consent was not an informed one or the contractual will was not free, the transaction is not a market-based one. Consequently, it shall not be enforceable. How the required information and level of voluntariness is to be determined depends on moral base-lines as well.[14] Protection of reliance on statements and conduct of the other party is equal for the parties in cases of equal bargaining power. The parties are, from this point of view, in equal positions in contracting. The basic evaluation is that each party has to take care of his own interest. If, due to changes in the circumstances or of the position of parties the performance becomes so burdensome that it is not reasonable to enforce it anymore, or the changes make the

12 Walter Wilburg, Entwicklung eines beweglichen Systems im Bürgerlichen Recht (Rede gehalten bei der Inauguration als Rector magnificus der Karl-Franzes Universität in Graz am 22 November 1950), Graz, Kienreich, 1950; Walter Wilburg, 'Zusammenspiel der Kräfte im Aufbau des Schuldrechts', *AcP*, Vol. 163, 1964, p. 364.

13 Franz Bydlinski, 'A "Flexible System" Approach to Contract Law', in H. Hausmaninger et al. (Eds), *Developments in Austrian and Israeli Private Law*, 1999, p. 9 ff.

14 Michael J. Trebilcock, *The Limits of Freedom Contract*, Cambridge, MA, Harvard University Press, 1997, p. 78 ff.

performance burdensome while the risk of such changes shall not be implied in the contract (hardship), the court may amend the contract or establish that it shall not be enforceable (frustration of purpose, impossibility of performance). The objective evaluation of the intended exchange is less relevant if contracting was informed and voluntary, while less voluntary or less informed contracting indicates a lower probability of enforcement of the bargain if there is an objective imbalance between the value of performances. This is the ground for judicial and legislative control of contracting with standard contract terms too. Responsibility and self-reliance mean that as a moral value, promises are to be kept.[15]

In the context of tort law, the general rule of liability is designed with similar content in different jurisdictions: the tortfeasor shall have the obligation to pay damages if loss was caused unlawfully and fault by the wrongdoer is established to have caused it. Thus, the prerequisites of liability are damage, unlawful conduct, a causal link between them, and fault. Compensable damage, relevant cause, fault, and unlawfulness are, as abstract legal norms, open for wide range of judicial interpretation. If the certain loss was compensable, it depends on moral evaluations as well: lost profit shall not be compensated if it was illicit and there are often fierce debates over the issue of whether childbirth can be a basis of a claim for damages. The concept of non-pecuniary loss has been emerged in court practice and the limits of it are to be drawn by courts. Fault is a concept expressing the required standard of conduct. Standards, by their nature, are always established and assessed by the courts on a case-by-case basis. To establish a causal link and establishing the relevant cause (legal cause) on the basis of the chain of natural causation (the condition *sine qua non* or the but-for test) is left to the courts also by all legal systems. That is, in addressing liability, the task of the legislator shall be restricted to providing specific rules where it is necessary and to give some basic evaluation (e.g. that fault is needed in order to establish liability) but not more.

Limits of liability are inherent to tort law and cases of pure economic loss are a good example for that. The main conceptual feature of pure economic loss is that it is a loss without antecedent harm to the plaintiff's person or property, which is not a consequential loss in the same patrimony in which property has been damaged and which is not the loss of the plaintiff, who as a person has been injured.[16] Pure economic loss is 'harm not causally consequent upon an injury to the person (life, body, health, freedom or other rights to personality) or to

15 Bernhard A. Koch, 'Wilburg's Flexible System in a Nutshell', in Helmut Koziol/Barbara C. Steininger (Eds), *European Tort Law 2001*, Wien/New York, Springer, 2002, pp. 545–548, 547; Franz Bydlinski, 'A "Flexible System" Approach to Contract Law', in Herbert Hausmaninger/Helmut Koziol/Alfredo M. Rabello/Israel Gilead (Eds), *Developments in Austrian and Israeli Private Law*, Wien/New York, Springer, 1996, pp. 9–20.

16 Mauro Bussani and Vernon Valentine Palmer (Eds), *Pure Economic Loss in Europe*, Cambridge, Cambridge University Press, 2003, p. 5.

property (tangible or intangible assets)'.[17] Compensating pure economic loss is a challenge for all jurisdictions for its quite unclear contours. Normally courts don't award compensation for such a loss in order to keep the floodgates shut against claims that are unpredictable in their amounts as well as concerning the number of potential plaintiffs. Helmut Koziol, considering the compensability of pure economic loss and searching for the elements of risk allocation in the flexible system of tort law identifies the following factors of evaluation: number of potential plaintiffs, existence or absence of additional duty of care, proximity and special relations, dangerousness, dependence, obviousness and actual knowledge, clear contours, negligence and intent, the importance of violated financial interests, and the importance of the defendant's financial interests.[18] In general, judgments of court in tort cases are the result of counter-weighing these elements and balancing the interests of the tortfeasor and victim in line with the weight of the factors that are relevant under the given facts of the case. The risk allocation in the judgment is provided accordingly. Thus, the judgment is the outcome of balancing of the interests. The preconditions of liability are called for only in order to have the judgment anchored in the civil code and maintaining the conceptual framework for liability. There is, however, nothing to do with interpretation of written law in this context.

In this evaluation-based flexible model the content of the norm referred to by the court in the judgment is not provided as the result of interpretation of the written legal text but with establishing the social evaluation of the case. The social evaluation is actually provided by the court with the judgment. This mechanism is very close to the one according to which constitutional courts come to conclusions providing the 'interpretation'[19] of the constitution as a result of counter-weighing constitutional values and balancing interests.

4.5 Legislation against judicial interpretation: Two sides of the same coin?

Of course, the written rule provided by the legislator is not irrelevant in this model either. Its role, however, cannot be described as an order that comes from a higher level of a hierarchy. The function of written rules provided by the legislator is complex.

Written rules provide the basic evaluation and the set of values that can be relevant in the course of deciding cases. These are the freedom of contract (private

17 Helmut Koziol, 'Compensation for Pure Economic Loss from a Continental Lawyer's Perspective', in W. H. van Boom/H. Koziol/C. A. Witting (Eds), *Pure Economic Loss*, Wien/New York, ECTIL Tort and Insurance Law, 2004, Vol. 9, p. 141 ff.

18 Helmut Koziol, 'Compensation for Pure Economic Loss from a Continental Lawyer's Perspective', in Wilhelm H. van Boom/Helmut Koziol/Christian A. Witting (Eds), *Pure Economic Loss*, Wien/New York, Springer, 2004, 141–161.

19 In details in Hungarian scholarship e.g. Tóth Gábor Attila, *Túl a szövegen – értekezés a magyar alkotmányról*, Budapest, Osiris, 2009.

autonomy), the rules addressing unequal bargaining (gross disparity, unfair standard contract terms, hardship), the specific rules in tort law providing for liability for extra-hazardous activity (consequences of dangerousness and avoiding externalities), the opportunity to reduce damages on equitable grounds (relevance of financial situation of the tortfeasor and that of the victim), or declaring exclusion clauses that make liability for death, personal injury, and health damage unenforceable (ranking the protected interests). The court has to overrule the basic evaluation provided by the legislator only if – and in so far as – another relevant risk allocation element (value) is strong enough to establish such overruling. On the level of legislation such opportunity for overruling written rules is provided with general clauses.

One important difference between legislative and judicial law-making is the different level of legitimacy. In democracies the source of legitimacy of legislative power is the election (which provides a strong legitimacy in a proper election system), while the legitimacy of the courts is supported by the system of choosing and appointing judges. The legitimacy of judicial power primarily seems to be a question of state organization. The legitimacy of legislative power comes to the foreground in cases where social evaluation is uncertain or there is no consent among the community of lawyers about understanding and evaluating a case. Such questions emerged in Hungarian court practice in the context of the concept of exclusive state property[20] or damages claims for childbirth.

One specific group of cases in medical malpractice is where a child was born with a genetic or teratological deficiency (e.g. Down syndrome) due to the failure of the doctor who was negligent in revealing and disclosing the obvious risk to the pregnant mother during pregnancy, depriving the parents of the opportunity to decide for an abortion permitted by law in such situation. In such cases, the parents may have a claim for damages as a compensation for giving life to a child with a mental or physical handicap ('wrongful birth' claims). It is also a question if the child could have such a claim in her own name ('wrongful life' claims). While wrongful birth claims are normally accepted, there are considerable arguments against allowing wrongful life claims. In Hungary, the Supreme Court established[21] that the child shall not be entitled to claim either pecuniary or non-pecuniary damages from the medical service provider for being born with genetic or teratological deficiencies on the ground that, during the pregnancy,

20 Supreme Court, Legf. Bír. Pfv. I. 21.446/2008. sz. (BH 2009. 175). The question was whether exclusive state property should mean that objects (real estates or tangible things) belonging to this category do not exist in the eyes of private law (French model) or only that such ownership is limited to its public functionality (German model). The courts were divided upon this issue. Finally, the Supreme Court followed the French model, but legitimacy provided too weak and the legislator provided specific rules for that with Act no. CXCVI of 2011 on national property.

21 Supreme Court, Unificatory Resolution no. 1/2008, 12 March 2008: No Damages for Wrongful Life, Magyar Közlöny (*Official Journal of the Hungarian Republic*) no. 2008/50 (26 March 2008).

her mother could not have decided for an abortion because of the incorrect information given to her by the medical service provider if an abortion would have been otherwise permitted in such a case. The scope of the unificatory resolution is to be restricted to wrongful life cases, i.e. to cases where the genetic or teratological deficiency is of a natural origin and developed independently of the activity of the medical service provider or its employees. Thus, claims for damages as compensation for prenatal injuries (compensation for injury suffered as a result of intervention of doctors during the pregnancy) are not covered by the resolution. The resolution does not affect the claims of parents.

The necessity to pass such a resolution concerning damages for wrongful life arose because, although the Supreme Court followed a settled practice of accepting such claims,[22] this interpretation did not correspond to the practice of some of the high courts in Hungary which also declared and published their interpretation rejecting such claims brought by the child.[23] Not only the tension created by diverging practice of high courts but also the obvious deviation from the trends presented by European legal systems[24] led the Supreme Court to revise its practice in such cases. As a result, obviously influenced by court practice of other European jurisdictions and with the clear intention of harmonizing Hungarian court practice with the trend of rejecting such claims in most European jurisdictions, the Supreme Court decided to revise its former decisions and to adopt a uniform practice of rejecting claims for damages for wrongful life.

The result of passing such a resolution in Hungarian law is laying down the law covered by the resolution with the effect of an authoritative interpretation which might – perhaps should – have been given by the legislator too. The necessity of passing such a resolution in Hungarian law supports the argument that such sensitive issues may and should be addressed by the legislator even if this does not seem to be compatible with the flexible system of tort law. The process of making law, in a democratic society, designed for channeling and harmonizing different social values and interests – in such sensitive areas – seems to be a more appropriate way of fixing such principles than court decisions.

The question, whether giving life to a child, whether the child is healthy or not could be a basis of damages claims may impose a heavy moral burden on judges. It may not be appropriate to impose such a burden on judges, or courts may not have enough strong legitimacy for deciding such issues. In France, the court

22 Supreme Court, Legf. Bír. Pfv. III. 22.193/2004. sz. – EBH 2005. 1206. sz. Reported by Attila Menyhárd, 'Hungary', in H. Koziol/B. C. Steininger (Eds), *European Tort Law 2005*, Wien/New York, Springer, 2005, 2006, no. 9–11.

23 Opinion of the Civil Law College to the Regional Court of Pécs no. 1/2006. (VI. 2.), Opinion of the Csongrád County Court, referred to in the explanatory notes to the Unificatory Resolution of the Supreme Court.

24 Explicitly referred to in the explanatory notes to the Unificatory Resolution of the Supreme Court. See also B. A. Koch, 'Comparative Overview', in H. Koziol/B. C. Steininger (Eds), *European Tort Law 2005*, Wien/New York, Springer, 2006, 608.

practice was reversed by legislative acts;[25] upon the same issue, in Hungary, the same revision has been performed by the courts. It made no difference if the step was made with legislative or judicial measures.

In Hungary, as happened in other central European countries, a great part of the citizens had become overburdened with bank loans denominated in Swiss Francs. These consumer loans became a huge social problem threatening with mass insolvency of the households. Many claims were brought to the courts arguing that shifting the risk of changes in currency rates to the debtor consumer was unfair and unenforceable. In order to avoid the flood of claims the legislator enacted a law which declares such clauses explicitly unenforceable.[26] The same conclusion with the same result could have been reached by the courts by applying the rules providing for unenforceability of unfair standard terms in the Civil Code.[27] It seemed, however, more efficient to provide a legislative solution instead of deciding thousands of claims in court procedure. The only difference between the legislative step and the solution provided with judicial adjudication was the efficiency.

These examples demonstrate that the difference between judicial and legislative measures cannot be found in hierarchy but in legitimacy and efficiency. Consequently, there is no huge difference in judicial and legislative power.

4.6 Conclusions

Interpretation is establishing the content of the written provision. As it is the task of the court to interpret the rule, the judge provides the content and with this, establishes the norm. In the course of establishing the norm the courts necessarily go beyond the textual interpretation. The text itself cannot be the sole source of the legal norm, that is, of the law. Judges should supplement it according to established practice, former judgments, and social morality. With this, the distinction between *making* the rule and the *application* of it cannot be justified. If we seek the answer to the question of what courts really do if they are engaged in judicial review on the basis of changing and unwritten moral principles instead of the written norm, we have to confront with the consequence that the courts may have the authority of a legislative power.

It is a failure to overestimate the importance of written law. The content of law is described with preliminary statements (predictions) on (hypothetical) judgments of courts. Thus, in order to define law or providing the proper model of it, we need to know the actual process of adjudication, which involves setting up priorities of values. According to the model suggested by Walter Wilburg, private law is a flexible system of open rules, allowing great power to the courts

25 Loi no. 2002/303 du 4 mars 2002 ("Loi Perruche").

26 Act no. LXXVII of 2014 upon amendment of certain consumer loan contracts relating to their currency and interests.

27 Hungarian Civil Code (2013) § 6:103.

and letting them establish and apply the proper guidelines to assess the cases. As a result of this system, a great part of the private law is shaped by the courts, which apply a complex system of criteria to assess and decide the cases. Even in codified legal systems, private law as a law in action is a flexible system where the decision of the court is a result of weighing different elements in each of the cases. In so far as legal adjudication is concerned, there is no difference between the codified legal systems and common law. The real difference between the role of judges and the role of legislator is the question of legitimacy and efficiency much more than the difference of legislative power and judicial power (which does not constitute a difference). This is supported by understanding the process of interpretation of abstract norms, concretizing general clauses, assessment of 'hard cases', procedural solutions like reversal of the burden of proof, and regulatory solutions where the legislator leaves the balancing of interests and establishing priorities to the courts. Courts may be required to anchor their judgments in written law. This is, however, far more an issue of argumentation and seeking for legitimacy for the legislative authority than a substantive issue.

References

M. Bussani, V. V. Palmer & V. Valentine (Eds), *Pure Economic Loss in Europe*, Cambridge, UK, Cambridge University Press, 2003.

F. A. Bydlinski, 'A "Flexible System" Approach to Contract Law', in H. Hausmaninger, H. Koziol, A. M. Rabello & I. Gilead (Eds), *Developments in Austrian and Israeli Private Law*, Wien/New York, Springer, 1996, pp. 9–20.

R. Dworkin, *Law's Empire*, Oxford, Hart Publishing, 1998.

J. H. Ely, 'The Wages of Crying Wolf: A Comment on Roe v. Wade', *Yale Law Journal*, Vol. 82, 1973, pp. 920–949.

T. C. Grey, 'The Constitution as Scripture', *Stanford Law Review*, Vol. 37, 1984–1985, pp. 1–25.

J. Habermas, *Between Facts and Norms*, Cambridge, Polity Press, Blackwell, 1997.

B. A. Koch, 'Wilburg's Flexible System in a Nutshell', in H. Koziol & B. C. Steininger (Eds), *European Tort Law 2001*, Wien/New York, Springer, 2002, pp. 545–548.

B. A. Koch, 'Comparative Overview', in H. Koziol & B. C. Steininger (Eds), *European Tort Law 2005*, Wien/New York, Springer, 2006, pp. 602–612.

H. Koziol, 'Compensation for Pure Economic Loss from a Continental Lawyer's Perspective', in W. H. van Boom, H. Koziol & C. A. Witting (Eds), *Pure Economic Loss*, Wien/New York, Springer, *ECTIL Tort and Insurance Law*, Vol. 9, 2004, pp. 141–161.

H. Koziol, 'Das bewegliche System – Die goldene Mitte für Gesetzgebung und Dogmatik' *Austrian Law Journal*, March, 2017, pp. 160–182.

A. Menyhárd, 'Hungary', in H. Koziol & B. C. Steininger (Eds), *European Tort Law 2005*, Wien/New York, Springer, 2006, pp. 332–347.

B. Rüthers, *Die unbegrenzte Auslegung. Zum Wandel der Privatrechtsordnung im Nationalsozializmus*, 5. erw. Aufl., Heidelberg, C. F. Müller Verlag, 1997.

G. Tóth, *Túl a szövegen – értekezés a magyar alkotmányról (Beyond the Text – Treatise on the Hungarian Constitution)*, Budapest, Osiris, 2009.

M. J. Trebilcock, *The Limits of Freedom Contract*, Cambridge, MA, Harvard University Press, 1997.

J. Wanner, *Die Sittenwidrigkeit der Rechtsgeschäfte im totalitären State*, Ebelsbach, Druck & Verlag GmbH, 1996.

W. Wilburg, Entwicklung eines beweglichen Systems im Bürgerlichen Recht (Rede gehalten bei der Inauguration als Rector magnificus der Karl-Franzes Universität in Graz am 22 November 1950), Graz, Kienreich, 1950.

W. Wilburg, 'Zusammenspiel der Kräfte im Aufbau des Schuldrechts', *AcP*, Vol. 163, 1964, pp. 346–379.

5 Supreme courts in Sweden

Are they "real" judges?

Mauro Zamboni

5.1 Introduction

To many readers, the title of this work will most likely seem to be a rhetorical (if not absurd) question. Since the supreme courts are the pinnacle of the judicial system in a country, it should go without saying that they are judges, or at least aim to operate as such, i.e., their positioning is that of a third party interpreting the law applicable to disputes among private and/or public actors. Actually, one of the features characterizing a democratic form of state, embracing the rule of law as its cardinal principle, is the idea that citizens (among others) can find in the judicial body an impartial party to settle disputes between them and other citizens or between them and public authorities.[1] However, if one considers more closely such general agreement as to the natural connection between democracy and a supreme court as a third party, one can see how the situation may be more complex and articulated under the surface, both from a general perspective and in the Swedish case.

From a broader viewpoint, the particular task of the supreme courts, i.e., being the authoritative interpreter of law, requires them to be in an intermediate position on the institutional map of a democracy based on the rule of law. This tends to be stretched across several different arenas simultaneously: the legal one (as the ultimate authority on what constitutes valid law); the political one (limiting and/or expanding the operating space of the political actors and their legislative tools); and – last but not least – the social arena in a broad sense (through their role in adapting the regulatory regimes to the constant changes in socio-economic realities).[2] In this respect, as also pointed out in the heated debate among many (legal and non-legal) scholars, the 'purely judicial' nature of the

1 T. Jagland, State of Democracy, Human Rights and the Rule of Law, pp. 17–19, available at https://edoc.coe.int/en/an-overview/7345-pdf-state-of-democracy-human-rights-and-the-rule-of-law.html.

2 H. M. Kritzer, 'Martin Shapiro: Anticipating the New Institutionalism', in N. Maveety (Ed.), *The Pioneers of Judicial Behavior*, Ann Arbor, MI, University of Michigan Press, 2003, p. 409. See M. Zamboni, *The Policy of Law*, Oxford, Hart Publishing, 2007, p. 160.

supreme courts is far from being settled simply based on their position at the pinnacle of the legal order.[3]

Moving the focus to the case of Sweden, this 'natural' assumption of the supreme courts as being among the 'judges' becomes even more tenuous. In both the political and the legal debate, it has traditionally been claimed in Sweden, almost undisputedly, that the three powers in the Scandinavian country are the legislative, the executive, and the mass media. This assertion certainly serves its aims: it underlines the fundamental dogma underlying the Swedish concept of democracy, namely the necessity to protect the freedom of the media and the freedom of expression in general (going so far as to devote a specific and separate constitutional document thereto). However, this claim also raises some questions as to what it does not say: the judicial body is not considered one of the fundamental pillars of the constitutional architecture in Sweden.[4] Thus, it should not come as a surprise that supreme courts in this Scandinavian country are traditionally considered (and consider themselves) an integral part of one of the other pillars: public administration.

The primary goal of this work is to investigate the reasons that a fully mature democracy like Sweden, which by most standards fulfills the basic criteria of being a rule of law state, has been able to prosper based on only two of the traditional pillars in the rule of law, namely the political (or legislative) power and the administrative (or executive) apparatus. This case study of the institutional positioning of supreme courts in Sweden may at first glance appear rather uninteresting to an international audience, because this country has always been considered to be 'living its own life' due to its isolation in the Nordic regions of Europe. However, the implicit scope of this work is to introduce reflections of a broader and more general character: to extrapolate from the Swedish case considerations that may be applicable to other European countries as to the question whether a supreme court with a fully judicial nature is a *conditio sine qua non* for every democracy.

Before beginning the analysis, it is necessary to offer one clarification as to the terminology used in this work. As will be seen in the following, most of the discussion revolves around the positioning (or not) of the Swedish supreme courts among the public agencies and, consequently, the issue of judges being seen (and considering themselves) as civil servants, rather than 'real' judges. In this work, the basic assumption is that *public servant* is anyone who 'serves the public' and is hired by either the state or a local government; thus it includes these judges.[5] A *civil servant* is part of the public service, but constitutes a much narrower

3 E.g. C. Guarnieri & P. Pederzoli, *The Power of Judges: A Comparative Study of Courts and Democracy*, Oxford, Oxford University Press, 2002, pp. 68–76; and M. Shapiro, *Courts: A Comparative and Political Analysis*, Chicago, IL, University of Chicago Press, 1981, p. 28.

4 O. Petersson, *Report from the Democratic Audit of Sweden 1999: Democracy the Swedish Way*, Stockholm, SNS Förlag, 1999, p. 27.

5 J. C. N. Raadschelders, 'Changing European Ideas about the Public Servant: A Theoretical and Methodological Framework', in F. Sager & P. Overeem (Eds), *The European Public Servant*, Colchester, ECPR Press, 2015, pp. 20–26.

category, not including the judges, as it identifies staff working in public administration, i.e., the apparatus of the state specifically devoted to the 'management of public programs'.[6]

5.2 Swedish supreme courts as civil servants

Moving our attention to the case of this chapter, it is interesting to note that the Swedish supreme courts, i.e., both the Supreme Administrative Court and the regular Supreme Court, are considered and consider themselves as part of the larger public administration within legal and constitutional discourse. As pointed out by several Swedish legal scholars, the highest judges tend to operate as an extension of the public administration into the higher legal instance rather than as a third party in disputes among public and private actors.[7] This does not mean that the Supreme Courts tends to deliver decisions in favor of the public administration; more accurately, it means that the judges consider themselves as internal reviewers of the public agencies (aiming at shaping a 'good administration' according to the criteria set by the legislator) rather than external referees (determining winners and losers in legal disputes, based on the valid law).[8]

A classic example of this positioning within the public administration's perspective is a series of decisions on tax avoidance made by the Swedish Supreme Administrative Court. The Act against Tax Avoidance (1995:575) has a quite general wording and, to some extent, vague terms, in order to be able to capture as many forms of tax avoidance as possible (both present and future). As this is the goal of the legislation, the Swedish Tax Agency, in its role of a public agency, has implemented the act in a rather broad way. It has included legal schemes devised by taxpayers, which, though officially created for other purposes, have had the avoidance of taxes as their 'true purpose' (by lowering the total taxable income). In many cases, the Supreme Administrative Court has followed the line of the Tax Agency, in this way (implicitly) considering this agency's decisions as authoritative when it comes to identifying the 'true intention' of the legislator. For example, the Supreme Administrative Court has in some cases simply copied and pasted into their *ratio decidendi* parts of policy documents produced by the Tax Agency. The judges of the Supreme Administrative Court do not then regard themselves as external interpreters of the letter of the law, but instead as reviewers of the interpretation offered by the public agency. This attitude on the part of the Supreme Administrative Court is even more peculiar in tax issues, where there is a good deal of potential for maneuvering on the part of the judicial

6 R. B. Denhardt, J. V. Denhardt & T. A. Blanc, *Public Administration*, 7th ed., Belmont, CA, Thomson Wadsworth, 2014, p. 2. *But see* A. Massey, 'Civil Service Systems', in A. Massey (Ed.), *International Handbook on Civil Service Systems*, Cheltenham, Edward Elgar, 2011, pp. 3–4.

7 R. Lavin, *Domstol och administrativ myndighet*, Stockholm, Norstedt, 1972, p. 7–9.

8 J. Reichel, *God förvaltning i EU och i Sverige*, Stockholm, Jure, 2006, p. 336. See SOU, *Domaren i Sverige inför framtiden*, Stockholm, *Statens offentliga utredningar, 1994, p. 48.*

bodies as the true interpreters of the tax legislation (e.g., due to a constitutional discourse which construes the legality principle in a way which is rather restrictive of the public agency's operations). Similar cases and *modus operandi* can be detected also in the regular Supreme Court, for example when it comes to regulation of the financial market and the opinions expressed by Sweden's Financial Supervisory Authority.[9]

It should further be noted (though this will not be investigated in this work) how this positioning (on the part of both the judges and the outside actors) of the supreme courts as public agencies, in its turn, fuels another shift: the perception of public agencies not simply as 'implementers', but also as authoritative 'interpreters' of the law. It is rather common that public agencies autonomously produce and advertise on their websites policy documents regarding how various legislative provisions should be interpreted by the recipients of the administrative services. As mentioned above, such policy documents are not rarely used by the supreme courts as the legal basis for their decisions, as if they were legally binding documents (when it comes to legal interpretation). In other words, there is a perception of the role of judges as a compliance agency as regards public administration decisions, which in turn stimulates the public agencies to operate not only as executive, but also as quasi-judicial actors.[10]

The idea that the judges sitting in the supreme courts consider themselves (and are regarded by the external world) as a prolongation of the public administration, has extremely complex and articulated origins. However, it is possible to sketch at least three fundamental (interconnected and mutually reinforcing) sets of reasons, related to factors of political, legal, and purely administrative nature.

As the first set of reasons, one can point out the Swedish or 'social-democratic' version of the welfare state.[11] The basic goal behind this political model consisted of transforming the state into the 'house of the people' (in Swedish, *folkhemmet*), i.e., to render the state and its apparatus servants of the citizens, who should feel 'at home' when dealing with public authorities.[12] As a fundamental step, this model requires the building of 'a home', that is the creation of an extremely articulated public apparatus which, through a deep integration and coordination of all its components, could realize the social and economic equality of all

9 E.g. T. Ingvarsson, 'Allmänna råd och jämkning av borgensåtaganden', *Svensk Juristtidning*, Vol. 2008, 2008, pp. 867–876.

10 H. Wenander, Sweden: Deference to the Administration in Judicial Review, 2017, pp. 3–4, available at https://portal.research.lu.se/portal/files/35406219/Wenander_Sweden_Deference_to_the_Administration_in_Judicial_Review.pdf. E.g. SOU, En uthållig demokrati!, Stockholm, *Statens offentliga utredningar*, 2000, p. 132.

11 G. Esping-Andersen, *The Three Worlds of Welfare Capitalism*, Princeton, NJ, Princeton University Press, 1990, p. 27. See E. Ferragina & M. Seeleib-Kaiser, 'Welfare Regime Debate', *Policy & Politics*, Vol. 39, 2011, pp. 583–611; and A. Bergh, 'The Universal Welfare State: Theory and the Case of Sweden', *Political Studies*, Vol. 54, 2004, pp. 749–754.

12 E. Åsard & W. Lance Bennet, *Democracy and the Marketplace of Ideas*, Cambridge, UK, Cambridge University Press, 1997, pp. 86 and 91–95.

citizens. The law and its actors are considered and used as essential parts of such a construction, but are of a 'soft' nature. This expression simply means that within the Swedish concept of the welfare state, the implementation of welfare ideals into society has to be done mainly by using legal regulatory tools, e.g., tax law.[13] However, in order to be used for implementing such a non-legal value (a welfare eco-political model), the legal instruments, culture, and actors must necessarily be 'softened'. The legal discourse and its main actors have to be ready and willing to see their basic principles and dogmas molded or bent in all cases where such legal paradigms conflict with principles of a non-legal nature, as indicated by the political actors through the legislation and as implemented by the civil servants.[14] For example, as previously seen, the judges of the Swedish Supreme Administrative Court must be ready to see their dogma of legal certainty in taxation matters 'sacrificed' at the altar of the political and social ideals of equal redistribution through taxation, as interpreted and implemented by the Swedish Tax Agency in its attempt at capturing all the incomes obscured through complex taxation schemes.[15]

The incorporation of judicial bodies within a strongly integrated system to promote the implementation of socio-political values has also been reinforced by one of the causes (or effects) of the success in Sweden of such a strongly integrated welfare state model. The Swedish model is rooted in (or, according to other interpretations, it created) an environment with a relatively low level of political, social, and economic conflicts. In turn, this environment is based on the idea (and, at least until recently, also the reality) that most of the major public and private actors agreed as to the fundamental values to be implemented through such a political system and its laws.[16] It is easy to understand how, unlike in other systems with greater tensions, the need of having a high court operating as a 'third' party, i.e., as an independent 'explicator of the law' among radically conflicting and diverging potential interpretations and implementations, vanished in this rather value-homogenous landscape.[17]

13 V. Aubert, 'The Rule of Law and the Promotional Funcion of Law', in G. Teubner (Ed.), *Dilemmas of Law in the Welfare State*, Berlin, de Gruyter, 1986, pp. 32–39; J. Habermas, *Between Facts and Norms,* Cambridge, MA, The MIT Press, 1998, pp. 405–407; and H. V. Dean, 'The Juridification of Welfare', in A. Kjonstad & J. Wilson (Eds), *Law, Power and Poverty*, Bergen, CROP Publications, 1997, pp. 3–27.

14 A. Peczenik, *Vad är rätt?*, Stockholm, Norstedts Juridik, 1995, pp. 46–47; and D. Bjerstedt, *Tryggheten inför rättan*, Lund, Lund University, 2009, pp. 40–42. E.g. K. Uggerud, 'Uønskede *menneskerettigheter*?', *Retfaerd*, Vol. 90, 2000, pp. 21–45.

15 J. W. F. Sundberg, *High-Tax Imperialism*, 2nd ed., Stockholm, Institutet för offentlig och internationell rätt, 2000.

16 B. Rothstein & L. Trägårdh, 'The State and Civil Society in a Historical Perspective', in L. Trägårdh (Ed.), *State and Civil Society in Northern Europe*, New York, Bergbahn Books, 2007, p. 235. See F. Lagergren, *På andra sidan* välfärdsstaten, Stockholm, Brutus Östlings Bokförlag, 1999, p. 181.

17 J. Lindvall & B. Rothstein, 'Sweden: The Fall of the Strong State', *Scandinavian Political Studies*, Vol. 29, 2006, pp. 49–50.

As to the second set of reasons why Swedish supreme courts operate as civil servants rather than as independent judicial bodies, these are connected to the Swedish constitutional architecture and discourse, which are the result of a welfare state with strongly integrated legislative, administrative, and judicial components. Starting with the Swedish constitutional architecture, one of its major components is a refusal of the principle of division of powers, unlike in most countries among the so-called Western-style democracies. Instead, there is an endorsement of the separation of functions. Legal actors have traditionally taken a rather strict interpretative stand when it comes to the Swedish constitutional document the Instrument of Government (1974), art. 1: 'All public power in Sweden proceeds from the people ... It is realized through a representative and parliamentary form of government and through local self-government'. As a result, the Parliament (i.e., the primary legislative law-making agency) is regarded as the only true power (being the only one representing 'the people'), and it, in turn, delegates the other two functions (judicial and executive) to the courts and the public agencies.[18]

It is natural then that the courts, operating in this kind of constitutional architecture, do not perceive themselves (and are not perceived by the other legal actors) as an autonomous power (whose goal is to evaluate whether the public and private actors operate in accordance with the law). Instead, the courts, including the supreme courts, consider themselves as ancillary bodies, serving to review the actions of private and public actors so that they fit the will of the highest (and only) power, namely the Parliament. In other words, due to the rebuttal of the principle of the separation of powers, the judges, including those sitting in the highest benches, tend to operate not as third parties, but as part of the executive body. They are civil servants aiming at fulfilling, as far as possible, the will of the people as expressed by the one and only power: the legislative one.[19]

As another factor contributing to the Supreme Court judges viewing themselves as civil servants rather than judges, one should add a feature of the Swedish constitutional system which directly affects the constitutional discourse within the country: the lack of a proper constitutional court and the rather ineffective constitutional review procedure. As comparative and historical scholarship has shown, the presence of a strong constitutional court usually produces waves strengthening the judicial bodies and work throughout the entire legal system.[20] In particular, a constitutional court increases the legitimacy of a widespread 'judicial' control of the political work, i.e., a sense shared by all the judges (even at

18 H. Strömberg & B. Lundell, *Allmän förvaltningsrätt*, 26th ed., Stockholm, Liber, 2014, p. 95. See J. Nergelius, *Constitutional Law in Sweden*, Alphen aan den Rijn, Wolters Kluwer, 2011, p. 15.

19 M. Sjöberg, 'Den långa vägen till en generell regel om domstolsprövning av förvaltningsbeslut', in G. Regner, M. Eliason & H.-H. Vogel (Eds), *Festskrift till Hans Ragnemalm*, Lund, Juristförlaget, 2005, p. 302. See T. Bull & F. Sterzel, *Regeringsformen*, 3rd ed., Stockholm, SNS förlag, 2015, p. 259 and pp. 275–278.

20 A. Stone Sweet, *Governing with Judges*, Oxford, Oxford University Press, 2000, pp. 116–124.

lower levels) that one of their primary duties is the evaluation, as external actors, of whether private and, even more importantly, public actors operate in accordance with the law.[21] Leaving aside the historical and institutional reasons for such 'deficiencies' in this Scandinavian country, the lack of a proper constitutional court (with its self-legitimizing force for the entire judicial body as a guardian of the law) has, in the Swedish legal discourse, led to a devaluation of the constitutional role of the supreme courts in the public law area (e.g., their focus, as a matter of course, on the protection of intangible rights for individuals) in favor of their administrative function (e.g., focusing primarily on finding the 'true' intention of the legislator when facing unclear legislative issues).[22]

The third motive behind the Swedish supreme courts' self-perception as an integral part of the public administration has a purely administrative nature, i.e., it is based on the specific career system a judge has to follow in order to be likely to be selected for such courts. A widespread and established recruitment policy is that a judge applying for a position in a supreme court has a better chance if she or he can show a few years' working experience within the Department of Justice or (to a lesser extent) the Government Offices.[23] This requirement is justified by the idea that, having spent some years within the Department of Justice, the candidate to the supreme court will have had the opportunity to gain a deeper knowledge of all aspects of legislation, not only its interpretation, but also its creation (as the Department of Justice is usually the place within the state apparatus where Acts are drafted) and its implementation (as the department is part of the executive structure of the state).[24]

This reasoning may be correct, but this prerequisite of having served a few years among civil servants leaves obvious traces in the way that future Supreme Court judges view themselves and their position on the state apparatus map. A judge enters the Supreme Court with strong ties to the administrative apparatus. Firstly, she or he has during her/his time at the Department of Justice developed professional and personal networks within that department and the other departments forming the core of the state administration. Even more importantly, the future judge of the Supreme Court is usually rather heavily influenced by the administrative culture permeating her or his years within the public administration. She or

21 Stone Sweet, 2000, pp. 114–115.

22 A. Lagerqvist Veloz Roca, 'Utvecklingslinjer inom svensk offentlig rätt under de senaste hundra åren', in K. Källström & J. Öberg (Eds), *Juridisk Tidskrift–Jubileumshäfte*, Stockholm, Jure, 2007, pp. 49–50; and K. Tuori, Vilken vikt bör i rättstillämpningen läggas vid lagstiftarens synpunkter och signaler i och utanför lagstiftningsärendet?, 2011, p. 790, available at http://jura.ku.dk/njm/39/789-796-vilken-vikt-bor-i-rattstillampningen-korref-tuori-red.pdf/. See W. Warnling-Nerep, 'Till frågan om legalitet och retroaktivitet i svensk rätt', *Juridisk Tidskrift*, Vol. 4, 2009, pp. 837–838.

23 H. von Sydow, *Rättsstatens rötter-reformer av domarutnämningar*, Lund, Juridiska Fakulteten vid Lunds Universitet, 2007, pp. 46–49 and pp. 55–57. See K. Fast, *Regeringsrådens oberoende och roll*, Stockholm: Institutet Skatter & rättssäkerhet, 2001.

24 B. Bengtsson, 'Domare och lagstiftare i samverkan och konflikt', in Å. Frändberg (Ed.), *Festskrift till Stig Strömholm*, Uppsala, Iustus Förlag, Vol. 1, 1997, p. 109.

he tends to have the civil servant's perspective, rather than the judicial one, when approaching legal issues: she or he aims at finding the solution that will implement the will of the legislator in the best way, rather than, in the words of H. L. A. Hart, solving them from the perspective internal to the legal system.[25]

This custom in the recruitment process to the Swedish supreme courts, a policy which moves the judges closer to the civil servants' mind-set, was reinforced by a recruitment procedure used up until the constitutional reform of 2011, which rarely allowed any 'outside-the-administration' candidate to reach such courts. Until that date, judges were appointed to both supreme courts by the Government, in a closed, non-competitive procedure, and without formal preparation by an external body. Far from being an intrusion of the political power into the recruitment process, the constitutional praxis was that judges within the supreme courts would indicate their future peers to the Government, which would almost always take up these 'suggestions'.[26]

Because of the concurrence of these three reasons, the judges sitting in the Swedish supreme courts tend to consider themselves and operate as civil servants rather than as a third party in the legal issues coming up for their evaluation. However, it is necessary to point out that this positioning among the civil servants, i.e., among the actors with the primary task of implementing the political will as expressed in the legislation, does not render the Swedish supreme courts more 'political bodies'.[27] First, at least in a fully accomplished democratic system like the Swedish one, the civil service tends to be independent from the government, from an institutional perspective: it is composed mainly of career bureaucrats, who are hired on professional merits rather than being appointed or elected.[28] Moreover, their institutional tenure typically outlasts the frequent transitions of political leadership and their careers are based on their professional performances, i.e., accomplishments measured according to criteria internal to the administrative apparatus (e.g., their efficiency) rather than external (e.g., political affiliation).[29]

Second, the de-politicization of the Swedish civil service (i.e., its robust autonomy from the control of the political parties) is also reinforced by a legal feature strongly demarcating the relationship between the legislative function (as both Parliament and Government) and the public agencies (i.e., the administrative

25 H. L. A. Hart, *The Concept of Law*, Oxford, Clarendon Press, 1961, pp. 55–56. See Guarnieri & Pederzoli, 2002, pp. 9–11.

26 von Sydow, 2007, pp. 10–14.

27 F. Sterzel, *Författning i utveckling*, Uppsala, Iustus Förlag, 1998, pp. 47–50.

28 J. Reichel, 'Svenska myndigheter som EU-myndigheter', in K. Källström & J. Öberg (Eds), 2007, pp. 104–105.

29 B. M. Jones, 'Sweden', in J. Kingdom (Ed.), *The Civil Service in Liberal Democracies*, Oxon, Routledge, 1990, p. 153. But see C. Dahlström & A. Sundell, *Budgetary Effects of Political Appointments*, 2013, pp. 10–11, available at https://ecpr.eu/Filestore/PaperProposal/fcd89d7b-851d-4e0c-a076-e66300e98f72.pdf. See also Guarnieri & Pederzoli, 2002, pp. 49–50.

apparatus outside the departments). The Swedish constitutional document of the Instrument of Government clearly states the prohibition of 'ministerial rule' over the public agencies in performing their primary task: implementing the law.[30] For various historical, political, and structural reasons (which cannot be discussed here), this prohibition is firmly respected by both (often reluctant) politicians, public agencies, and, last but not least, administrative courts.[31]

The political influence over the public administration in general is thus rather limited in Sweden, making it (in practice) a two-power system, where administrative practices tend to have a strong quasi-legislative status in many areas of both private and public law, from the control of the financial market to welfare law issues. As a result, the positioning of the supreme courts very close to (if not within) the area of civil service does not brings with it the 'politicization' of their work and culture, but rather their being considered a component within the strongly independent and powerful Swedish public administration.

5.3 Things are (maybe) changing

As it appears now, the panorama is rather clear: judges operating in the Swedish supreme courts tend to perceive themselves, and to be identified by others, as civil servants and to operate as such (i.e., they aim to find the best way to implement the true meaning of the legislator's intention) rather than as 'real judges' (i.e., focusing on assessing the law applicable to a dispute). However, in the last few years, small but important (and mutually reinforcing) signals indicate that this may be changing, and the supreme courts may be moving closer to the core of the judicial role, namely to operate as a third party in disputes among private and public actors.

First, in recent years, the activities of the supreme courts (in particular, but not exclusively, in the regular Supreme Court) have been characterized by a rather strong feature of judicial activism, i.e., a situation where 'the courts impose a judicial solution over an issue erstwhile subject to political resolution' by intervening and, for example, striking down properly enacted legislation.[32] It is thus easy to understand how this new opening on the part of the supreme courts is shifting them toward a more accentuated role as a third party in the constitutional panorama. By becoming judicial activists, the judges sitting in the higher courts are being guided by the idea that their primary role is neither to find the

30 Instrument of Government, Chapter 12, Art. 2: 'No public authority, including the Parliament, may determine how an administrative authority shall decide in a particular case relating to the exercise of public authority vis-à-vis an individual or a local authority, or relating to the application of law.' See also Chapter 7, Art. 3 and Chapter 12, Art. 1.

31 A. Jonsson, 'Förvaltningens självständighet och förbudet mot ministerstyre', in L. Marcusson (Ed.), *God förvaltning -ideal och praktik*, Uppsala, Iustus, 2006, pp. 174–177.

32 D. L. Anderson, 'When Restraint Requires Activism', *Stanford Law Review*, Vol. 42, 1990, p. 1570. *See* F. Werksäll, 'En offensiv Högsta domstol', *Svensk Juristtidning*, Vol. 2014, 2014, p. 1.

true intention of the legislative bodies nor to review the work done by the public agencies. The supreme courts, instead, aim to operate directly as guardians of the legal system, within the general framework of the valid law. In other words, with judicial activism, the judges position themselves as a third actor looking for solutions to fundamental legal issues, which have not been contemplated by the legislative bodies and/or whose regulation within the administrative practices can be considered as either non-existent or (from a general legal perspective) unsatisfactory.[33]

Second, Sweden's entry into the EU (in 1995) and the role that the European courts play have considerably strengthened the process of hardening of the law in Sweden, i.e., of making the law more difficult to mold to non-legal (e.g., political or financial) goals. In particular, being part of the European legal system has, in Swedish legal discourse, highlighted the inalienable and absolute nature of certain individual legal rights and the corresponding unconditional duty to operate (or not to interfere) on the part of public actors, *in primis* (but not solely) the administrative apparatus.[34] This influence has contributed to a more general growth in the Swedish legal, political, and social environments of a 'rights culture', where rights are now seen in a more Anglo-American sense. These are legal qualities assigned to individuals and ought to be protected by the judiciary, regardless of what the national statutory provisions prescribe or what the administrative practices indicate.[35] In this situation, and paralleling the role of the judiciary in the Anglo-American reality, the supreme courts are required more than ever to operate as a third and truly independent judicial body, in order to guarantee the fulfillment of these rights, in particular in relation to the actions of other public authorities. It is worth mentioning that this rights culture has started peeping through not only in the Supreme Administrative Court but also in the regular Supreme Court in areas usually disconnected from the idea of rights, at least in Swedish legal discourse, e.g., in matters of commercial law or contract law.[36]

33 J. Kleineman, 'Från prejudikatinstans till lagstiftare? Högsta domstolens ökade aktivism', *Juridisk Tidskrift*, Vol. 3, 2015, pp. 526–527.

34 T. Bull, 'Rättighetsskyddet i Högsta förvaltningsdomstolen', *Svensk Juristtidning*, Vol. 2017, 2017, pp. 216–244; U. Bernitz, 'Europarättens genomslag i svensk rätt', *Juridisk Tidskrift*, Vol. 3, 2010, p. 480; and J. Hirschfeldt, 'Domstolarna som statsmakt', *Juridisk Tidskrift*, Vol. 1, 2011, p. 19. See T. Risse, M. Green Cowles, & J. Caporaso, 'Europeanization and Domestic Change', in M. Green Cowles, J. Caporaso, & T. Risse (Eds), *Transforming Europe: Europeanization and Domestic Change*, Ithaca, NY, Cornell University Press, 2001, p. 3.

35 B. Rothstein, 'Välfärdsstat, förvaltning och legitimitet', in B. Rothstein (Ed.), *Politik som organization*, Stockholm, SNS Förlag, 2010, p. 57. See R. H. Pildes, 'Why Rights Are Not Trumps', *Journal of Legal Studies*, Vol. 27, 1998, p. 727; M. A. Glendon, *Rights Talk: The Impoverishment of Political* Discourse, New York, Free Press, 1993, p. 13; and R. Dworkin, *Taking Rights Seriously*, London, Duckworth, 1977, pp. 90–94.

36 E.g. M. Schultz, 'Rights Through Torts: *The Rise of a Rights Discourse in Swedish Tort Law*', *European Review of Private Law*, Vol. 3, 2009, pp. 305–333.

One can observe a third signal, of a more political nature, partially resulting from EU membership, which pushes the Swedish supreme courts closer to a more 'judicial' role in the constitutional architecture. Like many other places in Western Europe, Sweden is increasingly being portrayed as on the way toward becoming a post-welfare system.[37] Leaving aside an in-depth discussion as to what characterizes this situation, it is nevertheless necessary to draw attention to the fact that the post-welfare society has as one of its central dogmas a strong idea of the rule of law.[38] This implies moving away from the traditional Swedish model of the welfare state and its basic idea that legal actors (and in particular the judicial bodies) should consider and use the law as structurally soft in relation to the values expressed by the political environment (and implemented by the administrative apparatus). In a post-welfare system, it is the other way around: the political, social, and economic discourses are perceived by the judges as generally bending when conflicting with fundamental legal principles, either explicitly in the constitutional documents or through the legal system. Non-legal programs are supposed to stop and give way when confronted with general legal principles like legal certainty or equality in front of the law, but also when encountering private legal principles, like 'good faith' or 'equality between contracting parties'.[39] As a result, the judges operate as a true third party in the disputes, as their focus is mainly inserting and evaluating the disputes under discussion not in relation to the political will or the administrative practices, but rather in relation to the systems of rules and fundamental principles superseding the legal system.[40]

As to the fourth component indicating a shift of the Swedish supreme courts toward a more judicial role, this has to do with the changes which took place in constitutional reform of 2011. Among other innovations, the reform introduced a new system of recruitment to the higher courts.[41] In particular, the process has become competition-based (i.e., an open call is made, advertised as a vacant position to which anyone can apply) and is led by an independent authority, namely the Judicial Board, where five of the nine members are (or have been) ordinary

37 S. E. Olsson Hort, 'Sweden: Towards a 21st Century Post-Modern People's Home', in P. Koslowski & A. Føllesdal (Eds), *Restructuring the Welfare State*, Berlin, Springer, 1997, pp. 332–336. See also J. Reichel, 'Den svenska förvaltningsmodellen i det europeiska samarbetsprojektet', in I. Mattson & E. Sjögren (Eds), *Statsförvaltningen efter 20 år i EU*, Stockholm, Statskontoret, 2016, pp. 57–82, available at www.statskontoret.se/globalassets/publikationer/2016/om-offentlig-sektor-28_statsforvaltning-eu.pdf.

38 T. Wilhelmsson, 'Contract and Equality', *Scandinavian Studies in Law*, vol. 40, 2000, p. 153. See G. Skapska, *'Facing Past Human Rights Abuse'*, in J. Priban (Ed.) *Liquid Society and Its Law*, Aldershot, Ashgate, 2007, pp. 115–129.

39 Å. Frändberg, *Rättsordningens idé*, Stockholm, Iustus Förlag, 2005, pp. 251–263. See J. E. Fleming, *Getting to the Rule of Law*, New York, New York University Press, 2011, p. 96.

40 E.g. C. Carlson, 'Rätten att inte lämna ut uppgifter vid beslut om tredjemansrevision', *Juridisk Tidskrift*, vol. 2, 2012, pp. 418–420; or R. Påhlsson, *Likhet inför skattelag*, Uppsala, Iustus förlag, 2007, kap. 3.

41 Instrument of Government, Chapter 11, Art. 6 and Lag (2010:1390) om utnämning av ordinarie domare.

judges. This Board receives advice from the supreme courts, but this is not binding (as has been shown several times); meanwhile, the Board's indications to the Government, though not binding, carry a certain legal weight (requiring the Government to consult the Board again if it is considering appointing someone not nominated by this panel).

This system has brought with it two novelties, both strengthening the idea of the supreme courts as true and independent judicial bodies. First, the reform of the entire recruitment procedure has sent out a clear signal, immediately recognized by the judges (both within and outside the higher courts), that the institutional independence of the Swedish supreme courts within the constitutional architecture has been strengthened (in particular in relation to the political parties).[42] Second, as the new system is based on an open competition, it has encouraged from the very first day candidates outside the usual 'judge-formed-in-the-Department-of-Justice' model. In particular, a relatively high number of candidates coming from the private sector or from academia have successfully applied for vacant positions in recent years.[43] As a result, this new open recruitment procedure has led to the installment as judges in the Swedish supreme courts of prominent jurists whose professional cultures (and networks) are quite far from the civil servants' world.

Finally, there is an indication of a more general and societal nature that the positioning of the supreme courts in Sweden may be moving closer to the judicial ideal. The Swedish political, social, and financial atmospheres have changed considerably in the last decade, becoming more conflictual. The fragmentation of the community (or, more accurately, the surfacing of parts of the community forcibly hidden before) has forced the Swedish legal world into a new position.[44] Today, the legal arena is located in the middle of a plurality of value systems, which often stand in competition (if not in conflict) with each other in trying to gain recognition for their instances in the legal field. A classic case of this is the debate between supporters and critics of private religious schools financed with public money.[45]

As an immediate effect, the need for truly 'third party' judges at the top of the judicial body is felt even more strongly. In such a climate of value conflicts,

42 SOU, *En reformerad grundlag 2008: 125*, Stockholm, *Statens offentliga utredningar*, 2008, pp. 319–323.

43 For example, as to 1 April 2019, 6 of the actual 16 members of the ordinary Supreme Court have had a professional career (to a large extent) outside the public administration (either in law-firms or in academia). See www.hogstadomstolen.se/Justitierad/. The Supreme Administrative Court presents the exact same distribution between judges with (mostly) a non-administrative career and judges with an administrative professional background. See www.hogstaforvaltningsdomstolen.se/Justitierad/.

44 L. Wennberg & A. Pylkkänen, 'Intersektionalitet i rätten', *Retfærd*, Vol. 138, 2012, pp. 12–28. See Lindvall & Rothstein, 2006, pp. 55–56.

45 E.g. H. Bernitz, 'En icke-konfessionell skola', *Juridisk Tidskrift*, Vol. 3, 2017, pp. 566–579; and H. I. Roth, *Är religion en mänsklig rättighet?*, Stockholm, Norsteds, 2012, pp. 177–213.

supreme courts must often position themselves outside the various political, financial, social, and administrative systems in order to decide which value system is to be defended, based exclusively on the valid law (and not, for instance, on the often confusing intention of the legislative bodies or the conflicting practices developed by the various public agencies). As recently pointed out in a joint editorial by the Presidents of both the Swedish Administrative Supreme Court and the regular Supreme Court, the legal world is not only at the center of this never-ending battle among different value systems.[46] Even more importantly, Swedish positive law is considered and used by the higher courts as a connecting point for such systems with the decisive role of offering (at least in its intentions) 'objective' criteria for determining which value system is to prevail and to be used as to the 'lawful' one.[47]

Despite the many indications of a possible shifting of the supreme courts from the public administration's culture to the 'real' judicial one, one should not overestimate the true strength of these signals. If, on the one hand, all these hints suggest a possible evolution of the institutional and cultural positioning of the Swedish supreme courts, reality, on the other hand, indicates that these highest judicial bodies still have a foot and a half within the world of public administration. Generally, as pointed out by many scholars, the legal discourse and its actors in the Western world are characterized by structural inertia: legal culture usually presents a certain degree of path dependence or rigidity toward innovation and repositioning of actors on the legal map.[48]

More specifically, in the case of Sweden, two of the factors which have made the Swedish supreme courts lean toward the administrative pillar are still rather strong. First, separation of functions (instead of separation of powers) is still a dogma within the Swedish constitutional discourse and there are no indications signaling that it is going to fade away within the foreseeable future (unless there are quite unexpected, and henceforth unplanned, radical reforms to the Constitution).[49] Second, despite the attempt (through the 2011 constitutional reform) at broadening the recruitment of supreme court judges to sectors of the legal world other than that of the traditional career judges, one can observe that the majority of the judges in the courts still come from the ranks of professional

46 M. Melin & S. Lindskog, 'Domstolarnas oberoende behöver stärkas', *Svensk Juristtidning*, Vol. 2017, 2017, pp. 245–251.

47 As clearly stated by mainstream socio-legal scholarship, modern law remains a crucial indicator of a society's capacity to preserve the peaceful co-existence of a plurality of life-worlds. E.g. M. Deflem, *Sociology of Law*, Cambridge, UK, Cambridge University Press, 2008, p. 224.

48 E. A. *Christodoulidis, Law and Reflexive Politics*, Dordrecht, Springer Science+Business, 1998, pp. 212–224; and R. A. Posner, *Frontiers of Legal Theory*, Cambridge, MA, Harvard University Press, 2004, pp. 153–158.

49 E.g. T. Otter Johansson, 'Regeringens styrning av förvaltningsmyndigheterna efter den 1 januari 2011', *Svensk Juristtidning*, Vol. 2012, 2012, p. 834.

judges.[50] Moreover, the recruitment policy of giving preference to those who have worked at the Department of Justice stubbornly remains one of the fundamental selection criteria.

5.4 Conclusion

To conclude this brief work regarding the positioning of the Swedish supreme courts within the administrative landscape, one could easily state (as it is often and correctly done when it comes to this Scandinavian country) that Sweden's particular history and rather isolated location allow for this kind of exception. Moreover, the same critical voice could also add that the Swedish case, due to the specific historical and institutional context in which it has developed, does not offer much contribution to the European and global discourse as to the role of the highest courts in relation to the other powers. These critiques are certainly correct, but there is at least one consideration from the Swedish situation that may be general in character and can be used to draw conclusions applicable to most of the Western or Western-based legal systems.

When tackling the critical situations in many European countries (e.g., Russia, Poland, or Hungary), one point is often made: the reforms directed at transforming the judges sitting in the highest courts into civil servants are *per se* endangering one of the essential legal components of a democratic form of state.[51] While this critique may be correct for such realities, one should also point out that its validity is not due to an ontological connection between democracy as a political form of organization and a fully judicial culture in the highest courts (i.e., its position as third party). The Swedish case shows that it is possible to have a fulfilled democracy even with supreme courts that do not have 'thoroughbred' judges, instead having judges who operate as civil servants. In other words, this Scandinavian oddity suggests that there may be an ontological gap between a democratic form of state and one of the components of the legal institutional architecture traditionally attached to this political system, namely a fully third-party supreme court.

The critical assessments of the recent trends within certain European countries should instead be evaluated by setting the dependency relation between courts and administration within a contextual framework: a dependency culture within the public administration in general toward the legislative powers. In other words, despite the globalization of law, its institutions, and legal discourse,

50 E. Exelin, Domstolarnas oberoende och självständighet, 2014, p. 190, available at www.rattsfonden.se/pdf/domarens_oberoende_2014.pdf. See B. C. Smith, *Judges and Democratization: Judicial Independence in New Democracies*, London, Routledge, 2017, p. 1.

51 E.g. International Federation for Human Rights, Hungary: Democracy under Threat, 2016, pp. 15–21, available at www.refworld.org/docid/5825f72a4.html. See also D. P. Kommers, 'Autonomy versus Accountability: The German Judiciary', in P. H. Russell & D. M. O'Brien (Eds), *Judicial Independence in the Age of Democracy*, Charlottesville, University Press of Virginia, 2001, p. 137.

as highlighted by many legal scholars, the 'local' historical and political circumstances still play a role in better, and more fully, understanding a certain constitutional system.[52] The risk of losing the democratic character of a certain system once the supreme courts are incorporated within the executive power may be real in cases like Russia or Hungary. These are realities where, due to the historical and institutional contexts, politicians tend to have a more direct control over the administration in general and thus, indirectly, over the judges.[53] However, when looking instead to the case of Sweden and its strong administrative culture of independence from the legislative power, such danger has not materialized in the past decades.[54]

One could use the case of the judicial bodies in the People's Republic of China as a counterexample confirming the relevance of 'local' factors. At least until 2006, judges were considered an integral part of the public administration and were addressed in official documents as civil servants '*tout court*'.[55] Due to a series of reforms, nowadays they are institutionally and functionally separated from the public administration far more than their counterparts in Sweden. However, due the coexistence of other contextual frameworks (e.g., a historical culture of the administration being directly at the service of the political powers), not many would dare to claim that the Chinese constitutional architecture generates judicial bodies which are more independent from politicians (and therefore at a higher level of Western-style democracy) than in Sweden.

Ultimately, the real measurement of the level of democracy in a certain legal system may not primarily relate to the degree to which the highest courts operate as a third party in relation to the other powers, but rather the extent to which the public sector in general (i.e., including the courts) is institutionally and legally independent from the political powers.

References

E. Åsard & W. Lance Bennet, *Democracy and the Marketplace of Ideas*, Cambridge, UK, Cambridge University Press, 1997.

V. Aubert, 'The Rule of Law and the Promotional Function of Law', in G. Teubner (Ed.), *Dilemmas of Law in the Welfare State*, Berlin, de Gruyter, 1986.

B. Bengtsson, 'Domare och lagstiftare i samverkan och konflikt', in Å. Frändberg (Ed.), *Festskrift till Stig Strömholm*, Vol. 1, Uppsala, Iustus Förlag, 1997.

52 R. Hirschl, 'From Comparative Constitutional Law to Comparative Constitutional Studies', *International Journal of Constitutional Law, Vol. 11, 2013, pp.* 1–12. See Venice Commission, Report on Judicial Appointments, 2007, para. 5–6, available at www.venice.coe.int/webforms/documents/default.aspx?pdffile=CDL-AD(2007)028-e.

53 E.g. A. Körösényi, *Government and Politics in Hungary*, Budapest, Central European University Press, 1999, pp. 212–216.

54 Nergelius, 2011, p. 84.

55 K. Blasek, *Rule of Law in China*, Berlin, Springer, 2015, p. 69.

A. Bergh, 'The Universal Welfare State: Theory and the Case of Sweden', *Political Studies*, Vol. 54, 2004.

U. Bernitz, 'Europarättens genomslag i svensk rätt', *Juridisk Tidskrift*, Vol. 3, 2010.

H. Bernitz, 'En icke-konfessionell skola', *Juridisk Tidskrift*, Vol. 3, 2017.

D. Bjerstedt, *Tryggheten inför rättan*, Lund, Lund University, 2009.

K. Blasek, *Rule of Law in China*, Berlin, Springer, 2015.

T. Bull, 'Rättighetsskyddet i Högsta förvaltningsdomstolen', *Svensk Juristtidning*, Vol. 2017, 2017.

T. Bull & F. Sterzel, *Regeringsformen*, 3rd ed., Stockholm, SNS förlag, 2015.

C. Carlson, 'Rätten att inte lämna ut uppgifter vid beslut om tredjemansrevision', *Juridisk Tidskrift*, Vol. 2, 2012.

E. A. Christodoulidis, *Law and Reflexive Politics*, Dordrecht, Springer Science+Business, 1998.

C. Dahlström & A. Sundell, Budgetary Effects of Political Appointments, 2013, https://ecpr.eu/Filestore/PaperProposal/fcd89d7b-851d-4e0c-a076-e66300e98f72.pdf

H. V. Dean, 'The Juridification of Welfare', in A. Kjonstad & J. Wilson (Eds), *Law, Power and Poverty*, Bergen, CROP Publications, 1997.

M. Deflem, *Sociology of Law*, Cambridge, UK, Cambridge University Press, 2008.

R. B. Denhardt, J. V. Denhardt & T. A. Blanc, *Public Administration*, 7th ed., Belmont, CA, Thomson Wadsworth, 2014.

R. Dworkin, *Taking Rights Seriously*, London, Duckworth, 1977.

G. Esping-Andersen, *The Three Worlds of Welfare Capitalism*, Princeton, NJ, Princeton University Press, 1990.

E. Exelin, Domstolarnas oberoende och självständighet, 2014, www.rattsfonden.se/pdf/domarens_oberoende_2014.pdf

K. Fast, *Regeringsrådens oberoende och roll*, Stockholm: Institutet Skatter and rättssäkerhet, 2001.

E. Ferragina & M. Seeleib-Kaiser, 'Welfare Regime Debate', *Policy & Politics*, Vol. 39, 2011.

J. E. Fleming, *Getting to the Rule of Law*, New York, New York University Press, 2011.

Å. Frändberg, *Rättsordningens idé*, Stockholm, Iustus Förlag, 2005.

M. A. Glendon, *Rights Talk: The Impoverishment of Political Discourse*, New York, Free Press, 1993.

C. Guarnieri & P. Pederzoli, *The Power of Judges: A Comparative Study of Courts and Democracy*, Oxford, Oxford University Press, 2002.

J. Habermas, *Between Facts and Norms*, Cambridge, MA, The MIT Press, 1998.

H. L. A. Hart, *The Concept of Law*, Oxford, Clarendon Press, 1961.

J. Hirschfeldt, 'Domstolarna som statsmakt', *Juridisk Tidskrift*, Vol. 1, 2011.

R. Hirschl, 'From Comparative Constitutional Law to Comparative Constitutional Studies', *International Journal of Constitutional Law*, Vol. 11, 2013.

T. Ingvarsson, 'Allmänna råd och jämkning av borgensåtaganden', *Svensk Juristtidning*, Vol. 2008, 2008.

International Federation for Human Rights, Hungary: Democracy under Threat, 2016, www.refworld.org/docid/5825f72a4.html

T. Jagland, State of Democracy, Human Rights and the Rule of Law, https://edoc.coe.int/en/an-overview/7345-pdf-state-of-democracy-human-rights-and-the-rule-of-law.html

B. M. Jones, 'Sweden', in J. Kingdom (Ed.), *The Civil Service in Liberal Democracies*, London, Routledge, 1990.

A. Jonsson, 'Förvaltningens självständighet och förbudet mot ministerstyre', in L. Marcusson (Ed.), *God förvaltning -ideal och praktik*, Uppsala, Iustus, 2006.

J. Kleineman, 'Från prejudikatinstans till lagstiftare? Högsta domstolens ökade aktivism', *Juridisk Tidskrift*, Vol. 3, 2015.

D. P. Kommers, 'Autonomy versus Accountability: The German Judiciary', in P. H. Russell and D. M. O'Brien (Eds), *Judicial Independence in the Age of Democracy*, Charlottesville, VA, University Press of Virginia, 2001.

A. Körösényi, *Government and Politics in Hungary*, Budapest, Central European University Press, 1999.

H. M. Kritzer, 'Martin Shapiro: Anticipating the New Institutionalism', in N. Maveety (Ed.), *The Pioneers of Judicial Behavior*, Ann Arbor, MI, University of Michigan Press, 2003.

F. Lagergren, *På andra sidan välfärdsstaten*, Stockholm, Brutus Östlings Bokförlag, 1999.

A. Lagerqvist Veloz Roca, 'Utvecklingslinjer inom svensk offentlig rätt under de senaste hundra åren', in K. Källström & J. Öberg (Eds), *Juridisk Tidskrift – Jubileumshäfte*, Stockholm, Jure, 2007.

R. Lavin, *Domstol och administrativ myndighet*, Stockholm, Norstedt, 1972.

J. Lindvall & B. Rothstein, 'Sweden: The Fall of the Strong State', *Scandinavian Political Studies*, Vol. 29, 2006.

A. Massey, 'Civil Service Systems', in A. Massey (Ed.), *International Handbook on Civil Service Systems*, Cheltenham, Edward Elgar, 2011.

M. Melin & S. Lindskog, 'Domstolarnas oberoende behöver stärkas', *Svensk Juristtidning*, Vol. 2017, 2017.

J. Nergelius, *Constitutional Law in Sweden*, Alphen aan den Rijn, Wolters Kluwer, 2011.

S. E. Olsson Hort, 'Sweden: Towards a 21st Century Post-Modern People's Home', in P. Koslowski & A. Føllesdal (Eds), *Restructuring the Welfare State*, Berlin, Springer, 1997.

T. Otter Johansson, 'Regeringens styrning av förvaltningsmyndigheterna efter den 1 januari 2011', *Svensk Juristtidning*, Vol. 2012, 2012.

R. Påhlsson, *Likhet inför skattelag*, Uppsala, Iustus förlag, 2007.

A. Peczenik, *Vad är rätt?*, Stockholm, Norstedts Juridik, 1995.

O. Petersson, *Report from The Democratic Audit of Sweden 1999: Democracy the Swedish Way*, Stockholm, SNS Förlag, 1999.

R. H. Pildes, 'Why Rights Are Not Trumps', *Journal of Legal Studies*, Vol. 27, 1998.

R. A. Posner, *Frontiers of Legal Theory*, Cambridge, MA, Harvard University Press, 2004.

J. C. N. Raadschelders, 'Changing European Ideas about the Public Servant: A Theoretical and Methodological Framework', in F. Sager & P. Overeem (Eds), *The European Public Servant*, Colchester, ECPR Press, 2015.

J. Reichel, *God förvaltning i EU och i Sverige*, Stockholm, Jure, 2006.

J. Reichel, 'Svenska myndigheter som EU-myndigheter', in K. Källström & J. Öberg (Eds), *Juridisk Tidskrift –Jubileumshäfte*, Stockholm, Jure, 2007.

J. Reichel, 'Den svenska förvaltningsmodellen i det europeiska samarbetsprojektet', in I. Mattson & E. Sjögren (Eds), *Statsförvaltningen efter 20 år i EU*, Stockholm, Statskontoret, 2016, www.statskontoret.se/globalassets/publikationer/2016/om-offentlig-sektor-28_statsforvaltning-eu.pdf

T. Risse, M. Green Cowles & J. Caporaso, 'Europeanization and Domestic Change', in M. Green Cowles, J. Caporaso & T. Risse (Eds), *Transforming Europe: Europeanization and Domestic Change*, Ithaca, NY, Cornell University Press, 2001.

H. I. Roth, *Är religion en mänsklig rättighet?*, Stockholm, Norsteds, 2012.

B. Rothstein, 'Välfärdsstat, förvaltning och legitimitet', in B. Rothstein (Ed.), *Politik som organization*, Stockholm, SNS Förlag, 2010.

B. Rothstein & L. Trägårdh, 'The State and Civil Society in a Historical Perspective', in L. Trägårdh (Ed.), *State and Civil Society in Northern Europe*, New York, Bergbahn Books, 2007.

M. Schultz, 'Rights Through Torts: The Rise of a Rights Discourse in Swedish Tort Law', *European Review of Private Law*, Vol. 3, 2009.

M. Shapiro, *Courts: A Comparative and Political Analysis*, Chicago, IL, University of Chicago Press, 1981.

M. Sjöberg, 'Den långa vägen till en generell regel om domstolsprövning av förvaltningsbeslut', in G. Regner, M. Eliason & H.-H. Vogel (Eds), *Festskrift till Hans Ragnemalm*, Lund, Juristförlaget, 2005.

G. Skapska, 'Facing Past Human Rights Abuse', in J. Priban (Ed.) *Liquid Society and Its Law*, Aldershot, Ashgate, 2007.

B. C. Smith, *Judges and Democratization: Judicial Independence in New Democracies*, London, Routledge, 2017.

SOU (Statens offentliga utredningar), *Domaren i Sverige inför framtiden*, Stockholm, Statens offentliga utredningar, 1994.

SOU (Statens offentliga utredningar), *En uthållig demokrati!*, Stockholm, Statens offentliga utredningar, 2000.

SOU (Statens offentliga utredningar), *En reformerad grundlag 2008: 125*, Stockholm, Statens offentliga utredningar, 2008.

F. Sterzel, *Författning i utveckling*, Uppsala, Iustus Förlag, 1998.

A. Stone Sweet, *Governing with Judges*, Oxford, Oxford University Press, 2000.

H. Strömberg & B. Lundell, *Allmän förvaltningsrätt*, 26th ed., Stockholm, Liber, 2014.

J. W. F. Sundberg, *High-Tax Imperialism*, 2nd ed., Stockholm, Institutet för offentlig och internationell rätt, 2000.

K. Tuori, Vilken vikt bör i rättstillämpningen läggas vid lagstiftarens synpunkter och signaler i och utanför lagstiftningsärendet?, 2011, http://jura.ku.dk/njm/39/789-796-vilken-vikt-bor-i-rattstillampningen-korref-tuori-red.pdf/.

K. Uggerud, 'Uønskede menneskerettigheter?', *Retfaerd*, Vol. 90, 2000.

Venice Commission, Report on Judicial Appointments, 2007, www.venice.coe.int/webforms/documents/default.aspx?pdffile=CDL-AD(2007)028-e.

H. von Sydow, *Rättsstatens rötter-reformer av domarutnämningar*, Lund, Juridiska Fakulteten vid Lunds Universitet, 2007.

W. Warnling-Nerep, 'Till frågan om legalitet och retroaktivitet i svensk rätt', *Juridisk Tidskrift*, Vol. 4, 2009.

H. Wenander, Sweden: Deference to the Administration in Judicial Review, 2017, https://portal.research.lu.se/portal/files/35406219/Wenander_Sweden_Deference_to_the_Administration_in_Judicial_Review.pdf.

L. Wennberg & A. Pylkkänen, 'Intersektionalitet i rätten', *Retfærd*, Vol. 138, 2012.

F. Werksäll, 'En offensiv Högsta domstol', *Svensk Juristtidning*, Vol. 2014, 2014.

T. Wilhelmsson, 'Contract and Equality', *Scandinavian Studies in Law*, Vol. 40, 2000.

M. Zamboni, *The Policy of Law*, Oxford, Hart Publishing, 2007.

6 From separation of powers to superiority of rights*

The Italian Constitutional Court and end-of-life decisions (the Cappato case)

Monica Bonini

6.1 Introduction

The framers of the 1948 Italian Constitution opted for a rigid constitution. Therefore, the system of judicial review was included among several guarantees within the Constitution (i.e. Arts 134 ff.). Following the one especially developed by Hans Kelsen, the framers adopted a system of centralized review grounded in an organ of constitutional justice (separated from the judiciary).[1] Based on this background, along the decades the Constitutional Court has protected rights and law. In 2018, a Court order regarding an end-of-life decisions case raised a few questions among legal scholars.[2]

This chapter aims to reflect upon said Court's order. Indeed, the Italian constitutional system is grounded on separation of powers. Nevertheless, when the Parliament does not regulate sensitive matters, the Constitutional Court may act as a stand-in for the Parliament. Therefore, it is important to reflect upon the Constitutional Court's activism. As a matter of fact, the latter may break separation of powers to protect constitutional values at risk.

6.2 Balancing complex values: Judicial choices versus separation of powers

Balancing complex values is a challenge for any legal order. Years ago, political and legal scholars started a debate regarding the parliament's and the courts' role in such matter.[3] Nowadays, whether 'courts are well suited

* The author wishes to thank Paolo Zicchittu for helpful remarks concerning the thesis of the present essay and Dario Scarpa for the review of the work.

1 Literature regarding the issue is wide: see G. Zagrebelsky and V. Marcenò, *Giustizia costituzionale*, Bologna, Il Mulino, 2012.

2 Corte costituzionale, ordinanza n. 207, 16 novembre 2018.

3 Regarding judicial review of parliamentary acts see the renowned writing of R. Bellamy, *Political Constitutionalism: A Republican Defence of the Constitutionality of Democracy*, Cambridge, Cambridge UP, 2007; M. Tushnet, *Taking the Constitution Away from the Courts*, Princeton, NJ, Princeton UP, 1999; L. D. Kramer, *The People Themselves: Popular Constitutionalism and Judicial Review*, New York, OUP, 2004.

to balancing complex values through doctrinal tools'[4] is a question to be rediscovered.

The issue is grounded on the relationship between – roughly speaking – politics and law. As it is well known,[5] theoretically the tension marking this correlation may be described as follows. Politics and law experience a double-sided liaison: 'symbiotic'[6] and conflicting at the same time. Unrestrained popular will[7] needs constituted power 'ensuring the on-going and effective exercise of that same sovereignty'.[8] Then, 'constitutionalism refers to efforts to prevent arbitrary government'.[9] Two different paths may achieve that same goal. According to Richard Bellamy, political constitutionalism focuses on political equality. From mixed government to representative democracy, it balances powers in order to prevent arbitrariness.[10] On the other hand, legal constitutionalism safeguards individual rights by separating powers and by judicially protecting the constitution. 'Both traditions are present within most democracies and can be found side by side in many constitutions'.[11] The Italian experience does not differ from this model. Nonetheless, it is marked by some distinctive characteristics.[12]

4 E.g. 'as rationality/proportionality': P. Craig, 'Political Constitutionalism and the Judicial Role: A Response', *International Journal of Constitutional Law*, Vol. 9, No. 1, 2011, pp. 112–131, p. 127.

5 This chapter does not want to deepen origins and models of constitutionalism: for literature regarding the issue see ff. footnotes.

6 P. Scott, '(Political) Constitutions and (Political) Constitutionalism', *German Law Journal*, Vol. 14, No. 12, 2014, pp. 2158–2183, p. 2165.

7 Regarding the 'pouvoir constituant' and the written constitution see P. Barile, 'Potere costituente', in *Novissimo Digesto Italiano*, Torino, UTET, Vol. 13, 1966, pp. 443–450; P. Barile, 'Potere costituente', in P. Barile, *Scritti di Diritto costituzionale*, Padova, Cedam, 1967, pp. 592–611; F. Lanchester (Ed.), *Costantino Mortati: potere costituente e limiti alla revisione costituzionale*, Padova, Wolter Kluwers-Cedam, 2017; M. Dogliani, R. Bin, R. Martinez Dalmau, *Il potere costituente*, Napoli, Editoriale Scientifica, 2017.

8 P. Scott (n. 6) 2167.

9 R. Bellamy, 'Constitutionalism and Democracy', in R. Bellamy, *Political Constitutionalism*, Cambridge, UK, Cambridge University Press, 2007, pp. 90–142; for the quotations see Ralph Bellamy, *Constitutionalism*, www.britannica.com/topic/constitutionalism.

10 R. Bellamy, 'The Norms of Political Constitutionalism: Non-domination and Political Equality', in Bellamy (n. 9) pp. 145–175; see also R. Bellamy, Introduction, www.britannica.com/topic/constitutionalism.

11 R. Bellamy, 'Bringing Together Norms and Forms: The Democratic Constitution', in Bellamy (n. 9), pp. 209–259; R. Bellamy, Introduction, www.britannica.com/topic/constitutionalism. See also M. Goldoni, 'What is Political Constitutionalism', *Diritto e questioni pubbliche*, Vol. 10, 2010, pp. 337–360; M. Goldoni, 'Two Internal Critiques of Political Constitutionalism', *International Journal of Constitutional Law*, Vol. 10, No. 4, 2012, pp. 926–949; Idem, 'Constitutional Reasoning according to Political Constitutionalism', *German Law Journal*, Vol. 14, No. 8, 2013, pp. 1053–1076; C. Pinelli, 'Constitutional Reasoning and Political Deliberation', 2013, *German Law Journal*, Vol. 14, No. 8, 2013, pp. 1171–1182.

12 F. Lanchester, 'La Costituzione del 1948 e l'organo di garanzia esterno', *Il Politico*, Vol. 74, Fasc. 3, 2009, pp. 51–66.

Under the Italian Constitution, democratic processes and constitutional review[13] should live together in harmony. Italian legal scholars never (or rarely) claimed that Parliaments 'are better equipped than courts in constitutional reasoning'; nor did they state that people's representatives ensure a better protection of rights than courts.[14] Furthermore,[15] in 'order to avoid any impression of usurping powers or competences' even the Constitutional Court 'must convincingly motivate its interventions'.[16] Nonetheless, the separation of powers between the Italian Constitutional Court and the Parliament is not founded on a proper non-justiciable area. Moreover, the perimeter of such an area changes given 'the concrete case, the socio-political context and the lawmaker's attitude'.[17] This abstract equilibrium must be set in the Italian historical background. As a matter of fact, since 1956 the Constitutional Court's attitude toward the issue at stake changed.[18] In order to understand this development[19] the chapter now briefly recalls the wider framework of such evolution.

As Annen Junji wrote, 'Constitutionalism is one of the best gifts that the West has given to the world'.[20] On the other hand, 'law' (i.e. the constitution) should never limit power by altering the nature of its judicial guardian.[21] Judicial review cannot replace 'political' – i.e. parliamentary – decisions. However, this threshold is only theoretically fixed. The contemporary era unveiled another side of the topic. 'Former' and 'new' individual rights[22] intertwine with separation of powers, political decisions, and judicial competences.[23] From the 'age of rights' to the

13 The paper will further delve into the matter reflecting on the position of P. Zicchittu, 'The Italian Way to the Political Question', *Italian Journal of Public Law*, No. I, 2015, pp. 222–262.

14 C. Pinelli (n. 11) p. 1171.

15 Given the separation of powers. See also P. Zicchittu, *Le zone franche del potere legislative*, Giappichelli, Torino, 2017.

16 P. Zicchittu, (n. 13), p. 262. Regarding the Constitutional Court see only R. Romboli (Ed.), *L'accesso alla giustizia costituzionale: carattere, limiti, prospettive di un modello*, Napoli, Edizioni Scientifiche Italiane–ESI, 2006; G. Zagrebelsky and V. Marcenò (n. 1). The topic must be set back in the framework of C. Mortati, *Problemi di politica costituzionale*, Milano, Giuffrè, 1972.

17 P. Zicchittu, (n. 13), p. 262.

18 P. Zicchittu, (n. 13), p. 262.

19 See 4.–7. and E. Lamarque, 'Interpreting Statutes in Conformity with the Constitution: The Role of the Constitutional Court and Ordinary Judges', *Italian Journal of Public Law*, No. I, 2010, pp. 87–120.

20 A. Junji, 'Constitutionalism as a Political Culture', *Pacific Rim Law & Journal Policy Association*, Vol. 11, No. 3, 2002, pp. 561–576, p. 563.

21 The issue is an even more complex one: G. Zagrebelsky, *La legge e la sua giustizia: tre capitoli di giustizia costituzionale*, Bologna, Il Mulino, 2008.

22 N. Bobbio, *L'età dei diritti*, Einaudi, 2014.

23 G. Longo, *Controllo di legittimità e monito di sovranità: per una teoria politica della giustizia costituzionale*, Roma, Aracne, 2012.

'era of new rights'[24] parliaments and courts must face an important evolution. As the Italian constitutional court judge Marta Cartabia states, all

> 'the most important issues and problems of social life are tentatively dealt within the legal framework on individual rights. [...]. The emphasis on individual rights brings about an emphasis on judges: after all every individual right is susceptible to be claimed before a judicial authority. That's why rights and courts are closely tight together.'[25]

However, 'when rights are controversial',[26] '*simplex*' is no more '*sigillum veri*'. Sometimes, judicial authorities also face matters which the national legal order has not yet qualified as a proper 'right'. Foreign parliaments may have already disciplined such issues, but not the internal one. In these circumstances, judicial authorities – especially constitutional courts – must solve complex situations. Individuals demand that what is a proper 'right' in another legal order may be qualified in the same way in the national one. If the Parliament does not respond, the only way to face the matter is the judicial one.

In Italy, end-of-life decisions exemplify both theoretical sides of such situation. Whether the Constitutional Court and other judges are well-suited for the purpose of balancing complex values characterizing this specific subject matter is a difficult question.[27] Whether the Constitutional Court shall balance complex values when the Parliament refuses to decide upon them raises serious doubts. As a matter of fact, parliamentary inertia may be a political choice – i.e. a political domain to be strictly left out of the Court's reach.[28]

Based on this background, Italian legal scholars rediscover legal constitutionalism on the one hand and the 'political question doctrine' on the other. Thus far and no further; sometimes only judicial activism may protect constitutional values at stake – but break the separation of powers.

6.3 Balancing complex values: Judicial choices versus parliamentary inertia

Theoretically, representatives should make political choices regarding significant matters; courts should protect rights and law. Nonetheless, the separation of powers functions well when and if parliaments, courts, and constitutional courts strictly observe their competences. Otherwise, difficulties may occur. In Italy,

24 M. Cartabia, 'When Rights are Controversial, Are Dialogues between Courts still Enough? Editorial', *Italian Journal of Public Law*, No. I, 2010, pp. 1–5, p. 2.

25 M. Cartabia, (n. 24) p. 2.

26 The expression is of M. Cartabia, (n. 24) pp. 1–5. See also M. Cartabia, 'La Corte costituzionale nella nuova età dei diritti', *Rivista Il Mulino*, Vol. 466, Fasc. 2 (marzo-aprile), 2013, pp. 364–371.

27 Such 'as rationality/proportionality': P. Craig, (n. 4), p. 127.

28 P. Zicchittu (n. 15).

parliamentary inertia often gave rise to 'the pressing need to fill [judicially a] systemic vacuum' – especially when fundamental rights were at stake.[29] Therefore, legal scholars had to clarify whether the Italian Constitutional Court's intervention 'to rectify the defect of the Parliament's failure to act or to minimize the consequences of political decisions' was justified.[30]

As it is well known, the European debate regarding such matters does not resemble the one developed in the United Kingdom and in the United States.[31] Continental legal scholars never (or rarely) claim that parliaments are better than courts in constitutional reasoning or in protecting rights. Nowadays, a further issue – Italian parliamentary inertia – must be set in this framework.

Cesare Pinelli examined political constitutionalism by wondering whether democracy's functioning reflects Richard Bellamy's and Jeremy Waldron's positions.[32] Pinelli argues that even political deliberations may endanger rights. This occurs

> 'whenever the constitution [...] requires that laws shape in advance, and in general terms, the discretionary powers of the executive regarding certain rights, or entrust parliament with the exclusive power of providing the financial resources that may be required for funding rights pertaining to certain categories.'[33]

In light of this the principles guiding the parliamentary action and the judicial function seem to be grounded on a fundamental need: limiting 'as far as possible the subjectivity of judges that [...] may amount to arbitrariness'.[34] However, it is also important to wonder whether the idealization of any parliamentary debate[35] is acceptable. As a consequence, 'overruling' – especially of the Italian Constitutional Court – must be set in the said complex background.

In Italy, the judicial adoption of political solutions is grounded on two theoretical premises. First, the Constitutional Court may believe 'it to be more relevant and sustainable for the entire legal system' to judge despite awaiting any parliamentary debate. Second, the Court may intervene because 'the Parliament is unable to find a political agreement' regarding certain matters.[36] In other words,

29 P. Zicchittu, (n. 13), p. 258; M. Quattrocchi, 'Corte e Parlamento, attraverso le decisioni di inammissibilità', in A. Ruggeri and G. Silvestri (Eds), *Corte costituzionale e Parlamento. Profili problematici e ricostruttivi*, Milano, Giuffré, 2000, pp. 179–197.

30 P. Zicchittu, (n. 13) 258.

31 See again footnote (3).

32 C. Pinelli, (n. 11), pp. 1171–1172. Regarding the position of Richard Bellamy see footnote (9) ff. Concerning the one of Jeremy Waldron see J. Waldron, 'The Core of the Case Against Judicial Review', *Yale Law Journal*, Vol. 115, 2006, pp. 1346–1360.

33 C. Pinelli, (n. 11), p. 1174.

34 Especially in the field of individual rights: C. Pinelli, (n. 11), p. 1174.

35 I.e. a highly participated in debate, carefully considering the issue of rights.

36 P. Zicchittu, (n. 13), p. 258 for both quotations.

'overruling' may be the result of different conditions. Therefore, it is impossible to establish *a priori* if the Constitutional Court wants to or must act as a stand-in for the Parliament. Moreover, in the Italian legal order a third, more complicated possibility occurs (see Section 6.6 in this chapter). Further analysis shall be made in order to clear up the issue.

6.4 The superiority of the political: A myth to dispel?

As is well known, two typical features characterize constitutionalism: an original and a recent one.[37] Nowadays, its former, limiting role – regarding public power – impacts on several decisional levels: 'below the state, or above it, [on] international or transnational context'. Indeed, the 'spread of constitutionalism can be understood as nothing more than a corollary of the multiplication of the examples of the phenomenon to which it is inextricably linked'. That's why, central 'to much of the discourse of constitutionalism, at least on national level, is a distinction between law and politics' too.[38] For the aims of this chapter, reflecting upon the Italian Constitutional Court and the separation of powers means thinking about law and politics in light of constitutionalism's evolution.

Law and politics experience a double-sided relationship (symbiotic and conflicting)[39] because, in any contemporary legal order, they are rooted in constitutionalism's duality.[40] In Italy, some time ago renowned legal scholars analyzed the issue.[41] Recently, Paul Scott rediscovered the matter. Constitutionalism's duality is grounded on – roughly speaking – 'regularization of power, whereby it is both constituted and limited by the same apparatus'.[42] If 'the same framework both constitutes and limits',[43] 'the relationship between its political and legal variants'[44] must be reconsidered.[45] First, by emphasizing that politics and law are the two parts of every constitutional whole. Second, by accepting that contemporary legal orders are grounded in a mixture of political and legal institutions and processes.[46]

Scott's position seems to develop former Italian analyses regarding political decisions and judicial activism. Antonio Ruggeri reflected upon the complexity

37 For this approach P. Scott, '(Political) Constitutions and (Political) Constitutionalism', *German Law Journal*, Vol. 14, No. 12, 2014, pp. 2158–2183.
38 For all three quotations, see P. Scott, (n. 36) p. 2159.
39 See n. 2.
40 P. Scott, (n. 36), p. 2174.
41 See only M. Fioravanti, *Costituzionalismo: percorsi della storia e tendenze attuali*, Roma, Laterza, 2009; G. Silvestri, *Dal potere ai principi. Libertà ed eguaglianza nel costituzionalismo contemporaneo*, Roma, Laterza, 2009.
42 P. Scott, (n. 36), p. 2174.
43 P. Scott, (n. 36), p. 2176 for all the quotations.
44 P. Scott, (n. 36), p. 2178.
45 P. Scott, (n. 36), p. 2177: obviously, if his suggestion is correct.
46 For both statements, ibidem.

of the Italian Constitutional Court.[47] According to his opinion, the relationship between the latter and the Italian Parliament cannot be reduced to an 'exclusionary understanding of political/legal constitutionalism'.[48] The phenomenon is more complex, because it is based on the two-faced essence of any constitution.[49] The latter is an 'act' and a 'process' grounded in dynamic elements.[50]

Scott expresses a similar concept in a different way. He believes that, often, 'the fact of being legal is presented (explicitly or implicitly) as a denial of the political'.[51] For Ruggeri, this 'exclusionary understanding' roots in the debate developed by Hans Kelsen and Carl Schmitt concerning the guardian of the constitution.[52] Thereafter legal scholars accepted a dichotomy based on a rigid distinction: Constitutional Courts are either political actors or judges.[53] However, this distinction denies the nature of such courts, which merges both marks – the political and the judicial one.[54] Such a nature depends on the essence of any constitution. According to Ruggeri,[55] it is impossible to segregate constitutional issues in the boundaries of one model.[56] Therefore, any attempt to face parliamentary inertia especially cannot be based on a clear-cut explanation of the separation of powers. Nor can it be based on a rigid acceptance of the superiority of politics.

47 A. Ruggeri, 'Corte costituzionale e Parlamento tra aperture del 'modello' e fluidità dell'esperienza', in A. Ruggeri and G. Silvestri (Eds), *Corte costituzionale e Parlamento. Profili problematici e ricostruttivi*, Milano, Giuffré, 2000, pp. 1–789, p. 6.

48 P. Scott, (n. 36), p. 2178.

49 For the complex nature of constitutions see C. Mortati, *La Costituzione in senso materiale. Ristampa inalterata con una premessa di G. Zagrebelsky*, Milano, Giuffré, 1998; C. A. Jemolo, *Che cos'è la Costituzione? Con un'introduzione di G. Zagrebelsky*, Roma, Donzelli, 2008.

50 A. Ruggeri, (n. 46), p. 7. See also A. Spadaro, 'Dalla Costituzione come 'atto' (puntuale nel tempo) alla Costituzione come 'processo' (storico). Ovvero della continua evoluzione del parametro costituzionale attraverso i giudizi di costituzionalità', *Quaderni costituzionali*, 1998, 341 ff and especially 416 ff; L. D'Andrea, 'Il progetto di riforma tra Costituzione-atto e Costituzione-processo', in AaVv (Eds), *La riforma costituzionale*, Padova, Cedam, 1993, 93 ff. Regarding Hans Kelsens' model of the 'negative legislator' see M. Bignami, 'Il caso Cappato alla Corte costituzionale: un'ordinanza ad incostituzionalità differita', *Questione giustizia*, 19 novembre 2018, 2018 http://questionegiustizia.it/articolo/il-caso-cappato-alla-corte-costituzionale-un-ordinanza-ad-incostituzionalita-differita_19-11-2018.php.

51 P. Scott, (n. 36), p. 2178.

52 Regarding Hans Kelsen's 'Verfassungsgerichtsbarkeit' see G. Volpe, *Il costituzionalismo del Novecento*, Roma, Laterza, 2000, especially 150 ff.

53 A. Ruggeri, (n. 46), p. 5.

54 A. Ruggeri, (n. 46), p. 7.

55 Ibidem.

56 Ibidem. Regarding the (potential) influence of the parliamentary election of five of the fifteen constitutional judges see G. Zagrebelsky, *Principî e voti: la Corte costituzionale e la politica*, Torino, Einaudi, 2005.

Paul Scott identifies the core of the matter: 'in the event of a clash between political and legal actors, which will triumph?'[57] If Ruggeri is right, legal scholars should not wonder whether parliaments embody the superiority of the political power. They must identify the institution which has the last word in controversial issues concerning rights. More specifically, they must identify what institution is competent when and if parliaments do not transform new claims in proper rights. For this chapter, such an answer cannot be found if legal scholars adopt an 'exclusionary understanding of political/legal constitutionalism'.[58] As Scott affirms, given the evolution of constitutionalism, a 'non-rivalrous conception' is preferable.[59] The Italian experience[60] sets that same approach in a concrete background.

6.5 Political decisions through judicial means: The Italian experience

In Italy, the adoption of a 'political solution through legal means'[61] may occur in two circumstances (see Section 6.3 of this chapter).[62] Anyway, 'overruling' may express the need to decide on certain issues. Therefore, it is difficult to affirm *a priori* if the Constitutional Court wants to or must act as a stand-in for the Parliament. Both possibilities must be set in the Italian constitutional background.

Fulco Lanchester analyzed some aspects regarding the Constitutional Court.[63] Through the decades, the Court safeguarded the constitutional foundations of the Italian legal order acting in a specific framework: a written, but dynamic Constitution and an evolving social and political system. Born out of the defeat of the Italian totalitarianism, the Italian Court faced 'the crucial problem of every modern legal system'.[64] Constitutional justice hovers between 'the political' and 'the judicial'. Reviewing legislation means challenging parliamentary assemblies or starting a dialogue with them.[65] Within this context, Italian legal scholars also reflected upon the 'political question' doctrine.[66] On principle, in Italy discre-

57 P. Scott, (n. 36), p. 2178.
58 Ibidem.
59 Ibidem, p. 2179.
60 See n. 3.; G. Zagrebelsky, *Intorno alla legge: il diritto come dimensione del vivere comune*, Torino, Einaudi, 2009; V. Onida, 'La Costituzione dal 1948 al 2008', *Il Politico*, Vol. 74, Fasc. 3, 2009, pp. 22–32; V. Onida, 'The Constitution Yesterday and Today', *Italian Journal of Public Law*, Vol. 4, No. 1, 2012, pp. 15–37.
61 The paper does not delve into the matter more than it is necessary here; see A. Cerri, *Corso di giustizia costituzionale*, Milano, Giuffré, 2008.
62 P. Zicchittu, (n. 13), p. 258.
63 F. Lanchester, (n. 12) pp. 51–66.
64 P. Zicchittu, (n. 13), p. 223. Zicchittu's position grounds in C.E. Rostow, 'The Democratic Character of Judicial Revier', *Harvard Law Review*, Vol. 66, No. 2, 1952, pp. 193–224; G. Zagrebelsky, *Il diritto mite. Legge, diritti, giustizia*, Torino, Einaudi, 1997.
65 P. Zicchittu, (n. 13), p. 224.
66 Literature regarding the 'political question' and the 'political question doctrine' is wide: see O. P. Field, 'The Doctrine of Political Question in the Federal Courts', *Minnesota Law*

tionary power over such a question belongs only to the politically accountable branches of government.[67] Thus, sometimes the Italian Constitutional Court cannot let them settle constitutional questions regarding the political one. Given this background, it is important to explain briefly how the Court decides that a certain matter concerns only the legislature. Then it will be possible to reflect upon parliamentary inertia and judicial intervention – setting it in the framework of the separation of powers.

Under current rules, the Constitutional Court must provide an answer to all the questions submitted to its review.[68] Therefore, in the Italian legal order a proper case selection mechanism is not foreseen[69] – the Court may only 'indirectly' select cases.[70] However, sometimes the Court ruled also on issues which, on principle, should have been left to the legislature.[71] Judicial activism broke the exclusive field featuring the 'political question'. Legal scholars wondered whether such activism is grounded on the absence of any written rule concerning the 'political question' domain.

In Italy, according to art. 28 of Statute Law no. 87/1953,[72] the 'constitutional review on a law or on enactments having force of law excludes any assessment of political character and any adjudicature of Parliamentary discretion'. The provision protects the principle of separation of powers: judicial review cannot be transformed in political control.[73] Nevertheless, the Court may check the

---

Review, Vol. 8, 1924, pp. 485–512; M. F. Weston, 'Political Questions', *Harvard Law Review*, Vol. 38, No. 3, 1959, pp. 296–333; R. E. Barkow, 'More Supreme than Court? The Fall of the Political Question Doctrine and the Rise of Judicial Supremacy', *Columbia Law Review*, Vol. 102, No. 2 (March), 2002, pp. 237–336; T. L. Grove, 'The Lost History of the Political Question Doctrine', *New York University Law Review*, Vol. 90, 2015, pp. 1908–1974.

67 Especially the members of both Italian Houses.

68 Given several rules regulating the Court's competence: see Legge costituzionale n. 1/1948, article 1, para. 1; Legge n. 87/1953, article 27; 'Norme integrative' (i.e. the rules adopted by the Court itself which regard its judicial activity: concerning the latter E. Lamarque, 'Le nuove norme integrative per i giudizi davanti alla Corte costituzionale', *Diritto e Società*, 2009, pp. 113–145; U. Adamo, 'Le nuove norme integrative per i giudizi davanti alla Corte costituzionale: la via principale', *Rivista AIC*, 4 novembre 2011, 2011, www.rivistaaic.it.

69 A case selection may be set in the framework of Legge n. 87/1953, article 37, para. 3 concerning any responsibility of the State's branches (P. Zicchittu, (n. 13) footnote [157], p. 253).

70 P. Zicchittu, (n. 13), footnote [157], p. 253.

71 P. Zicchittu, (n. 15).

72 P. Zicchittu, (n. 13), p 226.

73 I.e. the Constitutional Court cannot exercise judicial control on political choices. Regarding the Court's role toward Statute Laws which do not pursue constitutional aims see only L. Pegoraro, *Le sentenze-indirizzo della Corte costituzionale italiana*, Cedam, Padova, 1984, especially p. 90; L. Pegoraro, 'Giustizia costituzionale', in G. Morbidelli, L. Pegoraro, A. Rinella and M. Volpi (Eds), *Diritto Pubblico Comparato*, Torino, Giappichelli, 2016, pp. 547–600, pp. 579–584.

reasonableness[74] of legislative acts. However, even in such a case judicial review must respect specific requirements (to exclude that the Court judges on political assessments).[75] Along years, Statute Law no. 87/1953[76] and the Court's self-restraint contributed to compliance with the separation of powers.

Thus far and no further, the issue is resolved. Set in this background, the 'political question' relies, above all, 'on a Court's decision that defines a "non-justiciable area" in the specific case. This means that a question of unconstitutionality is only considered political if the Constitutional Court decides it is so in actual terms'.[77] The Constitutional Court's approach to this issue evolved along the decades.[78] Overall, the Court did 'not affirm its lack of competence [regarding "political questions"], but rather recognize[d] that the decisions and instruments in his hands [could not] adequately solve the concrete question'.[79] Furthermore, the reasonableness test[80] granted an acceptable equilibrium between denial of constitutional justice and respect for legislative power.[81] However, waiting for parliamentary action on fundamental rights-issues, in specific circumstances would have endangered those same liberties.[82]

For example, in 2014[83] new electoral rules had been created via 'judicial review'.[84] At that time, people's representatives were not able to adopt new rules

74 In Italy, the reasonableness test allows the Constitutional Court to evaluate whether statute law is proportional and adequate when compared to the aims it pursues.

75 Any judicial authority who must resolve a dispute that requires the application of a legal provision – where there is a doubt as to that provision's constitutionality – has both the power and the duty to certify that question to the Constitutional Court. The judge must offer the Court a reasoned decision as to whether the proposed question is necessary to decide the case ('*rilevanza*'). Secondly, the judge must determine whether in his opinion the challenge has any merit ('*non manifesta infondatezza*'). Moreover, the proposed question must be marked by the '*tono costituzionale*' ('constitutional tone'), which on principle puts any political assessment out of judicial reach.

76 I.e. its article 28.

77 P. Zicchittu, (n. 13), p. 230.

78 For the historical evolution of this attitude see T. Groppi (con la collaborazione di C. Meoli), *Le grandi decisioni della Corte costituzionale italiana*, Napoli, Editoriale Scientifica-ESI, 2010; for the distinction between procedural decisions ('*decisioni di ammissibilità*') and decisions regarding the substance of the case ('*decisioni di infondatezza*') see again P. Zicchittu, (n. 13), pp. 231–234.

79 P. Zicchittu, (n. 13), p. 235 especially his footnote [67] for wider literature.

80 See again (n. 78); for an in-depth reflection on the subject (as set in a wider theoretical framework) see also A. Cerri, 'Spunti e riflessioni sulla ragionevolezza nel diritto', *Diritto pubblico*, Vol. 2, Maggio-Agosto, 2016, pp. 625–668.

81 P. Zicchittu, (n. 13), p. 236.

82 Ibidem, p. 258.

83 Ibidem, p. 259 and the writings he recalls at footnote (86); see Legge no. 270/2005.

84 The Constitutional Court considered that Statute Law no. 270/2005 foresaw a majority premium with no minimum threshold. Such a mechanism could obviously invalidate the election's results; therefore, the Court replaced those Parliamentary provisions which would not respect the right to vote. By deciding in this way, the Court substantially changed the existing electoral law to a proportional one.

on such a strategic issue. In that situation, respecting discretionary power could have left 'the system with no instrument to exercise a fundamental right such as the right to vote'. After repeatedly 'calling the lawmaker to reconsider attentively the issues of national electoral provisions'[85] the Court had only one choice.[86] It intervened on the matter because of 'the Parliament's inertia and the need to guarantee the respect of fundamental rights'.[87]When rights are at stake, separating powers cannot mean denying justice.

6.6 End-of-life decisions between parliamentary inertia and judicial review

In Italy, the judicial adoption of political solutions may be grounded also on a third theoretical premise.[88] The Constitutional Court acts not only to protect rights, but also 'law', i.e. the 1948 constitutional order.[89] Given that some rules adopted during the Dictatorship are still in force, the Court must also intervene with the aim of interpreting those provisions according to the republican democratic principles and fundamental rights. It would be desirable to adopt new ones further to a parliamentary debate. Nonetheless, parliamentary inertia may hinder a proper democratic solution. On the other hand, parliamentary inactivity is problematic: sometimes, inertia is in real terms a political choice.[90]

Anyway, in both cases the Court's intervention may reaffirm the constitutional coherence of the legal order. Nonetheless, such intervention should never infringe separation of powers. In other words, the Italian Constitutional Court is not allowed to decide whether parliamentary inertia expresses or not a political choice. A recent end-of-life case clarifies the issue.

Article 580 of the Italian Criminal Code[91] (ICC) was adopted in 1930. If compared to present dilemmas concerning end-of-life decisions, it reveals its

85 For both quotations see again P. Zicchittu, (n. 13), p. 260.

86 In other words, the Constitutional Court should have dismissed the case (i.e. declared the question as inadmissible): A. Anzon-Demmig, 'Un tentativo coraggioso ma improprio di far valere l'incostituzionalità della legge per le elezioni politiche (e per coprire una 'zona franca' del giudizio di costituzionalità), *Rivista AIC*, No. 3, 2013, www.rivistaaic.it; B. Brancati, 'Le questioni della Cassazione sulla legge elettorale: una vicenda 'imbarazzante' per la Corte costituzionale? Nota a Cass., I sez. civ., n. 12060/2013 del 17 maggio 2013', *Consulta Online*, Vol. 2013, 12 novembre 2013, 2013, www.giurcost.org/studi/Brancati1.pdf.; R. Romboli, 'La costituzionalità della legge elettorale 270/05: la Cassazione introduce, in via giurisprudenziale, un ricorso quasi diretto alla Corte costituzionale?', *Foro italiano*, Vol. 138, Parte I, Fasc. 6, 2013, pp. 183–1838; E. Rossi, 'La Corte costituzionale e la legge elettorale: un quadro in tre atti e dall'epilogo incerto', *Federalismi*, 5 giugno 2013, 2013, www.federalismi.it.

87 P. Zicchittu, (n. 13), p. 260.

88 Regarding the explanation of the other two circumstances see the start and the end of n. 3.

89 See n. 2. The Italian Constitution came into force on 1 January 1948.

90 P. Zicchittu (15).

91 Regio Decreto 19 ottobre 1930, n. 1398.

anachronistic ethical and legal roots. During the Dictatorship, no one would tailor such decisions to the individual patient's cultural and emotional background.[92] Individual life 'belonged' to the State.[93] Therefore, art. 580 ICC regulates in the same manner two different behaviors. It does not distinguish between conducts consisting of soliciting someone (i.e. a patient) to commit suicide against his own will and others, such as those consisting in helping someone to realize his own free will (with the same tragic result).[94] Nowadays both types of conduct may be punished with imprisonment.[95] Given the existing constitutional and European framework,[96] some legal scholars believe that art. 580 ICC is out-of-date.[97]

Until 2017, Italy experienced a legal vacuum regarding end-of-life decisions. Only after the adoption of several regional and local acts, some rulings of the Constitutional Court regarding the latter and a few judicial decisions (mostly regarding the *Englaro* case),[98] the Parliament partially filled this vacuum. At the present time, Statute Law no. 219/2017[99] disciplines[100] only those specific situations where individuals decide whether to receive or not medical treatments. Even if the public debate was clearly orientated toward euthanasia, in 2017 the Italian representatives did not decriminalize the above-mentioned second type of conduct nor introduced assisted-suicide in the legal order. According constitutional principles and rules, in Italy only the Parliament may adopt statutes in order to criminalize or decriminalize specific conducts. Separation of powers is the most significant tool to protect individual freedom in sensitive fields such as

92 I. Pellizzone, 'Aiuto al suicidio, dal Codice Rocco alla Carta costituzionale alla Convenzione Europea dei Diritti dell'Uomo', *Giurisprudenza penale*, 17 settembre 2018, 2018, www.giurisprudenzapenale.com, especially para. 1.

93 I. Pellizzone, (n. 92), para. 1.

94 As Fabiano Antoniani, the patient at the core of the 'Cappato case'.

95 I.e. five to twelve years imprisonment (if the patient succeeds in committing suicide) or one to five years imprisonment (if the patient stays alive, but seriously hurts himself or herself).

96 I.e. the European Convention on Human Rights and the European Union Charter of Human Rights. See also AaVv. (Eds), 'Questioni di fine vita. Dalla legge 22 dicembre 2017, n. 219, alla ordinanza della Corte costituzionale nel caso Cappato', *Giurisprudenza penale*, No. 2019-1*bis*, 2019, www.giurisprudenzapenale.com.

97 See again I. Pellizzone, (n. 92), 2018, para. 1; A. Santuosso, P. Belloli, 'Paradossi nel procedimento Cappato. Tre aporie generate dall'art. 580 c.p. a proposito di aiuto al suicidio', *Giurisprudenza penale*, 13 giugno 2018, 2018, www.giurisprudenzapenale.com.

98 For the complete list of the recalled acts and judgments regarding the Englaro case see R. Fattibene, 'A chi spetta la 'disponibilità della vita'? La disciplina del fine-vita come occasione di riflessione sulla partecipazione democratica nelle questioni biogiuridiche', *Osservatorio costituzionale*, N. 3, 4 dicembre 2018, 2018, www.osservatorioaic.it.

99 Legge 22 dicembre 2017, n. 219, 'Norme in materia di consenso informato e di disposizioni anticipate di trattamento', *Gazzetta Ufficiale*, Serie Generale, N. 12, 16 gennaio 2018.

100 According to arts 2, 13 and 32 of the Italian Constitution and arts 1, 2 and 3 of the European Union Charter of Human Rights.

criminal law and liabilities.[101] Therefore, Statute Law no. 219 and even current art. 580 ICC are not apt to discipline specific cases – such as the *Cappato* one.

Since 2017 Fabiano Antoniani claimed the right to put an end to his life. He was a tetraplegic, blind but sound-minded patient, unable to breathe without a respirator or to eat autonomously. He needed assistance even for the most intimate activities; medicines couldn't sooth his physical pain. Marco Cappato[102] helped him to reach a Swiss hospital where he could commit a physician-assisted suicide. Cappato often tried to draw the public attention to the existing legal vacuum regarding assisted-suicide in Italy. After Antoniani's death, Cappato self-accused of the crime foreseen under art. 580 ICC. In the ordinary case the presiding judge raised the question of the constitutionality of that same provision. The Constitutional Court answered as follows.

The Court adopted an '*ordinanza*' (from now on 'order') which was compared by Italian legal scholars to the German '*Unvereinbarkeitserklärungen*'.[103] In brief, order no. 207/2018 urges the Parliament to adopt rules disciplining assisted-suicide within September 2019. In case of parliamentary inertia, the Court will intervene and issue a decision.

Usually, the Court issues decisions that either sustain or reject the challenge regarding the constitutionality of certain provisions (see again Section 6.5). For the first time in its history, the Court sustained the constitutional challenge concerning art. 580 ICC while not adopting a '*pronuncia di accoglimento*' (i.e. the decision which usually declares a legal provision unconstitutional). Normally, an unconstitutional provision automatically loses effect from the day after the decision's publication.[104] Order no. 207/2018 does not formally declare art. 580 ICC unconstitutional. Nonetheless, as the Court does when it adopts the '*pronunce di accoglimento*', the recent order carefully explained why art. 580 ICC violates the Constitution. Roughly said, the provision is unconstitutional but not yet judicially declared as such.[105] Latter circumstance may intervene only

101 For a recent and detailed analysis of the issue see P. Zicchittu, 'Incostituzionalità differita, sanzione penale e forma di governo', *Diritti fondamentali*, N. 2, (forthcoming), especially para. 3.1.

102 Member of the 'Luca Coscioni Association' (which is engaged in the fight for free end-of-life decisions) and of the 'Partito Radicale'.

103 See N. Fiano, 'Caso Cappato, vuoti di tutela costituzionale. Un anno al Parlamento per colmarli. Riflessioni a caldo a partire dal modello tedesco', *Forum di Quaderni costituzionali*, 25 ottobre 2018, 2018, www.forumcostituzionale.it.

104 According to art. 136 of the Italian Constitution.

105 Therefore, several technical problems may arise in future. E.g. if the Parliament does not intervene, the Court will have no other choice than to declare art. 580 ICC unconstitutional. However, the question is whether the Court is legally obliged to decide in this way – and whether new constitutional judges shall respect the decisions taken by former ones. The destiny of the new tool embodied in the 2018's '*ordinanza*' is not certain; legal scholars hope that the Court's wisdom will face this unknown challenge. For all negative consequences deriving from 2018's order see A. Ruggeri, 'Pilato alla Consulta: decide di non decidere, perlomeno ora … (a margine di un comunicato sul caso Cappato), *Consulta*

in case of parliamentary inactivity. Anyway, until that moment only the judiciary must not apply the provision – while other institutions may comply with it. Legal scholars wonder why the Court adopted such a problematic technique. Given the importance of end-of-life decisions, the Court could have refused to declare immediately unconstitutional art. 580 ICC because of a specific aim. Only a parliamentary debate may carefully regulate the widest framework in which end-of-life issues must be set – and not 'simply' fill the legal vacuum regarding assisted-suicide.

In light of the above mentioned issues, the question is whether the order respects separation of powers or is an unusual example of judicial activism. As the chapter will now delve into, the 2018 order is a new decisional technique which breaks separation of powers for a specific need.

6.7 The new clothes of judicial activism: When the Constitutional Court decides not to decide

The *Cappato* case must be set in the background marking separation of powers. The Italian Constitutional Court is not a third chamber of the Parliament. The Court must respect legislative decisional freedom – even if the latter seems inadequate or mistaken. Judicial review must 'only' avoid violations of the Constitution, bringing back within its framework parliamentary choices. Therefore, legal scholars have opposite views regarding such new technique. Only a few of them believe that it introduces a new equilibrium between judicial review and parliamentary discretion. Most legal scholars think that it severely endangers the separation of powers.[106]

The Court recognizes that time has come to discipline assisted-suicide according to existing constitutional rights and new social expectations (not yet transformed into proper rights). Therefore, the Constitutional Court urges the Parliament to adopt a legislative solution which grounds any end-of-life decision on unrestrained individual self-determination. To achieve said goal, the Court could have adopted other solutions, different from the mentioned order. For that reason, the recent legal debate wonders why the Court chose the latter and not one of the following ones.

For example, the Court could have adopted a '*sentenza di accoglimento*' (i.e. a decision) sustaining the challenge regarding art. 580 ICC. Given that the Court's declaration is definitive and generally applicable, the presiding judge in the ordinary case would have resolved the latter. This same effect would have concerned

Online, No. 3, 26 ottobre 2018, 2018, www.giurcost.org/studi/ruggeri81.pdf, p. 568; A. Ruggieri, 'Venuto alla luce alla Consulta l'ircocervo costituzionale (a margine della ordinanza n. 207 del 2018 sul caso Cappato)', *Consulta Online*, No. 3, 26 ottobre 2018, 2018, www.giurcost.org/studi/ruggeri82.pdf; M. Bignami, (n. 49) http://questionegiustizia.it/articolo/il-caso-cappato-alla-corte-costituzionale-un-ordinanza-ad-incostituzionalita-differita_19-11-2018.php; P. Zicchittu (n. 101), paras 4.–5.1.

106 Respectively M. Bignami (n. 49) and P. Zicchittu (n. 104).

every other case involving art. 580 ICC; Parliament should have enacted other provisions to take the latter's place. Moreover, to reduce the risk of a legislative vacuum due to the declaration of unconstitutionality, the Court could also have adopted a '*sentenza manipolativa*' – i.e. a decision rewriting the provision in order to make it abide by the Constitution. Even a '*sentenza interpretativa di rigetto*' could have been an option (i.e. a decision which rejects the claim that art. 580 ICC is unconstitutional by interpreting the challenged provision in compliance with the Constitution).

Against this background, legal scholars wonder whether the Court adopted such an unusual order because end-of-life decisions are a political matter which must stay out of the Court's reach. The answer is negative.

Substantially, the order declares unconstitutional art. 580 ICC as any usual decision would do. But, given that it is not, for example, a '*sentenza di accoglimento*', the order does not have the effects of such a decision.[107] Furthermore, it does not simply urge parliamentary action. The order points out what the Parliament must regulate, how and when. The Court clearly limits representatives' decisional freedom in a field strictly belonging to the Parliament – i.e. criminal matters.[108] Maybe the latter consideration unveils the real concern of the Court.

Theoretically, the dialogue between the Constitutional Court and the Parliament is founded on loyal cooperation. Separation of powers should assure that sensitive matters stay out of the Court's reach; the Parliament must decide. On the other hand, parliamentary inertia shall not transform separation of powers (or political questions' field) in denial of protection of 'new' rights. In recent years, the latter possibility deeply worried the Court. That's why the Court seems to believe itself to be better equipped than both Houses in rights-oriented constitutional reasoning. Moreover, it seems to think that nowadays only constitutional judges may protect claims such as the one concerning assisted-suicide. However, by urging Parliament to decriminalize conducts which help a patient to commit suicide according to his own free will, the Court nearly trespassed an untouchable limit. Only the Parliament may decide whether a conduct must or not be punished (anyway, as said, the Court is 'only' asking for a conduct's decriminalization). But what might happen if acting within this threshold means denying the individual right to unrestrained self-determination in end-of-life decisions?

Maybe for this reason the Court did not dismiss the case but adopted an order trying to balance two opposite needs. The new technique seems to respect the separation of powers – the Court will decide upon the case only if a democratic solution will not be found. But, as the *Englaro* case shows (see Section 6.6 and footnote 98), it is highly probable that the Parliament will not be able – or want – to decide. Therefore, judicial activism is the only way to transform an assisted-suicide claim into a proper right.

107 See again (n. 104).

108 P. Zicchittu (n. 104), especially nos 3–3.2.

The threshold between political and judicial decision is thin. The real question is, whether in cases related to the 'new rights'[109] contemporary constitutionalism gives the last word only to one institution. According to the *Cappato* case, when Parliaments fail to decide, strongly judicially guided dialogue is the answer. However, such technique risks opening the gate to absolute supremacy of the judiciary. Therefore, even if the Court's intention is a good one, this kind of judicial activism must go along with judicial self-restraint.

The Constitutional Court tried to sow an old field with a new seed. But, if the political and the judicial must be grounded in the superiority of rights, both must be set back in principles protecting individual liberties for decades – as the separation of powers does. From now on, only this path may assure that justice and law will be served.

References

AaVv. (Eds), 'Questioni di fine vita. Dalla legge 22 dicembre 2017, n. 219, alla ordinanza della Corte costituzionale nel caso Cappato', *Giurisprudenza penale*, N. 2019-1bis, 2019, www.giurisprudenzapenale.com.

U. Adamo, 'Le nuove norme integrative per i giudizi davanti alla Corte costituzionale: la via principale', *Rivista AIC*, 4 novembre 2011, 2011, www.rivistaaic.it.

A. Anzon-Demmig, 'Un tentativo coraggioso ma improprio di far valere l'incostituzionalità della legge per le elezioni politiche (e per coprire una 'zona franca' del giudizio di costituzionalità)', *Rivista AIC*, No. 3, 12 luglio 2013, www.rivistaaic.it.

P. Barile, 'Potere costituente', in *Novissimo Digesto Italiano*, Vol. 13, UTET, 1966, pp. 443–450.

P. Barile, 'Potere costituente', in P. Barile (Ed.), *Scritti di Diritto costituzionale*, Cedam, 1967, pp. 592–611.

R. E. Barkow, 'More Supreme than Court? The Fall of the Political Question Doctrine and the Rise of Judicial Supremacy', *Columbia Law Review*, Vol. 102, No. 2, March 2002, pp. 237–336.

R. Bellamy, 'Bringing Together Norms and Forms: The Democratic Constitution', in R. Bellamy, *Political Constitutionalism. A Republican Defence of the Constitutionality of Democracy*, Cambridge, UK, Cambridge University Press, 2007a, pp. 209–259.

R. Bellamy, *Constitutionalism*, last update 30 July 2019, www.britannica.com/topic/constitutionalism.

R. Bellamy, 'Constitutionalism and Democracy', in R. Bellamy, *Political Constitutionalism. A Republican Defence of the Constitutionality of Democracy*, Cambridge, Cambridge University Press, 2007b, pp. 90–142.

R. Bellamy, 'Introduction', in R. Bellamy, *Constitutionalism*, last update 30 July 2019, www.britannica.com/topic/constitutionalism.

109 E. Lamarque, 'L'attuazione giudiziaria dei diritti costituzionali', *Quaderni costituzionali*, N. 2 (giugno 2008), 2008, pp. 269–296.

R. Bellamy, 'The Norms of Political Constitutionalism: Non-domination and Political Equality', in Idem, *Political Constitutionalism. A Republican Defence of the Constitutionality of Democracy*, Cambridge University Press, 2007c, pp. 145–175.

M. Bignami, 'Il caso Cappato alla Corte costituzionale: un'ordinanza ad incostituzionalità differita', *Questione giustizia*, 19 novembre 2018, 2018, http://questionegiustizia.it.

N. Bobbio, *L'età dei diritti*, Einaudi, 2014.

B. Brancati, 'Le questioni della Cassazione sulla legge elettorale: una vicenda 'imbarazzante' per la Corte costituzionale? Nota a Cass., I sez. civ., n. 12060/2013 del 17 maggio 2013', *Consulta Online*, Vol. 2013, 12 novembre 2013, 2013, www.giurcost.org/studi/Brancati1.pdf.

M. Cartabia, 'La Corte costituzionale nella nuova età dei diritti', *Rivista Il Mulino*, Vol. 466, Fasc. 2 (marzo-aprile), 2013, pp. 364–371.

M. Cartabia, 'When Rights are Controversial, are Dialogues between Courts Still Enough? Editorial', *Italian Journal of Public Law*, No. I, 2010, pp. 1–5.

A. Cerri, *Corso di giustizia costituzionale*, Giuffré, 2008.

P. Craig, 'Political Constitutionalism and the Judicial Role: A Response', *International Journal of Constitutional Law*, Vol. 9, No. 1, 2011, pp. 112–131.

L. D'Andrea, 'Il progetto di riforma tra Costituzione-atto e Costituzione-processo', in AaVv (Eds), *La riforma costituzionale*, Cedam, 1993, p. 93 ff.

M. Dogliani, R. Bin & R. Martinez Dalmau, *Il potere costituente (Lezioni del corso di Alta Formazione in diritto costituzionale 2017)*, Editoriale Scientifica, 2017.

R. Fattibene, 'A chi spetta la 'disponibilità della vita'? La disciplina del fine-vita come occasione di riflessione sulla partecipazione democratica nelle questioni biogiuridiche', *Osservatorio costituzionale*, No. 3, 4 dicembre 2018, 2018, www.osservatorio.aic.

N. Fiano, 'Caso Cappato, vuoti di tutela costituzionale. Un annoal Parlamento per colmarli. Riflessioni a caldo a partire dal modello tedesco', *Forum di Quaderni costituzionali*, 25 ottobre 2018, 2018, www.forumcostituzionale.it.

O. P. Field, 'The Doctrine of Political Question in the Federal Courts', *Minnesota Law Review*, Vol. 8, 1924, pp. 485–512.

M. Fioravanti, *Costituzionalismo: percorsi della storia e tendenze attuali*, GLF ed. Laterza, 2009.

M. Goldoni, 'Constitutional Reasoning according to Political Constitutionalism', *German Law Journal*, Vol. 14, No. 8, 2013, pp. 1053–1076.

M. Goldoni, 'Two Internal Critiques of Political Constitutionalism', *International Journal of Constitutional Law*, Vol. 10, No. 4, 2012, pp. 926–949.

M. Goldoni, 'What is Political Constitutionalism', *Diritto e questioni pubbliche*, Vol. 10, 2010, pp. 337–360.

T. Groppi (con la collaborazione di C. Meoli), *Le grandi decisioni della Corte costituzionale italiana*, Editoriale Scientifica-ESI, 2010.

T. L. Grove, 'The Lost History of the Political Question Doctrine', *New York University Law Review*, Vol. 90, 2015, pp. 1908–1974.

C. A. Jemolo, *Che cos'è la Costituzione? Con un'introduzione di G. Zagrebelsky*, Donzelli, 2008.

A. Junji, 'Constitutionalism as a Political Culture', *Pacific Rim Law & Journal Policy Association*, Vol. 11, No. 3, 2002, pp. 561–576.

L. D. Kramer, *The People Themselves: Popular Constitutionalism and Judicial Review*, New York OUP, 2004.

E. Lamarque, 'Interpreting Statutes in Conformity with the Constitution: The Role of the Constitutional Court and Ordinary Judges', *Italian Journal of Public Law*, No. I, 2010, pp. 87–120.
E. Lamarque, 'L'attuazione giudiziaria dei diritti costituzionali', *Quaderni costituzionali*, No. 2 (giugno 2008), 2008, pp. 269–296.
E. Lamarque, 'Le nuove norme integrative per i giudizi davanti alla Corte costituzionale', *Diritto e Società*, No. 1, 2009, pp. 113–145.
F. Lanchester (Ed.), *Costantino Mortati: potere costituente e limiti alla revisione costituzionale*, Atti del Convegno, Roma, 14 dicembre 2015, Wolter Kluwers-Cedam, 2017.
F. Lanchester, 'La Costituzione del 1948 e l'organo di garanzia esterno', *Il Politico*, Vol. 74, No. 3, 2009, pp. 51–66.
G. Longo, Controllo di legittimità e monito di sovranità: per una teoria politica della giustizia costituzionale, Aracne, 2012.
C. Mortati, *La Costituzione in senso materiale. Ristampa inalterata con una premessa di G. Zagrebelsky*, Giuffré, 1998.
C. Mortati, *Problemi di politica costituzionale*, Giuffrè, 1972.
V. Onida, 'La Costituzione dal 1948 al 2008', *Il Politico*, Vol. 74, No. 3, 2009, pp. 22–32.
V. Onida, 'The Constitution Yesterday and Today', *Italian Journal of Public Law*, Vol. 4, No. 1, 2012, pp. 15–37.
L. Pegoraro, 'Giustizia costituzionale', in G. Morbidelli, L. Pegoraro, A. Rinella & M. Volpi (Eds), *Diritto Pubblico Comparato*, Giappichelli, 2016, pp. 547–600.
L. Pegoraro, *Le sentenze-indirizzo della Corte costituzionale italiana*, Cedam, 1984.
I. Pellizzone, 'Aiuto al suicidio, dal Codice Rocco alla Carta costituzionale alla Convenzione Europea dei Diritti dell'Uomo', *Giurisprudenza penale*, 17 settembre 2018, 2018, www.giurisprudenzapenale.com
C. Pinelli, 'Constitutional Reasoning and Political Deliberation', *German Law Journal*, Vol. 14, No. 8, 2013, pp. 1171–1182.
R. Romboli (Ed.), *L'accesso alla giustizia costituzionale: carattere, limiti, prospettive di un modello*, Edizioni Scientifiche Italiane–ESI, 2006.
R. Romboli, 'La costituzionalità della legge elettorale 270/05: la Cassazione introduce, in via giurisprudenziale, un ricorso quasi diretto alla Corte costituzionale?', *Foro italiano*, Vol. 138, Parte I, Fasc. 6, 2013, 1831–1838.
E. Rossi, 'La Corte costituzionale e la legge elettorale: un quadro in tre atti e dall'epilogo incerto', *Federalismi*, 5 giugno 2013, 2013, www.federalismi.it.
C.E. Rostow, 'The Democratic Character of Judicial Review', *Harvard Law Review*, Vol. 66, No. 2, 1952, pp. 193–224.
A. Ruggeri, 'Corte costituzionale e Parlamento tra aperture del 'modello' e fluidità dell'esperienza', in A. Ruggeri & G. Silvestri (Eds), *Corte costituzionale e Parlamento. Profili problematici e ricostruttivi*, Giuffré, 2000, pp. 1–78.
A. Ruggeri, 'Pilato alla Consulta: decide di non decidere, perlomeno ora … (a margine di un comunicato sul caso Cappato)', *Consulta Online*, Fasc. 3, 26 ottobre 2018, 2018, www.giurcost.org/studi/ruggeri81.pdf.
A. Ruggeri, 'Venuto alla luce alla Consulta l'ircocervo costituzionale (a margine della ordinanza n. 207 del 2018 sul caso Cappato)', *Consulta Online*, Fasc. 3, 26 ottobre 2018, 2018, www.giurcost.org/studi/ruggeri82.pdf.

A. Santuosso & P. Belloli, 'Paradossi nel procedimento Cappato. Tre aporie generate dall'art. 580 c.p. a proposito di aiuto al suicidio', *Giurisprudenza penale*, 13 giugno 2018, 2018, www.giurisprudenzapenale.com.

P. Scott, '(Political) Constitutions and (Political) Constitutionalism', *German Law Journal*, Vol. 14, No. 12, 2014, pp. 2158–2183.

G. Silvestri, *Dal potere ai principi. Libertà ed eguaglianza nel costituzionalismo contemporaneo*, Laterza, 2009.

A. Spadaro, 'Dalla Costituzione come 'atto' (puntuale nel tempo) alla Costituzione come 'processo' (storico). Ovvero della continua evoluzione del parametro costituzionale attraverso i giudizi di costituzionalità', *Quaderni costituzionali*, No. 3, 1998, pp. 343–422.

M. Tushnet, *Taking the Constitution Away from the Courts*, Princeton, NJ, Princeton UP, 1999.

G. Volpe, *Il costituzionalismo del Novecento*, Laterza, 2000.

J. Waldron, 'The Core of the Case Against Judicial Review', *Yale Law Journal*, Vol. 115, 2006, pp. 1346–1360.

M. F. Weston, 'Political Questions', *Harvard Law Review*, Vol. 38, No. 3, 1959, pp. 296–333.

G. Zagrebelsky, *Intorno alla legge: il diritto come dimensione del vivere comune*, Einaudi, 2009.

G. Zagrebelsky, *Il diritto mite. Legge, diritti, giustizia*, Einaudi, 1997.

G. Zagrebelsky, *La legge e la sua giustizia: tre capitoli di giustizia costituzionale*, Il Mulino, 2008.

G. Zagrebelsky, *Principî e voti: la Corte costituzionale e la politica*, Einaudi, 2005.

P. Zicchittu, Incostituzionalità differita, sanzione penale e forma di governo', *Diritti fondamentali*, No. 2, 2019 (forthcoming).

P. Zicchittu, *Le zone franche del potere legislativo*, Giappichelli, 2017.

P. Zicchittu, 'The Italian Way to the Political Question', *Italian Journal of Public Law*, No. I, 2015, pp. 222–262.

Part III

Courts, constitution-making, and the separation between constituent and constituted powers

7 The negative legislator

On Kelsen's idea of a constitutional court

Paul Yowell

7.1 Introduction

In the post-war period of constitutional reconstruction in Europe, the US Supreme Court fired the moral imagination of constitutional framers. Hans Kelsen, however, inspired the basic institutional structure for the constitutional courts that were established across Europe. From 1945 to the mid-1990s, most European countries adopted systems of constitutional review that are (i) *centralized* in a single constitutional court, which is (ii) *separate* from the ordinary judiciary, and (iii) decides questions of constitutional law *abstractly* rather than by resolving a concrete case. The constitutional court created by the 1920 Austrian Constitution was an early model of this institutional structure. Kelsen personally drafted the key constitutional provisions, served as a justice on the court for a decade, and defended this model of constitutional adjudication in influential theoretical writings. Many scholars have termed this the 'Kelsenian' model and contrasted it to the 'American' model of judicial review. In the latter, every court has the power to engage in constitutional review but only in the course of deciding an ordinary case; thus review is *decentralized*, *concrete*, and *integrated* within the ordinary court system.

The purpose of this paper is to spell out and critically evaluate Kelsen's proposed model in light of a comparative study of the approaches taken by different legal systems. Although most European systems of judicial review have broadly followed Kelsen's institutional model, they generally depart from Kelsen's articulated view of the role and operation of a constitutional court in two significant respects. As Section 7.1 will show, European constitutional courts typically have jurisdiction to enforce a bill of rights, as in the American model. Kelsen opposed this on the ground that constitutional courts do not have the legitimacy to interpret and apply vague moral principles in contravening the decisions of democratic legislatures. Section 2 then introduces Kelsen's idea of a 'negative legislator', a proposal about how to conceive the role of constitutional courts within a system of separation of powers. This idea undergirds Kelsen's opposition to enforceability of rights, and it constitutes the second difference between European constitutional courts and the American model, which is considered in Section 7.3. As that section will show, Kelsen thought that the process of nullifying an unconstitutional law should be conceived in the same way as legislative repeal of a statute, and follow a similar mechanism. A determination of unconstitutionality should take effect *ex nunc*, from the moment of judgment forward, generally without retroactive effects. A judgment of unconstitutionality should thus be understood as a *constitutive* act, not a *declaratory* one. Kelsen structured the remedial mechanism of the Austrian Constitutional Court in this way. In his theoretical writings he criticized the alternative of treating unconstitutional laws as void *ab initio*, wherein a court that determines a law to be unconstitutional merely recognizes its invalidity and declares it. The unconstitutional law is considered to be void *ex tunc*, from the time of its creation. This is the formal doctrine in the US and the standard view in systems that follow the American model. The approach has also been adopted in Germany, and is reflected to some degree in several other continental systems. In both the American model and European systems, courts have devised techniques to avoid, at least in some cases, giving full retroactive effects after declaring a statute unconstitutional.

Section 7.5 shows that differences over how to deal with unconstitutional laws are driven in part by basic positions in legal theory. Kelsen's proposal for the annulment of unconstitutional laws *ex nunc* depends on conceiving the constitutional court as part of the *legislative* rather than the *judicial* arm of the state. It is on this basis that he designs the remedial mechanism of the Austrian Constitutional Court. I will argue that there is much good sense in Kelsen's model, when considered as a practical proposal for constitutional design, in comparison to the alternative of the void *ab initio* theory. Kelsen confuses the argument in favor of his model, however, by presenting it, at times, as a kind of conceptual or logical necessity. In arguing against the void *ab initio* approach, Kelsen frequently writes as if it is simply the product of theoretical or conceptual confusion. He fails to acknowledge clearly that the void *ab initio* theory is an option available to constitutional framers, and indeed one that better fits with standard accounts of adjudication. His argument would be more coherent if he had clearly acknowledged that considering a constitutional court to be a 'negative legislator' – as part of the legislative arm of the state – is not a conceptual necessity but a choice of constitutional design, and one that needs to be justified through practical reasons.

7.2 Kelsen on constitutional rights

European systems of judicial review of legislation generally follow the Kelsenian model, with review centralized in a single constitutional court. The court is not at the apex of the ordinary court system, as is typical for a supreme court in the American model, but separated from the ordinary system. The court usually resolves questions of constitutionality in the abstract, that is, without resolving a concrete case, though the question may be referred to the court from a concrete case by a court in the ordinary system. The most immediately obvious difference between Kelsen's view of the role of a constitutional court and many European systems involves the adjudication of abstract moral rights. Most European constitutional courts have the power to enforce a bill of rights, as in the American model. Kelsen opposed giving the constitutional court power to enforce principles formulated in abstract moral language, that is, those which make 'an appeal to the ideals of "justice", "freedom", "equality", "equity", "decency", and so on'.[1] He thought that such terms were legally 'vacuous', providing no determinate guidance to judges. They could serve as political norms, directing legislative organs in their creation of law, and law-making is rightly seen as a process that specifies vague principles into positive law.[2] But it would be 'highly dangerous' to make the principles a basis for constitutional adjudication, in particular for review of the constitutionality of statutes.[3]

> What the majority of the judges on the court regard as just may completely contradict what the majority of the state's inhabitants hold to be just, and it undoubtedly contradicts what the majority of the parliament that enacted the statute in question to be just.
>
> It is self-evident that it cannot be the purpose of a constitution to make every statute enacted by parliament dependent, through the use of an ill-defined and highly ambiguous word like "justice", or some other equally vacuous term, on the free discretion of a college whose members are as arbitrarily chosen, from a political point of view, as the members of a constitutional court.[4]

The arbitrary character of such an assignment arises from the fact that judges of the constitutional court are to be appointed on the basis of legal expertise, not political acumen or wisdom. Kelsen concluded that such a 'shift of power from parliament to an extra-parliamentary institution … is certainly not intended by the constitution'; it would 'concede to the constitutional court a fullness of power that must be regarded as altogether intolerable'.[5] To prevent such a transfer of power, Kelsen argued that a constitution must 'abstain from all phraseology of this kind'.[6] In other words, it should not have a bill of rights in the way that they are usually worded.

Despite Kelsen's warnings, nations that have otherwise generally followed Kelsen have also adopted a bill of rights. One explanation for this is that the framers who established the courts did not have Kelsen's willingness to trust the democratic system. The first wave of constitutional courts came after the fall of

1 H. Kelsen, 'On the Nature and Development of Constitutional Adjudication' in L. Vinx (Ed.), *The Guardian of the Constitution: Hans Kelsen and Carl Schmitt on the Limits of Constitutional Law*, Cambridge, Cambridge University Press, 2015, p. 60.
2 Ibid. p. 59.
3 Ibid. p. 60.
4 Ibid.
5 Ibid. p. 61.
6 Ibid.

fascist regimes in Germany, Italy, and Spain, and the second wave came after the fall of the Berlin Wall and communist regimes in eastern and central Europe. The Kelsenian court was seen as a ready-made model for keeping the legislature within constitutional limits. The addition of the bill of rights was seen as a way of building in a check against a possible lack of popular commitment to the values expressed therein.[7]

7.3 The negative legislature

Kelsen's opposition to a justiciable bill of rights is linked to his general view of the constitutional court as a 'negative legislator'. Kelsen thought that a constitutional court was fundamentally different from an ordinary court because its decision-making results in 'general norms'.

> If a "court" is endowed with the competence to annul a statute, it is thereby authorized to enact a general norm, since the annulment of a statute has the same general character as the enactment of a statute. The annulment of a statute, after all, is nothing but the inverse of enactment. The annulment of statutes is therefore itself *a legislative function*, and a court empowered to annul statutes is itself *an organ of legislative power*.[8]

Kelsen saw adjudication as a process resulting in the creation of norms, but only 'individual norms', which were used to resolve a particular case. 'Legislation creates general norms'.[9] The constitutional court must be conceived to be part of the legislative branch because of its power to annul statutes. This view of the court was the necessary answer to objections to constitutional adjudication on the ground of separation of powers.

> One should concede, at the outset, that the annulment of an act of legislation by an organ other than the legislative organ itself amounts to an interference with the legislative power, as we normally tend to put the matter. But we can see how problematic this whole argumentation is, once we consider the fact that the organ tasked with the annulment of unconstitutional statutes, even if it is referred to as a "court", and even if by virtue of its "independence", it is a court from an organizational point of view, is nevertheless, as a result of its function, engaged in an activity that makes into something more than a *mere court*.[10]

7 See M. Köpcke, *A Short History of Legal Validity and Invalidity: Foundations of Private and Public Law*, Cambridge, Intersentia, 2019, Ch. 9 III.
8 Kelsen (n. 1) p. 46 (emphasis added).
9 Ibid.
10 Ibid. pp. 45–46.

Although the constitutional court was not a 'mere court', and was to be considered part of the legislative branch in an operational sense, it was nevertheless not like the legislature in another sense. The 'positive' legislator is bound only by general principles and has a large area of freedom and flexibility – within the bound of those principles – in fashioning statutory norms.[11] The constitutional court, however, does not have such an extensive realm of discretionary judgment, in keeping with its lack of political accountability. The judgment of the constitutional court is to be within the narrower bounds of specific laws, as with ordinary courts. In this way, the court as a 'negative legislator' is distinguished from the 'positive legislator' with a wider remit. But if a constitutional court is given the power to enforce a bill of rights, it will have similar wide bounds of discretion as the legislature.

7.4 Unconstitutional laws: voidable or void *ab initio*?

Kelsen's recognition of the constitutional court as a negative legislator reflects the close attention he paid to the technical issues surrounding the abrogation of statutes by constitutional organs, and to the important difference between treating a constitutionally defective norm as (i) voidable (or annullable) and (ii) void (or null) *ab initio*. When he writes that the 'annulment of statutes' is a 'legislative function', he has a particular idea of what annulment involves. In his 1942 article 'Judicial Review of Legislation: A Comparative Study of the Austrian and the American Constitution', he states that is 'impossible to consider a statute enacted by the constitutional legislator as absolutely null or "void *ab initio*"'.[12] Kelsen appeals to what seems to be a view about what is conceptually possible within a legal system:

> Within a system of positive law there is no absolute nullity. It is not possible to characterize an act which presents itself as a legal act as null *a priori* (void *ab initio*). Only annulment of such an act is possible; the act is not void, it is only voidable. For the statement that an act is null is not possible without another statement, answering the question of who is competent to establish the nullity of the act. Since the legal order – to avoid anarchy – empowers certain authorities to establish whether an act is null, this establishment always has a constitutive, not a declaratory character. The act is "null" only if the competent authority declares it null. ... Before this declaration the act is not null, for being "null" means legally non-existent. *And the act must legally exist, if it can be the object of a judgment by an authority.*[13]

11 Ibid. pp. 47.

12 H. Kelsen, 'Judicial Review of Legislation: A Comparative Study of the Austrian and the American Constitution', *Journal of Politics*, Vol. 4, No. 2, 1942, pp. 183–200, p. 190.

13 Ibid. p. 186 (emphasis added).

In the article Kelsen also describes the system set up by the 1920 Austrian Constitution, which tracks this theoretical account on the practical plane, and the key provisions of which Kelsen personally drafted.[14] The power to review the constitutionality of statues was centralized in the Austrian Constitutional Court, and it was generally invoked upon referral by another court of the constitutional question. The Constitutional Court had the power to annul unconstitutional statutes, with the annulment taking effect from the date of judgment forward. The 'annulling decision of the court was in principle to be effective only *ex nunc*', Kelsen said, but there was one exception: the annulled statute would not be applied in the concrete case that prompted the referral to the court.[15] The annulment would have no further retroactive effect on prior cases decided or actions taken pursuant to the constitutionally defective statute. The Constitution further provided that the Court could delay the effectiveness of a decision for up to one year. If it did so, and the underlying case that prompted the referral was decided in the interim period, then it would be decided in accordance with the statute that had been determined to be unconstitutional.[16] A decision by the Court that a statute is unconstitutional thus annuls the statute for the concrete case (though not when the effectiveness of the judgment is delayed) and 'generally for all future cases'; the statute 'cease[s] to exist' as soon as the decision comes into force.[17] Kelsen described the judgments that the Court makes as *constitutive* (not declaratory) and as having 'the same character as a statute which abrogate[s] another statute';[18] in other words, the Court's power is essentially one of repeal. This is another important sense in which the Court is a 'negative legislator'.

In Section 7.5, I will show that Kelsen's arguments that unconstitutional statutes are voidable rather than void *ab initio* are ultimately *practical* arguments about how a constitutional system should be established rather than theoretical arguments about what is conceptually possible within a legal system. But first I will contrast Kelsen's practical approach – which is realized in the 1920 Austrian Constitution – with the approach in the American model and other systems.

In the major common law jurisdictions with judicial review of legislation – the United States, Canada, Australia, and Ireland – the generally accepted, formal theory is that unconstitutional statutes are void *ab initio*. The common law approach is traceable to *Marbury v Madison*.[19] The US Constitution is silent on

14 See also S. Lagi, 'Hans Kelsen and the Austrian Constitutional Court (1918–1929)', *Coherencia*, Vol. 19, No. 16, 2012, pp. 273–295.

15 Kelsen (n. 12), p. 187.

16 Ibid. 'This retroactive force, exceptionally granted to the judgement of annulment, was a technical necessity, because without it the authorities charged with the application of the law (that is, the judges of the Supreme Court and of the Administrative Court respectively) would not have had an immediate and consequently sufficiently cogent interest to cause the intervention of the Constitutional Court.' Ibid. p. 196.

17 Ibid. p. 186.

18 Ibid.

19 5 US 137 (1803).

the status of unconstitutional laws as well as the power of judicial review of legislation. In *Marbury*, Chief Justice John Marshall argued for judicial review on several grounds,[20] but his central appeal was to the nature of a constitution and its hierarchical superiority over other laws:

> Certainly all those who have framed written Constitutions contemplate them as forming the fundamental and paramount law of the nation, and consequently the *theory* of every such government *must* be that an act of the Legislature repugnant to the Constitution is *void*.[21]

To treat such a legislative act as binding on courts would, Marshall argues, run counter not only to the basic idea of a written constitution but also to 'one of the fundamental principles of our society'.[22] An unconstitutional statute is – 'must' be – 'entirely void' and 'not law'.[23]

Marshall's line of reasoning has been broadly followed in common law constitutional thought ever since, though with some qualification and dissent. In Canada and Ireland, the void *ab initio* doctrine was articulated by courts as an interpretation of constitutional provisions. The Canadian Constitution Act 1982, s. 52(1), provides that laws contrary to the constitution are 'of no force or effect,' and the Supreme Court has clarified that such laws 'are, *and always have been*, invalid and of no force or effect'.[24] The Constitution of Ireland, art. 15, provides that laws repugnant to the Constitution are 'invalid'; this has been interpreted by the Supreme Court to mean that an unconstitutional statute 'is to be deemed null and *void from the moment of its purported enactment*'.[25] One of the clearest statements of the void *ab initio* theory is by the High Court of Australia in *South Australia v Commonwealth* (1942):

> Common expressions, such as: "The courts have declared a statute invalid", sometimes lead to misunderstanding. A pretended law made in excess of power is not and never has been a law at all. Anybody in the country is entitled to disregard it. Naturally he will feel safer if he has a decision of a court in his favor – but such a decision is not an element which produces invalidity in any law. The law is not valid until a court pronounces against it – and thereafter invalid. If it is beyond power it is invalid *ab initio*.[26]

20 These included the oath that judges take to support the Constitution and the clause in art. 6 providing that laws made 'in pursuance' of the Constitution are supreme over state laws.
21 5 US 137 (1803), 177 (emphasis added).
22 5 US 137 (1803).
23 5 US 137 (1803), 177–178.
24 Reference re Manitoba Language Rights [1985] 1 SCR 721, 767 (emphasis added).
25 Murphy v Attorney General [1982] IR 241, 309 (emphasis added).
26 (1942) 65 CLR 373.

In the US the void *ab initio* theory was the prevailing approach in the late 19th and early 20th centuries. The classic statement is in *Norton v Shelby County* (1886).[27] Echoing Marshall's dictum in *Marbury* that a statute contrary to the constitution is 'not law', the Supreme Court held in *Norton*: '[A]n unconstitutional act is not a law; it confers no rights; it imposes no duties; it is, in legal contemplation, as inoperative as though it had never been passed'.[28] The academic orthodoxy at this time was expressed by Thomas Cooley:

> When a statute is adjudged to be unconstitutional, it is as if it had never been. Rights cannot be built up under it; contracts which depend upon it for their consideration are void; it constitutes a protection to no one who has acted under it, and no one can be punished for having refused obedience to it before the decision was made.[29]

A few courts, however, rejected the void *ab initio* theory. The leading statement in opposition to the view of the US Supreme Court in *Norton* is by Chief Justice Butler of Connecticut Supreme Court in *State v Carroll* (1871):

> Every law of the legislature, however repugnant to the constitution, has not only the appearance and semblance of authority, but *the force of law*. It [is] to all intents and purposes law, until questioned in and set aside by the courts. This principle is essential to the very existence of order in society.[30]

Butler rejected the theory that an unconstitutional law is void *ab initio*,[31] and he endorsed the view, which Kelsen would later propound, that a judgment that a law is unconstitutional is constitutive rather than declaratory.[32] Although most courts followed *Norton*, some cited Justice Butler with approval and refused to apply the void *ab initio* theory. The different views are captured by these contradictory statements made, respectively, by courts in New Jersey and Michigan in 1890 and in 1902:

27 118 US 425 (1886).
28 Ibid. 426.
29 T. Cooley, *A Treatise on the Constitutional Limitations Which Rest Upon the Legislative Power of the States of the American Union*, 7th edn, New York, Little, Brown & Co Publishers, 1903, pp. 382–383.
30 38 Conn. 449, 472 (1871) (emphasis added). This case concerned a judge appointed to office under a law later declared unconstitutional. Justice Butler held that the judge's decisions had legal effect as a *de facto* officer, and considered a long line of cases on this topic, some of which concerned constitutional irregularities while others considered broader questions of illegal appointment. His reasoning, however, did not rely only on the traditional doctrine regarding *de facto* officers.
31 Ibid. 472–473.
32 Ibid.

> An unconstitutional statute is not merely blank paper. The solemn act of the Legislature is a fact to be reckoned with.[33]
>
> [An unconstitutional act] is of no more force or validity than a piece of blank paper, and is utterly void.[34]

The void *ab initio* approach presents obvious practical problems, not least with regard to its potential for retroactive effects. The problem is particularly acute with long-standing statutes that have been relied on by individuals and public official over decades. In many cases it is practically impossible or enormously undesirable to reverse past judgments and transactions made pursuant to the putative statute.

Because of this potential for harsh and undesirable effects, the US Supreme Court eventually began to question the void *ab initio* doctrine. In *Chicot County Drainage District v Baxter State Bank* (1940), the Court cited *Norton* and cast doubt on the proposition that an unconstitutional law is as inoperative as if it had never existed:

> [S]uch broad statements as to the effect of a determination of unconstitutionality must be taken with qualifications. The actual existence of a statute, prior to such a determination, is an operative fact and may have consequences which cannot justly be ignored. ... The effect of the subsequent ruling as to invalidity may have to be considered in various aspects – with respect to particular relations, individual and corporate, and particular conduct, private and official. ... These questions are among the most difficult of those which have engaged the attention of courts, state and federal, and it is manifest from numerous decisions that *an all-inclusive statement of a principle of absolute retroactive invalidity cannot be justified*.[35]

In a general discussion of retroactivity in *Linkletter v Walker* (1965),[36] the Court connected *Norton*'s void *ab initio* theory to the 'Blackstonian' view that judges only have the power to declare and expound existing law, which the Court considered to be superseded by the 'Austinian' view that judges sometimes make law.[37] The US courts moved generally toward adopting a form of balancing test to determine whether to impose retroactive invalidity, considering reliance

33 Allison v Corker, 67 NJL 596 (1902).
34 Seneca Min. Co. v Secretary of State 82 Mich. 573 (1890) (Mich. Supreme Court).
35 308 US 371, 374 (1940).
36 381 US 618 (1965). This case did not deal directly with an unconstitutional statute but with the problem of retroactivity more generally. In the landmark case of Mapp v Ohio 367 US 643 (1961), the Court held that illegally seized evidence must be excluded from criminal trials, but in Linkletter the Court declined to apply the exclusionary rule to cases decided prior to Mapp.
37 Linkletter, 381 US 618 (1965) at 624.

interests, and looking to 'the prior history of the rule in question, its purpose and effect, and whether retrospective operation will further or retard its operation'.[38]

By 1973, the Supreme Court suggested, in *Lemon v Kurtzman*, that *Norton*'s void *ab initio* theory had been abandoned,[39] and it has been suggested that *Lemon* 'all but overruled' *Norton*.[40] The void *ab initio* theory, however, continues to be applied by some courts in some areas, including criminal statutes. In *Ex Parte Chance* (2014), for example, a Texas court granted a writ of *habeas corpus* that the applicant sought after the statute under which he was convicted was held unconstitutional in another case.[41] Although the applicant did not challenge the constitutionality of the statute in his original trial, the court granted the writ, stating that 'an unconstitutional law is void' and 'cannot be a legal cause of imprisonment', adding that it 'is void for all comers, those who have already been convicted of it before it was declared void, as well as those prosecuted under it after it had been declared void'.[42] The tension in the case law is reflected in a standard treatise that asserts in successive sections (i) the void *ab initio* theory as a general rule and (ii) the limitation principle of *Chicot County* as an exception to the rule.[43]

The US Supreme Court has never formally renounced the underlying theory that unconstitutional statutes are invalid from the time of the enactment, but the Court (like lower courts) has a strong tendency to mitigate the retroactive effects of the void *ab initio* theory. A similar pattern of development can be observed in other common law jurisdictions. As seen above, Ireland, Canada, and Australia have all embraced the void *ab initio* theory. I will now analyze cases in Ireland and Canada that show the reasoning behind this embrace, touching also on dissenting views, and show that when these jurisdictions encountered practical problems of retroactivity as in the US, they likewise responded by developing techniques to mitigate these problems.

38 Ibid. 629.

39 Lemon v Kurtzman (1973) 411 U.S. 192, 199 ('However appealing the logic of *Norton* may have been in the abstract, its abandonment reflected our recognition that statutory or even judge-made rules of law are hard facts on which people must rely in making decisions and in shaping their conduct').

40 E. F. Plave, 'Phenomenon of Antique Laws: Can a State Revive Old Abortion Laws in a New Era?', *George Washington Law Review*, Vol. 58, No. 1, 1989, pp. 111–24, 118.

41 Ex parte Chance (2014) 439 SW3d 918 (Tex. Crim. App.)

42 Ibid. 921.

43 See 'Constitutional Law' in American Jurisprudence, 2d, Minnesota, West Publishing, 2016 edn, ss 195–196. Section 195 states the void *ab initio* theory, citing Norton and similar cases: 'The general rule is that an unconstitutional statute, whether federal or state, though having the form and name of law, is in reality no law but is *wholly void and ineffective for any purpose*' (emphasis added). Section 196, citing Chicot County and similar cases, states: 'Though a statute declared unconstitutional is unenforceable, *it is not wholly without effect*; the existence of the statute prior to that declaration is an operative fact and may have consequences that cannot justly be ignored' (emphasis added).

In Ireland the leading case is *Murphy v Attorney General* (1982), where the Irish Supreme Court held that a provision in income tax law unconstitutionally discriminated against married taxpayers, who were required to pay more than couples merely cohabiting.[44] Henchy J construed the constitutional provision that laws repugnant to it are 'invalid'[45] to mean void *ab initio*:

> [The unconstitutional law] is to be deemed null and void from the moment of its purported enactment, no less than if it had emanated from a person or body with no power of legislation. In my judgment, the constitutional disposition of the powers of the State in this respect falls into line with the general principle that, when a constitution or a constitutional statute gives a specifically confined power of legislation to a legislature, laws found to have been enacted in excess of that delegation are *ultra vires* and therefore void *ab initio*. This is a principle which is inherent in the nature of such limited powers, but it is unequivocally spelled out in some constitutions and constitutional statutes.[46]

He explicitly rejected the argument, raised in dissent, that unconstitutional laws are merely voidable, and spelled out the consequences regarding retroactive effect:

> [T]he condemned provision will *normally* provide no legal justification for any acts done or left undone, or for transactions undertaken in pursuance of it; and the person damnified by the operation of the invalid provision will normally be accorded by the Courts all permitted and necessary redress.[47]

The term *normally* is crucial, because simultaneously with propounding the void *ab initio* theory, the Court adopted a principle of limitation or mitigation. Reasoning similarly to the US Supreme Court in *Chicot County*, and citing that case, Henchy J wrote:

> For a variety of reasons, the law recognizes that in certain circumstances, no matter how unfounded in law certain conduct may have been, no matter how unwarranted its operation in a particular case, what has happened has happened and cannot, or should not, be undone.[48]

44 Murphy v Attorney General [1982] IR 241.

45 Article 15 provides that any law 'repugnant to this Constitution ... shall, but to the extent only of such repugnancy, be invalid'.

46 Murphy (n. 84), 309–310.

47 Ibid. 310 (emphasis added).

48 Ibid. 313.

He declined to propose any general standard as to when the limiting principle should be activated, but indicated that a variety of doctrines, such as *res judicata* or waiver, could counteract what would otherwise be the retroactive effects of declaring a statute unconstitutional.[49] The claimants in *Murphy* were allowed to recover taxes paid under the unconstitutional law, but only for the two fiscal years dating from the time they challenged it. As one commentator noted, 'full redress would entail fiscal chaos'.[50]

Chief Justice O'Higgins, dissenting, argued that 'invalid' in art. 15 means 'voidable'. He noted that even in the absence of specific doctrinal and textual support for this view, he would reject the void *ab initio* theory because of the 'requirements of an ordered society'.[51] The doctrine means 'that all actions and conduct directed or permitted by [an unconstitutional] law would be deprived of all legal authority', affecting decisions regarding criminal punishment and expenditure of public monies; and the existence of such unconstitutional laws would encourage 'innocent people to enter into obligations and accept liabilities of a permanent nature'.[52] This, he argued, can have no place in an ordered society:

> It would appear to me to be unthinkable that a people, who adopted a Constitution in the interests, inter alia, of achieving a "true social order" (see Preamble) should have intended that, under that Constitution, laws, formally passed, which went into operation and which were respected and obeyed, could, years after their enactment, be declared never to have had the force of law. Such an interpretation of the Constitution would provide for our people the very antithesis of a true social order, an uneasy existence fraught with legal and constitutional uncertainty.[53]

Thus, he proposed the *ex nunc* approach, arguing that 'the invalidity of a law or any provision thereof *can only operate from the moment such invalidity is declared* in the High Court or in the Supreme Court'.[54] As we will see in Section 7.4 below, O'Higgins CJ's reasoning is similar to Kelsen's; he grounds his opposition to the void *ab initio* approach in the fundamental practical needs of a working legal order.

In 2006, the Irish Supreme Court declared unconstitutional a law prohibiting carnal knowledge of a child because it did not allow a defendant to claim honest

49 Ibid. 314.
50 N. Connolly, 'The Prospective and Retrospective Effect of Judicial Decisions in Ireland', in E. Steiner (Ed.), *Comparing the Prospective Effect of Judicial Rulings Across Jurisdictions*, Cham, Springer International Publishing, 2015, p. 52.
51 Ibid. p. 300.
52 Ibid. p. 297.
53 Ibid. pp. 300–301.
54 Ibid. p. 300.

mistake regarding the age of the child,[55] and in a later case the same year, *A v Governor of Arbour Hill*, a prisoner previously convicted under the law sought to have his conviction overturned.[56] Though the prisoner had known the child was twelve, the High Court held that his conviction was invalid because the statute under which he was convicted was void.[57] The Supreme Court, in a leading opinion by Chief Justice Murray, reversed the judgment. Murray CJ formally acknowledged *Murphy*'s doctrine of void *ab initio*, but his discussion emphasized the principle of limitation and evinced a negative view of the doctrine of void *ab initio*. He cited O'Higgins CJ's dissent in *Murphy* and said there are 'transcendent constitutional reasons why a declaration of constitutional invalidity as regards a statute should not in principle have retrospective effect so as *necessarily* to render void cases previously and finally decided and determined by the courts', and that these reasons include the interests of the common good in an ordered society, legal certainty, and the need to avoid incoherence and injustice.[58]

The statement in *Murphy* that retroactivity is the 'normal' result is consistent with Murray CJ's holding that a declaration of unconstitutionality does not 'necessarily' render past decisions void. Murray CJ's opinion 'reversed the principle and the exception'.[59] This is exactly what occurred in the US decisions over time. What we see in the movement from *Murphy* to *Arbour Hill* is a recapitulation of decades of experience in the US.[60]

Canada has also adopted the void *ab initio* theory but has taken a somewhat different path from Ireland and the US in applying it. With regard to criminal cases, it has been held that *res judicata* is a complete bar to reopening them even when the basis of the conviction is an unconstitutional statute. More generally, the preferred technique for avoiding the full implications of the void *ab initio* doctrine is issuing a judgment with suspended effect. This technique began with *Reference re Manitoba Language Rights* (1985),[61] in which the Supreme Court held that English-only statutes in Manitoba violated constitutional requirements

55 CC v Ireland [2006] 4 IR 1.

56 A v Governor of Arbour Hill Prison [2006] 4 IR 88.

57 Ibid.

58 Ibid. 142 (emphasis added).

59 O. J. Doyle, *Constitutional Law: Text, Cases and Materials*, Dublin, Clarus Press, 2008, p. 451.

60 The general statement of the void *ab initio* theory in Murphy is the exact equivalent of the articulation of the void *ab initio* theory in Norton and many cases that applied it with retroactive effect for decades. But as soon as Henchy J announced the general rule, he announced a broad principle of limitation, citing to Chicot County, which articulated the exception that is now applied more frequently than the rule in the US. The dissent by O'Higgins CJ in Murphy is equivalent to the minority view in the US represented by Butler J.'s rejection of the void *ab initio* theory and preference for the *ex nunc* approach. And Murray CJ's opinion in Arbour Hill is comparable to US decisions that have questioned the void *ab initio* theory without overruling it.

61 [1985] 1 SCR 721.

for provincial legislation to be bilingual, in French and English.[62] Questions about the validity of provincial laws had long been treated in accord with the UK Colonial Laws Validity Act, 1865, which by s. 2 provided that colonial laws in conflict with an Act of Parliament are 'absolutely void and inoperative'. Section 52 of the Constitution Act, 1982, provides that laws inconsistent with the Canadian Constitution are, to the extent of such inconsistency, 'of no force and effect', which the Court held to be equivalent to 'absolutely void and inoperative'. Thus, the Court held, all unilingual acts 'are, and always have been, invalid and of no force or effect'.[63] Since every law enacted in Manitoba since 1890 was unilingual, this threatened 'legal chaos' and created a state of emergency.[64] Public bodies and officials had acted without legal authority, and 'all legal rights, obligations and other effects which have purportedly arisen under all Acts of the Manitoba Legislature since 1890 would be open to challenge'.[65] This ran deeply contrary to the rule of law, which was held to be 'a fundamental principle of our Constitution', and the Court concluded that the 'Constitution will not suffer a province without laws'.[66] The Court's solution was to 'deem' the unconstitutional laws to be 'temporarily valid and effective' for the period required to translate, reenact, and publish legislation in bilingual form.[67] 'It is only in this way that legal chaos can be avoided and the rule of law preserved'.[68] As Ben Juratowitch noted, however, '[B]ecause the previous legislation was void ab initio, it follows as a matter of logic that for the chaos feared by the court to be avoided, it was necessary for the new bilingual legislation to have retroactive effect'.[69] The Manitoba legislature provided for such effect in the re-enacted statutes, and that approach has been used for other cases as well.[70]

62 See Constitution Act 1867, s. 133, and the Manitoba Act 1870.

63 [1985] 1 SCR 721, paras 51–52. The phrase 'force and effect' inserted into the Constitution Act 1982 (Canada) is doubtless taken from the Colonial Laws Validity Act 1865, s. 2.'2. Any Colonial Law which is or shall be in any respect repugnant to the Provisions of any Act of Parliament extending to the Colony to which such Law may relate, or repugnant to any Order or Regulation made under Authority of such Act of Parliament, or having in the Colony the Force and Effect of such Act, shall be read subject to such Act, Order, or Regulation, and shall, to the Extent of such Repugnancy, but not otherwise, be and remain absolutely void and inoperative'.

64 Ibid. paras 55, 96.

65 Ibid. para. 58.

66 Ibid. para. 107.

67 Ibid. para. 109. The Court observed that in many cases past decisions could be immune from challenge under principles such as *res judicata* or the *de facto* officer doctrine, but that many decisions and transactions would not be protected from retroactive invalidity without deeming past legislation temporarily valid: ibid. para. 82.

68 Ibid. para. 207.

69 B. Juratowitch, *Retroactivity and the Common Law*, Oxford, Bloomsbury-Hart Publishing, 2008, p. 207.

70 See The Re-Enacted Statutes of Manitoba 1987, s. 8 ('The Re-enacted Statutes of Manitoba, 1987, *shall not be held to operate as new law but shall be construed and have effect as a consolidation and as declaratory of the law* as contained in the Acts repealed by section 5 and

The potential for 'legal chaos' is created by the void *ab initio* theory, and is inherent in every decision that applies it. The *Language Rights* decision had an unusually wide scope, but it is not the scope alone that threatens rule of law principles and portends 'chaos'. Every decision applying the void *ab initio* theory is a microcosm for which the *Language Rights* case represents the macrocosm. Thus, it is not surprising that, once the precedent had been set, it became common for Canadian courts to suspend the effect of a declaration of unconstitutionality. The use of suspended judgments 'has grown by leaps and bounds, so that they now verge on the routine', according to Sujit Choudry and Kent Roach, who in 2003 counted 42 such judgments, with 14 of those by the Supreme Court.[71] The Court has used suspended judgments in recent high-profile cases declaring unconstitutional statutes on prostitution,[72] a law prohibiting assisted suicide,[73] and a law prohibiting private medical insurance.[74]

It is not only common law systems that have adopted the void *ab initio* theory as a formal constitutional doctrine. In Germany, the Federal Constitutional Court Act, s. 95(3), provides that when a court makes a judgment of unconstitutionality, the law is void (*nichtig*). A leading treatise explains the standard approach: an

> unconstitutional law is from its inception (*ex tunc*) and without need for any further act (*ipso iure*) inoperative. ... The German view is that the Federal Constitutional Court does not annul a statute. [The court] does not invalidate: it merely establishes the invalidity [in a declaratory way].[75]

However, just as common law courts have come up with workarounds, the Federal Constitutional Court developed an alternative remedy of declaring a law incompatible (*unvereinbar*) with the Basic Law, allowing the legislature a set period in which to change the law (if necessary, in a way that avoids problems of retroactivity), and the use of this remedy has been authorized by the legislature in the law regulating the Court.[76] The situation in Spain is similar to that of

---

for which the Re-enacted Statutes of Manitoba, 1987, are substituted) (emphasis added). A similar sequence occurred with *Re Eurig* (1998) [1998] 2 SCR 565, where the Supreme Court held unconstitutional a system of probate fees that had been in place since 1950, because it had been enacted in secondary rather than primary legislation. This could have required the repayment of fees paid over decades. The Court issue a suspended judgment, and the Ontario legislature enacted new legislation deemed to have retroactive effect. See Juratowitch (n 106) 207 & n 66.

71 S. Choudry and K. Roach, 'Putting the Past Behind Us? Prospective Judicial and Legislative Constitutional Remedies', *Supreme Court Law Review (2nd)*, Vol. 21, 2003, pp. 205–266.

72 Canada (AG) v Bedford [2013] 3 SCR 1101

73 Carter v Canada (AG) [2015] 1 SCR 331.

74 Chaoulli v Quebec (AG) [2005] 1 SCR 791.

75 K. Schlaich, *Das Bundesverfassungsgericht*, 3rd edn, Munich, C.H. Beck Verlag, 1994, pp. 220–221.

76 G. Vanber, *The Politics of Constitutional Review in Germany*, Cambridge, Cambridge University Press, 2004, p. 92 & n. 36.

Germany, though not as systematized either in theory or practice.[77] In Italy, art. 136 of the Constitution provides that following a judgment of the constitutional court determining the unconstitutionality of a law, the law ceases to have effect from the date of judgment (*ex nunc*). But this does not preclude the possibility of retroactive effects, which are expressly authorized by art. 27 of the Law of 11 March 1953, no. 87. This law provides that a determination that penal legislation is unconstitutional has retroactive effects, and, more generally, when the 'Constitutional Court declares an impugned law to be unconstitutional it may also declare the invalidity of other legislative dispositions when this follows logically from the court's holding the principal law impugned to be unconstitutional'.[78] It has been noted of European constitutional systems generally that most allow for unconstitutional laws to be treated as void *ab initio* in at least some cases, with only Austria adhering rigorously to Kelsen's exclusion of this.[79]

7.5 The void *ab initio* debate and legal theory

The aim of this section is to analyze the relationship between different constitutional practices and doctrines, and the problems they can generate, and legal theory about the precise status (in regard to validity) of an unconstitutional statute. The section focuses on Kelsen, but before taking up his work, it is worth noting that the debate among judges in this area, as Section 7.4 has shown, commonly involves appeals to the basic principles of legal order. The judges reach beyond textual interpretation of the constitution and rely on fundamental theory. John Marshall contended that the theory of every government with a written constitution 'must be that an act of the Legislature repugnant to the Constitution is void' and that this is 'one of the fundamental principles of our society'. In Ireland, Henchy J in *Murphy* argued that the void *ab initio* theory 'is a principle which is inherent in the nature of such limited [constitutional] powers'. Judges who reject the void *ab initio* theory outright, or resisted its logical implication of retroactive effects, argue at the same fundamental level. Dissenting in *Murphy*, O'Higgins CJ said the void *ab initio* theory is contrary to the basic 'requirements of an ordered society' and is the 'very antithesis of a true social order', echoing the reference in the Preamble to the Irish Constitution to 'true social order'. Earlier in the US, Justice Butler argued that a declaration of unconstitutionality should take effect from the judgment forward, and this 'is essential to the very existence of order in society'. Even when accepting the void *ab initio* theory, courts have appealed to fundamental principles to avoid retroactive effects in some cases. In *A v Governor of Arbour Hill*, Murray CJ referred to 'transcendent constitutional

77 A. Pizzorusso, *Law in the Making: A Comparative Survey*, Heidelberg, Springer, 1988, pp. 177–185.

78 M. Evans, 'The Italian Constitutional Court', *The International and Comparative Law Quarterly*, Vol. 17, No. 3, 1968, pp. 602–633, p. 606.

79 A. Pizzorusso (n. 77), p. 181.

reasons', including 'the interests of the common good in an ordered society', not to render previously decided cases void. In the *Manitoba Language Rights* case, the Canadian Supreme Court justified its suspended judgment on the basis of the rule of law as a fundamental, unwritten principle of the constitution.

The debate among judges is also illustrative of tensions in Kelsen's thoughts. As we will see, Kelsen acknowledged the possibility, from a theoretical viewpoint, that there could be purported laws that are void *ab initio* due to their failure to conform to the constitution (or other legal requirements). Indeed, such a possibility is integral to his theory of legal validity and the hierarchy of norms. At the same time, however, Kelsen had a clear and marked conviction that a constitutional system should treat unconstitutional laws as voidable rather than void *ab initio* (except, perhaps, for certain purported laws that utterly lack any plausible claim to validity – about such an exception he was not entirely clear). Often this conviction sounds like a dogma of legal theory. Close examination, however, shows that Kelsen grounded it in the practical need to avoid 'anarchy' (or what the Canadian Supreme Court called 'legal chaos'), retroactive effects of annulments, and contradictory rulings on the constitutionality of statutes; more generally, to avoid confusion and to promote what Anglo-American theory terms the Rule of Law.

Kelsen's general legal theory teaches that a legal norm is valid in virtue of its creation's conformity with a higher legal norm. All legal norms must conform in their making (both procedurally and in substantive requirements) to the constitution, and the constitution itself is valid pursuant to the *Grundnorm.*[80] Since a statute derives its validity from being duly enacted in conformity with the constitution, an *unconstitutional statute* is a contradiction in terms: an unconstitutional statute would be invalid, and 'an invalid statute is no statute at all; it is legally nonexistent'.[81] But this does not mean that a statute is void *ab initio* when its content is inconsistent with the constitution. Kelsen argues that the claim that 'a statute is unconstitutional' cannot be taken 'literally', but only as a reference to constitutional procedures that allow the statute to be invalidated.[82]

This discussion, drawn from the second edition of the *Pure Theory of Law* (1967) was preceded by similar arguments in the first edition (1934) as well as in *General Theory of Law and the State* (1945). In *General Theory* Kelsen said, with regard to statutes inconsistent with the constitution, 'The so-called "unconstitutional" law is not void *ab initio*, it is only voidable; it can be annulled for special reasons'.[83] He asks, 'Under what conditions is something which presents itself as a norm null *ab initio* and not a norm which has to be annulled in a legal

80 H. Kelsen, *Pure Theory of the Law*, tr. M. Knight, 2nd English edn, Berkeley, CA, University of California Press, 1967, pp. 198–201.

81 Ibid. p. 271.

82 Ibid.

83 H. Kelsen, *General Theory of Law and the State*, tr. A. Wedberg, Cambridge, MA, Harvard University Press, 1945, p. 157.

procedure?'[84] His answer: 'Only the legal order itself could answer that question'. Kelsen proceeds, however, to deny that the legal order can provide for declaratory judgments that recognize nullity, and claims instead that all judgments must be constitutive. At the conclusion of the argument he reaches for a metaphor: 'Just as everything King Midas touched turned into gold, everything to which the law refers becomes law, i.e., something legally existing. The case of absolute nullity lies beyond the law'.[85]

In both the first[86] and second editions[87] of *Pure Theory*, Kelsen argued that constitutions set up 'alternative' paths for enacting laws, one in which statutes have content that conforms to the constitution, and one in which statutes are non-conforming. The constitution 'prefers' the conforming path but cannot exclude the non-conforming one.[88] Kelsen argues:

> That the constitution does aim for the validity of the so-called unconstitutional statute is shown in the fact that it prescribes not only that statutes should be created in a certain way and have (or not have) a certain content, but also that if a statute was created other than in the prescribed way or has other than the prescribed content, *it is not to be regarded as null and void, but is to be valid until it is invalidated by the designated authority – say, a constitutional court – in a procedure governed by the constitution.*[89]

This is from the first edition of *Pure Theory* in 1934, written shortly after Kelsen had finished serving on the Austrian Constitutional Court. His argument fits the Austrian Constitution, but as Section 7.4 has shown, a number of common law systems follow the void *ab initio* approach as formal constitutional doctrine, and sometimes apply it with retroactive effect.[90] Kelsen's statement seems to assume that the constitution expressly addresses the situation of an unconstitutional statute and authorizes some organ to resolve it. In the second edition of *Pure Theory*, Kelsen also states that if the constitution is silent regarding the power of judicial review, the power is diffused among courts generally, and they 'are usually only authorized to refuse the application of this statute in the concrete case, that is,

84 Ibid. p. 160–161.
85 Ibid. p. 161.
86 Kelsen (n. 127, 2nd edn), pp. 270–274.
87 H. Kelsen, *Introduction to the Problems of Legal Theory: A Translation of the First Edition of the Reine Rechtslehre or Pure Theory of Law*, trs. B. L. Paulson and S. Paulson, Oxford, Oxford University Press, 1997, pp. 71–74.
88 Pure Theory (n. 71, 2nd edn.), p. 274.
89 Kelsen (n. 76), p. 72 (emphasis added).
90 Another claim by Kelsen in the same passage further shows that his argument depends on contingent facts, which were true in 1934 but no longer: '[M]ost constitutions do not provide for overturning unconstitutional statutes at all, and – leaving the validity of such statutes untouched – are satisfied simply with the possibility of holding certain authorities (chief of state or minister, for example) personally responsible for enacting the unconstitutional statute.' Ibid.

to suspend its validity for the concrete case; but the statute remains valid for all other cases'.[91]

Kelsen moved to the US in 1940, and two years later published the article on judicial review of legislation referenced above in Section 7.4, which compares the US and Austrian systems of judicial review of legislation.[92] In describing the US approach to determining the constitutionality of laws, he states: 'Nonapplication of the unconstitutional norm could be effected by authorizing the law-applying organs to test the constitutionality of the norm which they had to apply in a concrete case, and to refuse its application in this particular case if they found that the norm was unconstitutional'.[93] He adds that '[t]his is in principle the legal situation in the United States', further describing it as follows:

> The fact that a law-applying organ declares a general rule unconstitutional and does not apply it in a given case means that this organ is authorized to invalidate the general rule for the concrete case; but only for the concrete case, since the general rule as such – the statute, the ordinance – remains valid and can, therefore, be applied in other concrete cases.[94]

Kelsen significantly misunderstands the US constitutional system. First, he mischaracterizes the force of precedent:

> Inasmuch as the American courts consider themselves bound by the judgments of the Supreme Court a decision of that Court refusing to apply a statute in a concrete case because of unconstitutionality has practically almost the same effect as general annulment of the statute. But the rule of *stare decisis* is not at all an absolute principle. It is not very clear to what extent it is recognized as valid. Above all it is assumed that it is not valid in the case of an interpretation of the Constitution. "Constitutional questions are always open to examination." [The quotation is from an old case from Montana state court, O.V. and S.K.R.R, v. Morgan County, 53, Mo. 156 (1873).] Hence it is possible that the Supreme Court declares one and the same statute in one case constitutional and in another case unconstitutional as well as vice versa. The same is true as far as other courts are concerned. And, in fact, such cases have occurred.

While Kelsen is correct to identify the possibility of diverging rulings, he substantially underplays the force of precedent when the US Supreme Court declares a

91 Pure Theory (n. 71, 2nd edn), p. 274.

92 H. Kelsen, 'Judicial Review of Legislation: A Comparative Study of the Austrian and the American Constitution', *Journal of Politics*, Vol. 4, No. 2, 1942, pp. 183–200, p. 190.

93 Ibid. p. 185.

94 Kelsen (n. 81), p. 185.

statute unconstitutional. It is misleading to suggest that such a statute 'remains valid and can, therefore, be applied in other concrete cases'.

Moreover, Kelsen dismisses the void *ab initio* theory as an accurate account of US law without substantial analysis of the relevant cases. Acknowledging controversy regarding the theory, he argues that 'many outstanding American lawyers do not accept it', citing *Chicot County* (1940)[95] and *Wellington et al. Petitioners*, a 1834 Massachusetts case holding that unconstitutional laws are voidable, not void, which he said has 'the best formulation of the problem'.[96] He also opines that the void *ab initio* theory would violate the prohibition on *ex post facto* laws in the US Constitution.[97] Kelsen, however, ignores the clear articulation of and application of the theory in *Norton* and many other cases contrary to *Wellington*, and he seems unaware of the long period in which the void *ab initio* theory was the prevailing approach. In Section 7.4, I argued that *Chicot County* did not formally overrule the void *ab initio* theory, but allowed for mitigation of the effects. Even if the theory had been overruled by *Chicot County* in 1940, the experience of the previous decades cannot be dismissed as irrelevant to Kelsen's argument.

Curiously, at precisely the point at which it would have been helpful to analyze cases, articulations of doctrine, and actual practice in more depth, Kelsen resorts to an argument that seems to be based almost wholly on theory. In order to track the flow of Kelsen's argument, I quote at length, setting in context the remarks that opened the discussion above in Section 7.4:

> It is also controversial whether the statute which the [US] Supreme Court has declared unconstitutional has to be considered as void *ab initio*. Such an interpretation of the Supreme Court's decision would mean that this decision annuls the statute generally and with retroactive force so that all the legal effects which the statute had before are abolished. Within a system of positive law there is no absolute nullity. It is not possible to characterize an act which presents itself as a legal act as null *a priori* (void *ab initio*). Only annulment of such an act is possible; the act is not void, it is only voidable. For the statement that an act is null is not possible without another statement, answering the question of who is competent to establish the nullity of the act. Since the legal order – to avoid anarchy – empowers certain authorities to establish whether an act is null, this establishment always has a constitutive, not a declaratory character. The act is "null" only if the competent authority declares it null. This declaration is an annulment, an invalidation. Before this declaration the act is not null, for being "null" means legally

95 Kelsen (n. 81), p. 199 & n. 9.

96 16 Pick. 87, 96 (1834) (Mass. Sup. Ct.) ('Perhaps, however, it may be well doubted whether a formal act of legislation can ever with strict legal propriety be said to be void; it seems more consistent with the nature of the subject, and the principles applicable to analogous cases, to treat it as voidable'.)

97 US Constitution, art. I, s. 9, para. 3. See Kelsen (n. 81), p. 200.

> non-existent. And the act must legally exist, if it can be the object of a judgment by an authority. The annulment may be retroactive in effect; and the legal order may authorize every individual to establish the nullity of the act, that is, to annul the act with retroactive force. But normally only certain organs of the legal community are authorized to establish the "nullity" of acts presenting themselves as legal acts.
>
> It is especially impossible to consider a statute enacted by the constitutional legislator as absolutely null or "void *ab initio.*" Only courts have the power to decide the question whether a statute is unconstitutional. … Such a declaration has, therefore, always a constitutive and not a declaratory character. But the act by which a court declares a statute unconstitutional may, according to the Constitution, abolish the statute with retroactive force. In that case the decision of the court has, as we have previously pointed out, the character of a legislative act. Legislative acts with retroactive force are, however, hardly compatible with the prohibition of the American Constitution according to which no *ex post facto* law shall be passed. But this interpretation which excludes the "void *ab initio* theory" is not generally accepted.[98]

While the argument above appears to be grounded mainly in conceptual or logical necessity, there is an awareness of practical choice running just below the surface. Midway through the first quoted paragraph he notes that, 'to avoid anarchy', the legal order empowers authorities to determine whether an act is 'null and thereby prevents them from being treated as 'absolutely null' or 'void *ab initio*'. A bit later in the same discussion, Kelsen gives an example of lack of clarity over whether a certain 1935 regulation in the US was constitutional, and contends that the ability of private parties to challenge the constitutionality of statutes in ordinary lawsuits creates a standing possibility of similar confusion:

> For the lawsuit in itself can neither invalidate nor confirm the validity of the statute. The only thing we can say is that any lawsuit in which the constitutionality of a statute is contested creates a period of doubt and uncertainty concerning the validity of the statute and its legal effects. That is, from the point of view of legal technique, not at all satisfactory.[99]

Here we have a clear acknowledgment that we are dealing with a practical choice of legal technique, which theory itself does not answer. He proceeds to contrast the US approach with that of Austria, favorably to the latter:

> In the absence of a clear provision of the [US] Constitution all questions concerning the effect of an unconstitutional statute may be answered in contradictory ways. To avoid such an uncertainty was one of the reasons leading

98 Ibid. pp. 189–91.
99 Ibid. p. 191.

> to a centralization of the judicial review of legislation in Austria and to vesting jurisdiction in the Constitutional Court to abolish generally and not only for a given case the unconstitutional statute. The actual practice in the United States has the same aim but it pursues it by juristically imperfect means.[100]

For Kelsen the 'greatest difference' between the US and the Austrian constitutions 'concerns the procedure by which a statute is declared unconstitutional by the competent organ':

> According to the Constitution of the United States judicial review of legislation is possible only in the course of a process the chief aim of which is not the establishment of the unconstitutionality or constitutionality of a statute. This question can only arise incidentally when a party maintains that the application of a statute in a concrete case is an illegal violation of its interests because the statute is unconstitutional. Hence it is in principle only the violation of a party-interest which puts in motion the procedure of the judicial review of legislation. *The interest in the constitutionality of legislation is, however, a public one which does not necessarily coincide with the private interest of the parties concerned. It is a public interest which deserves protection by a special procedure in conformity with its special character.* The disadvantages resulting from the lack of such a procedure are widely recognized in American juristic literature.[101]

Kelsen's footnote on the 'literature' is to Oliver Field's 1935 work, *The Effect of an Unconstitutional Statute*, a comprehensive account of the debate among US judges over the void *ab initio* theory recounted in Section 7.3, and of the variable ways of applying that theory.[102]

What we are dealing with, then, is fundamentally a question of constitutional design, not of general legal theory. Constitutional framers should take care to make practical choices that protect the public interest in determining the constitutionality of legislation, and that avoid the confusion and uncertainty inherent in a decentralized, party-initiated system of judicial review like that of the US. In this article Kelsen does not clearly acknowledge that constitutional framers could choose the void *ab initio* approach, but nor does he definitively exclude the possibility either. While much of his argument seems to imply that the void *ab initio* approach is unavailable as a matter of theory, other parts of his argument imply that treating unconstitutional laws as voidable is the result of wise and prudent practical choice.

100 Ibid. p. 192.
101 Ibid. p. 193 (emphasis added).
102 See O. Field, *The Effect of an Unconstitutional Statute*, Minneapolis, MN, University of Minnesota Press, 1935.

A clue for resolving these tensions is found in one of Kelsen's earliest works, his 1925 *Allgemeine Staatslehre.*[103] Here he distinguishes between two viewpoints one can take when considering acts (whether public acts like statutes or regulations, or private transactions) that fail to conform to criteria for validity set by the law or constitution. One viewpoint is that of 'legal science' (*Rechtswisssenschaft* or *Staatstheorie*); that is the viewpoint represented in what I have generally called 'legal theory' in this chapter, occasionally connecting it to 'dogma', a term I use to capture the sense that the theorist is describing a conceptual or other reality beyond himself rather than shaping reality by practical choice. The other viewpoint, for Kelsen, is that of 'law and the state' (*Rechtsordnung*), which responds to legal and political reasons that can be evaluated as better or worse.

Kelsen argues that according to 'legal science', purported statutes or transactions that fail to conform to legal criteria are – or at least can be – invalid, null, void *ab initio.*[104] (Kelsen sometimes treats this as a question of degree: a purportedly valid act that is far removed from the criteria of validity is void ab *initio*, but this may not be true of an act that narrowly fails to meet criteria of validity.) When positive law sets out to regulate this area, it transforms this invalidity (absolute nullity) into one of two types of voidability: (1) voidness *ab initio* transformed into voidability, with retrospective effects; and (2) voidability proper, which amounts to annulment with prospective effect.[105] Usually, he says, the law treats invalid private transactions as (1), and invalid public acts, including statutes, as (2).

It is possible for the positive law to be silent on the question of voidability. In such a case, says Kelsen, legal science instructs us that the person who has the responsibility to check the validity of a purportedly legal act is any person charged with responsibility to apply the act.[106] (This corresponds to Kelsen's view in *Pure Theory of Law* (2nd edn), recounted above, that if a constitution is silent on the question of judicial review of legislation, the power to determine constitutionality belongs to every court.) But such a legal system would usually be socially damaging; when everyone is able to second-guess the validity of an act, there is a tendency toward uncertainty and 'chaos'.[107] Thus it is up to the positive law to prevent such confusion – to regulate invalidity.

The reasons to provide this regulation are legal-political. They are reasons of the *Rechtsordnung*; they do not come from legal science.[108] Any claim that legal science precludes the absolute nullity of a statute would, for Kelsen, be 'natural law thinking', an attempt to prescribe a solution to a practical problem from the nature of things.[109] Kelsen's dual methodological approach may explain the

103 H. Kelsen, *Allgemeine Staatslehre*, Berlin, Springer Verlag, 1925.
104 Ibid. pp. 277–278.
105 Ibid. p. 277.
106 Ibid. p. 289.
107 Ibid.
108 Ibid. p. 277.
109 Ibid. pp. 276–277, p. 289.

tensions that this chapter has grappled with. Kelsen often uses the term 'must' when describing the reasons of the *Rechtsordnung* in a way that sounds like conceptual dogma, without acknowledging that it is ultimately a matter of practical choice. He often refers to what is 'possible' within a system of law, stating that only voidability is possible and excluding absolute nullity as something that lies beyond the system of law. The reader unaware of Kelsen's dual methodology may take these as claims about theoretical necessity, thereby failing to appreciate that Kelsen is describing a state of affairs *after positive law has been adopted to reflect particular practical choices about regulating invalidity*. Moreover, Kelsen's pronouncements presume that such positive law has been adopted in a way that avoids uncertainty and chaos.

Awareness of Kelsen's dual methodology does not dispel the problems in his account. While he has dealt with the problem of unconstitutional laws and the regulation of invalidity more extensively than any other major legal philosopher, he has never, to my knowledge, systematically gathered and practically evaluated the possible approaches that a legal system might take. He does not fully acknowledge the possibility that a legal system might *choose* to treat unconstitutional laws as void *ab initio*, or that some legal systems have adopted the void *ab initio* theory as formal doctrine. As we have seen, he usually presents the choice that the *Rechstordnung* makes regarding judicial review of legislation as either between (1) a centralized system like Austria, with annulment that is typically prospective in its effects or (2) a decentralized system like America, which is the default position when the constitution is silent. He treats (2) as if it involves simply the refusal to apply an unconstitutional statute in an individual, concrete case. He does not deal either with the real force of precedent in a system like the US, or with the situation in which a decentralized system has adopted a formal doctrine of void *ab initio*.

Furthermore, Kelsen fails to acknowledge that the void *ab initio* theory may fit better with standard concepts of adjudication. The power to render unconstitutional statutes invalid *ex nunc* is a power to determine the content of future law, and in Kelsen's model this power has only a contingent relationship to the case *sub judice*. The 'annulling decision of the court [is] in principle to be effective only *ex nunc*'.[110] Kelsen provides that the judgment of unconstitutionality generally has retroactive effect in the case that prompted the referral to the constitutional court, as noted in Section 7.4, but this is given as an exception to what would otherwise be only prospective effects. The exception 'was a technical necessity, because without it the authorities charged with the application of the law ... would not have had an immediate and consequently sufficiently cogent interest to cause the intervention of the Constitutional Court'.[111] Furthermore, the exception is not applicable if the constitutional court allows the legislature

110 H. Kelsen, 'Judicial Review of Legislation: A Comparative Study of the Austrian and the American Constitution', *Journal of Politics*, Vol. 4, No. 2, 1942, pp. 183–200, p. 186.
111 Ibid. p. 196.

a period of time to reform the law before the judgment becomes effective; in this scenario, the case will be decided by the law that has been determined to be unconstitutional. The possibility that a constitutional court judgment might have only prospective effect indicates how far removed such a court is from ordinary conceptions of adjudication. In Ben Juratowitch's words, '[I]f a court severs the link between the case before it and the new rule that the court espouses in the course of that case, then the court's function becomes blatantly legislative'.[112] The remedial mechanism in the Austrian Constitutional Court is not fundamentally designed to ensure that only constitutionally compliant norms are applied in a given case; rather the case is treated as a means, almost an excuse, to invoke the power of the court to determine the content of future law.

7.6 Conclusion

It is perfectly understandable why most common law courts and judges – as well as many in civil law systems – are drawn to the void *ab initio* theory of unconstitutional laws. There is an intuitive appeal to John Marshall's argument that one of the basic aims of establishing a written constitution is to place legal limits on the activity of governing institutions, including lawmaking institutions. Since the limits are *legal*, it falls to the judiciary to enforce them. The basic function of adjudication is to give judgment according to the law. If two putative legal norms are in conflict, and one of them has a higher status as constitutional law, then it stands to reason that courts should render judgment in accordance with the higher law, judging the lower law to be invalid and hence unavailable as a source of judgment. As Marshall put it, the unconstitutional law is simply 'not law'. It is one short logical step further to say that what is not law *now* could *never have been law*, since the constitutional standard for judging the statute not law has been constant over time. While that temporal dimension was not yet present in *Marbury v Madison*, which in 1803 dealt with a recently minted statute under a new constitution, it is a straightforward move from Marshall's reasoning to the void *ab initio* theory.

Indeed this is precisely the kind of reasoning that Kelsen himself engages in when reflecting on the status of unconstitutional laws from the viewpoint of *legal science*. From that view, unconstitutional laws are invalid and void *ab initio*. The fundamental disjuncture between the common law void *ab initio* doctrine and Kelsen is his move to the viewpoint of the *Rechtsordnung*. But this move not only involves considerations about practical need and constitutional design (as Kelsen only equivocally acknowledges), it also involves the creation of a novel institution: the constitutional court as the kind of 'negative legislator' described in Section 7.2. The institution is novel because, in relation to the tripartite categories of the state recognized in standard separation of powers theory, the constitutional court

112 B. Juratowitch, *Retroactivity and the Common Law*, Oxford, Bloomsbury-Hart Publishing, 2008, p. 210.

belongs to the legislative branch. The mode of reasoning and decision-making of the constitutional court remains legal, because it responds to specific legal norms rather than general principles like a legislature. But its remedial mechanism – annulment of laws with prospective effect – is characteristic of legislative action. It amounts to enactment of a general norm as the inverse of a legislative act; the court effectively repeals a statute, much as a legislature would.

Everything would have been clearer if Kelsen had fully defended his preference for the Austrian system as a practical or political choice in constitutional design against an array of possible alternatives, clearly laid out (including the real possibility of the void *ab initio* approach). He often writes as if those working in other systems should reject the void *ab initio* theory as a theoretical confusion and adopt instead the approach of *ex nunc* annulment, without waiting for constitutional framers to set up a constitutional court on his model. His cuts his argument short by adverting to the 'musts' and apparent logical necessities of the viewpoint of the *Rechstordnung*. Section 7.4's account of the problems of applying the void *ab initio* theory could provide the materials for a full practical argument. Some of the most striking developments (such as the Irish cases and the *Language Reference* case in Canada) occurred after Kelsen had written, but the undercurrent of practical concern, expressed in his warnings about 'chaos' and 'anarchy', shows that he intuited the kind of problems that could develop in a void *ab initio* system. There is much to commend his model, but he confuses his case by arguing for it on the basis of what appear to be theoretical necessities but are ultimately practical reasons.

References

S. Choudry & K. Roach, 'Putting the Past Behind Us? Prospective Judicial and Legislative Constitutional Remedies', *Supreme Court Law Review (2nd)*, Vol. 21, 2003, pp. 205–266.

N. Connolly, 'The Prospective and Retrospective Effect of Judicial Decisions in Ireland', in E. Steiner (Ed.), *Comparing the Prospective Effect of Judicial Rulings Across Jurisdictions*, Cham, Switzerland, Springer International Publishing, 2015.

T. Cooley, *A Treatise on the Constitutional Limitations Which Rest Upon the Legislative Power of the States of the American Union*, 7th ed., New York, Little, Brown & Co Publishers, 1903.

O. J. Doyle, *Constitutional Law: Text, Cases and Materials*, Dublin, Clarus Press, 2008.

M. Evans, 'The Italian Constitutional Court', *The International and Comparative Law Quarterly*, Vol. 17, No. 3, 1968, pp. 602–633.

O. Field, *The Effect of an Unconstitutional Statute*, Minneapolis, MN, University of Minnesota Press, 1935.

B. Juratowitch, *Retroactivity and the Common Law*, Oxford, Bloomsbury-Hart Publishing, 2008.

M. Köpcke, *A Short History of Legal Validity and Invalidity: Foundations of Private and Public Law*, Cambridge, UK, Intersentia, 2019.

H. Kelsen, *Allgemeine Staatslehre*, Berlin, Springer Verlag, 1925.

H. Kelsen, *General Theory of Law and the State*, tr. A. Wedberg, Cambridge, MA, Harvard University Press, 1945.

H. Kelsen, *Introduction to the Problems of Legal Theory: A Translation of the First Edition of the Reine Rechtslehre or Pure Theory of Law*, trs. B. L. Paulson and S. Paulson, Oxford, Oxford University Press, 1997.

H. Kelsen, 'Judicial Review of Legislation: A Comparative Study of the Austrian and the American Constitution', *Journal of Politics*, Vol. 4, No. 2, 1942, pp. 183–200.

H. Kelsen, 'On the Nature and Development of Constitutional Adjudication', in L. Vinx (Ed.), *The Guardian of the Constitution: Hans Kelsen and Carl Schmitt on the Limits of Constitutional Law*, Cambridge, UK, Cambridge University Press, 2015.

H. Kelsen, *Pure Theory of the Law*, 2nd English ed., tr. M. Knight, Berkeley, CA, University of California Press, 1967.

S. Lagi, 'Hans Kelsen and the Austrian Constitutional Court (1918–1929)', *Co-herencia*, Vol. 19, No. 16, 2012, pp. 273–295.

A. Pizzorusso, *Law in the Making: A Comparative Survey*, Heidelberg, Springer, 1988.

E. F. Plave, 'Phenomenon of Antique Laws: Can a State Revive Old Abortion Laws in a New Era?', *George Washington Law Review*, Vol. 58, No. 1, 1989, pp. 111–124.

American Jurisprudence, 2d, Minnesota, MN, West Publishing, 2016.

K. Schlaich, *Das Bundesverfassungsgericht*, 3rd ed., Munich, C. H. Beck Verlag, 1994.

G. Vanber, *The Politics of Constitutional Review in Germany*, Cambridge, UK, Cambridge University Press, 2004.

8 Constitutional courts as ultimate players in multilevel constituent power games

The Bulgarian case

Martin Belov

8.1 Introduction[1]

This chapter will expose the several roles played simultaneously by the constitutional courts which make them ultimate players in multilevel constituent power games. The constitutional courts are gatekeepers of the bridge between the constitutionalism 'within' and 'beyond statehood'.[2] They are safeguards, promoters, or limiters of constitutional nationalism, constitutional internationalism, constitutional supranationalism, and constitutional globalism. Last but not least, they are mediators of the participation of the member states in the European Union (EU). The analysis will be limited to the Bulgarian case not only due to space constraints, but also because of the principal need to broaden the analysis of the role of constitutional courts to less researched constitutional jurisdictions which do not actively engage in intense judicial dialogue with the Court of Justice of the EU (CJEU). The Bulgarian case requires attention because the jurisprudence and the general stance of the Bulgarian Constitutional Court (BCC) with regard to Bulgaria's integration in the EU's multilevel constitutionalism are still rather under-researched. Nevertheless, some good work has already been undertaken in that area.[3]

Disregard of 'peripheral EU jurisdictions' such as Bulgaria may be quite dangerous. Indeed, the jurisprudential multilevel constituent power games are played predominantly by the CJEU and few activist constitutional courts of member states belonging to the EU's 'first speed'. This is especially true for the German Federal Constitutional Court, the Italian Constitutional Court, the French Constitutional Council, and the constitutional jurisdictions of Austria, Portugal, Spain, and Poland. However, the explicit or implicit Eurofriendliness or

1 I am grateful to Michael Hein and Mihail Vatsov for their useful comments and suggestions for improvement of my chapter.

2 For the 'constitutionalism beyond statehood' see P. Dobner and Martin Loughlin (Eds), *Twilight of Constitutionalism?*, Oxford, Oxford University Press, 2010; and N. Walker, 'Taking Constitutionalism beyond the State', *Political Studies*, Vol. 56, No. 3, 2008, pp. 519–543.

3 See M. Vatsov, 'European Integration Through Preliminary Rulings? The Case of the Bulgarian Constitutional Court', *German Law Journal*, Vol. 16, No. 6, 2015, pp. 1592–1622.

Euroscepticism of the constitutional courts of the rest of the EU member states is also important. This is due to the fact that they are not always blind followers of doctrines established in the course of the judicial dialogue led by the European mainstream. There are instances of passive resistance of such 'low profile' constitutional courts to the mainstream paradigms shaped by judicial dialogue. An example of this is BCC's implicit non-recognition of the doctrine of primacy of EU law. This doctrine is of paramount importance for the EU integration and for the development of EU constitutionalism. There can equally be deviating patterns developed by other such 'low profile' constitutional courts. Ignoring them, thus, may produce distorted understandings of the jurisprudential tendencies in promoting or hampering EU constitutionalism and, in turn, EU integration.

The Bulgarian case also exemplifies how EU integration allows domestic constitutional courts to become key players of constituent and external powers by virtue of a specific combination of tactics. That combination consists of domestic judicial activism on EU-related issues in parallel with absolute self-restraint for engagement in supranational judicial dialogue. The BCC is a giant on the domestic constitutional scene, sitting on the bridge between the Bulgarian and the EU constitutional orders. Simultaneously it is rather 'the sleeping beauty' or the 'invisible man' in the context of the judicial dialogue on sovereignty, primacy of EU law, constitutional supremacy, constitutional identity, 'counter-limits', etc. Moreover, the BCC combines explicit EU friendliness with implicit constitutional nationalism.

Consequently, the question may be raised whether the BCC actually participates in multilevel constituent power games if its engagement is limited to the domestic scene. Put differently, is BCC's case-law relevant for the EU if it is deliberately and durably refraining from participation in judicial dialogue. The EU-related decisions of the BCC are not only important for its strategic position as gatekeeper of the sovereignty and the supremacy of the Bulgarian Constitution. The BCC, being able to substantially influence and shape key constitutional principles and normative ideologies of constitutionalism, is also in a position to massively influence Bulgarian EU integration. Some of the BCC's competences (e.g. constitutional review of the ratification of primary EU law, giving abstract interpretation of the Bulgarian Constitution and declaring the procedure for transfer of constitutional competences to the EU as an 'unconstitutional constitutional amendment'[4]) may have an important impact on the EU and, indirectly, on other EU member states. Thus, the BCC is an important actor of the constituent power on the edge between national and supranational constitutionalism. It is an

4 For the concept of unconstitutional constitutional amendments see Y. Roznai, *Unconstitutional Constitutional Amendments. The Limits of Amendment Powers*. Oxford, Oxford University Press, 2017; M. Hein, 'Do Constitutional Entrenchment Clauses Matter? Constitutional Review of Constitutional Amendments in Europe', *International Journal of Constitutional Law*, Vol. 17, 2019, forthcoming. See also Michael Hein's chapter in this volume.

explicit player in domestic EU-related constitutional games and produces indirect and implicit effects also on the EU level.

8.2 The transfer of constitutional competences to the EU as a precursor for the increasing role of domestic constitutional courts

The analysis provided in this chapter will demonstrate how EU membership creates further opportunities for domestic courts – in this case the BCC – to engage with 'multilevel constituent power games' and to become key players in the 'ordering of constitutional orders'[5] overcoming the constitutionally entrenched separation between constituent and constituted powers. This case study should serve as an example of activist engagement of domestic constitutional courts in constitutional politics even through limited number of cases and with visible avoidance of engagement with judicial dialogue with the CJEU.

Intergovernmentalism and the more traditional and conservative constitutional theory of separation between constituent and constituted powers suggest that EU member states are transferring only competences and not sovereignty to the EU. Even if transfer of sovereignty is assumed it is not unconditionally handed over to the EU but is rather 'shared' with the rest of the EU member states for the achievement of common aims and for more efficient joint management of policies.[6] This transfer should be accomplished only by 'political powers' – the governments and the parliaments – which possess sufficient 'input' democratic legitimacy.[7] Courts should only check the observance of the legal framework for transfer of competences and powers stemming out of the domestic legal order. The transfer of constitutional competences should be accomplished by virtue of ratification of primary EU law or treaties concluded outside the EU framework (such as the Treaty on Stability Coordination and Governance) by the member states' parliaments. Such ratifications (depending on the relevant constitutional

5 For the concept of 'ordering of constitutional orders' see E. Tanchev, 'The Contemporary Supranational Constitutional Pluralism or the Ordering of Constitutional Orders', in P. Kirov (Ed.), *Constitutional Studies 2012–2013, Sofia*, 'St. Kliment Ohridski' University Press, 2014, pp. 171–198 (in Bulgarian).

6 See J. H. H. Weiler, 'The Transformation of Europe', *Yale Law Journal*, 1991, pp. 2403–2483; N. Walker (Ed.), *Sovereignty in Transition*, Oxford, Hart Publishing, 2006; R. Keohane, 'Ironies of Sovereignty: The European Union and the United States', *Journal of Common Market Studies*, Vol. 4, 2002, pp. 743–765; W. Wallace, 'The Sharing of Sovereignty: The European Paradox', *Political Studies*, 47 (3), 1999, pp. 503–521; and B. Fekete, 'The Limits of Sovereignty Pooling: Lessons from Europe', in M. Belov (Ed.), *Global Constitutionalism and Its Challenges to Westphalian Constitutional Law*, Oxford, Hart Publishing, 2018, pp. 133–161.

7 For the input legitimacy see F. Scharpf, *Governing in Europe. Effective and Democratic?*, Oxford, Oxford University Press, 1999; P. Craig and G. de Búrca, *EU Law. Text, Cases and Materials*, Oxford, Oxford University Press, 2008, p. 65; and Ph. Kiiver, *The National Parliaments in the European Union: A Critical View on EU Constitution-Building*, The Hague, Kluwer Law International, 2006, p. 95.

context) should be preceded by a constitutional amendment by the institutions of the domestic constituent power – typically the parliaments or special constituent assemblies, sometimes supplemented or replaced by direct consultation of the people via constitutional referendum.

This established practice is challenged by the increasing role of constitutional courts in promoting or impeding (1) constitutional change related to EU integration and (2) EU reforms preconditioned on domestic constitutional change. The engagement of constitutional courts in judicial dialogue[8] with the CJEU and their role as 'gatekeepers' of the 'domestic constitutional temple' makes them ultimate players in multilevel constituent power games. Such activity is accomplished through drawing of demarcation lines between the EU and the domestic legal order and by easing or rendering difficult the transfer of constitutional competences belonging to the member states towards the EU. Often it is constitutional courts which determine the possibility of engagement of the state with new level of political integration in the EU. It is typically framed as a two-track constitutional amendment resulting in amendment of the EU treaties and of the domestic constitution. Moreover, very frequently, the constitutional change is not explicit. It does not consist of formal amendment of the written constitution. There is an increasing number of instances of (1) 'creeping' constitutionalization and de-constitutionalization and (2) 'creeping' or implicit constitutional reform accomplished not by the institutions of the constituent power but by the constitutional courts on the basis of 'virtual amendment of the constitution'[9] preconditioned on the 'open texture' of constitutional law.[10] Furthermore, constitutional courts are also often 'paving the way' for constitutional reform by virtue of permissive constitutional interpretation favoring transfer of sovereignty, 'open statehood',[11] and further constitutional integration of the EU.

8 See G. Martinico and O. Pollicino, *The Interaction Between Europe's Legal Systems: Judicial Dialogue and the Creation of Supranational Laws*, Cheltenham, Edward Elgar, 2012; A. Muller and H. E. Kjos, *Judicial Dialogue and Human Rights (Studies on International Courts and Tribunals)*, Cambridge, Cambridge University Press, 2017; P. Lobba and T. Marinello (Eds), *Judicial Dialogue on Human Rights. The Practice of International Criminal Tribunals*, Leiden, Brill-Nijhoff, 2017; and M. Claes, M. de Visser, P. Popelier and C. Van de Heyning (Eds), *Constitutional Conversations in Europe*, Cambridge, Intersentia, 2012.

9 A. Tzanakopoulos suggests that 'law-interpretation and law-development are but points on a spectrum—only a thin line separates interpretation from "amendment"'. See A. Tzanakopoulos, 'Domestic Courts in International Law: The International Judicial Function of National Courts', *Loyola of Los Angeles International and Comparative Law Review*, Vol. 34, 2011, p. 134. Available at: http://digitalcommons.lmu.edu/ilr/vol34/iss1/7. In that regard see also M. Akehurst, 'The Hierarchy of the Sources of International Law', *The British Yearbook of International Law*, 1974–75, p. 273, p. 277.

10 See H. L. A. Hart, *The Concept of Law*, Oxford, Oxford University Press, 1997, pp. 124–136.

11 S. Hobe, 'Statehood at the End of the 20th Century – The Model of the 'Open State': A German Perspective', *Austrian Review of International and European Law*, Vol. 12, 1996, pp. 127–154. For the principle of open statehood in the Bulgarian constitutional order see M. Belov, 'The Opening of the Constitutional Order of Democracy in Transition Towards Supranational Constitutionalism: The Bulgarian Case', in B. Fekete and F. Gardos-Orosz

8.3 The concept of 'multilevel constituent power game'

Multilevel constitutionalism[12] is a phenomenon which has been present since the emergence of federations or even since the emergence of modern constitutionalism because the 1787 US constitution (and the constitutions of the states which became part of the USA) established for the first time in history a multilevel constitutional order. Multilevel constitutionalism consists of the existence of at least two levels of constitutional orders, e.g. national and sub-national or national and supranational, both possessing constitutions, constitutional systems of institutions of public power and constitutionally enshrined human rights. Since the end of the 20th century we are also witnessing the emergence of multilevel constitutionalism 'beyond statehood'. The two-track or even three-track constitutional orders consisting of the supranational constitutionalism of the EU and the domestic constitutional orders of the EU member states (as well as of the sub-national constitutional orders of the federal units of the federations which are members of the EU) are the paradigmatic examples of multilevel constitutionalism.

Multilevel constitutionalism 'beyond statehood' challenges key concepts of nation states' constitutionalism. It is not at ease with the principles of sovereignty and supremacy of the national constitution. It poses a range of interrelated questions such as: what is the role of domestic constitutional courts; should they be guardians of sovereignty and constitutional supremacy or facilitators of EU integration easing the transfer of sovereign powers to the EU and contributing to the absolute or relative primacy of the EU law; does the enhanced role of constitutional courts in multilevel constitutionalism endanger the status of the domestic institutions for accomplishment of constituent power; and how can we justify the role of constitutional courts as ultimate players in sovereignty games on the edge between national and supranational constitutionalism?

There is a general tendency for multilevel constitutionalism to enhance the role of the supreme and constitutional courts allocated on the upper constitutional level. In other words, even in domestic multilevel constitutional regimes, namely in federations, the supreme and constitutional courts of the federation gain additional importance as ultimate interpreters of the federal constitution and as arbiters in competence conflicts related to the vertical separation of powers. The historical precedent has been the US Supreme Court. However, this role has been quite visible also in Europe as early as the beginning of the 20th century when the Austrian Constitutional Court was empowered to resolve conflicts between the federation and the Bundesländer. Currently, most of the constitutional courts have the competence to be guardians of the vertical separation

(Eds), *Central and Eastern European Socio-Political and Legal Transition Revisited*, Frankfurt am Main, Peter Lang, 2017, pp. 213–231.

12 For the concept of multilevel constitutionalism see I. Pernice, 'The Global Dimension of Multilevel Constitutionalism. A Legal Response to the Challenges of Globalization', in *Völkerrecht als Wertordnung: Festschrift für Christian Tomushat*, Stuttgart, Engel Verlag, 2006, p. 973 and the following.

of powers. This competence is paralleled by the power to interpret the constitutional provisions which frequently leads to evolution of the constitutional model.

These functions of domestic supreme and constitutional courts raise issues related to the separation between constituent and constituted powers. However, they have somehow been accommodated by the theory of national constitutional law in the context of a balance between liberalism and democracy, the rule of law and the separation of powers, majoritarianism and counter-majoritarian safeguards for constitutional values, and constitutional supremacy as key components of nation-state constitutionalism. These issues are more novel and increasingly problematic in the context of 'constitutionalism beyond statehood'. They are problematic because they challenge the autonomy of the domestic constitutional order and the independence of the national community which is legally structured around the principles of state sovereignty and constitutional supremacy and safeguarded by the separation between constituent and constituted powers.

Indeed, the problem may also be posed the other way around, namely that the domestic constitutional courts may have specific legitimacy to be ultimate players in multilevel constituent power games. This role may be justified on the basis of requirements for coherence of the composite multilevel constitutional order, for adjustment of the EU and the domestic constitutional law, and for 'ordering of constitutional orders'.[13] Moreover, the domestic constitutional courts may function not only as transmitters of domestic sovereignty toward the EU and as promoters of the primacy of EU law. They may also be safeguards for the national constitutional identity and for the principles of the constitutional supremacy and state sovereignty. They may engage in 'pro-integration' judicial politics but also in 'nationalist jurisprudential games' via judicial dialogue.

This chapter will demonstrate how the BCC is performing such rather controversial and highly arguable roles and functions. It will outline the BCC's role as ultimate player in multilevel constituent power games.

8.4 The concept of constituent power and external power according to the Bulgarian constitutional model

The idea of separation between constituent and constituted powers is fundamental for the contemporary Bulgarian constitutional model. It is perceived as continuation of the pre-communist tradition of rigid procedure for constitutional amendment via special covenant – the Grand National Assembly (GNA). At the same time, it is a negation of the *de facto* power monism provided by the 1947 and 1971 communist constitutions which rejected the division between constituent and constituted powers. Indeed, both constitutions provided for the differentiation between statutory law and the much more rigid constitution.[14] However,

13 See E. Tanchev, op. cit.

14 See art. 99 of the 1947 Constitution and art. 143 of the 1971 Constitution.

the *de facto* constituent power was concentrated in the power elite and especially in the leadership of the Bulgarian Communist Party.

The contemporary Bulgarian constitutional model of the constituent power is rather rigid. It consists of a two-track amendment procedure due to the fact that the 1991 Constitution can be amended by either a special covenant – the GNA – or by the Parliament (National Assembly) via enhanced procedural hurdles and procedure which is more complicated in comparison to the ordinary legislative process.[15]

The most important constitutional amendments, enlisted in the entrenchment clause of art. 158 of the Constitution, should be adopted by a special covenant – the GNA. The entrenchment clause of art. 158 of the 1991 Bulgarian Constitution provides that the GNA shall exercise the following powers: adopt a new Constitution; resolve on the matters concerning a change of the territory of the Republic of Bulgaria, and ratify any international treaties providing for such changes; amend the form of state structure or the form of government; resolve on the matters concerning amendment of art. 5, paras 2 and 4 of the Constitution providing for the direct effect of the Constitution and the primacy of international treaties in the Bulgarian legal order and of art. 57, paras 1 and 3 of the Constitution concerning the protection of human rights in state of emergency; and amend Chapter IX of the Constitution devoted to the procedure for constitutional amendment.

The summoning of the GNA may be requested by half of the MPs of the National Assembly and by the President of the Republic. The decision for holding of elections for the GNA should be adopted by majority of two-thirds of all MPs in the National Assembly. The GNA adopts the constitutional amendments in three readings held in three different days with majority of two-thirds of all its members. The GNA functions instead of the regular parliament and will be dissolved immediately after the adoption of the constitutional amendments.

The rest of the constitutional amendments can be introduced by the National Assembly via qualified legislative procedure requiring qualified constitutional initiative belonging to one-quarter of the MPs and the President of the Republic, additional readings and qualified majorities. Acts of Parliament are adopted in two readings by virtue of majority of all of the MPs. A constitutional amendment is approved in three readings by virtue of a three-quarter majority of all MPs. If such majority is not achieved but at least two-thirds of the MPs have voted in favor, then the constitutional amendment can still be adopted in a fourth reading by virtue of a two-thirds majority of all MPs. There are no constitutional provisions regarding a constitutional citizens' initiative and constitutional referendum.

The rigid outlook of the contemporary Bulgarian model of the constituent power can be explained by reasons related to both the past and the future. The

15 See M. Hein, 'Bulgaria', in A. Fruhstorfer and M. Hein (Eds), *Constitutional Politics in Central and Eastern Europe: From Post-Socialist Transition to the Reform of Political Systems*, Wiesbaden, Springer VS, 2016, pp. 145–171.

authors of the 1991 Constitution wanted to deliberately draw upon a democratic tradition from the pre-communist Bulgarian history. Thus, they have adopted a modified version of model of constituent power provided by the first Bulgarian Constitution – the 1879 Tarnovo Constitution.[16] Moreover, they were aware of the fact that the period of transition to democracy would inevitably be turbulent. That is why they aimed to create a durable constitutional foundation for this transition by providing for a moderately rigid constitution.

The constituent power is not a concept which is explicitly used by the Bulgarian constitution and constitutional law. However, it has an established and stable use in constitutional theory. Moreover, the institutions and procedure for accomplishment of the constituent power have been initially concentrated in Chapter IX of the 1991 Constitution devoted to the amendment of the Constitution and the adoption of a new Constitution. Since the 2005 constitutional amendment this codification of the constituent power provisions in a single chapter has been undermined by the provision of a procedure for transfer of constitutional competences to the EU by the National Assembly.

Despite the initially rigid outlook of the constitutional model of the constituent power there have been five instances of constitutional reform accomplished by the National Assembly in 2003, 2005, 2006, 2007, and 2015.[17] Some of them, such as the introduction of the constitutional foundations of the Bulgarian EU membership, have been rather important. The BCC has played a pivotal role in the constitutional amendment procedure in two ways. First, it approved the constitutional amendments to be accomplished by the National Assembly and not by the GNA. This has been done by virtue of activist and extensive interpretation of the Constitution which was explicitly politically in favor of the EU integration of Bulgaria. Such interpretation has *de facto* redrawn the demarcation lines between the constituent and constituted powers and has shifted the competence load from the GNA to the National Assembly. Second, the BCC accomplished virtual amendment of the Constitution through extensive teleological interpretation. This interpretation constituted a mixture of overt Europeanism and implicit nationalism.

Equally, however, the BCC has recently gone back to the drawing board and reshuffled the divisions. It did so in a case concerning the constitutionality of certain referendum questions. While the case itself did not concern EU integration, its ramifications could theoretically concern EU integration. This can happen where an important EU integration-related question is proposed in a referendum and the BCC decides that it is of such high importance that the people cannot decide on it because the National Assembly itself cannot decide on it. While in

16 See M. Hein, *Verfassungskonflikte zwischen Politik und Recht in Südosteuropa.* Bulgarien und Rumänien nach 1989 im Vergleich, Baden-Baden, Nomos, 2013, pp. 102–103 and pp. 109–111.

17 See M. Belov, 'The Republic of Bulgaria', in *International Encyclopedia of Laws*, Deventer, Kluwer, 2018, pp. 34–35; Hein, op. cit. footnote 15, pp. 152–162.

the times of Brexit, such reasoning can be appreciated, it is not seen by some in the literature as necessarily reflecting the true meaning and spirit of the Bulgarian Constitution.[18]

The external power is the power for representation and participation of the state in the international and supranational relations.[19] It is not institutionalized in a special chapter of the Bulgarian Constitution. It is also rarely used by the Bulgarian theory. Most of the principles and competences in the external power domain are usually ascribed to the executive power and – to a lesser extent – to the legislative power. The lack of a clear concept of external power in the Bulgarian constitutionalism in parallel to the extremely modest debate on the constitutional background for the Bulgarian EU membership and participation in international organizations and the dispersed and fragmented provision of the EU-related constitutional provisions is creating a rather fuzzy and unclear constitutional foundation of the Bulgarian EU integration.

This combination of factors triggers huge opportunities for the BCC to become an ultimate player on the edge between domestic and European supranational constitutionalism. In the rest of this chapter it will be shown that the BCC is engaging in 'multilevel constituent power games' related to activist interpretation of the 1991 Constitution, redrawing of the demarcation lines between constituent and constituted powers, paving the way for transfer of sovereignty or, vice versa, for implicit and hidden domestic constitutional protectionism and nationalism. Such engagement of the BCC in constitutional politics seems to go against the initial idea of the founding fathers and mothers of the 1991 Constitution of the establishment of a moderately rigid constitution and for drawing clear distinction between constituent and constituted powers. Moreover, the BCC is becoming an unexpected player in the external power of the state. Last but not least, the BCC has established itself as the gatekeeper of the bridge between the EU and the Bulgarian constitutional orders.

8.5 The Bulgarian Constitutional Court: activist court accomplishing virtual constitutional amendment based on the 'open texture' of the 1991 Constitution

The vagueness of the constitutional foundations of the Bulgarian EU membership, their dispersion throughout the constitutional text, and the lack of clear constitutional conceptualization of the Bulgarian participation in the supranational constitutionalism of the EU are important preconditions for the BCC's judicial

18 M. Vatsov and P. Vakleva, 'The Shadow of Bicameralism in a Unicameral State: Dispersed Functional Bicameralism in Bulgaria?', in R. Albert, A. Baraggia, and C. Fasone (Eds), *Constitutional Reform of National Legislatures*, Cheltenham, Edward Elgar (forthcoming).

19 See M. Belov, 'Separation of Powers Reconsidered: A Proposal for a New Theoretical Model at the Beginning of the 21st Century', in A. Geisler, M. Hein and S. Hummel (Eds), *Law, Politics and the Constitution. New Perspectives from Legal and Political Theory*, Frankfurt am Main, Peter Lang, 2014, pp. 55–56.

activism. They allow the BCC to define the boundary between the domestic and the European legal order without clear basis, framework, and restriction. The lack of explicit restraints for jurisprudential shaping of the constitutional foundations of the Bulgarian EU membership, the precedent for redefinition of the competence delimitation between the institutions of the constituent power by the BCC[20] produced by its decisions from 2003, 2004, and 2005 which will be discussed below and the already established pattern of activist 'virtual' amendment of the Constitution by the constitutional jurisdiction put the BCC in the position of ultimate player in multilevel constituent power games.

The Bulgarian 1991 Constitution has no systematic approach to the participation of the state in international relations and especially in supranational constitutionalism. The constitutional foundations of Bulgarian EU membership are spread throughout the text of the Constitution. The EU is the only international or supranational organization which is mentioned by the Constitution after a constitutional amendment introduced in 2005. There are no specific provisions concerning the relationship between EU law and the 1991 Constitution.

The EU integration clause is rather vague. It just proclaims that 'the Republic of Bulgaria shall participate in the construction and development of the EU'. The EU integration clause is enshrined in art. 4, para. 3 of the Constitution. This is a rather awkward situation since art. 4 is generally devoted to the rule of law and not to the participation of the state in the EU. Indeed, the EU integration clause is the bearer of important political meaning and semiotic message. However, it has no chance to serve a framing function for BCC's jurisprudential activity.

The vagueness of the EU integration clause and the lack of explicit provisions on the hierarchical standing of the EU law in the Bulgarian constitutional order contribute a lot to the central role of the BCC as key moderator between the supranational and the domestic constitutional orders. This problem is additionally aggravated by the lack of a clear position of the constitutional legislator, Bulgarian constitutional theory, and the key state institution, the BCC itself, on the nature of the EU, the hierarchical standing of the EU law in the Bulgarian legal order, and the relationship between the constitutionalism 'within' and 'outside of statehood'.

Moreover, the BCC is an activist constitutional jurisdiction. It takes very low number of decisions and some of them are rather descriptive and declaratory, thus not really implying new meaning into the constitutional provisions. The main reasons for the BCC's low workload are the lack of direct constitutional complaints and the very restricted concrete review for constitutionality. However, there is a limited but very important number of cases when the BCC has developed the meaning of the constitutional text in a direction which cannot be derived from the intent of the constitutional legislator. Thus, the BCC is a *de*

20 See M. Belov, 'The Republic of Bulgaria', in *International Encyclopedia of Laws*, Deventer, Kluwer, 2018, pp. 34–35.

facto key player in the constituent power in Bulgaria despite or maybe because of the formal rigidness of the 1991 Constitution.

The BCC rarely takes decisions related to the EU and the Bulgarian membership in it. However, when it does the BCC is rather activist and makes use of its powerful competences for abstract and concrete control for constitutionality and especially for abstract interpretation of the Constitution. There are four most important decisions which demonstrate the central and even crucial and pivotal role played by the BCC with regard to the participation of the state in the EU. They are clear examples of judicial activism. These are Decision No. 3 of 2003, Decision No. 3 of 2004, Decision No. 8 of 2005,[21] and Decision No. 7 of 2018.

Decision No. 3 of 2003 has interpreted the concept of the form of governance in an extremely broad way. It has declared almost every amendment of the constitutional design to be relevant for the form of governance. Thus, it has reserved almost all constitutional amendments for the GNA. Such an interpretation was against the concept of the constituent power provided by the 1991 Constitution and would have made impossible the accomplishment of the EU related constitutional amendments necessary for the Bulgarian accession to the EU.

The BCC comes to rather different conclusions in its Decision No. 3 of 2004. This is the decision which radically changed the results of the previous Decision No. 3 of 2003. Thus, it made possible swift constitutional amendments accomplished by the National Assembly which paved the way for the Bulgarian EU accession in 2007. According to Decision No. 3 of 2004 the accession to the EU does not concern the form of territorial distribution of powers, the absolute supremacy of the Bulgarian Constitution, and the primacy of the international treaties.[22] It is really interesting and bizarre that the judge-rapporteur Vasil Gotzev who wrote the previous Decision No. 3 of 2003 was one of the two judger-apporteurs who prepared also Decision No. 3 of 2004.

Finally, Decision No. 8 of 2005 made some additional clarifications on which constitutional amendments related to the judiciary can be accomplished by the National Assembly instead of the GNA. Again, all the three decisions served as precursors of constitutional change. They are the result of pro-European judicial activism of the BCC, which has been put in the position of the inevitable partner of the National Assembly in the constituent power. This is due to the fact that the National Assembly could not have amended the Constitution without the preceding BCC decisions. This is further evidence that the BCC became the ultimate factor for the engagement of Bulgaria with the multilevel constitutionalism of the EU.

21 For an earlier analysis of these three judgments, see also M. Hein, op. cit. footnote. 16, pp. 204–210, 223–227 and 232–236.

22 The impact of the EU integration on the supremacy of the constitution is admitted by B. Punev, judge of the BCC in the period 2006–2015, in a scientific paper. See B. Punev, 'From Protection of the National Constitution towards Protection of the European Legal Order', in E. Tanchev (Ed.), *Classic and Contemporary Tendencies in Constitutional Control*, Sofia, Feneya, 2012, p. 227 (in Bulgarian).

There are several strategies and roles performed by the BCC which make it an ultimate player in multilevel constituent power games. They have their own semi-autonomous logic, but in the long run are mutually interrelated.

The first strategy consists of the full self-restraint of the BCC from engaging in judicial dialogue. There is no single demand for preliminary ruling addressed to the CJEU by the BCC.[23] Moreover, the BCC rarely uses the case-law of the CJEU as a source of legal argumentation in its own decisions. Explicit mentioning of the case-law of the CJEU or any other supranational and international court is an exotic rarity.[24] It is not part of the Court's style to ground its decisions on affirmation or rejection of the CJEU's jurisprudence, let alone to engage with the CJEU through a preliminary reference procedure for which it has been criticized.[25] This disengagement of the BCC with the CJEU has not gone unnoticed in Luxembourg either.[26]

The BCC has not developed a doctrine related to the national constitutional identity, the permissible limitations for transfer of constitutional competences to the EU or other international or supranational organizations, or for the permissible penetration of international or supranational legal standards in the Bulgarian legal order.[27] The primacy of EU law is just mentioned *obiter dictum* in some decisions of the BCC. This mentioning consists in merely asserting the fact that there is such primacy without any analysis or ascription of meaning to it. The most extensive analysis of the primacy of the EU law is given by the BCC in its Decision No. 7 of 2018. However even this decision does not clearly engage with the issue of the relationship between the 1991 Constitution and the EU law.[28] The BCC's Decisions No. 3 of 2003, No. 3 of 2004, and No. 8 of 2005 which have paved the way for the Bulgarian EU integration avoid any engagement with the principle of primacy of the EU law. Thus, reading the recent jurisprudence of the BCC, one can be informed of the existence of such primacy but cannot

23 For a missed opportunity for preliminary ruling which should have been demanded see the critical analysis of Decision No. 5 of 2008 provided by A. Kornezov. See A. Kornezov, 'The Jurisprudence of the Constitutional Court in the Light of the Community Law (2007–2008)', *Obstestvo i Pravo*, 2009, No. 2, pp. 24–25 (in Bulgarian).

24 Such rare examples of decisions in which the Constitutional Court refers to the case-law of the CJEU are Decision No. 2 of 2015 and Decision No. 7 of 2018. Decision No. 2 of 2015 pronounced the unconstitutionality of some provisions of the Electronic Communications Act which implemented the EU Data Retention Directive in Bulgaria. Decision No. 7 of 2018 (also known as the CETA Decision) clarified the status of the mixed agreements concluded simultaneously by the EU and its member states with a third party (such as CETA) in the Bulgarian legal order.

25 See M. Vatsov, op. cit.

26 See Opinion of AG Bot in Case C-614/14 Criminal proceedings against Atanas Ognyanov EU:C:2016:111, [13].

27 See M. Belov, *Bulgarian Constitutional Identity*, Sofia, Sibi, 2017, pp. 1–239 (in Bulgarian).

28 For a critical analysis of the reluctance of the BCC to engage with the issue of the relationship between the EU law and the Bulgarian Constitution see A. Kornezov, op. cit., p. 26 (in Bulgarian).

infer any consequences stemming out of it or come to any conclusions regarding its effect on the supremacy of the Bulgarian Constitution or the relationship between EU law and international treaties ratified by the Republic of Bulgaria.[29]

It should be mentioned that the BCC tries to provide for EU-friendly interpretation of the Bulgarian law. There are several decisions which are clear instances of interpretation of the 1991 Constitution in conformity with the EU law.[30]

The national constitutional identity is mentioned only once and as late as 2018 in Decision No. 7 of 2018. However, it is not conceptualized in such a way as to function as a device for mastering the relationship between the 1991 Constitution and the EU law and to serve its typical functions expected in all EU member states.[31]

Thus, the BCC has not developed doctrines for the relationship between the domestic and the EU legal order comparable to the extensive case-law of the German Federal Constitutional Court or to the '*contro-limiti*' doctrine of the Italian Constitutional Court. This is rather opaque situation because it may be interpreted in different and even controversial ways. It may mean that the BCC is very EU-friendly thus deliberately not developing any limitations to the EU integration. Or it may indicate hidden constitutional nationalism based on implicit tactics for preservation of the autonomy of the Bulgarian constitutional order and the supremacy of the 1991 Constitution over the EU law. In order to come to a clearer conclusion further analysis of the other EU related strategies of the BCC is needed.

The second strategy of the BCC is overtly pro-European. The BCC has paved the way to the swift Bulgarian EU integration by virtue of adopting its interrelated decisions No. 3 of 2003, No. 3 of 2004, and No. 8 of 2005 in the context of the late pre-accession period. This has been done at the price of having a questionable definition of the model for distribution of the competences between the National Assembly and the GNA.

The BCC functioned as a *de facto* constitutional legislator shifting the competence load in favor of the National Assembly. Indeed, this was not only result of deliberate activism of the Court but was necessitated by the very abstract formulation of the competences in the text of art. 158 of the Constitution. Nevertheless, the BCC made extensive use of its interpretative power.

29 The Bulgarian doctrine remains largely silent regarding the relationship between the EU law and the Bulgarian Constitution implicitly suggesting the absolute domestic constitutional supremacy. The primacy of the EU law over the 1991 Constitution is admitted (without any clarification and further argumentation) only by B. Punev. See B. Punev, op. cit., pp. 237–238 (in Bulgarian). For an in-depth analysis of the relationship between the EU law and the Bulgarian constitution admitting the relative primacy of the former over the latter see M. Belov, *Bulgarian Constitutional Identity*, Sofia, Sibi, 2017, pp. 195–229 (in Bulgarian).

30 Examples are Decision No. 11 of 2007 and Decision No. 6 of 2008. See A. Kornezov, op. cit., pp. 11–12 (in Bulgarian).

31 See M. Belov, 'The Functions of Constitutional Identity Performed in the Context of Constitutionalization of the EU Order and Europeanization of the Legal Orders of EU Member States', *Perspectives on Federalism*, Vol. 9, No. 2, 2017, www.on-federalism.eu/attachments/260_download.pdf.

What is particularly problematic is the inconsistency of the case-law. The BCC through its Decision No. 3 of 2003 made the constitutional reform necessary for the EU accession of Bulgaria practically impossible by reserving it for the GNA. This is due to the fact that summoning of GNA in a short period of time was practically impossible. Less than a year later, the BCC radically changed its practice. Decision No. 3 of 2004 was clear departure from the conclusions set by Decision No. 3 of 2003. It allowed the National Assembly to accomplish constitutional reforms which actually concerned the form of territorial distribution of powers, the supremacy of the Constitution, and the primacy of the international treaties – issues clearly reserved for the GNA. The result was activist defense of the European future of Bulgaria even at the expense of the separation of powers, legal certainty, and the coherency of the jurisprudence of the BCC which are key requirements of rule of law.

What is important here is that despite the contestable character of these decisions with regard to their constitutionality they allowed the BCC to establish itself as ultimate player in the context of the Bulgarian EU integration and membership and thus in multilevel constituent power games. The BCC became an ultimate player in such games in a twofold way. First, it has established itself as a promoter of the EU integration and as an insurmountable factor for its fostering or potential hampering. Second, the BCC has practically demonstrated that its pivotal status cannot be challenged. This is due to the fact that there is no legal way to abolish or otherwise invalidate its decisions apart from the unrealistic last resort option of explicit curtailment of its competences by virtue of constitutional amendment.

The third strategy of the BCC is implicitly nationalist-protectionist. It results in the protection of the absolute supremacy of the Bulgarian Constitution over the EU law. This strategy consists of the avoidance of explicit engagement with the issue of the relationship between the domestic constitution and EU law in parallel with implicit approval of the absolute supremacy of the 1991 Constitution to EU law. The BCC systematically accomplished control for compliance of Acts of Parliament with the EU law. However, there is no explicit competence for such control granted to the Court by the 1991 Constitution. Hence, the BCC subrogates EU law under the category of international treaties which automatically grants it sub-constitutional status.[32] This is due to the fact that according to

32 Such a rather problematic approach is visible also in the Bulgarian constitutional theory. For example, Prof. Emilia Drumeva – former judge of the BCC during the time of adoption of Decisions No. 3 of 2004 and 8 of 2005 – suggests that the Bulgarian constitutional legislator has had a clear idea that there is no need for new competence for control of compliance of the acts of Parliament with the EU law. The reason is that EU law actually equals international law and thus the BCC can accomplish such control on the basis of the existing competence for control for compliance of the Acts of Parliament with international treaties. See E. Drumeva, 'Preliminary Rulings of the Bulgarian Constitutional Court?', in E. Tanchev (Ed.), *Classic and Contemporary Tendencies in Constitutional Control*, Sofia, Feneya, 2012, pp. 170 and 172 (in Bulgarian). For criticism of this approach and the practice of the BCC to treat the EU law (especially the primary EU law) as traditional international treaties hav-

art. 5, para. 4 of the Constitution international treaties are allocated above the domestic legislation with the exception of the Constitution. This fact corresponds with the lack of explicit constitutional provision on the hierarchical standing of the EU law in the Bulgarian legal order. Finally, the Constitutional Court has stipulated, in the reasoning of Decision No. 3 of 2004, albeit only ***obiter dictum***, that EU law has the status of international treaties.

Consequently, a conclusion can be drawn that the BCC performs several roles in the context of the participation of Bulgaria in the multilevel constitutionalism of the EU. It is a promoter of Europeanism and supranational constitutionalism and facilitator of the EU integration, but also a protector of constitutional nationalism especially with regard to the absolute supremacy of the Bulgarian Constitution. The BCC is performing as an explicitly pro-European player, unwilling to participate in judicial dialogue, but also as an implicit nationalist player.

The reluctance of the BCC to engage in judicial dialogue can be explained by context-related factors such as a lack of clear understanding and recognition of this concept and the inexistence of a tradition of participation in exchange of judicial decisions especially with international and supranational courts.[33] However, it may also be conceptualized in a very contradictory way. On the one hand, this passive attitude may be considered as a result of affirmative pro-European stance which makes the drawing of limitations to supranational constitutional integration unnecessary. On the other hand, it may stem out of the desire to preserve constitutional supremacy and an absolute and holistic version of sovereignty. The latter stance of the BCC is not in parallel with the simplified procedure for transfer of constitutional competences to the EU which is eased in comparison to the procedure for constitutional amendment. Both the transfer of constitutional competences and the amendment of the constitution concern sovereignty, constitutional supremacy, and the division between constituent and constituted powers. Hence, they are relevant for the role of the BCC as a key player on the border between constituent and constituted powers and between the domestic and the European legal order.

8.6 The procedure for transfer of constitutional competences to the EU as 'unconstitutional constitutional amendment' enhancing the potential of the Constitutional Court to be ultimate player in multilevel constituent power games

The general model for approval of the Bulgarian engagement with deepening of the constitutionally relevant EU integration is to an extent problematic. This is due to several reasons. First, the GNA is rather conservative institution for

ing sub-constitutional status in the Bulgarian legal order see A. Kornezov, op. cit., p. 26 (in Bulgarian).

33 For a detailed discussion of the possible legal reasons for BCC's silence see M. Vatsov, op. cit.

constitutional amendment. It is reminiscent of the belief, which was widespread in 18th and 19th century constitutionalism that the rigidity of the constitution is precondition for its longevity.[34] If the division of competences for EU-related constitutional amendments between the GNA and the National Assembly is taken seriously and implemented in a consistent way adhering to strict interpretation of the entrenchment clause of the Bulgarian Constitution it may render very difficult the accomplishment of more profound EU reforms. In fact, not only Bulgarian EU integration may be brought to a halt if EU treaties' reforms with constitutional implications must be preceded by constitutional amendment produced by the GNA. The whole process of EU reform may be stalled if such treaties must be preceded by a constitutional reform accomplished by the GNA.

This is one of the main reasons why the Bulgarian constitutional legislator by virtue of the 2005 constitutional amendment decided to allow for ratification by the National Assembly of treaties which transfer constitutional competences. This procedure should be read in conjunction with Decision No. 3 of 2003, Decision No. 3 of 2004, and Decision No. 8 of 2005 of the BCC which paved the way for the accomplishment of important EU-related constitutional amendments without recourse to a GNA.

Second, the current Bulgarian constitutional model leads to a phenomenon which can be defined as 'democratic entrapment of the *demos*'. It consists of the pending issue whether constitutional referenda and referenda for denouncement of international treaties are allowed by the 1991 Constitution. Currently the Bulgarian Act of Parliament regulating direct democracy unconstitutionally prohibits the referenda for denouncement of international treaties. Here, it should be taken into account that there has been no referendum for Bulgarian EU accession.

Hence, the people are explicitly proclaimed by art. 1, para. 2 of the 1991 Constitution to be sovereign. However, they are not allowed to pronounce on key constitutional issues falling into the scope of the entrenchment clause and thus belonging to the exclusive sphere of competence of the GNA. The entrenchment clause is subject to rather activist, discretionary, and voluntary interpretation by the BCC shifting competences in favor of the National Assembly. Thus, the people have in fact no impact on the constitutional dimension of the Bulgarian EU integration. Moreover, they are deprived of important parts of 'negative sovereignty' in terms of 'counter-democracy'[35] by being prohibited to vote on referenda for denouncement international treaties and on constitutional referenda. The procedure for transfer of constitutional competences provided by art. 85, para. 1, point 9 and para. 2 of the Constitution also suggests that such process is reserved for the Parliament and not for the people.

34 See E. Tanchev, *Introduction in Constitutional Law*, Sofia, Sibi, 2003, pp. 237–238 (in Bulgarian).

35 See P. Rosanvallon, *Counter-Democracy Politics in an Age of Distrust*, Cambridge, Cambridge University Press, 2008, pp. 121–191.

What is important here is that the ultimate decision for the constitutionality or unconstitutionality of many sovereign decisions related to EU integration actually belongs to a composite veto player[36] consisting of the National Assembly and the BCC. The BCC is the competent institution to decide whether the provisions of the Act of Parliament shaping the constitutional, ratification, and denouncement referendum are in compliance with the 1991 Constitution. It is the institution which will pronounce on the constitutionality of the international treaty for transfer of constitutional competences to the EU.

The BCC may even be approached to pronounce on the constitutionality of the 2005 constitutional amendment which has introduced the procedure for transfer of constitutional competences to the EU. There has been no pronouncement so far but no temporal limitation exists for future engagement of the Constitutional Court with this issue. The BCC in its Decision No. 3 of 2003 has explicitly approved its own competence to control the constitutionality of Acts of the National Assembly for amendment of the Constitution. The BCC can accomplish only formal, procedural, and *ultra vires* control for constitutionality of such unconstitutional amendment safeguarding or in fact determining the separation of powers between the National Assembly and the GNA.

Hence, the conclusion whether art. 85, para. 1, point 9 and para. 2 of the Constitution are an 'unconstitutional constitutional amendment' is implicitly pending which is comparable to a 'ticking atomic bomb'. If Bulgaria ratifies a treaty for amendment of the primary law of the EU by virtue of the procedure provided by art. 85, para. 1, point 9 and para. 2 of the Constitution and this procedure is subsequently declared to be unconstitutional by the BCC, this will be extremely problematic for both the Bulgarian and the EU legal order. The effect of the BCC's decision in the domestic legal order will make the transfer of constitutional competences null and void. This will produce an entanglement because according to the *pacta sunt servanda* principle Bulgaria will have to fulfill its obligations to the EU and the other EU member states stemming out of the treaty, whereas the constitutional foundations of this treaty will be shaken since its ratification will be based on 'unconstitutional constitutional amendment'. Hence, art. 85, para. 1, point 9 and para. 2 of the Constitution can be defined as 'the most dangerous provisions' of the Bulgarian Constitution.

The procedure for transfer of constitutional competences is enshrined in art. 85, para. 1, point 9 and para. 2 of the Constitution. According to art. 85, para. 1, point 9 the National Assembly ratifies and denounces by virtue of an Act of Parliament international treaties which transfer to the EU competences stemming out of this Constitution. Furthermore, art. 85, para. 2 provides that the Act

36 For the concept of veto players see G. Tsebelis, *Veto Players. How Political Institutions Work*, Princeton, NJ/New York, Russell Sage Foundation and Princeton University Press, 2002.

of Parliament for ratification of such treaties should be adopted in two readings by virtue of a two-thirds majority of all MPs.

The introduction of the procedure for transfer of constitutional competences via ratification of international treaties constitutes an 'unconstitutional constitutional amendment'. This is due to the fact that it has been introduced in the Constitution by the National Assembly but should have been accomplished by the GNA. The transfer of constitutional competences defined by art. 85, para. 1, point 9 as 'competences stemming out of this Constitution' is in fact transfer of sovereignty to a supranational polity – the EU.[37] The constitution is a result of sovereign decision. It is the depot of sovereignty. Hence, the transfer of constitutional competences is transfer of sovereignty.

Traditionally constitutional reforms can be accomplished only via explicit amendment of the text of the constitution. However, judicial activism allows for indeed rather questionable 'virtual amendment' of the constitution by the BCC. Furthermore, constitutional reform may be produced also via combined tactics of transfer of constitutional competences to the EU through ratification of international treaty which will be subsequently legalized and consolidated by affirmative BCC decision. Such constitutional tactics have a very fragile constitutional basis and may lead to informal but substantial 'creeping' amendment of the constitution.

An important problem consists also of the fact that transfer of constitutional competences based on art. 85, para. 1, point 9 and para. 2 of the Constitution will not be accomplished by the GNA or the National Assembly acting as an institution of the constituent power. They will not be done through the forms and procedures for accomplishment of constituent power. Such a transfer will be performed via the special legislative procedure by the National Assembly acting as institution of the legislative power.

This procedure, which itself constitutes an 'unconstitutional constitutional amendment', potentially increases the role of the BCC as 'gatekeeper' of the Bulgarian constitutional order. It fosters the chances that the BCC will *de facto* exercise constituent power. Further, the power potential stemming out of the competence of the BCC to control the constitutionality of the Acts of Parliament for transfer of constitutional competences to the EU puts the BCC in the role of ultimate player in multilevel constituent power games.

The procedure provided by art. 85, para. 1, point 9 and para. 2 of the Constitution creates potential risks for constitutionalization or deconstitutionalization of the Bulgarian constitutional order by virtue of the transfer of constitutional competences by the National Assembly. Deconstitutionalization may consist in the transfer of constitutional competences to the EU by the National Assembly with the explicit or implicit approval of the BCC. A reversed trend of

37 The fact that the EU member states (Bulgaria included) are transferring sovereignty and not just competences is admitted also by the BCC judge Blagovest Punev. See B. Punev, op. cit., p. 236 and p. 238 (in Bulgarian).

peculiar constitutionalization via Europeanization of the Bulgarian constitutional order may emerge out of its opening towards supranational constitutional standards having validity in the domestic constitutionalism, last but not least, with the consent of the BCC.

8.7 Conclusions

Stringent amendment procedures for domestic constitutional change enhance the role of domestic constitutional courts as players in constituent power games in the context of the EU multilevel constitutionalism. In light of the Bulgarian case it is highly questionable whether rigid constitutions really protect sovereignty or foster alternative ways for amendment and even surpassing the restraints to EU integration imposed by the domestic constitution. Rigid constitutions may foster 'unconstitutional constitutional amendments' accomplished by alliances of constituted powers – parliaments and constitutional courts – acting as *de facto* constituent powers.

The model of Bulgarian EU integration demonstrates that the principle of popular sovereignty has been bypassed by a joint accomplishment of sovereign powers by the National Assembly and the BCC. Such shared 'parliamentary-judicial sovereignty' is not legitimate from the viewpoint of the ideal constitution (the predominant official normative ideologies) and the written constitution and more precisely its art. 1, para. 2 proclaiming popular sovereignty. However, it is rather efficient and seems justified from the viewpoint of pro-European integration constitutional politics and in the context of post-democracy.[38]

The open texture of the 1991 Constitution, the fuzziness of the EU integration clause, the lack of a clear and coherent concept underlying the constitutional foundations of the Bulgarian EU membership and the already established tradition of judicial activism and jurisprudential virtual amendment of the Constitution make the BCC an ultimate player in multilevel constituent power games. The BCC is even the ultimate player in the strategic shaping of the framework, principles, and range of the constituent power. This strategic placement of the BCC is the result of tactical use of a combination of explicit pro-European activism in seminal decisions paving the way to the EU integration and implicit constitutional nationalism in instances that keep control of domestic players over the points of interaction between the supranational and the national constitutional orders. Clear examples of such constitutional nationalism are the implicit non-recognition of the primacy of the EU law over the Bulgarian Constitution and the strategic self-restraint in engagement with judicial dialogue with the CJEU.

38 The term 'post-democracy' has been introduced by Colin Crouch but I am using it here with a slightly different meaning. See Crouch, C., *Postdemocracy*, Cambridge, Polity Press, 2004.

References

M. Akehurst, 'The Hierarchy of the Sources of International Law', in *The British Yearbook of International Law*, Oxford, Oxford University Press, Volume 47, Issue 1, 1975, pp. 1–53.

M. Belov, *Bulgarian Constitutional Identity*, Sofia, Sibi, 2017a (in Bulgarian).

M. Belov, 'Separation of Powers Reconsidered: A Proposal for a New Theoretical Model at the Beginning of the 21st Century', in A. Geisler, M. Hein & S. Hummel (Eds), *Law, Politics and the Constitution. New Perspectives from Legal and Political Theory*, Frankfurt am Main, Peter Lang, 2014.

M. Belov, 'The Functions of Constitutional Identity Performed in the Context of Constitutionalization of the EU Order and Europeanization of the Legal Orders of EU Member States', *Perspectives on Federalism*, Vol. 9, No. 2, 2017b, www.on-federalism.eu/attachments/260_download.pdf.

M. Belov, 'The Opening of the Constitutional Order of Democracy in Transition Towards Supranational Constitutionalism: The Bulgarian Case', in B. Fekete & F. Gardos-Orosz (Eds), *Central and Eastern European Socio-Political and Legal Transition Revisited*, Frankfurt am Main, Peter Lang, 2017c.

M. Belov, 'The Republic of Bulgaria', in *International Encyclopedia of Laws*, Deventer, Kluwer, 2018.

M. Claes, M. de Visser, P. Popelier & C. Van de Heyning (Eds), *Constitutional Conversations in Europe*, Cambridge, Intersentia, 2012.

P. Craig & G. de Búrca, *EU Law: Text, Cases and Materials*, Oxford, Oxford University Press, 2008.

P. Dobner & M. Loughlin (Eds), *Twilight of Constitutionalism?*, Oxford, Oxford University Press, 2010.

E. Drumeva, 'Preliminary Rulings of the Bulgarian Constitutional Court?', in E. Tanchev (Ed.), *Classic and Contemporary Tendencies in Constitutional Control*, Sofia, Feneya, 2012 (in Bulgarian).

B. Fekete, 'The Limits of Sovereignty Pooling: Lessons from Europe', in M. Belov (Ed.), *Global Constitutionalism and Its Challenges to Westphalian Constitutional Law*, Oxford, Hart Publishing, 2018.

H. L. A. Hart, *The Concept of Law*, Oxford, Oxford University Press, 1997.

M. Hein, 'Bulgaria', in A. Fruhstorfer & M. Hein (Eds), *Constitutional Politics in Central and Eastern Europe. From Post-Socialist Transition to the Reform of Political Systems*, Wiesbaden, Springer VS, 2016.

M. Hein, 'Do Constitutional Entrenchment Clauses Matter? Constitutional Review of Constitutional Amendments in Europe', *International Journal of Constitutional Law*, Vol. 17, 2019, forthcoming.

M. Hein, *Verfassungskonflikte zwischen Politik und Recht in Südosteuropa. Bulgarien und Rumänien nach 1989 im Vergleich*, Baden-Baden, Nomos, 2013.

S. Hobe, 'Statehood at the End of the 20th Century – The Model of the 'Open State': A German Perspective', *Austrian Review of International and European Law*, Vol. 12, 1996.

R. Keohane, 'Ironies of Sovereignty: The European Union and the United States', *Journal of Common Market Studies*, Vol. 4, 2002, pp. 743–765.

Ph. Kiiver, *The National Parliaments in the European Union: A Critical View on EU Constitution-Building*, The Hague, Kluwer Law International, 2006.

A. Kornezov, 'The Jurisprudence of the Constitutional Court in the Light of the Community Law (2007–2008)', *Obstestvo i Pravo*, No. 2, 2009, pp. 24–25 (in Bulgarian).

P. Lobba & T. Marinello (Eds), 'Judicial Dialogue on Human Rights', *The Practice of International Criminal Tribunals*, Leiden, Brill-Nijhoff, 2017.

G. Martinico & O. Pollicino, *The Interaction Between Europe's Legal Systems: Judicial Dialogue and the Creation of Supranational Laws*, Cheltenham, Edward Elgar, 2012.

A. Muller & H.E. Kjos, *Judicial Dialogue and Human Rights (Studies on International Courts and Tribunals)*, Cambridge, UK, Cambridge University Press, 2017.

I. Pernice, 'The Global Dimension of Multilevel Constitutionalism. A Legal Response to the Challenges of Globalization', in *Völkerrecht als Wertordnung. Festschrift für Christian Tomushat*, Stuttgart, Engel Verlag, 2006.

B. Punev, 'From Protection of the National Constitution Towards Protection of the European Legal Order', in E. Tanchev (Ed.), *Classic and Contemporary Tendencies in Constitutional Control*, Sofia, Feneya, 2012.

P. Rosanvallon, *Counter-Democracy Politics in an Age of Distrust*, Cambridge, UK, Cambridge University Press, 2008.

Y. Roznai, 'Unconstitutional Constitutional Amendments', in *The Limits of Amendment Powers*, Oxford, Oxford University Press, 2017.

F. Scharpf, *Governing in Europe. Effective and Democratic?*, Oxford, Oxford University Press, 1999.

E. Tanchev, *Introduction in Constitutional Law*, Sofia, Sibi, 2003.

E. Tanchev, 'The Contemporary Supranational Constitutional Pluralism or the Ordering of Constitutional Orders', in P. Kirov (Ed.), *Constitutional Studies 2012–2013*, Sofia, 'St. Kliment Ohridski' University Press, 2014, pp. 171–198 (in Bulgarian).

G. Tsebelis, *Veto Players. How Political Institutions Work*, Princeton, NJ/New York, Russell Sage Foundation and Princeton University Press, 2002.

A. Tzanakopoulos, 'Domestic Courts in International Law: The International Judicial Function of National Courts', *Loyola of Los Angeles International and Comparative Law Review*, Vol. 34, 2011, p. 134. http://digitalcommons.lmu.edu/ilr/vol34/iss1/7

M. Vatsov, 'European Integration Through Preliminary Rulings? The Case of the Bulgarian Constitutional Court', *German Law Journal*, Vol. 16, No. 6, 2015, pp. 1591–1622.

M. Vatsov & P. Vakleva, 'The Shadow of Bicameralism in a Unicameral State: Dispersed Functional Bicameralism in Bulgaria?', in R. Albert, A. Baraggia & C. Fasone (Eds), *Constitutional Reform of National Legislatures*, Cheltenham, Edward Elgar (forthcoming).

N. Walker (Ed.), *Sovereignty in Transition*, Oxford, Hart Publishing, 2006.

N. Walker, 'Taking Constitutionalism beyond the State', *Political Studies*, Vol. 56, No. 3, 2008, pp. 519–543.

W. Wallace, 'The Sharing of Sovereignty: The European Paradox', *Political Studies*, 47 (3), 1999, pp. 503–521.

J. H. H. Weiler, 'The Transformation of Europe', *The Yale Law Journal*, Vol. 100, Issue 8, 1991, pp. 2403–2483.

9 Courts in the constitution-making process

Paradoxes and justifications

Antonios Kouroutakis

9.1 Introduction

Without doubt, the constitution-making process is a highly political process. It is the expression of the sovereignty and the constituent power that is entrusted to special constituent assemblies and a variety of representative bodies.[1] Only the sovereign has the constituent power, which in theory is superior and predates the positive constitutional norms, which determine how the constituted power (legislative, executive, and judicial) is exercised.

As it is accurately remarked, 'the notion of *pouvoir constituant* is often associated with the unquestioned affirmation of unrestrained or even arbitrary processes of constitutional politics'.[2] Indeed, the orthodoxy among lawyers, philosophers, and political theorists was that the constitution-making process is unrestrained and arbitrary, with the exception of the imposed constitutions (also known as *constitutions octroyées*) such as the monarchical constitutions,[3] because in principle the constituent assembly preexists any other institution and in practice it has the unlimited and uncontrolled power to decide the process of the constitution drafting and the substance of the constitution. Furthermore, Jon Elster has argued

1 The concept of sovereignty is a dynamic concept, a concept that changed and evolved. Initially there was a tautology between the Sovereign and the institution with the 'ultimate coercive power of command'. For instance Bodin has remarked that 'There are none on earth, after God, greater than sovereign princes, whom God establishes as His lieutenants to command the rest of mankind'. See J. Bodin, *Six Books of the Commonwealth*, in M. J. Tooley (Ed.), Oxford, Basil Blackwell Oxford, 1995, p. 40. Then, it evolved to the idea of a power 'to found, to posit, to constitute' the legal order. See A. Kalyvas, 'Popular Sovereignty, Democracy, and the Constituent Power', *Constellations*, Vol. 12, No. 2, 2005, p. 223.

2 M. Patberg, 'Constituent Power: A Discourse-Theoretical Solution to the Conflict between Openness and Containment', *Constellations*, Vol. 24, No. 1, 2017, p. 51.

3 For more details about the imposed constitutions see R. Albert, X. Contiades and A. Fotiadou, *The Law and Legitimacy of Imposed Constitutions*, Routledge, 2018; Y. Hasebe, 'Imposed Constitutions (Constitutions Octroyées)', in R. Grote and others (Eds), *Max Planck Encyclopedia of Comparative Constitutional Law*, Oxford, Oxford University Publishing, 2017; N. Feldman, 'Imposed Constitutionalism', *Connecticut Law Review*, Vol. 37, No. 4, 2004–2005, p. 857; S. Chesterman, 'Imposed Constitutions, Imposed Constitutionalism, and Ownership', *Connecticut Law Review*, Vol. 37, No. 4, 2004–2005, p. 947.

that constituent power might be subject to constraints, but as it will be shown below, such constraints have relative force.[4]

However, during the last decades, court interventions, direct or indirect, have been recorded in the constitution-making process. Obviously, the presence of the courts and their interventions in the constitution-making process is seen as a limit and as a control on the constituent power. In particular, this chapter will examine the role of the judiciary in four constitutional orders, Colombia, South Africa, Honduras, and Nepal in the constitution-making process in 1991,[5] 1993,[6] 2009,[7] and 2011,[8] respectively.

The close examination of these cases will show the role of the judiciary in the constitution-making process under different circumstances. Methodologically, the analysis will compare and contrast the conditions that allowed the judiciary to intervene in the constitution-making process and will examine its impact. Hence, this chapter aims to highlight paradoxes but also to offer justifications, both formal and substantive, for the intervention of the courts in the constitutionalization of a new legal order.

This chapter argues that the existence of an interim constitution or a total revision of the existing constitution may grant direct authority to the court to intervene in the constitution-making process, for instance by controlling the constituent assembly, reviewing its acts and even certifying the final constitutional document. In addition, the courts' participation in the constitution-making process might be justified on substantive grounds such as natural law principles, common constitutional principles, or the so-called supra-constitutional principles that exist in every democratic society and pervade the general belief of the people.

The chapter is organized in the following way. The first part will revisit the concept of the constituent power in order to highlight the paradoxes from judicial intervention in the constitution-making process. In the second part, it will examine the formal justifications for the courts' intervention. In particular, it will focus on the case of South Africa, and it will show that the existence of an interim constitution may provide the positive law ground for the courts' intervention. Furthermore, the chapter will examine the theoretical framework of the total

4 See below, section 9.2.2.

5 Supreme Court, Case No. 138, May 24, 1990; available at www.teoriajuridicayconstitucion.com/app/download/13243974430/Sentencia++138+1990+de+la+CSJ.pdf?t=1485478996 [Accessed 20 April 2019].

6 Certification of the Constitution of the Republic of South Africa, 1996 (CCT 23/96) [1996] ZACC 26; 1996 (4) SA 744 (CC); 1996 (10) BCLR 1253 (CC) (6 September 1996).

7 Corte Suprema de Justicia, Comunicado Especial, June 30, 2009; and Comunicado del 20 de Julio, July 20, 2009; both available at www.poderjudicial.gob.hn [Accessed 20 April 20, 2019].

8 Bharatmani Jungam & others v Office of the President and others, [Supreme Court] Nov. 25, 2011, 68 ws 0014 (4) (Nepal); available at www.supremecourt.gov.np/web/assets/downloads/judgements/Constitution_Assembly_Case.pdf [Accessed 20 April 2019].

revision of the constitution and it will argue that such a process also offers formal justifications for the courts' intervention.

Finally, the last part will examine the cases of Nepal, Colombia, and Honduras. In Nepal the interim constitution did not recognize any formal justification for the participation of the judiciary in the constitution-making process, and likewise, in Colombia and in Honduras, when a total revision of the Constitution was initiated, the Constitution did not recognize a role for the judiciary. Nonetheless, in Nepal the Supreme Court played a constructive role on the constitution-making process. Regarding the cases of Colombia and Honduras, in the former case, the Supreme Court of Colombia allowed the total revision. In the latter case of Honduras, the Supreme Court blocked that process. By examining these two cases, the chapter will elaborate on the substantive grounds that permit the courts' intervention in such process, when formal justifications are absent.

9.2 The paradoxical role of the courts in the constitution-making process

9.2.1 Constituent power

The constitution-making process is a special and exceptional procedure. It is entrusted to a special body, the constituent assembly,[9] and such process, unlike the formation of the legislature, is not periodic. In most of the cases, the formation and the composition of the constituent assembly is not regulated in advance, but *ad hoc*. In principle, *a priori* regulation *de facto* limits procedurally the sovereignty of the constituent power.[10] Hence, it is a highly political process that requires wide and deep deliberation. Such power is exercised based on a pure political process. Such a process is pure because it is not constrained by the law, as it preexists the legal framework.[11]

9 However, in recent years a new type of constitution-making process occurred in Iceland, which was more open and transparent as the people participated in the process of the drafting of the new constitution with the support of new technology and social media. See H. Landemore, 'Inclusive Constitution-Making: The Icelandic Experiment', *The Journal of Political Philosophy*, Vol. 23, No. 2, 2015, p. 166; H. Fillmore-Patrick, 'The Iceland Experiment (2009–2013): A Participatory Approach to Constitutional Reform', *DPC Policy Note New Series*, Vol. 2, 2013; S. Suteu, 'Constitutional Conventions in the Digital Era: Lessons from Iceland and Ireland', *Boston College International and Comparative Law Review*, Vol. 38, No. 2, 2015, p. 251.

10 However, in the case of total revision of the constitution, such as the case of Spain, Argentina, and Bulgaria where the constitution-making process is regulated, the constituent assembly is regulated in advance. See below, (n 41).

11 Bruce Ackerman, highlights 'the arbitrary character of acts of constituent power,' which is distinct from his theory of constitutional politics and he explicitly disclaims because it implies that 'where the law ends … pure politics (begins)'. See B. Ackerman, *We the People II: Transformations*, Cambridge, MA: Harvard University Press, 1998, p. 11, p. 425.

Furthermore, the constituent power is also defined as primary power because the legislative, executive, and judicial power emanate, are defined by, and depend on the constituent power.[12] Sieyès has stated that

> the constituent power can do everything [in relationship to constitutional making]. It is not subordinated to a previous constitution. The nation that exercises the greatest, the most important of its powers, must be, while carrying this function, free from all constraints, from any form, except the one that it deems better to adopt.[13]

While the concept of sovereignty evolved, the core definition of sovereignty remains the same as it was first articulated by Bodin: 'sovereignty is that absolute and perpetual power.'[14] Having said that, the following part will examine the constraints on the constituent power.

9.2.2 Limits of the constituent power

In his seminal article 'Forces and Mechanisms in the Constitution-Making Process'[15] Jon Elster has examined the first Constitution of the US, the first Constitution of France, and the Basic Law of Germany. He has accurately remarked that upstream and downstream constraints exist in the constitution-making process.[16]

12 Locke has identified that the legislative power is supreme, but he clarified that at the same time such power is entrusted by the sovereign, and thus subordinate to the sovereign power which is the ultimate power: see J. Locke, The Second Treatise of Government: An Essay Concerning the True Original, Extent, and End of Civil Government, in J. Bennett (Ed.), 2017, Ch. 13, par. 149, 48. '[T]here can be only one supreme power, the legislative power, to which all the rest are and must be subordinate. But this is only a fiduciary [= 'entrusted'] power to act for certain ends, so that the people retain a supreme power to remove or alter the legislature when they find it acting contrary to the trust that had been placed in it. [The root of 'fiduciary' is the Latin fide = 'trust'.] All power that is given with trust for attaining a certain end is limited by that purpose; when the purpose is obviously neglected or opposed by the legislature, the trust is automatically forfeited and the power returns into the hands of those who gave it'.

13 E. J. Sieyès, Reconnaissance et exposition raisonnée des droits de l'homme et du citoyen, Bruxelles Chez F Hayez, rue de l'Escalier, 1792, p. 13 (in French).'Les pouvoirs compris dans l'établilfement public font tous fournis à des loix, à des réglés, à des formes , qu'ils ne font point les maîtres de changer. Comme ils n'ont pas pu se constituer eux-même , ils ne peuvent pas non plus changer leur constitution; de même ils ne peuvent rien sur la constitution les uns des autres. Le pouvoir constituant peut tout en ce genre. Il n'est point soumis d'avance à une constitution donnée. La Nation qui exerce alors le plus grand, le plus important de ses pouvoirs, doit être dans cette fonction, libre de toute contrainte, et de toute forme, autre que celle qu'il lui plaît d'adopter'.

14 See Bodin, 1995, p. 24.

15 J. Elster, 'Forces and Mechanisms in the Constitution-Making Process', *Duke Law Journal*, Vol. 45, No. 2, 1995, p. 364.

16 Ibid.

In particular, Elster categorizes the constraints into two broad categories: upstream and downstream. The upstream constraints are the 'constraints [that] are imposed on the assembly before it starts to deliberate', and the downstream 'constraints are created by the need for ratification of the document the assembly produces'.[17] Regarding the upstream constraints, Elster remarks that the constituent assemblies formed for the drafting of the US, French, and German constitutions were subject to some constraints because they were not self-created; for instance the first was formed by the Continental Congress in the United States in 1787, the French was formed by the King in France in 1789, and the German was formed by the Western Occupying Powers in Germany in 1949 respectively.[18] Hence such assemblies had some upstream constraints about their composition, the decision-making process, etc.

Furthermore, such constituent assemblies may have also downstream constraints which are the ratification process. For instance, Elster identifies that in the US paradigm, the Philadelphia Convention was bound about the ratification process which required unanimity from the states in federal policies or in the German paradigm there was the provision for a popular referendum to ratify the new constitution.[19]

However, such constraints were proven in practice as having relative force. For instance, in the US the constitutional convention adopted a completely new constitution while it has also defined a new ratification formula.[20] Likewise, in Germany, the constituent assembly drafted a constitution prescribing a more centralized federation while the ratification process did not take place with a referendum.[21]

That said, there is no reference to the courts as a constraint in the constitution-making process. In theory, it is paradoxical for the judiciary to have a role in the constitution-making process, as the judicial power is a constituted power, which emanates from the constituent power. In addition from a more pragmatic perspective, the judiciary cannot have a role because the formation of the courts always follows the drafting and/or promulgation of the constitution, and, therefore, courts cannot intervene in the constitution-making process.

Furthermore, and from an institutional perspective, the judiciary is a counter-majoritarian institution and compared to the popular branches, the legislature and the executive, has less political legitimacy to participate in a highly political process such as constitution-making.[22] Moreover, judges are not elected by the

17 Ibid., p. 373.

18 Elster, 1995, p. 364.

19 Ibid., p. 373.

20 For more details, see R. Albert, 'Four Unconstitutional Constitutions and their Democratic Foundations', *Cornell International Law Journal*, Vol. 50, No. 2, 2017, p. 169.

21 See Hasebe, 2017, pp. 28–30.

22 See G. Zhu and A. Kouroutakis, 'The Role of the Judiciary and the Supreme Court in the Constitution Making Process: The Case of Nepal', *Stanford International Law Journal*, Vol. 55, 2019, pp. 69–71.

people; in fact, judges are expected to be politically insulated. Thus, the institution has limited democratic legitimacy.

Having said that and given the political nature of the constitution-making process, it seems that it is paradoxical for an institution like the judiciary with limited democratic legitimacy to participate in the drafting of a constitution or even to act as a constraint in the process.

9.3 Formal and substantive justifications

While a number of paradoxes emerge regarding the role of the courts in the constitution-making process, in practice, courts have participated in the constitution-making process of a number of countries the recent years, namely in Colombia, South Africa, Honduras, and Nepal in the constitution-making process in 1991, 1993, 2009, and 2011, respectively.

The close examination of these cases will show the role of the judiciary in the constitutionmaking process under different circumstances. In particular, the existence of an interim constitution or a total revision of the existing constitution provides formal justification for the intervention of the judiciary in the constitution-making process. As will be shown below, the provisions of the interim constitution may grant direct authority to the court to intervene in the constitution-making process to control the constituent assembly, to review its acts, and even to certify the final constitutional document.

In addition, the courts' participation in the constitution-making process might be justified on substantive grounds such as natural law principles, common constitutional principles, or the so-called supra-constitutional principles that exist in every democratic society and pervade the general belief of the people.

9.3.1 Formal justifications

As was mentioned previously, the existence of an interim constitution offers the conditions for the participation of the courts in the constitution-making process. This was the case in South Africa. In South Africa, an interim constitution was adopted in 1993 to officially end the apartheid period and to serve as transitional until the adoption of a new constitution.[23] Indeed the aim of the interim constitution was to define the framework for the adoption of a new and permanent constitution.[24]

23 About interim constitutions and sunset clauses in the constitution drafting, see A. Kouroutakis, *The Constitutional Value of Sunset Clauses*, Routledge, 2017, p. 163.

24 The preamble of the Constitution of the Republic of South Africa in 1993, prescribed that 'in order to secure the achievement of this goal, elected representatives of all the people of South Africa should be mandated to adopt a new Constitution in accordance with a solemn pact recorded as Constitutional Principle'. See Constitution of the Republic of South Africa, 1993, [Preamble].

Article 71 of the Interim Constitution entitled 'Constitutional Principles and Certification'[25] prescribes the principles and the procedure of the approval of the new and permanent constitution. In particular:

> (1) A new constitutional text shall– (a) comply with the Constitutional Principles contained in Schedule 4; and (b) be passed by the Constitutional Assembly in accordance with this Chapter. (2) The new constitutional text passed by the Constitutional Assembly, or any provision thereof, shall not be of any force and effect unless the Constitutional Court has certified that all the provisions of such text comply with the Constitutional Principles referred to in subsection (1) (a). (3) A decision of the Constitutional Court in terms of subsection (2) certifying that the provisions of the new constitutional text comply with the Constitutional Principles, shall be final and binding, and no court of law shall have jurisdiction to enquire into or pronounce upon the validity of such text or any provision thereof.

Hence, the drafters of the Constitution, the members of the constitutional assembly,[26] had upstream and downstream constraints based on the classification by Elster.[27] Upstream constraint was the compatibility of the text of the constitution with 34 principles that were included in Schedule 4 of the Interim Constitution.[28]

Accordingly, once the drafters of the Constitution finalized the text of the new constitution, which was approved by 86 per cent of the members of the constitutional assembly,[29] it was sent to the Court for certification. Before the Court, a number of objections were submitted opposing the certification of the new text of the Constitution by political parties and private members alike.[30] Interestingly, the Court set the interpretation principles based on which it would apply the constitutional principles prescribed in Schedule 4.[31] Furthermore, it acknowledged

25 Constitution of the Republic of South Africa, 1993, Article 71.

26 Constitution of the Republic of South Africa, 1993, Article 68.

27 See n. 18.

28 Among them, the drafters of the interim constitution included the principle of the democratic governance and the equality (I) the protection of fundamental rights; (II) the prohibition of discrimination; (III) the supremacy of the constitution; (IV) the principles of equity and substantive equality; (V) the principle of separation of powers and checks and balances; (VI) the independence and impartiality of the judiciary; (VII) the principle of representation; (VIII) of accountability in the administration; (IX) the protection of minority political parties; (XIV) the rigidity of the amendment process; (XV) the different levels of government; (XVI) the relationship between central and regional governments (XVIII). For more details see Constitution of the Republic of South Africa, 1993, Schedule 4.

29 Certification of the Constitution of the Republic of South Africa, 1996 (CCT 23/96) [1996] ZACC 26; 1996 (4) SA 744 (CC); 1996 (10) BCLR 1253 (CC) (6 September 1996) [21].

30 Ibid., [24].

31 Certification of the Constitution of the Republic of South Africa, 1996 (CCT 23/96) [1996] ZACC 26; 1996 (4) SA 744 (CC); 1996 (10) BCLR 1253 (CC) (6 September

its limited jurisdiction in the internal processes followed by the constitutional assembly on the drafting of the new text of the constitution, the so-called *interna corporis* of the constitutional assembly.[32]

Eventually, the Constitutional Court ruled that several provisions of the text of the newly adopted Constitution did not comply with a number of constitutional principles of Schedule 4 of the interim Constitution.[33] In particular, the Constitutional Court found that the provision of Art. 23 of the new text was not compatible with the 'Right of Individual Employers to Bargain Collectively'.[34] Also, it found that a law, the Labour Relations Act 66 of 1995 which was excluded from constitutional review based on provision 241(1) of the new text was incompatible with the 34 principles.[35] In addition, it found that the failure of the drafters of the new constitution to entrench some provisions did not comply with the 34 principles.[36] Furthermore, it found that the offices of the Public Protector and Auditor regulated by provisions 182(1) and 188 of the new text respectively did not receive the safeguards expected by the 34 principles.[37] Finally, the Constitutional Court found that some specific regulations about the competence of the local government did not comply with the 34 constitutional principles.[38]

Regardless of the outcome of the case, the intervention of the Constitutional Court of South Africa was a mandatory process, proscribed in the ratification process.[39]

1996). '[33] In the light of the background described and in the context discussed above, the CPs have to be applied and interpreted along the following lines. [34] The CPs must be applied purposively and teleologically to give expression to the commitment "to create a new order" based on "a sovereign and democratic constitutional state" in which "all citizens" are "able to enjoy and exercise their fundamental rights and freedoms. [35] The CPs must therefore be interpreted in a manner which is conducive to that objective. Any interpretation of any CP which might impede the realisation of this objective must be avoided. [36] The CPs must not be interpreted with technical rigidity. They are broad constitutional strokes on the canvas of constitution making in the future. [37] All 34 CPs must be read holistically with an integrated approach. No CP must be read in isolation from the other CPs which give it meaning and context. [38] It accordingly follows that no CP should be interpreted in a manner which involves conflict with another. The lawmaker intended each of the CPs to live together with the others so as to give them life and form and nuance'.

32 Ibid., [28]. 'Nor do we have any power to comment upon the methodology adopted by the CA'.

33 For a complete list with the provisions of the new text that violated the 34 principles see Certification of the Constitution of the Republic of South Africa, 1996 (CCT 23/96) [1996] ZACC 26; 1996 (4) SA 744 (CC); 1996 (10) BCLR 1253 (CC) (6 September 1996) [482].

34 Ibid., [69].

35 Ibid., [149].

36 Ibid., [152–156].

37 Ibid., [161–165]

38 Ibid., [301].

39 See Zhu and Kouroutakis, 2019, p. 69, 81. About the role of the Constitutional Court see also J. Sarkin, 'The Political Role of the South African Constitutional Court', *African Law Journal*, Vol. 114 S, 1997, p. 134.

Having said that, it is worth noting that the Constitutional Court itself tried to distinguish its role from the political process. In particular, it clarified the following:

> First and foremost it must be emphasized that the Court has a judicial and not a political mandate. Its function is clearly spelt out in IC 71(2): to certify whether all the provisions of the NT comply with the CPs. That is a judicial function, a legal exercise. Admittedly a constitution, by its very nature, deals with the extent, limitations and exercise of political power as also with the relationship between political entities and with the relationship between the state and persons. But this Court has no power, no mandate and no right to express any view on the political choices made by the CA in drafting the NT, save to the extent that such choices may be relevant either to compliance or non-compliance with the CPs. Subject to that qualification, the wisdom or otherwise of any provision of the NT is not this Court's business.[40]

Finally, besides the existence of an interim constitution, the role of the courts in the constitution-making process is justified when a total revision of the existing constitution is initiated. The total revision of the constitution may be a procedure explicitly regulated in the existing constitution, such as the case of Spain,[41] Argentina,[42] and Bulgaria.[43] The drafters of the Constitution may explicitly recognize a role for the judiciary in such process. However, as of today, there is no provision on total revision of the constitution that recognizes the role of the courts in the total revision process.

9.3.2 Substantive justifications

Having explored the formal justifications for the participation of the judiciary in the constitution-making process, this section will examine the substantive justifications. To begin with, the idea that unconstitutional constitutional norms

40 Certification of the Constitution of the Republic of South Africa, 1996 (CCT 23/96) [1996] ZACC 26; 1996 (4) SA 744 (CC); 1996 (10) BCLR 1253 (CC) (6 September 1996) [27].

41 See for instance, the Constitution of Spain, 1978, Article 168: '1. If a total revision of the Constitution is proposed, or a partial revision thereof, affecting the Preliminary Title, Chapter Two, Section 1 of Title I, or Title II, the principle shall be approved by a two-thirds majority of the members of each House, and the Cortes shall immediately be dissolved. 2. The Houses elected must ratify the decision and proceed to examine the new Constitutional text, which must be approved by a two-thirds majority of the members of both Houses. 3. Once the amendment has been passed by the Cortes Generales, it shall be submitted to ratification by referendum'.

42 Likewise, see the Constitution of Argentina 1994, Article 30: 'The Constitution may be totally or partially amended. The necessity of reform must be declared by Congress with the vote of at least two-thirds of the members; but it shall not be carried out except by an Assembly summoned to that effect'.

43 See also the Constitution of the Republic of Bulgaria 1991, Article 158.

exist was first articulated by German courts after World War II. Judges expressed the idea that 'superior' constitutional norms exist based on natural law principles, which were superior compared to ordinary and positive law constitutional norms.[44]

Substantive justifications exist regardless of the existence or not of formal justifications. By default, the substantive justifications are abstract and theoretical. For instance, some general legal principles about what is fair and just preexist the constitutional documents, and are omnipresent.

As we have said elsewhere,

> such principles, which are not written and do not depend on the existence of a constitutional document, might be seen as natural law or as supra-constitutional principles. Such principles might be common features across countries that share common constitutional traditions, or they might be specific norms based on the constitutional history of each country. Such norms, in reality, create a general framework within which the constituent power is exercised and thus form limitations in the constitution-making process. Accordingly, if there is a violation of these norms, then the courts might intervene during the constitution-making process.[45]

In particular, in Nepal, the justification for the role of the court was not explicit, and based on the text of the interim constitution like the case of South Africa. More precisely, an interim constitution was adopted in 2007.[46] According to the interim constitution, the lifespan of the constituent assembly was limited into two years.[47] However, after two years, there was no final document. Thus, with an amendment to the interim constitution, the lifespan of the constitution assembly was extended, in total four times.[48]

When such extensions were challenged before the Supreme Court, it found that such extensions violated the principle of periodic elections, which was set out in the Preamble of the Interim Constitution.[49] In particular, it ruled that:

44 See G. Dietze, 'Unconstitutional Constitutional Norms', *Virginia Law Review*, Vol. 42, No. 1, 1957, p. 1, 3. 'It was soon claimed that the judges could not only review a statute for its constitutionality, but also the compatibility of constitutional norms with those "superior" constitutional norms that contained natural law. This gave rise to the problem of unconstitutional constitutional norms. Closely tied up with the compatibility of constitutional norms with natural law, that issue became one of the most fascinating juristic phenomena of recent years. It reflects the German jurists' farewell to a positivistic tradition in which most of them had been brought up'.

45 Zhu and Kouroutakis, 2019, p. 69, 81.

46 See Constitution (INTERIM) of Nepal, 2007.

47 See Constitution (INTERIM) of Nepal, 2007, Art 63–64.

48 International IDEA, 'Nepal's Constitution Progress: 2006–2015: Progress, Challenges, and Contributions of the International Community', 2015.

49 Bharatmani Jungam v Office of the President, Writ No. 68-ws-0014, at 4–5 (Nov. 25, 2011).

> In case the Constitution did not come into force within the stipulated time, there may ipso facto rise a political question about which the Preamble of the Constitution suggests that the only way out of the problem is to go into the periodic election. In such a situation the act of frequent extension of time limit about which the Article 64 of the Interim Constitution clearly specifies shall be ipso facto void in the eyes of law.[50]

The jurisdiction of the Supreme Court of Nepal was based on the ordinary jurisdiction of Art. 102 Clause 4 of the Interim Constitution of Nepal 2063 (2007), according to which the Supreme Court 'shall have the final authority to interpret [the interim] Constitution and the laws in force'.[51]

Furthermore, in the case of a total revision of the Constitution, in case there is no provision regulating the total revision, *a fortiori* there is no such provision about the role of the courts. Likewise, the jurisdiction of the courts might be justified on their ordinary jurisdiction. Such are the cases of Colombia and Honduras.

In fact, in Colombia in 1990, the National Commission proposed to hold a referendum in parallel to the elections of 11 March 1990 so as to form a constituent assembly to propose a new constitution.[52] Despite the fact that an official referendum did not take place, an unofficial one was organized and the result was an overwhelming support for a new constituent assembly. This led President Virgilio Barco to use his emergency powers in order to call for an official referendum along with the presidential elections of 27 May 1990. The use of presidential emergency powers was challenged before the Supreme Court which uphold this unconstitutional total revision of the constitution. Fox, Gallon-Giraldo, and Stetson argue that 'the Court considered that according to general principles of Colombian Constitutional Law, governance of the state derives from the people's will. Consequently, if the Colombian people decide to reform their constitution they are free to do so without restraint'.[53]

The justification for a total revision of the constitution was offered by Madison who stated on the unconstitutional adoption of the US Constitution in 1999 that

> [Citizens] must have reflected, that in all great changes of established governments, forms ought to give way to substance; that a rigid adherence in such cases to the former, would render nominal and nugatory the transcendent

50 Ibid., at 4.

51 Constitution (INTERIM) of Nepal, 2007, Article 102.

52 D. T. Fox Gustavo Gallon-Giraldo, and A. Stetson, 'Lessons of the Colombian Constitutional Reform of 1991', in Laurel E. Miller and Louis Aucoin (Eds), *Framing the State in Times of Transition – Case Studies in Constitution Making*, Washington DC, United States Institute of Peace Press Washington DC, 2010, p. 470.

53 Ibid., p. 471.

and precious right of the people to abolish or alter their governments as to them shall seem most likely to affect their safety and happiness.[54]

Thus, the judiciary in Colombia has also intervened in the constitution-making process, as it approved the formation of a constituent assembly,[55] regardless of the fact that such a process contradicted the amendment process of the existing constitution.[56]

On the other hand, in Honduras, in 2009, when the President Manuel Zelaya attempted a total revision of the constitution, the Supreme Court similarly intervened but in order to block the process. The Supreme Court of Honduras[57] did not approve the total revision of the constitution through popular referendum, 'on the argument that [the President] had promoted presidential re-election, and had attempted to alter the unamendable provisions in the Constitution'.[58] Having said that, the Supreme Court of Honduras' intervention in the constitution-making process, which led to a constitutional crisis as the President was ousted from his position,[59] had a completely opposite effect from the deferential stance of the Supreme Court of Colombia.

9.4 Conclusions

This chapter has examined the role of the judiciary in the 'constitutionalization' process. It has examined the role of the courts in four legal orders, namely South

54 J. Madison, 'The Federalist No. 40', in Clinton Rossiter (Ed.), *The Federalist Papers*, New York, Modern Library, 1938, pp. 257–258. See also R. Albert, 'Four Unconstitutional Constitutions and their Democratic Foundations', *Cornell International Law Journal*, Vol. 50, No. 2, 2017, p. 169.

55 Supreme Court, Case No. 138, May 24, 1990; available at www.teoriajuridicayconstitucion.com/app/download/13243974430/Sentencia++138+1990+de+la+CSJ.pdf?t=1485478996 [Accessed 20 April 2019].

56 For details on the constitution-making process in Colombia during the early 1990s, see K. Merhof, 'Building a Bridge between Reality and the Constitution: The Establishment and Development of the Colombian Constitutional Court', *International Journal of Constitutional Law*, Vol. 13, 2015, p. 714, pp. 716–717.

57 Corte Suprema de Justicia, Comunicado Especial, June 30, 2009; and Comunicado del 20 de Julio, July 20, 2009; both available at www.poderjudicial.gob.hn [Accessed 20 April 2019].

58 L. Marsteintredet, 'The Honduran Supreme Court Renders Inapplicable Unamendable Constitutional Provisions', *International Journal of Constitutional Law Blog*, 2015, available at www.iconnectblog.com/2015/05/Marsteintredet-on-Honduras [Accessed 20 April 2019).

59 'An array of Honduran civil authorities – including all 15 members of the Supreme Court, the chief prosecutor, an overwhelming majority of Congress, and the new, *de facto* government insisted that his ouster was a lawful and constitutional action to defend Honduran democracy and the rule of law from a president who had defied both courts and Constitution, and who was maneuvering to amend the Constitution to allow him to run for a second term'. See D. Casse, 'Honduras: Coup d'Etat in Constitutional Clothing?', *American Society of International Law Insights*, Vol.13, No. 9, 2009, p. 9.

Africa, Nepal, Colombia, and Honduras. The examination of such cases reveals that the courts have participated in the constitution-making process under different circumstances.

Prima facie the role of the courts in the constitution-making process is paradoxical, as courts are purely legal institutions, while the constitution-making process is a highly political process. However, formal and substantive justifications explain their role. For instance, in case of a total revision of the constitution, or in case of an interim constitution, the role of the courts may be explicitly recognized. Such as the case of South Africa with the interim constitution of 1993.

However, in the absence of formal justifications, in the case of Nepal, Honduras, and Colombia, we have seen the courts have participated in the process either to spur or to block the constitution-making process. Such role is justified on natural law or supra-constitutional principles that transcend the legal orders. However, the intervention of the Courts, due to their limited political legitimacy, needs to strike a balance between deference to the popular will and their role of safeguarding major constitutional principles.

References

B. Ackerman, *We the People II: Transformations*, Cambridge, MA: Harvard University Press, 1998.

R. Albert, 'Four Unconstitutional Constitutions and their Democratic Foundations', *Cornell International Law Journal*, Vol. 50, No. 2, 2017, pp. 169–198.

R. Albert, X. Contiades & A. Fotiadou, *The Law and Legitimacy of Imposed Constitutions*, London, Routledge, 2018.

J. Bodin, in M. J. Tooley (Ed.), *Six Books of the Commonwealth*, Oxford, Basil Blackwell Oxford, 1995.

D. Casse, 'Honduras: Coup d'Etat in Constitutional Clothing?', *American Society of International Law Insights*, Vol. 13, No. 9, 2009.

S. Chesterman, 'Imposed Constitutions, Imposed Constitutionalism, and Ownership', *Connecticut Law Review*, Vol. 37, No. 4, 2004–2005.

G. Dietze, 'Unconstitutional Constitutional Norms', *Virginia Law Review*, Vol. 42, No. 1, 1957.

J. Elster, 'Forces and Mechanisms in the Constitution-Making Process', *Duke Law Journal*, Vol. 45, No. 2, 1995.

N. Feldman, 'Imposed Constitutionalism', *Connecticut Law Review*, Vol. 37, No. 4, 2004–2005.

H. Fillmore-Patrick, 'The Iceland Experiment (2009–2013): A Participatory Approach to Constitutional Reform', *DPC Policy Note New Series*, Vol. 2, 2013.

D. T. Fox Gustavo Gallon-Giraldo & A. Stetson, 'Lessons of the Colombian Constitutional Reform of 1991', in L. E. Miller & L. Aucoin (Eds), *Framing the State in Times of Transition – Case Studies in Constitution Making*, Washington DC, United States Institute of Peace Press Washington DC, 2010.

Y. Hasebe, 'Imposed Constitutions (constitutions octroyées)', in R. Grote & others (Eds), *Max Planck Encyclopedia of Comparative Constitutional Law*, Oxford, Oxford University Publishing, 2017.

A. Kalyvas, 'Popular Sovereignty, Democracy, and the Constituent Power', *Constellations*, Vol. 12, No. 2, 2005.
A. Kouroutakis, *The Constitutional Value of Sunset Clauses*, London, Routledge, 2017.
H. Landemore, 'Inclusive Constitution-Making: The Icelandic Experiment', *The Journal of Political Philosophy*, Vol. 23, No. 2, 2015.
J. Locke, 'The subordination of the powers of the commonwealth', in J. Bennett (Ed.), *The Second Treatise of Government: An Essay Concerning the True Original, Extent, and End of Civil Government*, Jonathan Bennett, 2017.
J. Madison, 'The Federalist No. 40', in C. Rossiter (Ed.), *The Federalist Papers*, New York, Modern Library, 1938.
L. Marsteintredet, 'The Honduran Supreme Court Renders Inapplicable Unamendable Constitutional Provisions', *International Journal of Constitutional Law Blog*, 2015, www.iconnectblog.com/2015/05/Marsteintredet-on-Honduras [Accessed 20 April 2019].
K. Merhof, 'Building a Bridge Between Reality and the Constitution: The Establishment and Development of the Colombian Constitutional Court', *International Journal of Constitutional Law*, Vol. 13, 2015.
M. Patberg, 'Constituent Power: A Discourse-Theoretical Solution to the Conflict between Openness and Containment', *Constellations*, Vol. 24, No. 1, 2017.
J. Sarkin, 'The Political Role of the South African Constitutional Court', *African Law Journal*, Vol. 114 S, 1997.
E. J. Sieyès, 'Reconnaissance et exposition raisonnée des droits de l'homme et du citoyen', *Bruxelles Chez F Hayez, rue de l' Escalier*, 1792.
S. Suteu, 'Constitutional Conventions in the Digital Era: Lessons from Iceland and Ireland', *Boston College International and Comparative Law Review*, Vol. 38, No. 2, 2015.
G. Zhu & A. Kouroutakis, 'The Role of the Judiciary and the Supreme Court in the Constitution Making Process: The Case of Nepal', *Stanford International Law Journal*, Vol. 55, 2019.

10 The least dangerous branch?

Constitutional review of constitutional amendments in Europe

Michael Hein[1]

10.1 Introduction

On 4 March 2016, the Constitutional Court of Moldova declared a constitutional amendment unconstitutional, which had been enacted 15 years prior.[2] Upon the request of a group of deputies, the Court invalidated the introduction of the parliamentary election of the president, which, back in 2000, had replaced the direct presidential election by the people.[3] Following the plaintiffs' argument, the Court argued that an infringement of the constitutional amendment rules had occurred. According to the constitution, the Court must issue an 'advisory opinion' on any amendment initiative regarding its compatibility with the constitutional entrenchment clauses and international law (Art. 135, para. 1., lit c, and Art. 141, para. 2. Const.). After the Court had issued its advisory opinion in 1999,[4] the parliament made several changes to the original amendment draft. In particular, it introduced the requirement of a three-fifths majority (instead of an absolute majority) of the deputies for presidential elections. According to the 2016 court ruling, any changes to a draft require a new advisory opinion. Since this condition was not met in 1999/2000, the Court declared the respective amendment procedurally unconstitutional, without examining whether the amendment had substantively violated the constitution.

1 Adult Education Center Altenburger Land, Altenburg, Germany. E-mail: mail@michaelhein.de. I wish to thank Verena Frick, Anna Fruhstorfer, Lisa Harms-Dalibon, Ran Hirschl, Alexander Hudson, and Eugénie Mérieau for their helpful comments and suggestions. For their help with data collection on certain countries, I am grateful to Athanasia Hadjigeorgiou (Cyprus), Alkmene Fotiadou (Greece), Peter Bußjäger (Liechtenstein), and Maria Haimerl and Zeynep Yanasmayan (Turkey). This research was supported in part by the Alexander von Humboldt Professorship in Comparative Constitutionalism at the University of Göttingen.

2 Moldova 2016b: Judgment No. 7 2016, 4 March. A detailed list of all countries and court decisions studied is available at http://data.michaelhein.de.

3 A. Fruhstorfer, 'Moldova', in A. Fruhstorfer & M. Hein (Eds), *Constitutional Politics in Central and Eastern Europe. From Post-Socialist Transition to the Reform of Political Systems*, Wiesbaden, Springer VS, 2016, pp. 359–387, at pp. 370–371.

4 Moldova 1999f: Advisory Opinion 6/1999, 16 November.

This decision was a complete surprise.[5] Although it was highly controversial among both politicians and legal observers, it was nevertheless eagerly accepted by the political elite. This was probably caused by the fact that the three-fifths majority requirement had caused a long-lasting political crisis from 2009 until 2012, including two snap parliamentary elections, since due to slight parliamentary majorities and high polarization between left and right parties, the parliament had failed several times to elect a new president.[6] For the same reasons, the parliament had been unable to re-amend the constitution in that respect. In any case, the Court changed the character of the Moldovan governmental system literally overnight.

The above example shows that constitutional and supreme courts are not only veto players concerning statutory legislation, but may play a similar role in the field of constitutional politics. Whereas the former phenomenon has been capturing the attention of comparative political scientists for decades,[7] the latter has been studied to date exclusively by legal scholars.[8] The theoretical debate on the democratic compatibility of judicial review has not considered the impact of court decisions on constitutional amendments at all.[9] This double neglect has most

5 M. Popşoi, 'Controversial Ruling by Moldova's Constitutional Court Reintroduces Direct Presidential Elections', *Moldovan Politics*, 9 March 2016. Available at: https://moldovan-politics.com/2016/03/09/controversial-ruling-by-moldovas-constitutional-court-reintroduces-direct-presidential-elections [Accessed 26 March 2019].

6 See Fruhstorfer, 2016, p. 371. The Constitutional Court even supported this critique in its judgment (Moldova 2016b, para. 180).

7 See K. M. Holland, (Ed.), *Judicial Activism in Comparative Perspective*, Basingstoke, Macmillan, 1991; J. L. Gibson, G. A. Caldeira & V. A. Baird, 'On the Legitimacy of National High Courts', *American Political Science Review*, Vol. 92, No. 2, 1998, pp. 343–358; A. Stone Sweet, *Governing with Judges: Constitutional Politics in Europe*, Oxford, Oxford University Press, 2000; G. Vanberg, 'Legislative-Judicial Relations: A Game-Theoretic Approach to Constitutional Review', *American Journal of Political Science*, Vol. 45, No. 2, 2001, pp. 346–361; A. Dyevre, 'Unifying the Field of Comparative Judicial Politics: Towards a General Theory of Judicial Behaviour', *European Political Science Review*, Vol. 2, No. 2, 2010, pp. 297–327; M. Hein & S. Ewert, 'How Do Types of Procedure Affect the Degree of Politicization of European Constitutional Courts? A Comparative Study of Germany, Bulgaria, and Portugal', *European Journal of Legal Studies*, Vol. 9, No. 1, 2016, pp. 62–102.

8 See O'Connell, 1999; K. Gözler, *Judicial Review of Constitutional Amendments: A Comparative Study*, Bursa, Ekin Press, 2008; R. Albert, 'Nonconstitutional Amendments', *Canadian Journal of Law and Jurisprudence*, Vol. 22, No. 1, 2009, pp. 5–47; L. Garlicki, & Z. A. Garlicka, 'Review of Constitutionality of Constitutional Amendments (an Imperfect Response to Imperfections?)', *Anayasa Hukuku Dergisi*, Vol. 1, No. 1, 2012, pp. 185–224; G. Halmai, 'Judicial Review of Constitutional Amendments and New Constitutions in Comparative Perspective', *Wake Forest Law Review*, Vol. 50, 2015, pp. 951–984; Y. Roznai, *Unconstitutional Constitutional Amendments: The Limits of Amendment Powers*, Oxford, Oxford University Press, 2017.

9 See R. Dworkin, *Taking Rights Seriously*, Cambridge, MA, Harvard University Press, 1977; J. H. Ely, *Democracy and Distrust: A Theory of Judicial Review*, Cambridge, MA, Harvard University Press, 1980; J. Waldron, 'Judicial Review and the Conditions of Democracy', *Journal of Political Philosophy*, Vol. 6, No. 4, 1998, pp. 335–355; J. Waldron, 'The Core of the Case against Judicial Review', *Yale Law Journal*, Vol. 115, No. 6, 2005, pp. 1346–1406; R. Bellamy, *Political Constitutionalism: A Republican Defence of the Constitutionality of Democracy*, Cambridge, Cambridge University Press, 2007; A. Lever, 'Democracy and

likely been caused by the false assumption that constitutional review of constitutional amendments occurs very rarely.[10] As I will demonstrate in this chapter, European constitutional and supreme courts have delivered no fewer than 154 decisions on the constitutionality of constitutional amendments from 1945 until 2016. In 44 of these cases, the courts completely (N = 26) or partially (N = 18) invalidated the respective constitutional amendments.

On the one hand, constitutional review of constitutional amendments is a last resort against threats to the foundations of democracy.[11] On the other hand, the annulment of constitutional amendments constitutes a serious intervention into the democratic decision-making process and causes legitimacy problems that are more serious than those courts face when reviewing statute legislation.[12] By invalidating statutory law or reinterpreting a constitutional right, the court's 'adversary' is the parliamentary majority, which might – at least in principle – react by searching for a qualified majority and/or the people's consent to amend the constitution. Therefore, judicial activism may even be a helpful complement to parliamentary decision-making, as some human rights activists insist.[13] When reviewing constitutional amendments, however, the court's adversary is the amending power of the parliament or even the constitution-making power of the citizenry itself. This means that the only remaining reaction would be a new form of constitution-making or a breach of the existing constitutional order.

Against this background, this chapter examines the following question: Does constitutional review of constitutional amendments empirically contribute to the protection of modern democracy, or is it endangering the people's democratic right of self-government? I address this question by analyzing the abovementioned 154 decisions that European national courts have made on the constitutionality of constitutional amendments from 1945 until 2016. I will demonstrate that when invalidating constitutional amendments, European courts predominantly do so in a democracy-adverse, judicial activist manner. To explore this topic, I substantively assess all court decisions to determine whether they constitute a case of judicial activism encroaching on the people's democratic right of self-government instead of protecting democracy, or a case of judicial restraint, that is, a decision that accepts the people's democratic right of self-government and intervenes only insofar as the court is (at least implicitly) entitled and called upon by the constitution to do so.

In what follows, I first develop a framework for the substantive analysis of court decisions and embed the phenomenon of constitutional review of constitutional amendments in the literature on judicial activism. After providing a brief overview of the development of constitutional review of constitutional

Judicial Review: Are They Really Incompatible?', *Perspectives on Politics*, Vol. 7, No. 4, 2009, pp. 805–822.

10 See e.g., Garlicki & Garlicka, 2012, p. 220.

11 See Albert, 2009; Roznai, 2017.

12 See Roznai, 2017, pp. 105–175.

13 See C. Rodriguez-Garavito, 'Beyond the Courtroom: The Impact of Judicial Activism on Socioeconomic Rights in Latin America', *Texas Law Review*, Vol. 89, 2011, pp. 1669–1698.

amendments in Europe since 1945, I examine the 154 court decisions regarding their protective or endangering consequences for democracy. In the concluding section, I summarize the key findings and discuss their implications for the normative debate on, and the constitutional practice of reviewing constitutional amendments.

10.2 Judicial activism and constitutional review of constitutional amendments

10.2.1 What is 'judicial activism'?

For several decades, both political scientists and legal scholars have identified a global trend of the 'expansion of judicial power',[14] the 'judicialization of politics',[15] and even 'juristocracy'.[16] These terms describe how courts 'have become increasingly important, even crucial, political decision-making bodies'.[17] This trend coincides with an increase in judicial activism. Since the 1940s,[18] judicial activism has been defined in several ways, for instance, as ignoring precedent, as a departure from accepted interpretive methodology, as judicial legislation, as result-oriented judging, or as striking down arguably constitutional actions of other state bodies.[19] Applying the last-mentioned definition, and using a formulation provided by Lino A. Graglia, I interpret judicial activism as 'the practice by judges of disallowing policy choices by other governmental officials or institutions that the Constitution does not clearly prohibit'.[20] For the study of the constitutional review of constitutional amendments, this understanding of judicial activism is particularly favorable. It enables political scientists to analyze the democratic compatibility of constitutional review in its relationship to the other, 'political' branches of the state. This is based on a 'thick' definition of democracy, which requires not only all actions of the state to be legitimized and controlled by citizens, but also to be framed by fundamental rights, the rule of law, and the separation of powers to protect both democratic procedures and citizens' individual rights.[21] The function of constitutional review is to protect the constitutional framework, but since constitutional and supreme courts are merely checked and balanced by other state bodies, the courts may themselves threaten the democratic order.

14 C. Neal Tate & T. Vallinder, *The Global Expansion of Judicial Power*, New York, New York University Press, 1995.
15 Stone Sweet, 2000.
16 R. Hirschl, *Towards Juristocracy: The Origins and Consequences of the New Constitutionalism*, Cambridge, MA, Harvard University Press, 2004.
17 Hirschl, 2004, p. 1.
18 See K. D. Kmiec, 'The Origin and Current Meanings of "Judicial Activism"', *California Law Review*, Vol. 92, No. 5, 2004, pp. 1441–1477, at pp. 1445–1450.
19 See Kmiec, 2004.
20 L. A. Graglia, 'It's not Constitutionalism, it's Judicial Activism', *Harvard Journal of Law and Public Policy*, Vol. 19, No. 2, 1996, pp. 293–300, at p. 296.
21 See L. Diamond, *In Search of Democracy*, New York, Routledge, 2015.

The term 'judicial activism' describes democracy-adverse behavior based on judges' personal preferences, ideological orientations, or political interests.[22] Generally, court decisions are to a greater or lesser extent (co-)determined by political influences.[23] This is an inevitable consequence of the relatively wide scope for decision-making in constitutional matters, because constitutional provisions are often generally and vaguely formulated.[24] However, judicial activism is a particularly strong and evitable form of politicization. Activist decisions enforce one possible interpretation of a certain constitutional principle or provision instead of leaving the parliament or the people to choose between differing, equally legitimate interpretations. Judicial activism disrespects the policy space of the legislature and tends to endanger (instead of protecting) the democratic order.

The opposite phenomenon is judicial (self-)restraint. It can be defined as self-limiting court behavior compatible with democracy. It acknowledges competing constitutional interpretations as equally legitimate and leaves it to the legislature (or the people) to choose between those interpretations. Judicial restraint thus 'stands for the idea that the judge applies the relevant law, and only the law, in the case before him – he "restrains" any inclination to do otherwise'.[25]

10.2.2 Identifying judicial activism in the constitutional review of constitutional amendments

Many legal scholars favor constitutional review of constitutional amendments. In the footsteps of Alexis de Tocqueville,[26] they fear 'the problematic possibilities of popular sovereignty when sovereignty is mediated through an ill-intentioned legislature'.[27] To protect against this danger, 'judicial review of constitutional amendments fulfils the vertical separation of powers'.[28] In such a perspective, one would expect courts to be 'the least dangerous branch',[29] showing judicial restraint toward constitutional amendments.

22 See D. N. Mayer, *Liberty of Contract: Rediscovering a Lost Constitutional Right*, Washington, DC, Cato Institute, 2011, p. 58.
23 See M. Hein & S. Ewert, 'What is "Politicisation" of Constitutional Courts? Towards a Decision-Oriented Concept', in A. Geisler, M. Hein & S. Hummel (Eds), *Law, Politics, and the Constitution: New Perspectives from Legal and Political Theory*, Frankfurt am Main, Peter Lang, 2014, pp. 31–45, at p. 39.
24 See R. A. Dahl, 'Decision-Making in a Democracy: The Supreme Court as a National Policy-Maker', *Journal of Public Law*, Vol. 6, 1957, pp. 279–295, at p. 280; D. Grimm, 'Constitutions, Constitutional Courts, and Constitutional Interpretation at the Interface of Law and Politics', in B. Iancu (Ed.), *The Law/Politics Distinction in Contemporary Public Law Adjudication*, Utrecht, Eleven International Publishing, 2009, pp. 21–34, at p. 27.
25 Mayer, 2011, p. 152.
26 See A. de Tocqueville, *Democracy in America: Volume I*, New York, George Adlard, 1839.
27 Albert, 2009, p. 35.
28 Roznai, 2017, p. 180.
29 A. M. Bickel, *The Least Dangerous Branch: The Supreme Court at the Bar of Politics*, 2nd ed., New Haven, Yale University Press, 1986.

As a look at the possible sources to declare amendments unconstitutional shows, this does not necessarily have to be the case. First and foremost, courts can assess whether the amendment procedure was followed properly. Procedurally irregular amendments are the least controversial kind of unconstitutionality. One could even say that in these cases, courts only ascertain whether an asserted amendment is an amendment at all.[30] Second, courts can base their decisions substantially on the supremacy of international laws over contradictory national laws, insofar as this is stipulated in the constitution.[31] That way, courts may force the legislative power to either refrain from a certain constitutional amendment or to change the respective international legal situation, for instance, by terminating the respective international treaty. This does not only circumvent international conflicts, but also leaves parliament (and the people) with the opportunity to amend the constitution in the desired way.

Third, courts can apply a theory of implicit substantial limitations on constitutional amendments and state that a given constitution contains unamendable principles or features, although they are not explicitly declared unamendable in the constitutional text.[32] This concept was applied for the first time by the Indian Supreme Court, which developed the famous 'basic structure doctrine' beginning with its landmark decision in Kesavananda Bharati v State of Kerala in 1973. The development and application of theories of implicit amendment limitations is a typical feature of judicial activism. They are inevitably nothing other than an ex post rationalization by a small group of judges of the assumed will of the people that had enacted the constitution. It is thus not surprising that, beginning with India, judges are often not able to reach a unanimous position amongst themselves. Even if proposed implicit limits aim to protect essential principles of the constitution, their genesis alone breaches the principle of democratic constitution-making.

Finally, courts can rely on substantial constitutional entrenchment clauses if available. These clauses can be understood as the explicit will of the people expressed when enacting the constitution. In general, almost all contemporary constitutions are basically entrenched; in other words, harder to amend than ordinary laws. This is typically achieved by requiring increased majorities in parliament, approval by two successive parliaments (i.e., the need for intervening elections), or an additional referendum. However, many constitutions take one or two further steps and contain additional entrenchment clauses.[33] These are provisions that make amendments to certain parts of a constitution or amendments under certain circumstances either more difficult than 'normal' amend-

30 See Gözler, 2008, at 27–28.

31 See Roznai, 2017, pp. 82–102.

32 See Roznai, 2017, pp. 39–70.

33 See M. Hein, 'Entrenchment Clauses in the History of Modern Constitutionalism', *Legal History Review*, Vol. 86, No. 3–4, 2018, pp. 434–481; M. Hein, *The Constitutional Entrenchment Clauses Dataset*, Göttingen, University of Göttingen, 2018. Available at: http://data.michaelhein.de [Accessed 26 March 2019].

ments ('constraint on amendments') or impossible, that is, legally inadmissible ('prohibition of amendments', 'eternity clauses', or 'unamendable provisions').

In contrast to the application of a 'basic structure doctrine', invalidating a constitutional amendment with reference to an entrenchment clause can be a restrained action, as long as it fulfills the abovementioned criterion of judicial restraint, that is, acknowledging competing constitutional interpretations as equally legitimate and leaving it to the democratically legitimated amending power to choose between them. If, for instance, a constitutional eternity clause protects the independence of the judiciary, the court would be allowed (and obliged) to invalidate any amendment that would infringe on that principle (e.g., the introduction of a right of the minister of justice to intervene in court proceedings). In contrast, amendments that only reform the way an independent judiciary is organized, for example, a change from the judicial self-management model to the management-by-the-executive model,[34] would have to be accepted.

In sum, judicial restraint regarding constitutional amendments can be understood as a court behavior that fulfills two criteria. In procedural terms, a restrained court reviews an amendment only and insofar as it is explicitly or at least implicitly[35] entitled to do so. If, in contrast, a constitution explicitly denies a court that competence or restricts it to certain aspects (e.g., to procedural aspects), a restrained court will not overstep these boundaries. In substantive terms, a restrained court strikes down a constitutional amendment only if it has violated the constitutional amendment procedure, contradicts international law (insofar as its supremacy is codified by the constitution), or clearly breaches a constitutional principle or provision that is protected by an entrenchment clause. A court decision that fulfills both criteria constitutes either a restrained intervention or a restrained non-intervention into the amendment process (depending on the characteristics of the reviewed amendment).

If one or both criteria are not fulfilled and a court nevertheless invalidates a constitutional amendment, this court decision must be assessed as an activist intervention. Finally, there is the fourth possibility, which I would like to call an activist non-intervention. In line with the presented understanding of judicial activism, 'activism' is not identical to 'intervention'. Instead, courts can also be activist by not intervening. This would be the case if a competent court did not invalidate a procedurally or substantively unconstitutional constitutional amendment. Such a case displays judicial activism, since the respective court follows a specific, counter-constitutional policy line.

Applying this framework, I will examine whether constitutional review of constitutional amendments contributes to the protection of democracy, or endangers the people's democratic right of self-government. Of course, these substantive assessments are anything but beyond doubt, since 'the line between proper

34 See S. Bartole, 'Organizing the Judiciary in Central and Eastern Europe', *East European Constitutional Review*, Vol. 7, No. 1, 1998, pp. 62–69.

35 For instance, by the competence to review the constitutionality of 'laws'.

judicial review and judicial activism depends on the speaker's understanding of the Constitution.'[36] Nevertheless, the approach seems reasonable because it reveals the 'democratic compatibility' of constitutional review. Assessing a judgment as an activist intervention thus only means that it is not clear how a non-intervention would have endangered democracy. Likewise, classifying a decision as an activist non-intervention only signifies that an intervention would have circumvented concrete encroachments on democratic constitutionalism.

10.3 Constitutional review of constitutional amendments in Europe since 1945

From 1945 to 2016, constitutional and supreme courts in the 49 European countries (and their predecessor states) with entrenched constitutions have delivered 154 decisions on the constitutionality of (potential)[37] constitutional (draft) amendments.[38] Decisions on national statutory legislation and on international treaties are included, if the claimants and/or the judges argue that the challenged norms would have been impossible to enact even by means of a regular constitutional amendment, because they are constrained or prohibited by a constitutional entrenchment clause.

The 154 decisions stem from 21 countries, that is, 28 European countries have not seen any relevant judgments. In 44 decisions (28.6%), amendments were completely (N=26/16.9%) or partially (N=18/11.7%) declared unconstitutional, whereas 110 decisions (71.4%) accepted the respective amendment entirely. The vast majority of all decisions (137 of 154 cases, 89.0%) were taken in countries whose constitutions contained a general[39] entrenchment clause at

36 Kmiec, 2004, p. 1466.

37 Potential constitutional amendments are considered in cases of so-called 'interpretation decisions'. The constitutional interpretation is a peculiarity of some post-socialist constitutional courts in Europe (e.g., in Bulgaria, Moldova, and Ukraine). It entitles state authorities to request the interpretation of a constitutional norm without any specific prerequisite. In some jurisdictions, the applicants can equip their interpretation requests with concrete questions dealing with law projects or potential constitutional amendments. Among the court decisions under study, four judgments in Bulgaria fall into this category (Constitutional Court Decision of 10 April, No. 3/2003; Constitutional Court Decision of 5 July, No. 3/2004; Constitutional Court Decision of 1 September, No. 8/2005; Constitutional Court Ruling of 17 September, No. 3/2015).

38 These decisions were found in the online databases of the courts, as well as in the literature on individual courts and on unconstitutional constitutional amendments.

39 As mentioned above, entrenchment clauses either constrain or prohibit amendments to certain parts of a constitution, or amendments under certain circumstances. These clauses can be further differentiated according to their scope: they can apply *generally* to any amendment initiative; *temporally* for a limited period of time; or *situationally* under certain "extra-constitutional" circumstances, such as emergency, war, or siege (See M. Hein, 'Impeding Constitutional Amendments: Why are Entrenchment Clauses Codified in Contemporary Constitutions?', *Acta Politica*, Vol. 54, No. 2, 2019, pp. 196–224, at pp. 199–200). Since no single court decision studied referred to a temporal or situational entrenchment clause,

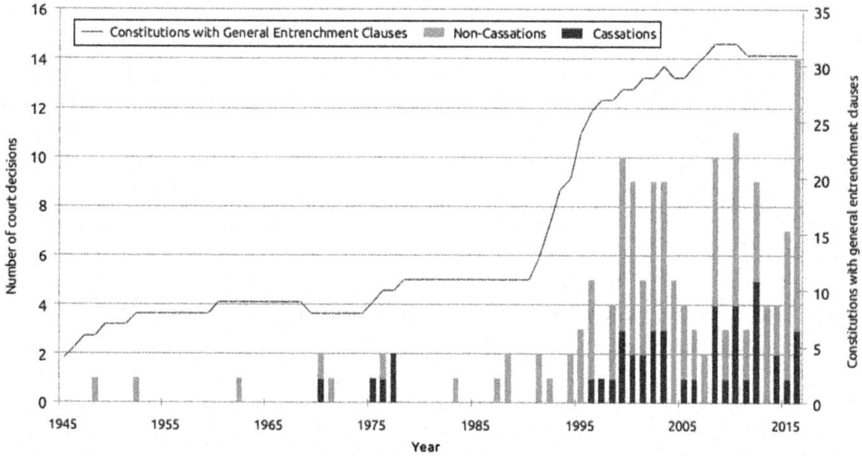

Figure 10.1 Unconstitutional constitutional amendments in Europe over time (1945–2016).

the time of the decision. Among the 44 invalidations, 38 were made based on a general entrenchment clause, whereas five decisions were made on procedural grounds, and one decision was based on the supremacy of international law. Not a single amendment was invalidated based on implicit amendment limitations.[40]

As Figure 10.1 demonstrates, both the number of court decisions on the constitutionality of constitutional amendments per year, and the share of amendment invalidations have considerably increased over time. Before 1996, only 23 relevant court decisions were recorded, whereas 131 decisions have been made since then. Likewise, only four of the 44 amendment invalidations were decided upon before 1996 – all of them in Turkey. In 2016, the court activity has reached

all the following considerations and results concerning constitutional entrenchment clauses exclusively refer to the two general types of entrenchment clauses: general prohibitions of amendments ('eternity clauses') and general constraints on amendments.

40 Only two courts (Turkey 1971: Decision of 3 April, No. 1971/37; Italy 1988: Judgment of 15 December, No. 1146) occasionally developed and applied theories of implicit substantial limitations on constitutional amendments, but this did not lead to amendment invalidations (see M. Hein, 'Do Constitutional Entrenchment Clauses Matter? Constitutional Review of Constitutional Amendments in Europe', *International Journal of Constitutional Law*, Vol. 18, 2020, forthcoming). On 30 January 2019 (i.e., after the period studied in this chapter), the Slovak Constitutional Court was the first court in Europe that invalidated a constitutional amendment based on a theory of implicit amendment limitations (see M. Domin, 'A Part of the Constitution is Unconstitutional, the Slovak Constitutional Court has Ruled', *Verfassungsblog*, 8 February 2019. Available at: https://verfassungsblog.de/a-part-of-the-constitution-is-unconstitutional-the-slovak-constitutional-court-has-ruled [Accessed 26 March 2019]).

a new peak with 14 decisions. Two factors might explain this increasing court activity. First, it mirrors the abovementioned global trend of the expansion of judicial power. Second, it runs parallel with the dissemination of entrenchment clauses. Whereas in 1945, only 40.0% of the studied constitutional states had an entrenchment clause (6 out of 15 constitutions), this share increased to 73.5% in 2016 (36 out of 49 constitutions). In statistical terms, the number of constitutions with entrenchment clauses and the number of court decisions on the constitutionality of constitutional amendments, both per year, correlate highly significantly (Pearson's $r = 0.80$; significant at the 0.001 level).

10.4 Judicial activism in court decisions on constitutional amendments

How do judicial restraint and judicial activism characterize the 154 court decisions under study? In other words: does constitutional review of constitutional amendments contribute to the protection of modern democracy, or is it endangering the people's democratic right of self-government? As a matter of course, it would be impossible to present the analyses of all 154 cases in detail here. To make my substantive assessments more comprehensible, however, I will demonstrate the detailed analyses of eight selected court decisions: one restrained intervention, one restrained non-intervention, one activist intervention, and one activist non-intervention.

10.4.1 Typical examples of judicial restraint

On 10 September 2009, the Czech Constitutional Court annulled a constitutional amendment that would have shortened the ongoing term of office of the Chamber of Deputies, the lower house of the Czech parliament.[41] The amendment had been designed to enable snap elections after the Chamber had dismissed the government by a no-confidence vote, since the Constitution did not contain the right of self-dissolution for the Chamber. Deputy Miloš Melčák challenged this amendment before the Constitutional Court. With a 13-to-2 vote, the Court ruled that an ad hoc constitutional amendment, which regulates an individual instance retroactively and divergently from the general constitutional rules without amending them, breaches 'the essential requirements for a democratic state governed by the rule of law', which are unamendable principles of the Czech Constitution (Art. 9, para 2. Const.). Almost all political actors criticized the ruling. They claimed that the Court had exceeded its competencies and deepened the political crisis in the country.[42] Nevertheless, the parliament accepted the

41 Czech Republic 2009a: Decision Pl. ÚS 27/09, 10 September.

42 I. Šlosarčik, 'Czech Republic 2009–2012: On Unconstitutional Amendment of the Constitution, Limits of EU Law and Direct Presidential Elections', *European Public Law*, Vol. 19, No. 3, 2013, pp. 435–448, at p. 438.

decision and adopted a new, 'regular' constitutional amendment, which introduced the right of self-dissolution for the Chamber of Deputies. Because of the 'fear of another constitutional challenge (based on a retroactivity argument)',[43] however, the next elections took place on their regular date in May 2010.

This decision is a typical example of a *restrained intervention*. The struck-down amendment breached several 'essential requirements for a democratic state governed by the rule of law' as protected by the Czech constitution, in particular, popular sovereignty (Art. 2, para. 1 Const.) and the prohibition of retrospective legislation, which is a key element of the rule of law (Art. 1, para. 1 Const.). Nonetheless, the court did not intervene in the contents of the amendment, but demanded only that the introduction of the right of self-dissolution of the Chamber of Deputies had to abide by the entrenched constitutional principles.

Several examples of restrained non-interventions into constitutional politics can be found in Ireland. Among all courts under study, the Irish Supreme Court has most explicitly and consistently emphasized the people's democratic right of self-government in the field of constitutional politics. Article 46 of the Irish Constitution states: 'Any provision of this Constitution may be amended', provided that the amendment law adopted by the parliament receives the approval of the people in a referendum. Nevertheless, the Court had to address four claims of unconstitutional amendments,[44] all of which it rejected. In 1995, for instance, the Irish President Mary Robinson challenged two constitutional amendments from 1992, which had added two new paragraphs to Art. 40, Sec. 3 Const. Without touching the absolute ban on abortion in Ireland,[45] the new paragraphs guaranteed the right 'to obtain or make available [...] information relating to [abortion] services lawfully available in another state,' and the 'freedom to travel' to obtain an abortion abroad.[46] President Robinson asked the Supreme Court whether there were any natural law norms superior to the constitution, which no amendment could contravene.

The Supreme Court rejected this claim. Referring to Art. 46 Const. and several related constitutional provisions, the judges stated that Ireland was a democratic state, where the people have the right 'in final appeal, to decide all questions of national policy' (Art. 6, Sec. 1). This includes the amendment of any part of the Constitution. Furthermore, the Court declared that although the constitution

43 Šlosarčik, 2013, p. 438.

44 Ireland 1983: Finn v Attorney General and others [1983] IR 154; Ireland 1995: In Re Article 26 and the Regulation of Information (Services outside the State for the Termination of Pregnancies) Bill 1995 [1995] IESC 9 (12 May 1995); Ireland 1999a: Riordan v An Taoiseach (No. 1) [1999] 4 IR 321; Ireland 1999b: Riordan v An Taoiseach (No. 2) [1999] IESC 1 (20 May 1999, Appeal No. 202/98).

45 This was finally removed from the constitution by an amendment adopted in May 2018; see H. McDonald & E. Graham-Harrison, 'Ireland Votes by Landslide to Legalise Abortion', *The Guardian*, 26 May 2018. Available at: www.theguardian.com/world/2018/may/26/ireland-votes-by-landslide-to-legalise-abortion [Accessed 26 March 2019].

46 O'Connell, 1999, pp. 63–66.

refers to 'natural rights' on some occasions, Ireland as 'a pluralist society' does not allow the courts to decide 'between the differing views, where they exist, of experts on the interpretation [...] of either the nature or extent of these natural rights'.[47] Since the challenged amendment was procedurally constitutional, the decision can be assessed as an example of restrained non-intervention.

10.4.2 Typical examples of judicial activism

Besides the 2016 decision of the Moldovan Constitutional Court mentioned at the outset of this chapter, another typical example of an activist intervention can be found in a decision taken ex officio and a priori in Ukraine. In 2000, President Leonid Kučma initiated a constitutional reform to strengthen his political position. Among others, the draft amendment envisaged the introduction of a second parliamentary chamber, the abolition of parliamentarians' immunity, the reduction of their number from 450 to 300, and the right of the President to dissolve parliament under certain conditions. The Constitutional Court invalidated the draft amendment with only one dissenting opinion.[48] The judges did not even consider the proposed changes in detail, but rejected the entire amendment as immature by stating that it would cause manifold contradictions within the constitution. Therefore, the Court stated that it was unable to assess the possible consequences for the human and citizens' rights and freedoms, which are protected by the eternity clause in Art. 157 Const.

With this move, the Court clearly overstepped the limits of constitutional review, which involves the examination of the constitutionality of constitutional amendments, not their quality.[49] Whereas a restrained court could have made recommendations for the improvement of the draft, the invalidation of an entire amendment due to alleged possible breaches of the eternity clause is clear-cut judicial activism.

A typical activist non-intervention is one of the few judgments issued before the 1990s. In 1968, Art. 10 of the (West) German Basic Law regulating the privacy of correspondence, posts, and telecommunications was amended. The amended Art. 10, para. 2 allowed specific restrictions of this fundamental right 'to protect the free democratic basic order or the existence or security of the Federation or of a Land'. In such cases, the wiretapped person does not have to be informed of this act and 'recourse to the courts shall be replaced by a review of the case by agencies and auxiliary agencies appointed by the legislature'. Two citizens, by means of individual complaints, and the government of the Land of Hesse challenged this amendment before the Federal Constitutional Court. They argued that the possibility of secret wiretapping and the replacement of judicial

47 Ireland 1995.
48 Ukraine 2000b: Constitutional Court Opinion of 17 June, No. 2-v/2010.
49 See U. K. Preuss, 'The Implications of "Eternity Clauses": the German Experience', *Israel Law Review*, Vol. 44, 2011, pp. 429–448, at p. 432.

by administrative review of surveillance measures infringed upon the fundamental principles of human dignity and the rule of law, which are protected by the entrenchment clause in Art. 79, para. 3 Basic Law.

In a highly controversial decision, the Court judges rejected the claims of the plaintiffs with a 5-to-3 majority.[50] The Court basically argued that the amendment must be interpreted in line with the proportionality principle. Consequently, wiretapping is only permissible if no other means are available, and a wiretapped person must be informed in retrospect if the free democratic basic order or the existence or security of the Federation or of a Land is no longer at risk. In addition, the Court demanded the administrative review to be 'substantively and procedurally equivalent to judicial control'.[51] By that interpretation, most judges arrived at the decision that the amendment was constitutional. However, as the three dissenting judges pointed out, replacing the recourse to the courts by the review of a politically appointed and controlled organ is, as such, an encroachment on the separation of powers and the rule of law, and would therefore have to be declared unconstitutional.[52]

10.4.3 Judicial activism in court decisions on constitutional amendments

The results of the analysis of the 154 court decisions are displayed in Table 10.1. As the table shows, the majority of the court rulings (N = 124) were assessed as complete (N = 104) or partial (N = 19) restrained non-interventions. The courts passed the respective amendment laws, which neither violated the constitutional amendment procedure, contradicted international law, nor breached a constitutional principle or provision protected by an entrenchment clause. Thus, constitutional review of those (potential) constitutional (draft) amendments did not essentially change the legal and political situation.[53] Thirteen decisions were assessed as complete (N = 5) or partial (N = 8) restrained interventions. Here, the respective courts struck down obvious procedural irregularities or substantive encroachments on the constitution, in most cases by referring to an entrenchment clause. The courts thus effectively contributed to the protection of the democratic order.

In contrast, almost twice as many decisions (N = 34) were complete (N = 22) or partial (N = 12) activist interventions, where the courts illegitimately interfered with the constitutional amendment process. Finally, six decisions were assessed as complete (N = 4) or partial (N = 2) activist non-interventions. The courts

50 Germany 1970: BVerfG, Judgment of the Second Senate of 15 December; BVerfGE 30, 1.

51 Germany 1970, para. 97.

52 Germany 1970, para. 123–156.

53 Of course, confirming the constitutionality of an amendment might strengthen the political position of the drafting actors (for instance the governing majority vis-à-vis the opposition), or clarify the legal situation by removing legal doubts.

Table 10.1 Judicial activism and judicial restraint in court decisions on the constitutionality of constitutional amendments in Europe (1945–2016)

		Court competencies not overstepped + (potential) constitutional (draft) amendment violated constitutional amendment procedure, contradicted supreme international law and/or breached a constitutional entrenchment clause	
		Yes	*No*
Invalidation of (potential) constitutional (draft) amendment by the court	Yes	Restrained intervention: • Austria 2001 • Czech Republic 2009a • Hungary 2012 (partly) • Moldova 1998, 2002a (partly) • Romania 1996, 2003a (partly), 2011 (partly), 2014 (partly) • Ukraine 1999a (partly), 2008a (partly), 2010a (partly), 2010b (partly)	Activist intervention: • Bulgaria 2003, 2005 (partly), 2006a • Kosovo 2012a (partly), 2012b (partly), 2012c (partly), 2015a • Lithuania 2014 • Moldova 1997 (partly), 1999a (partly), 1999c, 2002b (partly), 2008a, 2008b, 2016a, 2016b, 2016c • Romania 2000, 2011 (partly), 2014 (partly) • Turkey 1970, 1975, 1976b, 1977a, 1977b, 2008, 2010 (partly) • Ukraine 2000b, 2001a (partly), 2002, 2003a, 2010a (partly), 2010c, 2012a
	No	Activist non-intervention: • Azerbaijan 2016 • France 1962 • Germany 1970 • Moldova 2016h (partly) • Romania 2014 (partly) • Slovenia 1996	Restrained non-intervention: • Austria 1948; 1952, 1988, 1994, 1998, 2005, 2008a, 2008b, 2010a, 2010b, 2016 • Azerbaijan 2002, 2008 • Bulgaria 2004, 2005 (partly), 2006b, 2015 • Czech Republic 2008, 2009b • Estonia 2012 • France 2003 • Georgia 2010, 2012, 2013 • Germany 1991, 1996a, 1996b, 2004, 2009, 2011, 2012 • Hungary 1994, 1996, 1998, 2002, 2012 (partly) • Ireland 1983, 1995, 1999a, 1999b • Italy 1988 • Kosovo 2012a (partly), 2012b (partly), 2012c (partly), 2013, 2014, 2015b • Liechtenstein 2002, 2003 • Moldova 1995a, 1995b, 1997 (partly), 1999a (partly), 1999b, 1999d, 1999e, 1999f, 2000a, 2000b, 2000c, 2001a, 2001b, 2002a (partly), 2002b (partly), 2002c, 2002d, 2004, 2005, 2006, 2010a, 2010b, 2010c, 2011, 2014, 2015a, 2015b, 2016d, 2016e, 2016f, 2016g, 2016h (partly) • Norway 1991 • Romania 2003a (partly), 2003b, 2003c, 2011 (partly), 2014 (partly), 2016 • Slovenia 1998, 2000 • Spain 1992, 2004 • Turkey 1971, 1976a, 1987, 2007a, 2007b, 2010 (partly), 2016 • Ukraine 1999a (partly), 1999b, 2000a, 2000c, 2000d, 2001a (partly), 2001b, 2003b, 2003c, 2004a, 2004b, 2005, 2008a (partly), 2008b, 2008c, 2010a (partly), 2010b (partly), 2010d, 2012b, 2013a, 2013b, 2015a, 2015b, 2016a, 2016b

restrained themselves from invalidating the reviewed amendments, although they (would have) violated the constitutional amendment procedure, contradicted international law, or breached a constitutional entrenchment clause. Whereas two of those draft amendments failed to find the necessary parliamentary majority later,[54] the other four amendments became or remained established constitutional law.[55] In these cases, the courts refrained from circumventing damages to the democratic constitutional order.

These results disprove the optimistic assumption that courts predominantly protect the democratic constitutional order by reviewing constitutional amendments.[56] Excluding the many restrained non-interventions from consideration (because the constitution was not endangered in those cases), only 13 restrained interventions remain, in contrast to 40[57] activist interventions and non-interventions. That is, in only 13 out of 154 decisions (i.e., less than 10%), constitutional review safeguarded the respective constitution from encroachments of the democratic constitutional order. However, ten of those decisions were taken ex officio a priori in Moldova, Romania, and Ukraine. In all ten cases, it is highly likely that the invalidated draft amendments would not have found the necessary qualified majorities in parliament, given the highly polarized compositions of the parliaments in the respective periods and countries. Only in three cases in Austria, the Czech Republic, and Hungary,[58] one may convincingly argue that the constitutional courts were the last actors to protect the democratic constitutional orders from severe encroachments. Three out of 154 decisions (or 1.95%) – a convincing argument in favor of constitutional review of constitutional amendments – would appear differently.

How can this result be explained? The first, and most obvious, influencing factor are constitutional entrenchment clauses. As I have shown previously, the number of court decisions on the constitutionality of constitutional amendments and the number of constitutions with entrenchment clauses correlate highly significantly. Eighty-nine per cent of all decisions (137 of 154 cases) were taken in countries whose constitutions contain such a clause. However, judges are not just the Montesquieuean 'mouth that pronounces the words of the law, mere passive beings, incapable of moderating either its force or rigor'.[59] Instead, activist courts may also use entrenchment clauses to enforce a specific but controversial vision of the constitution and declare amendments unconstitutional although they are not clearly prohibited by the constitutional text. Indeed, 29 out of the 34 activ-

54 Romania 2014: Constitutional Court Decision of 7 April, No. 80/2014; Moldova 2016c: Advisory Opinion 2/2016, 16 March.

55 France 1962: Decision No. 1962-20 DC, 6 November; Germany 1970; Slovenia 1996: Decision of 11 April, Case No. U-I-332/94; Azerbaijan 2016: Decision of 25 July.

56 See Albert, 2009; Roznai, 2017

57 Not 41, since Romania (2014) appears in both categories.

58 Austria 2001: Decision of 10 March; VfSlg 16327; Czech Republic 2009a; Hungary 2012: Decision of 29 December, No. 45/2012 (partly).

59 C. B. de Montesquieu, *The Spirit of Laws*, New York, Cosimo, 2011 [1748].

ist interventions among the studied court decisions were based on constitutional entrenchment clauses. In other words, without those provisions, constitutional amendments would probably be a rare subject-matter before courts, and judicial activism would be likewise rarely to be observed.[60]

Second, recent studies have emphasized the role of the types of procedure in the political relevance of courts.[61] Types of procedure regulate access to courts, the possible contents of constitutional review, and the consequences of court decisions. Regarding decisions on the constitutionality of constitutional amendments, one type of procedure stands out: five constitutional courts in Central and Eastern Europe established after 1989 (Azerbaijan, Kosovo, Moldova, Romania, and Ukraine) are obliged to review ex officio all constitutional draft amendments before they reach the parliamentary debate stage (a priori). This transforms the respective courts from 'negative legislators' into 'positive legislators'.[62] They are not dependent on being called into play by another actor and cannot only retroactively annul amendments but can also actively influence their drafting. Therefore, it is reasonable to expect those courts to issue more activist decisions, and in particular, more activist interventions. Indeed, of all 154 studied court decisions, 82 (53.2%) were issued ex officio a priori. They led to 28 out of 44 amendment invalidations (63.6%), and, among them, to 19 out of 34 activist interventions (55.9%).

To sum up, constitutional entrenchment clauses and the ex officio a priori review mainly account for the high number of constitutional amendments brought before the courts and thus function as catalysts for judicial activism.

10.5 Conclusion

Constitutional review of constitutional amendments has become an important and regular feature in many European countries. Like constitutional review of statutory legislation, it fluctuates between judicial activism and judicial restraint. However, the invalidation of constitutional amendments is a much more serious intervention into democratic decision-making and causes more serious legitimacy problems. Against this background, I have demonstrated that only a small share of all 154 studied European constitutional or supreme court decisions on the constitutionality of constitutional amendments can be assessed as restrained interventions (N = 13). With these decisions, the courts struck down constitutional amendments that violated the constitutional amendment procedure, contradicted international law, or breached a constitutional principle or

60 For deeper insights into the role of constitutional entrenchment clauses for the constitutional review of constitutional amendments, see Hein, Constitutional Entrenchment Clauses, 2019.

61 See Hein & Ewert, 2016.

62 H. Kelsen, 'Judicial Review of Legislation: A Comparative Study of the Austrian and the American Constitution', *Journal of Politics*, Vol. 4, No. 2, 1942, pp. 183–200.

provision that was protected by a constitutional entrenchment clause. Since ten of those decisions were taken ex officio a priori and would have had no realistic chance of being adopted by the respective parliaments, in only three cases were the courts the last actors to protect the democratic constitutional orders from severe encroachments.

In contrast, most decisions were assessed as either complete or partial restrained non-interventions (N = 124), or as activist decisions (N = 40). Here, constitutional review either did not make a difference, or itself endangered the democratic constitutional order by illegitimately interfering with the constitutional amendment process or by restraining the invalidation of obviously unconstitutional amendments. These results disprove the positive expectations towards constitutional review of constitutional amendments. Instead, I conclude that constitutional review of constitutional amendments – although theoretically a reasonable feature of the protection of modern constitutional democracy – is empirically the opposite: a threat to democracy.

With this in mind, it might be worth considering for both democratic theory and constitutional practice whether constitutional texts should explicitly prohibit courts from reviewing constitutional amendments or restrict their competence to review the procedural regularity of the amendment. As empirical evidence shows, however, even explicit competence restrictions might not discourage activist courts from overstepping their responsibilities. The Turkish Constitutional Court ruled several times on the substantive constitutionality of amendments, although the Turkish Constitutions have explicitly limited the court's competence to formal review.[63] Thus, one may ask whether judicial activism is the inevitable destiny of democratic constitutional politics.

References

R. Albert, 'Nonconstitutional Amendments', *Canadian Journal of Law and Jurisprudence*, Vol. 22, No. 1, 2009, pp. 5–47.

S. Bartole, 'Organizing the Judiciary in Central and Eastern Europe', *East European Constitutional Review*, Vol. 7, No. 1, 1998, pp. 62–69.

R. Bellamy, *Political Constitutionalism: A Republican Defence of the Constitutionality of Democracy*, Cambridge, Cambridge University Press, 2007.

A.M. Bickel, *The Least Dangerous Branch: The Supreme Court at the Bar of Politics*, 2nd ed., New Haven, CT, Yale University Press, 1986.

A. de Tocqueville, *Democracy in America: Volume I*, New York, George Adlard, 1839.

R. A. Dahl, 'Decision-Making in a Democracy: The Supreme Court as a National Policy-Maker', *Journal of Public Law*, Vol. 6, 1957, pp. 279–295.

L. Diamond, *In Search of Democracy*, New York, Routledge, 2015.

M. Domin, 'A Part of the Constitution is Unconstitutional, the Slovak Constitutional Court has Ruled', *Verfassungsblog*, February 8, 2019. Available at: https://

63 Gözler, 2008, pp. 42–49.

verfassungsblog.de/a-part-of-the-constitution-is-unconstitutional-the-slovak-constitutional-court-has-ruled [Accessed 26 March 2019].

R. Dworkin, *Taking Rights Seriously*, Cambridge, MA, Harvard University Press, 1977.

A. Dyevre, 'Unifying the Field of Comparative Judicial Politics: Towards a General Theory of Judicial Behaviour', *European Political Science Review*, Vol. 2, No. 2, 2010, pp. 297–327.

J.H. Ely, *Democracy and Distrust: A Theory of Judicial Review*, Cambridge, MA, Harvard University Press, 1980.

A. Fruhstorfer, 'Moldova', in A. Fruhstorfer & M. Hein (Eds.), *Constitutional Politics in Central and Eastern Europe: From Post-Socialist Transition to the Reform of Political Systems*, Wiesbaden, Springer VS, 2016, pp. 359–387.

L. Garlicki & Z.A. Garlicka, 'Review of Constitutionality of Constitutional Amendments (An Imperfect Response to Imperfections?)', *Anayasa Hukuku Dergisi*, Vol. 1, No. 1, 2012, pp. 185–224.

J.L. Gibson, G.A. Caldeira & V.A. Baird, 'On the Legitimacy of National High Courts', American Political Science Review, Vol. 92, No. 2, 1998, pp. 343–358.

K. Gözler, *Judicial Review of Constitutional Amendments: A Comparative Study*, Bursa, Ekin Press, 2008.

L.A. Graglia, 'It's not Constitutionalism, It's Judicial Activism', *Harvard Journal of Law and Public Policy*, Vol. 19, No. 2, 1996, pp. 293–300.

D. Grimm, 'Constitutions, Constitutional Courts, and Constitutional Interpretation at the Interface of Law and Politics', in B. Iancu (Ed.), *The Law/Politics Distinction in Contemporary Public Law Adjudication*, Utrecht, Eleven International Publishing, 2009, pp. 21–34.

G. Halmai, 'Judicial Review of Constitutional Amendments and New Constitutions in Comparative Perspective', *Wake Forest Law Review*, Vol. 50, 2015, pp. 951–984.

M. Hein, 'Entrenchment Clauses in the History of Modern Constitutionalism', *Legal History Review*, Vol. 86, No. 3–4, 2018a, pp. 434–481.

M. Hein, *The Constitutional Entrenchment Clauses Dataset*, Göttingen, University of Göttingen, 2018b. Available at: http://data.michaelhein.de [Accessed March 26, 2019].

M. Hein, 'Do Constitutional Entrenchment Clauses Matter? Constitutional Review of Constitutional Amendments in Europe', *International Journal of Constitutional Law*, Vol. 18, 2020, forthcoming.

M. Hein, 'Impeding Constitutional Amendments: Why Are Entrenchment Clauses Codified in Contemporary Constitutions?', *Acta Politica*, Vol. 54, No. 2, 2019, pp. 196–224.

M. Hein & S. Ewert, 'What Is 'Politicisation' of Constitutional Courts? Towards a Decision-Oriented Concept', in A. Geisler, M. Hein & S. Hummel (Eds.), *Law, Politics, and the Constitution. New Perspectives from Legal and Political Theory*, Frankfurt am Main, Peter Lang, 2014, pp. 31–45.

M. Hein & S. Ewert, 'How Do Types of Procedure Affect the Degree of Politicization of European Constitutional Courts? A Comparative Study of Germany, Bulgaria, and Portugal', *European Journal of Legal Studies*, Vol. 9, No. 1, 2016, pp. 62–102.

R. Hirschl, *Towards Juristocracy: The Origins and Consequences of the New Constitutionalism*, Cambridge, MA, Harvard University Press, 2004.

K.M. Holland (Ed.), *Judicial Activism in Comparative Perspective*, Basingstoke, Macmillan, 1991.

H. Kelsen, 'Judicial Review of Legislation: A Comparative Study of the Austrian and the American Constitution', *Journal of Politics*, Vol. 4, No. 2, 1942, pp. 183–200.

K.D. Kmiec, 'The Origin and Current Meanings of 'Judicial Activism'', *California Law Review*, Vol. 92, No. 5, 2004, pp. 1441–1477.

A. Lever, 'Democracy and Judicial Review: Are They Really Incompatible?', *Perspectives on Politics*, Vol. 7, No. 4, 2009, pp. 805–822.

D.N. Mayer, *Liberty of Contract: Rediscovering a Lost Constitutional Right*, Washington, DC, Cato Institute, 2011.

H. McDonald & E. Graham-Harrison, 'Ireland Votes by Landslide to Legalise Abortion', *The Guardian*, 26 May 2018. Available at: www.theguardian.com/world/2018/may/26/ireland-votes-by-landslide-to-legalise-abortion [Accessed 26 March 2019].

C.B. de Montesquieu, *The Spirit of Laws*, New York, Cosimo, 2011 [1748].

C. Neal Tate & T. Vallinder, *The Global Expansion of Judicial Power*, New York, New York University Press, 1995.

R. O'Connell, 'Guardians of the Constitution: Unconstitutional Constitutional Norms', *Journal of Civil Liberties*, Vol. 4, 1999, pp. 48–75.

M. Popşoi, 'Controversial Ruling by Moldova's Constitutional Court Reintroduces Direct Presidential Elections', *Moldovan Politics*, 9 March 2016. Available at: https://moldovanpolitics.com/2016/03/09/controversial-ruling-by-moldovas-constitutional-court-reintroduces-direct-presidential-elections [Accessed 26 March 2019].

U.K. Preuss, 'The Implications of 'Eternity Causes': The German Experience', *Israel Law Review*, Vol. 44, 2011, pp. 429–448.

C. Rodriguez-Garavito, 'Beyond the Courtroom: The Impact of Judicial Activism on Socioeconomic Rights in Latin America', *Texas Law Review*, Vol. 89, 2011, pp. 1669–1698.

Y. Roznai, *Unconstitutional Constitutional Amendments: The Limits of Amendment Powers*, Oxford, Oxford University Press, 2017.

I. Šlosarčik, 'Czech Republic 2009–2012: On Unconstitutional Amendment of the Constitution, Limits of EU Law and Direct Presidential Elections', *European Public Law*, Vol. 19, No. 3, 2013, pp. 435–448.

A. Stone Sweet, *Governing with Judges: Constitutional Politics in Europe*, Oxford, Oxford University Press, 2000.

G. Vanberg, 'Legislative-Judicial Relations: A Game-Theoretic Approach to Constitutional Review', *American Journal of Political Science*, Vol. 45, No. 2, 2001, pp. 346–361.

J. Waldron, 'Judicial Review and the Conditions of Democracy', *Journal of Political Philosophy*, Vol. 6, No. 4, 1998, pp. 335–355.

J. Waldron, 'The Core of the Case against Judicial Review', *Yale Law Journal*, Vol. 115, No. 6, 2005, pp. 1346–1406.

Part IV

The role of courts in the context of democratic backsliding, illiberal democracies and populist constitutionalism

11 Constitutional courts in the context of constitutional regression

Some comparative remarks

Angela Di Gregorio

11.1 Introduction

Limitations on the independence of constitutional courts are among the main pointers of constitutional regression. Taking a cue from the best-known cases in Europe and Latin America (Hungary, Poland, Russia, Turkey, and Venezuela) the chapter considers how the 'normalization' or 'neutralization' of the courts has triggered and then maintained illiberal degeneration (since these institutions are the major counter-balance to the political majority). The chapter explores the role played by the 'reformed' courts in the new political reality, and also takes into account the dialog with international courts. The latter aspect is very sensitive, considering the tough implementation of the judgments of supranational courts in cases of constitutional 'sovereignism'. The analysis will be performed using the method of comparative law.

11.2 The involvement of constitutional courts in constitutional regression, and the end of the 'transition paradigm'

The aim of the present chapter is to make some comparative remarks on the role and destiny of constitutional courts in countries that, although they belong in different cultural and geopolitical contexts, have all experienced a constitutional deterioration in the last few years. This deterioration has occurred in cases of the apparent consolidation of democracy or the further decline of an already existing semi-authoritarian regime. In both cases, the courts were heavily implicated in the authoritarian degeneration and the maintenance of the status quo, being either 'assaulted' or manipulated. In examining the way in which constitutional regression has affected constitutional courts, we will try to underline their role and responsibility during regression (since they were either victims or protagonists) and after regression. Hungary, Poland, Russia, Turkey, and Venezuela[1] are the countries dealt with in this chapter.

1 In the case of Venezuela, we are referring to constitutional review provided for by the *sala constitucional* of the Supreme Court of Justice. Constitutional review can also be performed by other judges, according to Art. 334 of the Constitution.

Formally, the system in the countries under examination is not a fully authoritarian one, since these countries have constitutions that provide for the separation of powers and the guarantee of rights (as well as being members of supranational organizations that are based on liberal-democratic values). These countries are uncritically linked under the labels of 'populism' and 'sovereignism', although it would be preferable to talk about 'constitutional regression' or 'involution', meaning a modification (amendment or replacement) of the constitution, or the constitution being emptied or derogated from, in order to neutralize its system of checks and balances.

The involvement of constitutional courts in constitutional regression has several causes, particularly the will of the dominant political majority at a given moment in history, to which one can add mistakes by previous legislators or framers of the constitution, as was the case in Hungary and Poland.[2] This path has been influenced by the procedures for appointing judges and the possibility of their confirmation. The replacement of judges has been justified on the grounds of their alleged inefficiency, corruption, or compromise with the previous regime. However, even politically appointed or 'loyalist' judges can maintain a certain independence (as emerges from some dissenting opinions).[3] One should also consider the 'natural' deference of constitutional judges towards the executive power and especially towards the head of state (as seen, for example, in Russia and Turkey). In some of the cases examined, constitutional courts that had played a prominent role in the past and that had turned against ruling majorities suffered a drastic reduction of their role, through both the supply of 'loyalists' and the constitutional limitation of competences (Hungary, Turkey). Consequently, we can distinguish between countries in which illiberal rulers had a penalizing attitude towards the constitutional courts (Hungary, Poland, Turkey) and countries where the rulers tried to subdue the courts regardless of their previous behavior (Russia, Venezuela).

The political capture of the constitutional courts (and of other checks and balances) has been reached in different ways, depending on constitutional and political peculiarities. In Hungary and Poland, the 'majoritarian principle' of the ruling party prevails, assisted by the charismatic approach of the leader (more evident in the case of Orbán, while Kaczyński is a 'shadow' leader). In other cases, a 'personalized' and 'extra-party' culture predominates, where the constitutional framework and party system are modeled after the dominant leader.

The main aspects on which attention should be focused are the ways in which degeneration occurred (through the modification of or derogation from the

2 See A. Di Gregorio, 'Lo stato di salute della rule of law in Europa: c'è un regresso generalizzato nei nuovi Stati membri dell'Unione?', *DPCE on-line*, 4/2016.

3 See the comment by V. Partlett, 'Russia's contested constitutional review', *International Journal of Constitutional Law Blog*, 13 February 2018, in which some dissenting opinions are used to address the possibility of a positive evolution of the Russian Constitutional Court, more in line with a liberal-democratic vision of constitutionalism. Nevertheless, at present, such a prediction is dubious.

constitution), the role of the constitutional courts in this regression (as victims or co-protagonists), and after it, the responsibility and failure of supranational actors.

The role that constitutional courts play in contexts of illiberal degeneration, where the constitutional system becomes hybrid (semi-autocratic) or almost autocratic, is particularly relevant as it is in cases of transition to democracy. In some respects, the 'degeneration' and 'transition' paradigms seem to overlap. Until a few years ago the paradigm of transition or democratization was dominant, especially with reference to the former communist countries. Today the paradigm has been replaced with that of constitutional regression or involution, which concerns not only these countries but also so-called 'consolidated' democracies. The change of reconstructive setting, despite being necessary as events develop, is likely to merge situations that are different without distinction. It would be preferable to have a short-term goal of describing what is happening. This could avoid the application of quantitative indices of democracy and authoritarianism: at the moment, in fact, there is a struggle to consolidate broader hypotheses that are aimed at identifying new hermeneutical categories, despite the crisis of the traditional pattern of classification.

11.3 The political and constitutional environment in the countries concerned

Constitutional regression in the countries examined presents common trends and many differences, depending on the political environment and the historical heritage. Some of the countries analyzed experienced important democratic phases (Hungary and Poland from 1989 to 2010 and from 1989 to 2015;[4] Venezuela was considered among the most stable Latin American countries after 1958 and until the political crises of the 1980s), while others (Russia, Turkey) include in their genetic code authoritarian elements that periodically surface or become stable for a long time.[5]

In Hungary and Poland, democracy appeared stable up to the parliamentary elections in 2010 and 2015, respectively, and Russia's democratic performance has worsened since 2004. In Turkey, which in its history has experienced several phases of 'confusion' between civil and military power and the dominance of the latter, the authoritarian degeneration, with the concentration of powers in the hands of the President, increased after the coup attempt of July 2016 (although the decline started with the constitutional amendments of 2007),[6] as evidenced

4 Poland also had liberal and democratic traditions even in its pre-socialist history.

5 See the opinion of B. Mathieu, '25 ans d'élections démocratiques à l'Est. Propos conclusifs', *Est Europa*, 2016–2017, pp. 265–269, regarding the imperial perspective of some countries that have a natural inclination to deny liberal values.

6 Constitutional reforms over the last 30 years have had mixed results: until 2007 there was progressive liberalization (especially through the amendments of 1995, 2001, and 2004) but since 2007 there has been a centralization of power in the hands of the President and the reduction of counterweights and the role of parliament.

by the 2017 constitutional amendments. As for Venezuela, which, like almost all the Latin American countries, has alternated over history between military regimes and more democratic phases, the populist degeneration began in the last part of the Chavez presidency[7] and the country has become openly authoritarian under Maduro, especially since 2016. The 1999 Bolivarian constitution (with a post-liberal content and a strong emphasis on social rights and popular participation) gradually came to be disregarded.[8]

Despite having different constitutional systems (in terms of their system of government), both Russia and Turkey, where a charismatic leader has held power for many years, have experienced a further consolidation of the executive power, and, in particular, the power of the President, in recent years: in Turkey through specific constitutional amendments and in Russia through political practice and legislation (plus the increase in the length of the presidential term that was introduced in 2008). The constitutional crises in Hungary and Poland take different forms, since they are based on the dominance of a majoritarian power that does not formally affect the constitutional competences of the leader of the executive (the real leader is not the President of the Republic, but the premier in Hungary and the leader of the majority party in Poland).

All these countries have been subjected to the democratic conditionality of (regional) organizations for the protection of human rights and, in the case of Hungary and Poland, also to the complex path of democratic conditionality that precedes entry into the European Union.[9] Because of this membership, the violation of rule of law principles and of a set of fundamental rights inherent in a liberal democracy appears in all its seriousness. In fact, the violation of such rules appears more serious in the context of the Council of Europe, of which four out of the five countries under consideration are members, and the European Convention on Human Rights (ECHR).[10] However, the lack of effective sanctioning mechanisms within the Council of Europe has concentrated punitive efforts within the European Union.[11] Regarding Venezuela, its relationship with the Organization

7 According to A. R. Brewer-Carías, *Los jueces constitucionales controlando al poder o controlados por el poter. Algunos cases notorios y recentes*, San José Costa Rica, Editorial Investigaciones Jurídicas, 2017, this began with the consultative referendum for the election of the Constituent Assembly in 1999.

8 A. R. Brewer-Carías, *Dismantling Democracy in Venezuela: The Chávez Authoritarian Experiment*, New York, Cambridge University Press, 2010; J. Couso, 'Venezuela's recent constitutional crisis: Lessons to be learned from a failed judicial coup d'etat', *International Journal of Constitutional Law Blog*, 12 April 2017.

9 Turkey has also been subjected to a long-standing democratic EU conditionality – with results in terms of significant reforms until the beginning of the 2000s – and formally this is still the case.

10 This Convention, together with a court system and numerous additional protocols, was written to protect fundamental rights in a democratic society.

11 Different tools are used, with different practical impacts and involving different institutions: an infringement procedure (EU Commission, CJEU: specific violations of EU law), a rule of law framework (Commission: systemic approach), a rule of law dialogue (Council of the

of American States (OAS) and with the Inter-American Court of Human Rights has been marked by a growing distance, leading to the adoption of an OAS resolution in June 2018 that declared the re-election of Maduro in May 2018 to be illegitimate (and therefore initiated the procedure for the suspension of Venezuela). In April 2017, Venezuela had itself submitted a request to leave the organization, and this has been finalized in April 2019. Declarations have been made by Russian and Hungarian politicians about the possibility of exiting the ECHR system in order not to have to comply with unwelcome judgments of the Strasbourg Court.

Although this conditionality could be considered unsuccessful, if we take a long-term view the situation appears to be more nuanced. Pressure by the Council of Europe made important reforms possible in both Russia and Turkey, and during some periods the dialog with the Strasbourg Court has been fruitful in both countries.

11.4 The role of constitutional courts in constitutional regression

Despite the peculiarities of each case, there are many similarities in the efforts of political leaders or ruling parties to 'atrophy' their judicial counterweights (Poland, Hungary, Turkey) or, vice versa, to make the courts support them more strongly in their nationalist projects to re-build society (Russia, Venezuela). In the long term, after their neutralization the courts have become submissive and therefore supportive of the political leadership, although in Poland and Hungary there are still glimmers of a positive evolution, at least with reference to the ordinary courts. The political involvement of the constitutional courts also depends on their competences (in Turkey and Hungary, they were very large and with a potential political impact). Venezuela demonstrates the risk of granting broad powers of constitutional control to judicial institutions in weakly institutionalized democracies.[12] In fact, without strong democratic institutions and a strong sense of judicial virtue, constitutional courts can favor authoritarian constitutionalism.[13]

EU: limited impact), Art. 7 (activated against Poland in December 2017 at the initiative of the Commission), European Parliament reports (see, among the most recent, the Sargentini report on Hungary which also called for the activation of Art. 7), etc. The literature on this topic is huge. For some aspects please refer to A. Jakab & D. Kochenov (Eds), *The Enforcement of EU Law and Values. Ensuring Member States' Compliance*, Oxford, Oxford University Press, 2017. For the list of the tools please refer to the study commissioned by the European Parliament, *An EU Mechanism on Democracy, the Rule of Law and Fundamental Rights*, Annex 1, Brussels, 2016.

12 C. García-Soto, 'Venezuela', *2017 Global Review of Constitutional Law*, p. 314.

13 M. Tushnet, 'Authoritarian constitutionalism', *Cornell Law Review*, Vol. 100, 2015, p. 391. Please see also T. Ginsburg & T. Moustafa (Eds), *Rule by Law. The Politics of Courts in Authoritarian Regimes*, New York, Cambridge University Press, 2008; M. Hailbronner & D. Landau, '*Introduction: Constitutional Courts and Populism*', *Global Review of Constitutional Law Blog*, 22 April 2017.

As far as Venezuela is concerned, significant judicial decisions were adopted before the Chavist 'colonization' of the top court; these had an ambiguous content that favored constitutional transformation. In two judgments of 19 January 1999 (Consultative Referendum I and II), the Supreme Court allowed the holding of a consultative referendum for the convocation of a national Constituent Assembly (Arts 245–246 of the 1961 Constitution provided for a confirmatory referendum on a new Constitution only after parliamentary approval of the text). This Supreme Court was replaced in the 1999 Constitution by the Supreme Court of Justice (SCJ) as a new supreme court to be elected by the new political majority,[14] which suddenly became a reliable instrument of the regime. A series of decisions, starting in 2003, have denied the superiority of international treaties on human rights despite the provisions of the Constitution (see infra). Subsequently, since the end of 2015, numerous decisions have been adopted to support the President and to challenge the authority of the newly elected National Assembly, for which the united opposition parties received the majority of the votes. With the decisions of 27 and 29 March 2017, the SCJ allowed a new Constituent Assembly to be convened and the National Assembly that had been elected on 6 December 2015 to be delegitimized. In particular, in its judgment no. 156 of 29 March, claiming to react to the refusal of the National Assembly to respect some of its previous decisions, the Supreme Court of Justice stated that 'in order to preserve the country's rule of law' it was forced to transfer all the powers of the parliament to itself ('or to the entity that the Court decides'). The judgment no. 378 of 7 June 2017 established that the President had the power to convene a Constituent Assembly without a prior consultative referendum since he acted in the name of popular sovereignty.[15]

In Turkey, the Constitutional Court (TCC) has played an important role in terms of secularization, democratization, and Europeanization since the 1960s, after its introduction in the Constitution of 1961. The Court was inspired by European models and, despite the heavy influences of the military on the Turkish legal system, it managed to gain credibility both nationally and internationally as an important barrier, especially in the secularist direction, as evidenced by the numerous judgments for the dissolution of Islamic-inspired political parties. This is a strong example of militant democracy, in which the Constitutional Court, along with other institutions, was built to protect the core values of the secular Kemalist Republic.[16]

14 The 32 *magistrados* are appointed by the National Assembly and serve non-renewable 12-year terms. Appointments are made by a two-thirds majority or by a simple majority if efforts to appoint a judge fail three times in a row.

15 For an accurate description of judicial degeneration please refer to ICJ (International Commission of Jurists), *The Supreme Court of Justice of Venezuela: An Instrument of the Executive Branch*, August 2017.

16 The guiding principles of Kemalist ideology, reaffirmed in all Turkish constitutions, were outlined in the famous speech held in 1927 and defined precisely the six arrows of Atatürk: nationalism (Turkish ethno-cultural identity), republicanism, populism (intended as the uni-

Over time the TCC compromised the interests of the ruling majority, which at different moments reduced the autonomy and competences of the Court. In particular, some judgments in 2007–2008 affected important political interests of the Justice and Development Party (AKP). One of them threatened even to dissolve the party.[17] Another case concerned the constitutional amendment that would have allowed the legislator to remove the ban on wearing the headscarf in universities; the Court considered this to be unconstitutional.[18] The decision about the majority required for the parliamentary election of the President was also a clear signal to the party to stop.[19] The arguments used to settle these cases with a high constitutional profile have been weak, and this has further undermined the Court's credibility.[20] After the constitutional reform of 2010, the number of constitutional judges[21] and the role of the head of state in their appointment[22] increased. A limit of 12 years was also imposed on the term that the judges could serve. Although the reform was presented as being one step closer to the requirements of European conditionality, and although it has indeed reduced the influence of the military, it actually exposed the institutions to more political influence.[23] Further minor changes have taken place as a result of the constitutional Act of 16 April 2017 (the number of judges has been reduced from 17 to 15),[24] and, although the competences of the Court remain the same, it has indirectly lost some of them, especially as a result of the strengthening of

---

tary concept of the people as opposed to the status and the social divisions of the previous legal order), statism (especially in the economic field), laicism, and reformism (social and political transformations had to continue to modernize the state). Please refer to C. Camposilvan, 'La Costituzione della Turchia', in L. Mezzetti (Ed.), *Codice delle Costituzioni*, Vol. VI.1, Padova, Cedam-Wolters Kluwer Italia, 2016, pp. 510–511.

17 E. 2008/1, K. 2008/2 of 30 July 2008.

18 E. 2008/16, K.2008/116 of 5 June 2008.

19 E. 2007/45, K. 2007/54 of 1 May 2007.

20 See M. C. Uzun, 'The protection of laicism in Turkey and the Turkish Constitutional Court: The example of the prohibition on the use of the Islamic veil in higher education', *Penn State International Law Review*, Vol. 28, No. 3, 2010; Y. Roznai, 'An unconstitutional constitutional amendment—The Turkish perspective: A comment on the Turkish Constitutional Court's headscarf decision', *International Journal of Constitutional Law*, Vol. 10, No. 1, 2012; O. O. Varol & L. Dalla Pellegrina & N. Garoupa, 'An Empirical Analysis of Judicial Transformation in Turkey', *The American Journal of Comparative Law*, Vol. 65, 2017.

21 From 11 permanent and four substitute judges to 17 permanent and no substitute judges.

22 The proportion of judges selected from the judicial system was reduced, while the President selects 14 out of the 17 judges (drawn from the high courts, the Council of Higher Education, etc.).

23 Varol & Dalla Pellegrina & Garoupa, 2017, p. 197. See also L. De Grazia, 'Constitutional coup e democrazie illiberali: l'esperienza della Turchia', *Rivista AIC*, 4/2018 and V. R. Scotti, 'L'indipendenza della Corte costituzionale turca fra legittimità delle leggi e tutela dei diritti. Quali segnali per la tenuta della democrazia in Turchia', *Rivista di diritti comparati*, 1/2019.

24 This is a result of the abolition of two military courts that had the authority to nominate candidates.

executive power.[25] The Court endorsed the regression with a series of decisions in sharp contrast to its earlier and settled case law.

The Russian Constitutional Court (RCC) has never been powerful or authoritative since its creation in 1990–1991. However, as a result of the Court's political involvement at a moment of institutional crisis (1991–1993), the 1993 Constitution reduced its responsibilities (for instance, it no longer checks political parties). There have been no major changes in the composition and competences of the Constitutional Court since the entry into force of the Constitution, although the change in the method of appointment of the Court's president and vice presidents in 2009 represented an evident reduction of its autonomy.[26] This Court, however, unlike others examined here, had not given evidence of insubordination to the executive. It stated that the war in Chechnya and the incorporation of the Crimea were legal, and disagreed with the Strasbourg Court on politically sensitive issues that touched on important public interests, such as in the Yukos case. A similar tendency is found in the jurisprudence concerning fundamental political rights, with the Court having substantially supported the restrictions on freedom of assembly and association. The most politicized decisions are those challenging the Strasbourg Court's authority (especially from 2015 to 2017, to be read through the prism of the speeches of RCC chairman Zorkin),[27] while others are more protective of social rights.

As far as Hungary and Poland are concerned, political pressure on constitutional judges is particularly unbearable because these countries have undergone a long and difficult process of constitutional transition from the communist system. In both cases, but especially in Hungary, these institutions played a relevant role in dismantling the remnants of the previous political regime and in the democratization process. The Polish Constitutional Tribunal (CT) started operating in the terminal phase of the regime (it was introduced by the 1982 constitutional

25 Following M. Haimerl, *'The Turkish Constitutional Court under the amended Turkish Constitution', VerfBlog*, 2017/1/27, other amendments risk having indirect consequences for the Court's autonomy. For example, there are amendments that make it easier to adopt emergency decrees: the President can now issue decrees in matters of competence of the executive without an authorization law, and consequently it is no longer possible for the Court to limit the executive power by checking whether the law itself meets the requirements of the Constitution.

26 While until 2009 the individuals appointed to these positions were selected by the same constitutional judges, the 2 June 2009 amendment of the constitutional Act on the Constitutional Court requires that the president and the two vice presidents are elected from among the constitutional judges by the Federation Council on a proposal from the head of state.

27 In a long interview given to the government newspaper *Rossijskaya Gazeta* on 9 October 2018, Zorkin made a number of philosophical observations on the concept of constitutional identity and the values underlying the Russian Constitution, which in his mind counterbalance the 'moral degeneration' being brought about by globalization. This is a trend that has been emerging from his speeches in the last few years, one which urges a 'nationalist' and conservative stance against western criticism of Russia. It should also be remembered that Zorkin is holding his sixth non-consecutive term as chairman of the RCC.

amendment and began functioning in 1986), while the Hungarian Constitutional Court (HCC) was introduced in 1989 and soon became an important counterweight on the political scene, adopting many anti-majority decisions. On this path of democratization and the approach to European standards, the constitutional courts enjoyed high prestige and authority. Furthermore, the initial composition of these courts (former dissidents or protagonists of regime change, especially in the Hungarian case, were appointed as judges) also reinforced their credibility at the international level.

In these two countries, the ruling parties, Fidesz (from spring 2010) and PiS (from November 2015) respectively, have influenced the appointment of constitutional judges[28] to paralyze the constitutional courts or to make them submissive, introducing judges who can be manipulated and are close to the ruling majority. They subsequently changed the rules to make the way the court functioned, and the quorums required,[29] more complex. In Hungary, the transformation of the Court began before the adoption of the new 2011 Fundamental Law, in relation both to the methods of the election of judges and to their number and competences.[30] The Court tried to 'resist', but the parliament constitutionalized the legislative provisions that it had declared unconstitutional. Although the reduction of the jurisdiction of the Constitutional Court is not significant (before 2010 it was super-equipped), the new methods for the selection of the judges and the president, the repealing of the jurisprudence preceding the entry into force of the 2011 Fundamental Law (IV constitutional amendment) and some other negative innovations have led to its subjugation. Particularly relevant are the decisions of the HCC on constitutional identity and the superiority of the Fundamental Law over international treaties (see, for instance, the judgments of 30 November 2016, 9 July 2018, and 25 February 2019). Poland appeared to follow the same path as Hungary, but in the absence of a political constitutional majority the conservative party acted differently by violating the CT's judgments, and therefore the Constitution, several times.[31] The CT tried to resist, with the help of ordinary and administrative judges, but after the replacement of the con-

28 However, in Poland everything started through a tactical error of the previous parliamentary majority (the Civic Platform), which, on 8 October 2015 at the end of the parliamentary session, elected more constitutional judges than were allowed.

29 See, for example, the new Polish Act on the CT criticized by the Venice Commission: Opinion on the Act on the Constitutional Tribunal, adopted by the Venice Commission at its 108th Plenary Session, Venice, 14–15 October 2016.

30 Since June 2010, in the parliamentary committee that selects the candidates for constitutional judges, political forces have been represented in proportion to the number of seats they have in parliament (previously, every parliamentary party had a member). From September 2011 the number of judges increased from 11 to 15 and in the new Fundamental Law the judges' term of office increased from 9 to 12 years.

31 Examples are the illegitimate appointment of three judges and the amendment of the Act on the Constitutional Tribunal to limit its competences and complicate its activity. In detail, see: W. Sadurski, *How Democracy Dies (in Poland): A Case Study of Anti-constitutional Populist Backsliding*, Sydney Law School Research Paper No. 18/01, January 2018; W. Sadurski,

stitutional judges there was paralysis or neutralization of this institution, both quantitatively and qualitatively. There has been an 'emptying' of the Constitution that can be compared to what happened during the communist system.

11.5 The constitutional identity doctrine and the new role of Courts after constitutional regression

One of the common features of the cases examined lies in the contrast with regional courts for the protection of human rights (and in the case of Hungary and Poland, with the European Court of Justice too). In fact, to legitimate constitutional regression a constitutional court must elaborate its own theory of 'constitutional identity'. This is especially the case in Russia, Hungary, and Venezuela, even though in the first two of these countries the content of this identity has not been clarified except with reference to generic principles, whereas in Venezuela this identity has an ideological content with a clear populist nature. It should also be stressed that the constitutional identity doctrine, although it is a new label for very old narratives on the protection of the core content of a constitution against the penetration of European law, means different things depending on the legal system that is taken into consideration, be it the EU or the ECHR one.

Both the Russian Constitutional Court and the Venezuelan SCJ have treated the unwelcome decisions of international courts for the protection of fundamental rights as inapplicable in their country, using different legal foundations. In the Russian case, the RCC has since 2013 become an instrument of 'sovereign' resistance against the Strasbourg Court, borrowing from some western countries, for example, the German Constitutional Tribunal, a narrative of the protection of the national identity that was born in another context and for other purposes.[32] First the Constitutional Court and then the legislature provided for a specific procedure to check the constitutionality of the judgments of international courts.[33] The legal reasoning of the RCC to justify the non-enforceability of international judgments was rather complex and sophisticated, referring to the doctrine of constitutional identity (the Court stated that the ECHR had been consistent with the Constitution at the time of its ratification but that the later 'evolutionary' case law of the European Court of Human Rights (ECtHR) was unconstitutional).[34]

'Polish Constitutional Tribunal under PiS: From an activist court, to a paralysed tribunal, to a governmental enabler', *Hague Journal on the Rule of Law*, 2018.

32 For critical comments please refer to A. Blankenagel, 'The ghost haunting decisions of European constitutional courts: What to do with constitutional identity?', *Sravnitel'noe konstitutsionnoe obozrenie*, Vol. 27, No. 5, 2018 and A. Dzhagaryan, 'Russian constitutionalism: In search of identity', *Sravnitel'noe konstitutsionnoe obozrenie*, Vol. 27, No. 6, 2018.

33 The RCC decision of 14 July 2015 and the Constitutional Act of 14 December 2015.

34 See especially the decisions of 6 December 2013 (Markin), 19 April 2016 (Anchugov and Gladkov), and 17 January 2017 (Yukos). In the Anchugov and Gladkov case, the RCC considered that no subordination existed between the European and Russian legal systems, but emphasized the need for dialogue, since 'the effectiveness of the norms of the ECHR

The *sala constitucional* of the Venezuelan SCJ was cruder, particularly in three decisions made in 2008, 2011, and 2015.[35] Despite the clarity of the constitutional provision regarding the prevalence of international human rights treaties if they contained provisions more favorable than those of the Venezuelan Constitution and legislation (Article 23), this provision was completely disregarded by the constitutional judge by referring to the prevalence of popular sovereignty. In judgment no. 1939 of 18 December 2008 (the Gustavo Álvarez Arias case) the *sala constitucional* of the SCJ argued for the subordination of law to politics, expressing the Venezuelan version of constitutional identity and sovereignty: 'law is a normative theory at the service of politics'. The standards to settle the conflict between principles and norms must be compatible with the 'political project of the Constitution' (that is, the '*Estado Democrático y Social de Derecho y de Justicia*').[36] The SCJ has even accused the Inter-American Court of abusing its powers and of having itself violated some international treaties.

As for Hungary, judgment 22/2016 on the interpretation of Article E(2) of the Fundamental Law was a rather vague decision. While stating that the HCC maintains the right to make two types of verification with regard to the joint exercise of powers between the EU and Hungary (sovereignty and identity control), the HCC did not clarify what constitutional identity is, referring to vague principles and to the concept of a 'historical constitution' (the protection of constitutional identity, deriving from the Hungarian historical constitution, cannot be called into question by the requirements of European integration). The petition was based on the constitutional prohibition on 'collective expulsion' from Hungary (Article XIV(1)), but the connection between this provision and the relocation of migrants/asylum seekers from other European countries was not clarified.[37]

Subsequent to constitutional regression, constitutional courts survive with the aim of strengthening political consensus because they enjoy a certain aura of

---

in the legal system of Russia depends on the respect by the European Court of Human Rights of the national constitutional identity'. The same argument was repeated in the Yukos judgment. On this subject, please refer to A. Di Gregorio, 'Russia', *2018 Global Review of Constitutional Law, forthcoming.*

35 No. 1939 of 18 December 2008, No. 1547 of 17 October 2011, No. 1175 of 10 September 2015.

36 In the Court's words, 'There cannot exist a system of absolute and ahistorical principles over the Constitution'. Theories that claim to limit sovereignty and national self-determination 'as a pretext of universal values' are unacceptable. If there is a conflict between the Constitution and an international treaty 'the constitutional norms that privilege the general interest and the common good must prevail, since the provisions that privilege the collective interests … over special interests must be applied'. For further comments, see Brewer-Carías, 2017.

37 T. Drinóczi, '*The Hungarian Constitutional Court on the limits of EU law in the Hungarian legal system*', *International Journal of Constitutional Law Blog*, 29 December 2016; G. Halmai, '*The Hungarian Constitutional Court and constitutional identity*' *and* R. Uitz, '*National constitutional identity in the European constitutional project: A recipe for exposing cover ups and masquerades*', both at http://verfassungsblog.de.

impartiality that can be useful for expanding the power of the regime.[38] This can be seen in Hungary, for example, with the ruling of 30 November 2016, and in Russia in the remarks of President Zorkin. In countries that had previously achieved a stable, even if fragile, democratization, the constitutional jurisprudence following constitutional regression has in fact deleted the guaranteeing role of the constitutional court.

Despite all the limitations observed, however, constitutional courts can still play a non-secondary role in legal systems that have undergone constitutional regression, a role that goes beyond the simple legitimation of the regime. In Russia, for example, the Constitutional Court focuses on specific issues that are relevant to citizens' economic and social rights, while in dealing with the rare cases of the restriction of political rights, it protects specific aspects. During the time when the most heated confrontation with the Strasbourg Court took place (2015–2017), the RCC issued a relevant judgment concerning the confiscation of property from *bona fide* buyers, in which it accepted the position of the European Court in Strasbourg, favoring an internal adaptation.[39] In some circumstances, therefore, the Russian Constitutional Court continues to refer to, or to align with, the case law of the Strasbourg Court.

Despite the unfavorable political context and the fact that the introduction of individual petitions decreased the number of judgments on systemic violations (as in the Hungarian case, where *actio popularis* previously existed),[40] there still is the 'daily' protection of individual rights and some dissent by a few judges. In Turkey, after the recent reforms and in the changed political climate following the 2016 coup, constitutional judges demonstrate continuing deference to the ruling party, particularly in politically sensitive issues (such as freedom of expression or the detention of members of parliament). The clearest examples of its political deference are found in the decisions that backtrack on the symbols of secularism (in a ruling of 11 December 2018, the ban on wearing the headscarf in universities was abolished), on the control of governmental emergency decrees,[41] on the autonomy of parliament (itself affected by the

38 Couso, 2017.

39 This is the decision of 22 June 2017, in which the RCC tried to make up for the delays of the legislator in implementing a series of decisions of the European Court of Human Rights on the protection of the right to housing when placed in competition with the right to property. This was a very sensitive social issue, with hundreds of petitions.

40 Since the 'packing', the HCC has avoided politically sensitive cases (using various ploys, including deferring the decision for as long as possible) or has supported the government. In general, the Court adopts a minimalist, non-activist attitude. See B. Eszter & F. Gárdos-Orosz, 'Hungary', *2017 Global Review of Constitutional Law*, p. 130. Also Z. Szende, 'The political orientation of the members of the Hungarian Constitutional Court between 2010 and 2014', *Constitutional Studies*, Vol. 1, No. 1, 2016; Z. Tóth, 'Changes which occurred in the role of the Hungarian Constitutional Court in protecting the constitutional system', *Acta Universitatis Sapientiae, Legal Studies*, Vol. 7, No. 1, 2018.

41 In eight decisions adopted between 12 October 2016 and 2 November 2016, the TCC unanimously rejected applications claiming the unconstitutionality of four emergency

constitutional reforms from 2007 onwards), and on offences against the head of state. However, in the context of individual petitions, the Court has sought to protect its reputation by deciding, more often than in the past, that there have been violations of constitutional rights and freedoms, especially in relation to the operation of individual petitions.[42] In fact, since 2012, the TCC has in many cases backed individual rights going against the interests of the ruling party (deleting the suspension of YouTube and Twitter, protecting the environment and the freedom of expression of journalists, etc.), although it declined to rule on the fairness of the electoral process, and deferred pronouncements in cases involving the detention of journalists.

11.6 Some concluding remarks on the courts under examination here on the problem how to label the 'deteriorated' constitutional systems and on their perspectives

The five cases examined can be grouped into three sub-groups: Poland and Hungary, Russia and Turkey, and Venezuela. In the first two countries, constitutional degeneration seems more serious because it takes place in the 'new' heart of the EU and the Council of Europe, where there is financial support from the EU, and despite protests in various European forums and institutions. The role of international organizations, especially the Council of Europe and the European Union, has been and is ambivalent for these countries. On the one hand, as mentioned, these organizations have for several years made the introduction of relevant institutional reforms possible. On the other hand, their model of integration has partially failed, since countries that had lived in communist solidarity were not ready for a purely liberal model. In the case of Russia and Turkey, the hegemonic ambitions and the cultural and geopolitical characteristics of the two former empires have led to the failure of European (ECHR) democratic conditionality. In Venezuela, the degeneration has been so crude and violent, even from a constitutional point of view, that the Maduro regime is completely isolated, both regionally and internationally.

As a further reflection on the five countries examined, we can distinguish three cases in relation to the impact of the degeneration on the constitution: the adoption of a new constitution (Venezuela in 1999,[43] and Hungary in 2011), the

decrees brought into force in the aftermath of the failed coup. Applying a literal interpretation of Article 148 of the Constitution, it made its former case law completely meaningless without any further argument.

42 S. Köybaşı, 'Turkey', *2017 Global Review of Constitutional Law*, p. 296. B. E. Oder, *'Populism and the Turkish Constitutional Court: The Game Broker, the Populist and the Popular'*, *International Journal of Constitutional Law Blog*, 2 May 2017. Following Köybaşı, 2017, in 2017 the Court found violations in 917 cases, the highest number since the introduction of individual petitions.

43 Ignoring the new constitutional process that has been in progress since 2017.

adoption of amendments to the constitution in force (Hungary both before 2011 and after, and Turkey especially in 2010 and 2017), and the derogation from and emptying of the constitution (Poland, Russia). As far as the constitutional courts are concerned, the degeneration goes through three phases: the replacement of judges (Hungary, Poland, Turkey, and Venezuela), the reduction of competences (Hungary, Turkey indirectly, and Russia in the past), and the imposition of difficulties in taking decisions (Poland). As regards the behavior of the courts, we can distinguish between those that favored degeneration (Venezuela), those that supported it with the doctrine of constitutional identity or similar (Russia and Hungary), and those that suffered it (Turkey). After regression, the support given by the courts is in some cases total and brutal (Venezuela) and in others it is almost total since the courts support the rulers in politically sensitive cases (Turkey, Russia and Hungary) while having greater autonomy in individual cases or aspects (dissenting opinions, social rights, and other rights). In Poland the CT became quite passive.

Notwithstanding this sad picture, there is still a chance of a positive evolution. For Poland and Hungary, the hope for change lies in the synergy between the internal opposition forces and the pressure from the European Union. In the Polish case particularly, one can speak of a sort of 'parallel' judicial system, and this is true to a lesser extent in Hungary,[44] although this system could be only temporary before a final purge. There is an interesting 'tug of war' in place between the 'loyalist' Constitutional Tribunal (and also the 'renewed' National Judicial Council) on the one hand and the Supreme Court and the ordinary judges on the other. The latter are raising several preliminary questions to the Court of Justice of the EU to challenge the legitimacy of the judicial reforms of the PiS. On the other hand, the Minister of Justice, who is also the Attorney General, is punishing the rebel judges through his controlled National Judicial Council with a series of disciplinary proceedings.[45]

In these countries, the courts are also resisting thanks to the European Court of Justice.[46] This has 'softened' some aspects of judicial reforms, like the early retirement of common judges (with different consequences in Hungary and

44 The Hungarian ordinary courts still maintain a certain level of independence. For this reason Fidesz has introduced a new order of administrative judges (the relevant Act was adopted on 12 December 2018), with the possibility of 'loyalists' being appointed, to deal with controversies with a high political content (taxation and public procurement, police misconduct, asylum cases, electoral issues, and freedom of information).

45 Please refer to J. Sawicki, 'La via giudiziaria come possibile soluzione alle minacce per lo stato di diritto: la Polonia dinanzi alla Corte di giustizia dell'Unione europea', *Osservatorio AIC*, Nr. 3 of 2019.

46 And to other courts in EU Member States: note the refusal to grant European arrest warrants for Polish citizens, on the basis that the principle of the rule of law in the judiciary is not guaranteed in Poland.

Poland: in the first case without practical effects,[47] and in the second pushing the parliament to have a temporary review of the law).[48]

In Venezuela, a partially dual or parallel system has been created, which symbolizes the overcoming of the authoritarian system after a long period of stabilization.[49] Another lesson that comes from this case is that strong international pressure can provoke reactions within a country. In other cases, therefore, the only hope for change lies in division within the ruling elites. This applies to countries such as Turkey and Russia, where the regime is virtually monolithic.

As has been rightly observed, when compared to the complete political subjugation of the Venezuelan SCJ even the Polish Constitutional Tribunal seems to be respectable. The Venezuelan supreme judges have behaved in an openly illegitimate manner and should face criminal prosecution. Instead, in less extreme cases, 'if a court restrains itself and tries to maintain a minimum of legal functionality in the face of overpowering politics, they deserve understanding and support from the European Club of Constitutional Courts'.[50] Also, while fully authoritarian regimes generally ignore counterweights established domestically or internationally, semi-authoritarian or hybrid regimes use the judiciary, especially the higher courts, instrumentally to justify their anti-liberal behavior. This happens because they come from traditions where there is a separation of powers, apparently successful democratic conditionality, the protection of fundamental rights, or secularization, or because they intend to maintain a certain international prestige for economic and political reasons.

The existence of hybrid systems leads us to reflect that the analysis of the ways in which constitutional regression occurs is useless without a few general considerations about the state of health of constitutionalism and the conceptual justifications that political leaders use to explain their behavior (they contrast the mechanisms of 'democracy', in fact, populist demagogy, and 'liberal constitutionalism', considered as a set of non-democratic, elitist and far from popular needs). It is not surprising that the regression in Poland and Hungary has given rise in recent years to a rich multidisciplinary debate concerning the decay of democracy. The merit of this research is to produce new explanatory formulas that go beyond the traditional categories of public law and political science and avoid the rigid alternative between autocracy and democracy, but are able to keep genetically different phenomena together.[51] However, some of these studies give

47 For further details please refer to A. Di Gregorio, 'The fundamental law of Hungary in the European context', in Z. Szente & F. Mandák & Z. Fejes (Eds), *Challenges and Pitfalls in the Recent Hungarian Constitutional Development. Discussing the New Fundamental Law of Hungary*, Paris, L'Harmattan, 2015.

48 Sawicki, 2019.

49 Without taking into account the most recent appearance of a counter-president in January 2019, the dualism began after the 2015 National Assembly elections.

50 M. Steinbeis, 'Piercing the hull', *VerfBlog*, 2019/1/12.

51 Linz draws a distinction between 'authoritarian regimes', which are 'non-democratic regimes that are not totalitarian' (based on a limited political pluralism without extensive

rise to reservations because they tend to unite cases in distant geographical areas and in places where democracy has never taken root. Both the terms 'populist regime'[52] and 'illiberal democracy'[53] are inaccurate in the constitutional law discourse, although they have a strong media impact. Moreover, the term 'illiberal democracy' is mainly suitable for the cases of Poland and Hungary. The cases of Turkey and Russia are quite different, as these countries have mostly had imperial size systems marked by a high power concentration.[54] Venezuela, despite being the most problematic country in the current Latin American political landscape (and criticized by most other countries in the region)[55] is an example of the fluctuating trends of Latin American political culture, with recurrent phases of democratic decline reflecting the culture of the leadership (*caudillismo*).

What happens in the contexts of fragile democratization or 'imperfect' authoritarian systems, with the capture and neutralization of the top courts, allows a broader reflection on the new perspectives of constitutional narrative and categorization. Even if efforts to find new formulas, so as not to jeopardize the enormous effort of the last decades aimed at the worldwide exportation of western liberal-democratic models, allow the reference to constitutionalism to be kept, albeit in a deteriorated form ('authoritarian constitutionalism', 'constitutions without constitutionalism', 'constitutional retrogression'),[56] constitutional scholars in fact tend to borrow classifications from political scientists, focusing on the characteristics or regressions of democracy,[57] or re-proposing old theories related

political mobilization) and 'authoritarian populist regimes' that are not considered as pluralist since they divide society between 'us' (the people) and 'them' (the elites)'. See J. Linz, *Totalitarian and Authoritarian Regimes*, Boulder, CO: Lynne Rienner Publishers, 2000, pp. 159–261.

52 In the Russian political tradition, the concept of 'populism' refers to a very specific historical heritage, which has nothing in common with the current trend. The reference to 'populism' in the Turkish constitutional tradition is also peculiar, being one of the six arrows of Kemalism, as mentioned above.

53 Prof. S. Cassese gives a clear picture of this, explaining why democracy dies if it becomes illiberal: 'La democrazia svanisce se diventa illiberale', *Corriere della sera*, 28 August 2018. See also G. A. Tóth, 'Constitutional markers of authoritarianism', *Hague Journal on the Rule of Law*, September 2018.

54 In Turkey, from a concentration of civilian and military powers, power became centralized in the hands of the leader of an (initially) moderate Islamic party; in Russia there is a horizontal and vertical centralization regardless of the existence of a 'party of power', which is a consequence and not the origin of the strong leadership.

55 C. de la Torre & F. Finchelstein, '"Democraduras"? Venezuela and National-Populism in Latin America', in A. Martinelli (Ed.), *When Populism Meets Nationalism. Reflections on Parties in Power*, Milano, Ledizioni LediPublishing, 2018.

56 Please refer to, among others, *University of Chicago Law Review*, Vol. 85, No. 2, March 2018 (*Symposium: The limits of constitutionalism – A Global Perspective*); T. Ginsburg & A. Simpser (Eds), *Constitutions in Authoritarian Regimes,* New York, Cambridge University Press, 2018*;* G. Stopler, 'Semi-liberal constitutionalism', *Global Constitutionalism*, Vol. 8, No. 1, March 2019.

57 For example V. Baldini, 'Populismo versus democrazia costituzionale', in "dialogo" con Andreas Voßkuhle', *Dirittifondamentali.it*, 2/2018. See also T. G. Daly, 'Democratic decay: Conceptualising an emerging research field', *Hague Journal on the Rule of Law*, 2019.

to the cyclical waves of democratization (and regression).[58] This may be a springboard for further and broader discussions.

References

V. Baldini, 'Populismo versus democrazia costituzionale. In 'dialogo' con Andreas Voßkuhle', *diritti fondamentali.it*, Vol. 2, 2018, pp. 1–27.

A. Blankenagel, 'The Ghost Haunting Decisions of European Constitutional Courts: What to Do with Constitutional Identity?', *Sravnitel'noe konstitutsionnoe obozrenie*, Vol. 27, No. 5, 2018.

A. Brewer-Carías, *Dismantling Democracy in Venezuela: The Chávez Authoritarian Experiment*, New York, Cambridge University Press, 2010.

A. Brewer-Carías, *Los jueces constitucionales controlando al poder o controlados por el poter. Algunos cases notorios y recentes*, San José, CA, Editorial Investigaciones Jurídicas, 2017.

C. Camposilvan, 'La Costituzione della Turchia', in L. Mezzetti (Ed.), *Codice delle Costituzioni*, Vol. VI.1, Padova, Cedam-Wolters Kluwer Italia, 2016.

J. Couso, 'Venezuela's Recent Constitutional Crisis: Lessons to be Learned from a Failed Judicial Coup D'etat', *International Journal of Constitutional Law Blog*, 12 April 2017, http://www.iconnectblog.com/2017/04/venezuelas-recent-constitutional-crisis-lessons-to-be-learned-from-a-failed-judicial-coup-detat-i-connect-column/

L. De Grazia, 'Constitutional coup e democrazie illiberali: l'esperienza della Turchia', *Rivista AIC*, Vol. 4, 2018.

A. Di Gregorio, 'Lo stato di salute della rule of law in Europa: c'è un regresso generalizzato nei nuovi Stati membri dell'Unione?', *DPCE Online*, Vol. 4, 2016.

A. Di Gregorio, 'Russia', in *2018 Global Review of Constitutional Law* (forthcoming)

A. Di Gregorio, 'The Fundamental Law of Hungary in the European Context', in Z. Szente, F. Mandák & Z. Fejes (Eds), *Challenges and Pitfalls in the Recent Hungarian Constitutional Development: Discussing the New Fundamental Law of Hungary*, Paris, L'Harmattan, 2015.

A. Dzhagaryan, 'Russian Constitutionalism: In Search of Identity', *Sravnitel'noe konstitutsionnoe obozrenie*, Vol. 27, No. 6, 2018.

B. Eszter & F. Gárdos-Orosz, 'Hungary', in R. Albert, D. Landau, P. Faraguna, S. Drugda (Eds.), *2017 Global Review of Constitutional Law*, I·CONnect-Clough Center, 2017.

C. García-Soto, 'Venezuela', in R. Albert, D. Landau, P. Faraguna, S. Drugda (Eds.), *2017 Global Review of Constitutional Law*, I·CONnect-Clough Center, 2017.

T. Ginsburg & T. Moustafa (Eds), *Rule by Law: The Politics of Courts in Authoritarian Regimes*, New York, Cambridge University Press, 2008.

T. Ginsburg & A. Simpser (Eds), *Constitutions in Authoritarian Regimes*, New York, Cambridge University Press, 2018.

58 I. Kenenova, 'Constitutionalism and political leadership in Central and Eastern European countries: challenges and perspectives', *Sravnitelnoe konstitutsionnoe obozrenie*, No. 5, 2018; A. Lürhmann & S. I. Lindberg, 'A third wave of autocratization is here: What is new about it?', *Democratization*, 2019.

M. Haimerl, 'The Turkish Constitutional Court under the Amended Turkish Constitution', *VerfBlog*, 27 January 2017, https://verfassungsblog.de/the-turkish-constitutional-court-under-the-amended-turkish-constitution/

ICJ (International Commission of Jurists), *The Supreme Court of Justice of Venezuela: An Instrument of the Executive Branch*, ICJ, August 2017.

A. Jakab & D. Kochenov (Eds), *The Enforcement of EU Law and Values: Ensuring Member States' Compliance*, Oxford, Oxford University Press, 2017.

I. Kenenova, 'Constitutionalism and Political Leadership in Central and Eastern European Countries: Challenges and Perspectives', *Sravnitelnoe konstitutsionnoe obozrenie*, No. 5(126), 2018.

S. Köybaşı, 'Turkey', in R. Albert, D. Landau, P. Faraguna, S. Drugda (Eds.), *2017 Global Review of Constitutional Law*, I·CONnect-Clough Center, 2017.

A. Martinelli (Ed.), *When Populism Meets Nationalism: Reflections on Parties in Power*, Milano, Ledizioni LediPublishing, 2018.

B. Mathieu, '25 ans d'élections démocratiques à l'Est. Propos conclusifs', *Est Europa*, 2016–2017.

E. Oder, 'Populism and the Turkish Constitutional Court: The Game Broker, the Populist and the Popular', *International Journal of Constitutional Law Blog*, 2 May 2017, http://www.iconnectblog.com/2017/04/populism-and-the-turkish-constitutional-court-the-game-broker-the-populist-and-the-popular/

V. Partlett, 'Russia's Contested Constitutional Review', *International Journal of Constitutional Law Blog*, 13 February 2019, http://www.iconnectblog.com/2018/02/russias-contested-constitutional-review/

Y. Roznai, 'An Unconstitutional Constitutional Amendment—The Turkish Perspective: A Comment on the Turkish Constitutional Court's Headscarf Decision', *International Journal of Constitutional Law*, Vol. 10, No. 1, January 2012.

W. Sadurki, *How Democracy Dies (in Poland): A Case Study of Anti-constitutional Populist Backsliding*, Legal Studies Research Paper No. 18/01, Sidney Law School, January 2018a.

W. Sadurski, 'Polish Constitutional Tribunal under PiS: From an Activist Court, to a Paralysed Tribunal, to a Governmental Enabler', *Hague Journal on the Rule of Law*, 2018b.

W. Sawicki, 'La via giudiziaria come possibile soluzione alle minacce per lo stato di diritto: la Polonia dinanzi alla Corte di giustizia dell'Unione europea', *Osservatorio AIC*, Nr. 3 of 2019.

V. R. Scotti, 'L'indipendenza della Corte costituzionale turca fra legittimità delle leggi e tutela dei diritti. Quali segnali per la tenuta della democrazia in Turchia', *Rivista di diritti comparati*, Vol. 1, 2019.

M. Steinbeis, 'Piercing the Hull', *verfassungsblog.de*, January 12, 2019.

G. Stopler, 'Semi-Liberal Constitutionalism', *Global Constitutionalism*, Vol. 8, No. 1, March 2019.

Z. Szende, 'The Political Orientation of the Members of the Hungarian Constitutional Court between 2010 and 2014', *Constitutional Studies*, Vol. 1, No. 1, 2016.

Z. Tóth, 'Changes which Occurred in the Role of the Hungarian Constitutional Court in Protecting the Constitutional System', *Acta University Sapientiae: Legal Studies*, Vol. 7, No. 1, 2018.

M. Tushnet, 'Authoritarian Constitutionalism', *Cornell Law Review*, Vol. 100, 2015.

M. C. Uzun, 'The Protection of Laicism in Turkey and the Turkish Constitutional Court: The Example of the Prohibition on the Use of the Islamic Veil in Higher Education', *Penn State International Law Review*, Vol. 28, 2010.

O. O. Varol, L. Dalla Pellegrina & N. Garoupa, 'An Empirical Analysis of Judicial Transformation in Turkey', *The American Journal of Comparative Law*, Vol. 65, 2017.

12 The use of the EU infringement procedures to protect *de facto* the rule of law via the development of the parameter

From obligations under the Treaties to the Charter of Fundamental Rights

Enrico Albanesi

12.1 Introduction

The principle of the rule of law and the other fundamental EU values under Art. 2 TEU (respect for human dignity, freedom, democracy, equality, respect for human rights) are under pressure in some Member States, e.g. in Hungary[1] and Poland.[2] This is due to far reaching amendments in their constitution or new pieces of legislation passed in recent years. These reforms could turn those states into 'illiberal democracies'.[3]

The main paths for the enforcement of EU values should be essentially political, namely the mechanisms under Art. 7 TEU.[4] On 20 December 2017 the European Commission (EC) proposed that the Council shall determine that there

1 On constitutional transformation in Hungary since 2010 see P. Sonnevend, A. Jakab & L. Csink, 'The Constitution as an Instrument of Everyday Party Politics: The Basic Law of Hungary', in A. von Bogdandy & P. Sonnevend (Eds), *Constitutional Crisis in the European Constitutional Area. Theory, Law and Politics in Hungary and Romania*, Oxford/Portland, OR, Hart, 2015, pp. 75–79; A. Vincze & M. Varju, 'Hungary The New Fundamental Law', *European Public Law*, Vol. 18, No. 3, 2012, pp. 437–453; and M. Bánkuti, G. Halmai & K. L. lin G. A. Tóth (Ed.), *Constitution for a Disunited Nation. On Hungary's 2011 Fundamental Law*, Budapest, Central European University Press, 2012, pp. 237–268.

2 On constitutional transformation in Poland since 2015 see T. T. Koncewicz, 'The Capture of the Polish Constitutional Tribunal and Beyond: Of Institution(s), Fidelities and the Rule of Law in Flux', *Review of Central and East European Law*, Vol. 43, 2018, pp. 116–173 and A. Śledzińska-Simon, 'The Rise and the Fall of Judicial Self-Government in Poland: On Judicial Reform Reversing Democratic Transition', *German Law Journal*, Vol. 19, No. 7, 2018, pp. 1839–1869.

3 According to the definition given by F. Zakaria, 'The Rise of Illiberal Democracy', *Foreign Affairs*, Vol. 76, No. 6, 1997, pp. 22–43.

4 And under the Communication from the EC to the EP and the Council, A new framework to strengthen the Rule of Law, COM (2014) 158.

is a clear risk of serious breach of the values under Art. 7(1) TEU in Poland.[5] On 12 September 2018 the European Parliament (EP) did the same, with regard to Hungary.[6] However, the path under Art. 7 TEU is seen as a sort of 'nuclear option' because of its politically devastating effects:[7] due to political obstacles, it has not been used so far and it is very unlikely that it will be used.

Alternative *new* or *revised* mechanisms for the enforcement of EU values have been proposed in the literature. Such mechanisms are the establishment of an *ad hoc* body or the protection of individuals' rights by national courts.[8] One of the main alternative mechanisms that has been proposed is the use of EU infringement procedures (under Arts 258–260 TFEU) in a 'revised' version,[9] as described later on in this chapter.

This chapter will focus on the use of an *already existing* mechanism (EU infringement procedures under Arts 258–260 TFEU), as used to protect *de facto* the values under Art. 2 TEU. The main aims of this chapter are: (i) to demonstrate how since 2012 the EC, then supported by the European Court of Justice (CJEU), has actually used infringement procedures to *de facto* protect the fundamental values under Art. 2 TEU in Hungary and Poland via the development of the relevant parameter: namely, obligations under the Treaties; and, more significantly, the Charter of Fundamental Rights of the European Union (CFREU), then; (ii) to analyze the factual and legal consequences of such a path followed by the EC. From a strictly legal perspective, the hypothesis underpinning this chapter is that the use of such parameters has allowed the EC and the CJEU to

5 Reasoned proposal in accordance with Article 7(1) of the Treaty on European Union regarding the rule of law in Poland COM (2017) 835 final.

6 EP resolution of 12 September 2018 on a proposal calling on the Council to determine, pursuant to Art. 7(1) of the Treaty on European Union, the existence of a clear risk of a serious breach by Hungary of the values on which the Union is founded P8_TA(2018)0340.

7 As the former President of the Commission Barroso called these mechanisms. See State of the Union 2012 Address, Plenary Session of the EP, Strasbourg 12 September 2012, SPEECH/12/596.

8 Müller proposed the establishment of an *ad hoc* body, like the Venice Commission, tasked with protecting Copenhagen criteria (namely a Copenhagen Commission). See J.-W. Müller, 'Protecting the Rule of Law (and Democracy!) in the EU. The Idea of a Copenhagen Commission', in C. Closa & D. Kochenov (Eds), *Reinforcing Rule of Law Oversight in the European Union*, Cambridge, Cambridge University Press, 2016, pp. 206–224. Von Bogdandy and other scholars proposed that national court should protect individuals' rights, as EU citizens, from the violation of EU values. See A. von Bogdandy, C. Antpöhler, J. Dickschen, S. Hentrei, M. Kottmann & M. Smrkolj, 'A European Response to Domestic Constitutional Crisis: Advancing the Reverse-Solange Doctrine)', in A. von Bogdandy & P. Sonnevend (Eds), *Constitutional Crisis in the European Constitutional Area*, Oxford, Hart, 2015, pp. 235–253. An overview of these and other academic proposals is offered by D. Kochenov, 'The Acquis and Its Principles. The Enforcement of the 'Law' versus the Enforcement of 'Values' in the EU', in A. Jakab & D. Kochenov (Eds), *The Enforcement of EU Law and Values. Ensuring Member States' Compliance*, Oxford, Oxford University Press, 2017, pp. 18–25.

9 K. L. Scheppele, 'Enforcing the Basic Principles of EU Law through Systemic Infringement Actions', in Closa & Kochenov, 2016, pp. 105–132.

keep their actions within the scope of the EU law and at the same time to protect *de facto* the rule of law within the Member States.

The chapter will proceed as follows. First, the reasons for the failure of the mechanisms under Art. 7 TEU will be described: political obstacles have so far prevented those mechanisms from working (Section 12.2). Second, the legal arguments against the use of the infringement procedures under Arts 258–260 TFEU to protect the fundamental values under Art. 2 TEU will be critically analyzed. However, the official legal position of the EC, supported by the EP, is that of the inability to use the infringement procedures to *expressly* protect fundamental values under Art. 2 TEU (Section 12.3).

This is the reason why, third, this chapter will try to show how since 2012 the EC has used the infringement procedures against Hungary and Poland ***without expressly mentioning Art. 2 TEU*** with regard to some violations of obligations under the Treaties and the CFREU which ***de facto*** affected fundamental values, such as, primarily, the rule of law. What especially matters here from a legal viewpoint is that the EC started following this path, first by resorting to obligations under the Treaties as parameters; and then, more significantly, by using the parameters of the CFREU (Section 12.4).

Fourth, before commenting on such a use from a legal viewpoint, the factual consequences of such an approach will also be examined here. The question will be posed whether such use of infringement procedures could be considered an effective way to protect those values, at least ***indirectly*** (Section 12.5).

Finally, from a strictly legal perspective, it will be argued that the use of such a parameter of the CFREU allowed the EC and the CJEU to keep their activity within the scope of the EU law but at the same time to use infringement procedures in order to ***de facto*** protect the rule of law within Member States (Sections 12.6 and 12.7).

12.2 The mechanism under Article 7 TEU and its failure

The principle of the rule of law and the other EU fundamental values are protected according to Art. 7 TEU through mechanisms that are essentially political.[10] These political mechanisms have actually failed in protecting constitutional democracy. As already mentioned, huge political obstacles have prevented the EU from using them.

First, there is a tendency of the EU to avoid such a 'nuclear option' because of its politically devastating effects. However, when President Barroso used this expression, he seemed to forget that Art. 7(1) is still not the last step, as there are two further steps under Art. 7(2) and 7(3). Moreover, it seems that he also

10 Besselink calls such a procedure one 'of a highly political nature'. See L. F. M. Besselink, 'The Bite, the Bark, and the Howl. Article 7 TEU and the Rule of Law Initiatives', in Jakab & Kochenov, 2017, p. 132.

wanted to reassure countries such as Hungary and Poland that no such procedures would be started.[11]

Second, the majorities to be achieved in these procedures are very high[12] by definition. Article 7(1) requires a majority of four-fifths and Art. 7(2) requires unanimity. The point is that the European parties usually close their ranks around Prime Ministers (who are threatening the rule of law in their own countries) when they belong to the same political families. The European People's Party tended to do this with regard to Viktor Orbàn in Hungary and the Party of European Socialists did the same with regard to Victor Ponta in Romania.[13] Better later than never, on 20 March 2019 the European People's Party Presidency suspended Orbàn's Fidesz membership in the EPP and established an evaluation committee. Its task is to accomplish monitoring of the implementation of some basic conditions. On 10 April 2019 the Party of European Socialists announced it would consider relations with the Romanian Social Democratic Party frozen, until the Romanian Government clarified its commitment to the rule of law and followed the European Commission's recommendations, pending a formal discussion at the next PES Presidency meeting in June 2019, where its membership will be discussed.

In 2016 the EC took the path of the *A new framework to strengthen the Rule of Law* as a kind of early warning mechanism (to be initiated before the beginning of Art. 7 TEU) concerning Poland by issuing recommendations.[14] However, no outcome from Poland has been achieved. As already said, in 2017, the EC proposed that the Council determine that there is a clear risk of serious breach of the values under Art. 2 TEU in Poland. In 2018 the EP did the same with regard to Hungary.

For the abovementioned reasons, it is very unlikely that the Council would do so. Even if the Council proceeds, it is unlikely that such a determination under Art. 7(1) TEU (without sanctions) would produce concrete effects, anyway. In any case, it seems unlikely that Art. 7(2) TEU will be initiated since those procedures require unanimity. The Hungarian Prime Minister Viktor Orbàn has already announced that Hungary will veto such a potential decision regarding Poland[15] and it is likely that Poland will do the same in a decision concerning Hungary.[16]

11 As argued by L. F. M. Besselink & J. H. Reestman, 'Editorial', *European Constitutional Law Review*, Vol. 13, 2017, pp. 207–220.

12 M. Dawson & E. Muir, 'Enforcing Fundamental Values: EU Law and Governance in Hungary and Romania', *Maastricht Journal of European and Comparative Law*, Vol. 4, 2012, pp. 471–472.

13 J.-W. Müller, 'Should the EU Protect Democracy and the Rule of Law Inside Member States?', *European Law Journal*, Vol. 21, No. 2, 2015, p. 149.

14 Commission Recommendations (EU) 2016/1374 of 27 July 2016, 2017/146 of 21 December 2016, 2017/1520 of 26 July 2017 and 2017/9050 of 20 December 2017.

15 Financial Times, 8 January 2016.

16 For an alternative path, see K. L. Scheppele, 'EU Can Still Block Hungary's veto on Polish Sanctions', *Politico.eu*, 11 January 2016.

12.3 The infringement procedures under Articles 258 and 260 TFEU and the legal arguments in favor or against its use to protect expressly the values provided by Article 2 TEU

In the light of the failure of EU political mechanisms to protect constitutional democracies in Member States, it is time to see whether infringement procedures can be used *expressly* with the same purpose. The underpinning legal issue here is the relationship between Arts 258–260 TFEU and Art. 7 TEU. In other words, the possible use of the procedures under Arts 258–260 TFEU in the event of a breach of fundamental values under Art. 2 TEU as such.[17]

On the one hand, some scholars have conceptualized this relation as one of *lex specialis*. Thus, the infringement procedures cannot be used with regard to the breach under Art. 2 TEU as such, because for this breach special procedures under Art. 7 TEU has been established.[18]

According to these authors, the rationale behind such a special procedure under Art. 7 TEU is to provide the EU with a tool to address Member States' behavior outside the scope of the EU law. Therefore, as the Union is competent under Art. 7 TEU to act on Member State behavior *outside* the scope of EU law, this brings that behavior *within* the scope of Union law in a broader sense: otherwise,

> a Member State could respect human dignity, freedom, equality, the Rule of Law, human rights [...] and be a democracy *only* when acting within the narrower confines of EU law, but then still persistently and seriously breach those values and denigrate human dignity, stifle freedom, crush equality, deny the Rule of Law, trample human rights, and act as a dictatorship in gross denial of minority rights outside the scope of EU law narrowly construed.[19]

The consequence of this view is that infringement procedures under Arts 258–260 TFEU can be used only *within the scope* of EU law, i.e. with regard to a breach of *specific* provision of EU law; the use of infringement procedures to protect fundamental values *expressly* under Art. 2 TEU would lead the EC to act *outside the scope* of EU law.

In the 2014 Communication mentioned above, the EC wrote that '[a]ction taken by the Commission to launch infringement procedures, based on Art. 258 TFEU, has proven to be an important instrument in addressing certain rule of

17 Kochenov, 2017, pp. 10–12.

18 M. Dawson, E. Muir & M. Claes, 'A Tool-box for Legal and Political Mobilisation in European Equality Law', in D. Anagnostou & M. Claes (Eds), *Rights and Courts in Pursuit of Social Change. Legal Mobilisation in the Multi-level European System*, Oxford/Portland, OR, Hart, 2014, pp. 117–118. See also L. Prete, *Infringement Proceedings in EU Law*, Alphen aan den Rijn, Kluwer Law International, 2017, p. 225.

19 Besselink, 2017, p. 143.

law concerns': but 'infringement procedures can be launched by the Commission only where these concerns constitute, at the same time, a breach of a specific provision of EU law'. On the other hand, '[t]here are situations of concern which fall outside the scope of EU law and therefore cannot be considered as a breach of obligations under the Treaties but still pose a systemic threat to the rule of law'.[20] In the case of the latter, the EC's implicit statement is that infringement procedures cannot be used.

This is also the view of the EP. In 2013 the EP called on the EC (as the Guardian of the Treaties) to launch an objective investigation and start infringement procedures whenever it considers that a Member State has failed to fulfil an obligation under the Treaties and, in particular, is violating the rights enshrined in the CFREU. Beside this, the EP demanded that the EC should focus not only on specific infringements of EU law, *to be remedied notably through Art. 258 TFEU*, but should respond appropriately to a systemic change in the constitutional and legal system and practice of a Member State where multiple and recurrent infringements unfortunately result in a state of legal uncertainty, which no longer meets the requirements of Art. 2 TEU.[21] For the latter, this is apparently the EP's view, Art. 258 TFEU should not be used.

It has been also noted that such use of Arts 258–260 TFEU to indirectly protect EU fundamental values under Art. 2 TEU would fall prey to the accusation of 'integration by stealth'.[22] Other scholars also underlined that the parameters under Art. 2 TEU cannot be systematically protected and assured by legal means, and in particular by courts.[23] A judicial approach could even be counter-productive.[24]

On the other hand, other scholars stated that infringement procedures under Arts 258–260 TFEU can be used by the EC when a Member State breaches fundamental values under Art. 2 TEU.

First, Hillion noted that the *lex specialis* argument finds no support in the text of the EU Treaties:[25] as has been noted, 'there is nothing in the treaty which informs us about the relationship between the two procedures'.[26]

20 Communication, 2014, p. 5.

21 EP resolution of 3 July 2013 on the situation of fundamental rights: standards and practices in Hungary (pursuant to the EP resolution of 16 February 2012) P7_TA(2013)0315, para. 70.

22 According to Dawson & Muir, 2012, p. 473.

23 M. Avbelj, 'The Inherent Limits of Law – the Case of Slovenia', *Verfassungsblog.de*, December 2013.

24 As argued by P. Blokker, 'Systemic Infringement Action: An Effective Solution or Rather Part of the Problem?', *Verfassungsblog.de*, December 2013.

25 C. Hillion, 'Overseeing the Rule of Law in the EU. Legal Mandate and Means', in Closa & Kochenov, 2016, p. 72.

26 F. Hoffmeister, 'Enforcing the EU Charter of Fundamental Rights: How Far Rome, Budapest and Bucharest from Brussels?', in Von Bogdandy & Sonnevend, 2015, p. 205.

Second, as for the impossibility to protect the fundamental values by legal means, it has been noted that Art. 2 TEU is underscored by several provisions in the Treaties[27] and those values are *legal* parameters, which are not so mysterious to the courts.[28]

Third, Komárek has noted that infringement procedures are used when the EC considers that a Member State has failed to fulfill *an obligation under the Treaties*. The obligation to respect the EU fundamental values under Art. 2 TEU is also *an obligation under the Treaties*. Therefore Arts 258–260 TFEU can be used in this case.[29]

Finally, from a different perspective (as her proposal is confined to violations of substantive area of EU law), it is worth mentioning here also Scheppele's proposal to use the infringement procedures expressly in relation to Art. 2 TEU in case of systemic breach of Treaty obligations. According to Scheppele's view, 'ordinary' infringement procedures under Arts 258–260 TFEU could be used to challenge breaches of fundamental values but they are often too narrow to address the structural problems which persistently noncompliant states pose in this field. This is the reason why she proposed a 'revised' version of infringement procedures, to be used as a mechanism to sanction Member States in cases of *systemic* infringements when the fundamental values under Art. 2 TEU are undermined by individual infringement of EU law. By grouping together related complaints thematically under Art. 2 TEU, 'the Commission would add the argument that the whole is more than the sum of the parts and that the set of alleged infringements rises to the level of a systemic breach of basic values'.[30] I agree with Scheppele's view.[31]

As said, it needs to be understood that the EC has never in fact used infringement procedures under Arts 258–260 TFEU by mentioning expressly Art. 2 TEU, because the EC looks at those two procedures as separate ones. However, it is worth analyzing here those cases in which the EC has used infringement procedures with regard to the breach of specific provisions of EU law that *implicitly* and *in the current Hungarian and Polish constitutional framework* had some impact on EU fundamental values.

27 M. Schmidt & P. Bogdanowicz, 'The Infringement Procedure in the Rule of Law Crisis: How to make effective use of Article 258 TFEU', *Common Market Law Review*, Vol. 55, 2018, pp. 1070–1071.

28 Scheppele, 2016, p. 115.

29 J. Komárek, 'The EU is More Than a Constraint on Populist Democracy', *Verfassungsblog.de*, March 2013. See also E. Albanesi, Pluralismo costituzionale e procedura d'infrazione dell'Unione europea, Torino, Giappichelli, 2018, p. 250 and Schmidt & Bogdanowicz, 2018, p. 1070.

30 Scheppele, 2016, pp. 108–125.

31 Albanesi, 2018, pp. 253–255.

12.4 The use of infringement procedures by the European Commission and the Court of Justice of the EU to protect *de facto* EU fundamental values under Article 2 TEU

12.4.1 Obligations under the treaties as parameter

12.4.1.1 Hungary and the system of retirement of judges (C-286/12)

The first case that should be mentioned is the case of infringement procedures brought against Hungary because of the system of retirement of judges having reached the age of 62.[32] This was one of the most dangerous provisions passed in Hungary since 2010 from the perspective of the respect for the principle of the rule of law, because it infringed abruptly and significantly the independence of the Judiciary:[33] 236 judges, 100 prosecutors, and 60 notaries (which means 10%, 5%, and 20% of the total number of each profession) had to retire.[34]

The EC decided to tackle these provisions under the violation of obligations under the Treaties, namely Directive 2000/78/EC establishing a general framework for equal treatment in employment and occupation. When the case was brought before it, the CJEU stated that such a system of retirement was a breach of that Directive, because it gave rise to a difference in treatment on grounds of age that, although reasonably justified, was not proportionate as regards with objective pursued.[35] Therefore, the relevant parameter, in this case, was an obligation under the Treaties: the CJEU found that Hungary had failed to fulfill its obligations because of such a violation of that Directive.

12.4.1.2 Hungary and vacating the office of the data protection supervisory authority (C-288/12)

The same happened when infringement procedures were brought against Hungary because of an Act of Parliament which compelled the data protection supervisory authority to vacate its office before serving its full term, due to the establishment of a new authority.[36] Once again, such a removal from office of the former authority before the expiry of the term prescribed by the law, raised concern from the perspective of the principle of the rule of law.[37]

32 Judgment of 6 November 2012 in Case 286/12, Commission v Hungary [2012], paras 77–81 in http://curia.europa.eu/.

33 G. Halmai, 'The Case of the Retirement Age of Hungarian Judges', in F. Nicola & B. Davies (Eds), *EU Law Stories*, Cambridge/New York, Cambridge University Press, 2017, p. 471.

34 As reported in A. Vincze, 'The CJEU as the Guardian of the Hungarian Constitution: Case C-286/12 Commission v. Hungary', *European Public Law*, Vol. 19, No. 3, 2013, p. 495.

35 Paras 57–80.

36 Judgment of 8 April 2014 in Case 288/12, Commission v Hungary, [2012], para. 54, in http://curia.europa.eu/.

37 Vincze & Varju, 2012, p. 444.

The EC started infringement procedures against Hungary due to the violation of an obligation under the Treaties. The CJEU stated that such provisions undermined the authority's independence and viewed this as a breach of Art. 28(1) of Directive 95/46/EC under which supervising authorities shall act with complete independence in exercising the functions entrusted to them. It is worth noting that the CJEU also mentioned Art. 8(3) CFREU which establishes that compliance with rules on protection of personal data 'shall be subject to control by an independent authority'.[38]

12.4.1.3 Hungary and the reform of the Central Bank (2012)

It is worth mentioning here also the infringement procedures brought against Hungary because of the constitutional and legislative reform of the Hungarian Central Bank. Such a reform was criticized from the perspective of the principle of the rule of law, as it undermined the independence of the Hungarian Central Bank: among other things, its Governor became a simple deputy chairman of a new controversial structure (the Budget Council) with relevant powers.[39] This would structurally encroach on his independence.

The EC issued a letter of formal notice in 2012,[40] against Hungary for having breached Art. 130 TFEU on the independence of National Central Banks. The EC then decided to close the infringement procedures when the Hungarian Parliament amended its Constitution and its legislation in line to the EC's concerns.[41]

12.4.2 The CFREU as parameter

12.4.2.1 Hungary and the Immigration Laws (2018)

Other controversial laws enacted by Hungary are those regarding migration and asylum, which have been called by Halmai 'anti-rule-of-law' Immigration Laws.[42] The EC referred Hungary to the CJEU in 2018 due to the violation of the Directive 2013/32/EU (Asylum Procedure Directive) and Directive 2010/64/EU (Directive on the right to interpretation and translation in criminal proceedings).

More significantly from the perspective of this analysis, in this case the EC also referred Hungary due to the violation of Art. 47 CFREU on the right to an effective remedy and to a fair trial, because, with regard to the judicial review of decisions rejecting an asylum application, a personal hearing of the applicant is

38 Paras 47 and 54.

39 M. Varju, 'Governance, Accountability, and the Market', in Tóth, 2012, p. 315.

40 EC, Press release, 17 January 2012.

41 EC, Press release, 19 July 2012. See also EC, Press release, 25 April 2012.

42 G. Halmai, 'How the EU Can and Should Cope with Illiberal Member States', *Quaderni costituzionali*, 2018, p. 317.

optional and because judicial decisions taken by court secretaries (a sub-judicial level) lack judicial independence.[43]

12.4.2.2 Hungary and the Higher Education Law (C-66/18)

Another case is the one of infringement procedures brought against Hungary due to the Hungarian Higher Education Law having the aim of shutting down the Central European University (CEU) in Budapest, by adding new requirements and authorizations with regard to foreign higher education institutions. The concerns regarding the endurance of the common values under Art. 2 TEU in Hungary in the light of this law[44] are evident, as the right of academic freedom (as part of freedom of expression) is a condition for democracy.

The EC considered this law a breach of the freedom of establishment and freedom to provide services under Arts 49 and 56 TFEU and more significantly from the perspective of this analysis the right of academic freedom, the right to education, and the freedom to conduct a business as provided respectively by Arts 13, 14, and 16 CFREU. It referred Hungary to the CJEU in 2018.[45]

12.4.3 Article 19(1) TEU in connection with 47 CFREU as parameter and the indirect mentioning of Article 2 TEU

12.4.3.1 Poland and the system of retirement of judges (C-192/18)

The EC also brought infringement procedures against Poland because of its reform of the judiciary, due to the retirement age of female judges (at the age of 60), different from those of their male counterparts (at the age of 65). The new legislation gave the Ministry of Justice the discretionary power to postpone the mandate of those judges who have reached the limit for retirement and the power to dismiss the Presidents of the Courts.

Like the aforementioned Hungarian Law on Judges, this was one of the most dangerous provisions passed in Poland from the perspective of the respect of the principle of the rule of law, because it infringed abruptly and significantly the independence of the judiciary and gave the aforementioned discretionary powers to the Ministry of Justice.[46]

The EC viewed this system as a discrimination on the basis of gender, thus a breach of Art. 157 TFEU and of Directive 2006/54/EC. More significantly from the perspective of the current analysis, the EC considered the discretionary

43 EC, Press release, 19 July 2018. See also 10 December 2015 and 7 December 2017.

44 G. Halmai, 'Much Ado About Nothing? Legal and Political Schooling for the Hungarian Government', *Constitutionalism and Politics*, 29 April 2017 (https://blogs.eui.eu/constitutionalism-politics-working-group/).

45 Action brought against Hungary on 1 February 2018, Case 66/18, Commission v Hungary, in http://curia.europa.eu/.

46 On the reform of the judiciary in Poland see Śledzińska-Simon, 2018.

powers of the Minister also as a breach of Art. 19(1) TEU, under which Member States shall provide remedies sufficient to ensure effective legal protection in the fields covered by Union law, in connection with Art. 47 CFREU, which recognizes the right to an effective remedy and a fair trial. The EC brought the case before the CJEU in 2018.[47]

12.4.3.2 Poland and the Law on the Supreme Court (C-619/18)

The most significant infringement procedures in the light of the current analysis are those brought by the EC[48] against Poland because of the new Polish Law on the Supreme Court. Under this law, the retirement age for Supreme Court judges has been lowered to 65 years: judges can continue their activity beyond that age only if the President of the Republic grants them permission. No judicial review of such a decision is allowed. The impact on the principle of the rule of law in the Polish constitutional framework is evident, because it infringed abruptly and significantly the independence of the judiciary; moreover without allowing any judicial review of the decision of the President of the Republic.[49]

The EC brought an action against Poland before the CJEU in October 2018 because such a law undermines the principle of judicial independence: Poland has fulfilled its obligations under Art. 19(1) TEU, read in connection with Art. 47 CFREU. The EC also requested the Court to order Poland via interim measures to suspend the application of those provisions, to take all necessary measures to assure that the Supreme Court judges may continue to perform their duties in the same post and to refrain from appointing new judges.

On 19 October 2018 the President of the CJEU granted those interim measures. Significantly, the order recalls that

> the requirement of judicial independence forms part of the essence of the fundamental right to a fair trial [under Art. 47 CFREU], a right which is of cardinal importance *as a guarantee* that all the rights which individuals derive from EU law will be protected and *that the values common to the Member States set out in Art. 2 TEU, in particular the value of the rule of law, will be safeguarded*.[50]

Although indirectly, the CJEU mentioned Art. 2 TEU for the first time in infringement procedures. As rarely happens in infringement procedures, it significantly also granted interim measures.

47 Action brought against Poland on 15 March 2018, Case 192/18, Commission v Poland, in http://curia.europa.eu/.
48 EC, Press release, 24 September 2018. See also 2 July 2018 and 14 August 2018.
49 Śledzińska-Simon, 2018.
50 Order of the President of the Court of Justice of 16 November 2018 in Case 619/18, Commission v Poland, [2018] in http://curia.europa.eu/. Emphasis added to quote.

On 24 June 2019 the CJEU found that by granting the President of the Republic the discretion to extend the periof of judicial activity of judges of the Supreme Court beyond the newly fixed retirement age, Poland had failed to fulfill its obligations under the second subparagraph of Art. 19(1) TEU.[51]

12.4.3.3 Poland and the new disciplinary regime for judges

On 3 April 2019 the EC lanunched infringement procedures against Poland because of the new disciplinary regime for judges. According to the EC, the new disciplinary regime undermines the judicial independence of Polish judges by not offering necessary guarantees to protect them form political control.

Once again, the EC stated that Poland failed to fulfill its obligations under Art. 19(1) TEU, read in connection with Art. 47 CFREU. It also indirectly mentioned Art. 2 TEU.[52]

The factual and legal consequences of such a development of the use of the relevant parameter in the infringement procedures against Hungary and Poland will be now analyzed.

12.5 The factual consequences of such use of the infringement procedure to protect indirectly the fundamental values under Article 2 TEU: from the (impracticable) political 'nuclear option' to (effective) legal targeted goals

As these cases clearly show, the EC has always started such types of infringement procedures on the grounds of breach of specific provisions of EU law only. For the legal reasons already mentioned, it has been said that it would be highly unlikely that the EC would seek a judgment solely finding an infringement of the values of Art. 2.[53]

However, it is worth underlining that in all these cases examined, the EC has protected values such as the independence of the judiciary, the independence of a supervisory authority, the independence of a central bank, or the right to academic freedom, whose breaches, especially due to the constitutional framework in which they arose in Hungary and Poland, have had an impact on the rule of law and the other EU fundamental values under Art. 2 TEU.

Some scholars have noted that the use of infringement procedures to protect EU fundamental values has actually some defects. Among other things,

51 Judgment of 24 June 2019 in Case 618/19, Commission v Poland, [2019], in http://curia.europa.eu/.

52 EC, Press release, 3 April 2019.

53 L. W. Gormley, 'Infringement Proceedings', in Jakab & Kochenov, 2017, p. 75.

infringement procedures cannot be used to legally restore the *ex ante* general picture tackled by the Member State.[54]

However, in the light of the political obstacles to the use of political mechanisms under Art. 7 TEU, via such infringement procedures the EC has been able to deal with, at least partially, some of the most dramatic constitutional issues which are arising in Hungary and Poland. And, more significantly, instead of using the (impracticable) politically devastating 'nuclear option', it has been able to achieve some targeted legal goals. First, the constitutional provisions and the legislation regarding the Hungarian Central Bank have been changed by Hungary due to the pressure brought to bear by the infringement procedures carried out by the EC. Second, Poland had to suspend the implementation of the Law on the Supreme Court thanks to the interim measures issued by the President of the CJEU. Third, Hungary has been found not to have fulfilled its obligations due to its laws on the system of the retirement of judges and on the data protection authority. Actions have been brought before the CJEU against Hungary with regard to its immigration laws and the Hungarian Higher Education Law, and against Poland due to its reform of the judiciary. The Sword of Damocles of monetary sanctions is pending on these two Member States.

More generally, as has been noted, the effectiveness of the infringement procedures is noteworthy. The EC does not have to wait, but can seize the initiative. The procedures can be used against general and persistent infringements, which seems to cover the ones Hungary and Poland are carrying out in threatening the principle of the rule of law. As seen, the CJEU can grant interim measures and this avoids irreparable damage to the interests concerned. The procedures are given teeth with the sanction procedure under Art. 260.[55] It can also play a preventive function, i.e. it can allow the EU to intervene at an earlier stage, before a serious and persistent breach of Art. 2 TEU.[56]

These are the factual consequences of such a use of the infringement procedures by the EC and the CJEU, in order to protect indirectly the values under Art. 2 TEU. However, it is now worth analyzing the path followed by the EC and the CJEU from a strict legal perspective.

12.6 The use of the CFREU as the relevant parameter

The most significant trend underpinning the cases examined above is the development of the relevant parameter used by the EC and the CJEU. In the first three cases (Section 12.4.1), concerning Hungary, which affected the principle of the rule of law under Art. 2 TEU if viewed from the perspective of the Hungarian

54 With specific regard to case C-286/12, some Authors noted that, given the legal effects of a judgement in an infringement case, once the Judges retired, the CJEU was not able to replace them. See Halmai, 2018, p. 316 and Scheppele, 2016, pp. 109–110.

55 Schmidt & Bogdanowicz, 2018, p. 1073.

56 Hillion, 2016, pp. 72–73 and Albanesi, 2018, pp. 253–254.

constitutional framework, Hungary was found not to have fulfilled its obligations because of a violation of obligations under the Treaties: breaches of the Directive on equal treatment in employment and occupation, of the Directive under which supervising authorities shall act with complete independence in exercising the functions entrusted to them, and of Art. 130 TFEU on the independence of National Central Banks.

In a second stage (Section 12.4.2), concerning Hungary, the EC *also* started using the CFREU as parameter: the Directives on asylum and criminal proceedings *and* Art. 47 CFREU on the right to a fair trial, with regard to the Hungarian immigration laws; the fundamental internal market freedoms *and* Art. 13, 14, and 16 CFREU on the right of academic freedom, the right to education and the freedom to conduct a business, with regard to the Hungarian Higher Education Law.

In these cases, the EC has raised the level of the issues to that of a constitutional nature, by involving the CFREU. However, as the extent of the application of the CFREU is controversial (according to some scholars, it could be applied even by domestic courts in purely domestic cases[57]), the EC did its best to keep its action within the scope of the EU law, namely within the area of freedom, security, and justice and within the area of the internal market.

The last three cases (Section 12.4.3), concerning Poland, marked a turning point.

The 2017 action against Poland concerning its reform of the judiciary was brought in the light of Art. 19(1) TEU and Art. 47 CFREU. The connection of such allegations with the substantive scope of the EU law only is formally the fact that Art. 19(1) refers to 'the fields covered by Union law': within this area Member States shall provide remedies sufficient to ensure effective legal protection. In particular the EC noted that its concerns rose from the fact that due to the reform of the judiciary there can be influence over judges when they are adjudicating cases *involving the application of EU law*.

However, this case shows that it is impossible to draw a line between what is within and what is outside the scope of EU law when speaking about horizontal issues of a constitutional nature: matters concerning independence of the judiciary are not with regard to specific remedies or specific fair trials 'in the fields covered by Union law' only but the essence of structure of the judiciary in Poland as a whole, *regardless of the application of EU law or not.*

In the order concerning the Polish Supreme Court, the President of the CJEU mentioned 'systemic concerns' which 'give rise to legal uncertainty and to *hinder the proper functioning of the EU legal order*' (emphasis added).[58] However, for the first time in infringement procedures, the CJEU mentioned Art. 2 TEU and recalled that the requirement of judicial independence (which forms part of the

57 A. Jakab, 'Application of the EU CFR by National Courts in Purely Domestic Cases', in Jakab & Kochenov, 2017, pp. 252–262 and von Bogdandy et al., 2015, pp. 235–253.

58 Case 619/18, Commission v Poland, para. 15.

essence of the right to a fair trial under Art. 47 CFREU) was a guarantee that *the values common to the Member States* set out in Art. 2 TEU, in particular the rule of law, will be safeguarded.

The turning point is clear here. Infringement procedures concerning the Polish Law on the Supreme Court were formally carried out under a specific right under the CFREU (Art. 47 CFREU) *in order to protect the functioning of the EU legal order*. However, albeit indirectly, the actual goal of the EC and of the CJEU in granting the interim measures, is guaranteeing the safeguarding of the values *common to the Member States* set out under Art. 2 TEU, in particular the rule of law.

It should be noted that three factors accompanied this turning point. In 2017 the EC announced it would specifically pursue cases in which national law provides no effective redress procedures for a breach of EU law or otherwise prevents national judicial systems from ensuring that EU law is specifically applied effectively in accordance with the requirements of the rule of law and Art. 47 CFREU.[59]

In 2018 the CJEU stated on a preliminary ruling that Art. 19 TEU

> gives concrete expression to the value of the rule of law stated in Art. 2 TEU, [and] entrusts the responsibility for ensuring judicial review in the EU legal order not only to the Court of Justice but also to national courts and tribunals.[60]

In 2018, in the famous preliminary ruling concerning Poland and the European arrest warrant, the CJEU pointed out that

> the requirement of judicial independence forms part of the essence of the fundamental right to a fair trial, a right which is of cardinal importance as a guarantee that all the rights which individuals derive from EU law will be protected and that the values common to the Member States set out in Art. 2 TEU, in particular the value of the rule of law, will be safeguarded.[61]

12.7 Conclusion

The analysis carried out here has shown that the use of infringement procedures to tackle *indirectly* issues concerning the violation of the EU fundamental values under Art. 2 TEU and in particular the rule of law, was effective and gained

59 Communication from the EC, EU Law: Better Results through Better Application, COM 2017/C 18/02.

60 Judgment of 27 February 2018 in Case 64/16, Associação Sindical dos Juízes Portugueses, [2018], para. 48, in http://curia.europa.eu/.

61 Judgment of 25 July 2018 in Case 216/18 PPU, LM [2018], para. 32, in http://curia.europa.eu/.

results. Hungary was compelled to change the provisions regarding its Central Bank due to the pressure exerted by the infringement procedures carried out by the EC; Poland was forced to suspend the implementation of its law on the Supreme Court; the Sword of Damocles of monetary sanctions is pending on both countries with regard to the other cases. Such a tool is not perfect but these goals are valuable, especially in the light of the ineffectiveness of the mechanisms under Art. 7 TEU.

What has been demonstrated here from a legal point of view is even more interesting. The EC and the CJEU have developed the use of the relevant parameter in the cases analyzed above: first, they used to refer to obligations under the Treaties; then they started using them in tandem with articles of the CFREU (and this, by all means, raised the level of the issues concerned to one of a constitutional nature); finally, beside the mention of the CFREU as a parameter, the CJEU expressly mentioned systemic concerns and recalled that the requirement underpinning the relevant parameter of the CFREU was a guarantee that the values common to the Member States set out in Art. 2 TEU, in particular the rule of law, will be safeguarded.[62]

In particular, the 2017–2019 cases of the Polish judiciary, the Polish Supreme Court and the Polish disciplinary regime for judges showed that it is impossible to draw a line between what is within and what is outside the scope of EU law when speaking about horizontal issues of a constitutional nature[63] or concerns related to values under Art. 2 TEU which are 'systemic'.

The protection of the independence of judges, when they are adjudicating cases *involving the application of EU law*, cannot be separated from the protection of their independence when they are adjudicating cases *outside the scope of EU law*. Similarly, when speaking about judicial independence, *the protection of the EU legal order* cannot be separated from the protection of the values *common to the Member States* set out under Art. 2 TEU.

That is why it can be argued that the development of the parameter and the very recent mention of Art. 2 TEU in the order issued by the President of the CJEU have allowed the EC and the CJEU to keep their action within the scope of EU law but at the same time to use the infringement procedures in order to protect *de facto* the rule of law within the Member States.

62 As has been noted, CFREU-based cases can lead to three different scenarios. A Charter right: is further specified by EU secondary law; is not underpinned by specific EU legislation; concerns horizontal guarantees on the rule of law and fair trial. See Hoffmeister, 2015, pp. 200–202. The second and the third stages mentioned in the text above coincide respectively with the first and the third scenarios.

63 Hoffmeister, 2015, p. 195.

References

E. Albanesi, *Pluralismo costituzionale e procedura d'infrazione dell'Unione europea*, Torino, Giappichelli, 2018.

D. Anagnostou & M. Claes (Eds), *Rights and Courts in Pursuit of Social Change. Legal Mobilisation in the Multi-level European System*, Oxford/Portland, OR, Hart, 2014.

M. Avbelj, 'The Inherent Limits of Law – The Case of Slovenia', *Verfassungsblog.de*, December 2013. Available at: https://verfassungsblog.de/ [Accessed 15 August 2019].

M. Bánkuti, G. Halmai & K. L. Scheppele, 'From Separation of Powers to a Government without Checks: Hungary's Old and New Constitutions', in G.A. Tóth (Ed.), *Constitution for a Disunited Nation. On Hungary's 2011 Fundamental Law*, Budapest, Central European University Press, 2012, pp. 237–268.

L. F. M. Besselink, 'The Bite, the Bark, and the Howl. Article 7 TEU and the Rule of Law Initiatives', in A. Jakab & D. Kochenov (Eds), *The Enforcement of EU Law and Values. Ensuring Member States' Compliance*, Oxford, Oxford University Press, 2017, pp. 128–144.

L. F. M. Besselink & J. H. Reestman, 'Editorial', *European Constitutional Law Review*, Vol. 13, 2017, pp. 207–220.

P. Blokker, 'Systemic Infringement Action: An Effective Solution or Rather Part of the Problem?', *Verfassungsblog.de*, December 2013. Available at: https://verfassungsblog.de/ [Accessed 15 August 2019].

C. Closa & D. Kochenov (Eds), *Reinforcing Rule of Law Oversight in the European Union*, Cambridge, UK, Cambridge University Press, 2016.

M. Dawson & E. Muir, 'Enforcing Fundamental Values: EU Law and Governance in Hungary and Romania', *Maastricht Journal of European and Comparative Law*, Vol. 4, 2012, pp. 469–476.

M. Dawson, E. Muir & M. Claes, 'A Tool-box for Legal and Political Mobilisation in European Equality Law', in D. Anagnostou & M. Claes (Eds), *Rights and Courts in Pursuit of Social Change. Legal Mobilisation in the Multi-level European System*, Oxford/Portland, OR, Hart, 2014, pp. 105–128.

L. W. Gormley, 'Infringement Proceedings', in A. Jakab & D. Kochenov (Eds), *The Enforcement of EU Law and Values. Ensuring Member States' Compliance*, Oxford, Oxford University Press, 2017, pp. 65–78.

G. Halmai, 'How the EU Can and Should Cope with Illiberal Member States', *Quaderni costituzionali*, 2018, pp. 313–339.

G. Halmai, 'Much Ado About Nothing? Legal and Political Schooling for the Hungarian Government', *Constitutionalism and Politics*, 29 April 2017a. Available at: https://blogs.eui.eu/constitutionalism-politics-working-group/ [Accessed 15 August 2019].

G. Halmai, 'The Case of the Retirement Age of Hungarian Judges', in F. Nicola & B. Davies (Eds), *EU Law Stories*, Cambridge/New York, Cambridge University Press, 2017b, pp. 471–487.

C. Hillion, 'Overseeing the Rule of Law in the EU. Legal Mandate and Means', in C. Closa & D. Kochenov (Eds), *Reinforcing Rule of Law Oversight in the European Union*, Cambridge, Cambridge University Press, 2016, pp. 59–81.

F. Hoffmeister, 'Enforcing the EU Charter of Fundamental Rights: How Far Rome, Budapest and Bucharest from Brussels?', in A. von Bogdandy & P. Sonnevend

(Eds), *Constitutional Crisis in the European Constitutional Area. Theory, Law and Politics in Hungary and Romania*, Oxford/Portland, OR, Hart, 2015, pp. 195–233.

A. Jakab, 'Application of the EU CFR by National Courts in Purely Domestic Cases', in A. Jakab & D. Kochenov (Eds), *The Enforcement of EU Law and Values. Ensuring Member States' Compliance*, Oxford, Oxford University Press, 2017, pp. 252–262.

A. Jakab & D. Kochenov (Eds), *The Enforcement of EU Law and Values. Ensuring Member States' Compliance*, Oxford, Oxford University Press, 2017.

D. Kochenov, 'The Acquis and Its Principles. The Enforcement of the 'Law' versus the Enforcement of 'Values' in the EU', in A. Jakab & D. Kochenov (Eds), *The Enforcement of EU Law and Values. Ensuring Member States' Compliance*, Oxford, Oxford University Press, 2017, pp. 9–27.

J. Komárek, 'The EU is More than a Constraint on Populist Democracy', *Verfassungsblog.de*, March 2013. Available at: https://verfassungsblog.de/ [Accessed 15 August 2019].

T. T. Koncewicz, 'The Capture of the Polish Constitutional Tribunal and Beyond: Of Institution(s), Fidelities and the Rule of Law in Flux', *Review of Central and East European Law*, Vol. 43, 2018, pp. 116–173.

K. Kovács & G. A. Tóth, 'Hungary's Constitutional Transformation', *European Constitutional Law Review*, 2011, pp. 183–203.

J.-W. Müller, 'Should the EU Protect Democracy and the Rule of Law inside Member States?', *European Law Journal*, Vol. 21, No. 2, 2015, pp. 141–160.

J.-W. Müller, 'Protecting the Rule of Law (and Democracy!) in the EU. The Idea of a Copenhagen Commission', in C. Closa & D. Kochenov (Eds), *Reinforcing Rule of Law Oversight in the European Union*, Cambridge, Cambridge University Press, 2016, pp. 206–224.

F. Nicola & B. Davies (Eds), *EU Law Stories*, Cambridge/New York, Cambridge University Press, 2017.

L. Prete, *Infringement Proceedings in EU Law*, Alphen aan den Rijn, Kluwer Law International, 2017.

K. L. Scheppele, 'Enforcing the Basic Principles of EU Law through Systemic Infringement Actions', in C. Closa & D. Kochenov (Eds), *Reinforcing Rule of Law Oversight in the European Union*, Cambridge, Cambridge University Press, 2016a, pp. 105–132.

K. L. Scheppele, 'EU Can Still Block Hungary's veto on Polish Sanctions', *Politico.eu*, 11 January 2016b. Available at: https://www.politico.eu/ [Accessed 15 August 2019].

M. Schmidt & P. Bogdanowicz, 'The Infringement Procedure in the Rule of Law Crisis: How to make effective use of Article 258 TFEU', *Common Market Law Review*, Vol. 55, 2018, pp. 1061–1100.

A. Śledzińska-Simon, 'The Rise and the Fall of Judicial Self-Government in Poland: On Judicial Reform Reversing Democratic Transition', *German Law Journal*, Vol. 19, No. 7, 2018, pp. 1839–1869.

P. Sonnevend, A. Jakab & L. Csink, 'The Constitution as an Instrument of Everyday Party Politics: The Basic Law of Hungary', in A. von Bogdandy & P. Sonnevend (Eds), *Constitutional Crisis in the European Constitutional Area. Theory, Law and Politics in Hungary and Romania*, Oxford/Portland, OR, Hart, 2015, pp. 75–79.

G.A. Tóth (Ed.), *Constitution for a Disunited Nation. On Hungary's 2011 Fundamental Law*, Budapest, Central European University Press, 2012.

M. Varju, 'Governance, Accountability, and the Market', in G.A. Tóth (Ed.), *Constitution for a Disunited Nation. On Hungary's 2011 Fundamental Law*, Budapest, Central European University Press, 2012, pp. 301–331.

A. Vincze, 'The CJEU as the Guardian of the Hungarian Constitution: Case C-286/12 Commission v. Hungary', *European Public Law*, Vol. 19, No. 3, 2013, pp. 489–500.

A. Vincze & M. Varju, 'Hungary The New Fundamental Law', *European Public Law*, Vol. 18, No. 3, 2012, pp. 437–453.

A. von Bogdandy, C. Antpöhler, J. Dickschen, S. Hentrei, M. Kottmann & M. Smrkolj, 'A European Response to Domestic Constitutional Crisis: Advancing the Reverse-Solange Doctrine', in A. von Bogdandy & P. Sonnevend (Eds), *Constitutional Crisis in the European Constitutional Area*, Oxford, Hart, 2015, pp. 235–253.

A. von Bogdandy & P. Sonnevend (Eds), *Constitutional Crisis in the European Constitutional Area. Theory, Law and Politics in Hungary and Romania*, Oxford/Portland, OR, Hart, 2015.

F. Zakaria, 'The Rise of Illiberal Democracy', *Foreign Affairs*, Vol. 76, No. 6, 1997, pp. 22–43.

Index

Page numbers in **bold** reference tables, Page numbers in *italics* reference figures.